# DESIGNING THE FRENCH INTERIOR

# DESIGNING THE FRENCH INTERIOR: THE MODERN HOME AND MASS MEDIA

*Anca I. Lasc, Georgina Downey, and Mark Taylor*

Bloomsbury Academic
An imprint of Bloomsbury Publishing Plc

BLOOMSBURY
LONDON • OXFORD • NEW YORK • NEW DELHI • SYDNEY

**Bloomsbury Academic**
An imprint of Bloomsbury Publishing Plc

50 Bedford Square
London
WC1B 3DP
UK

1385 Broadway
New York
NY 10018
USA

www.bloomsbury.com

**BLOOMSBURY and the Diana logo are trademarks of Bloomsbury Publishing Plc**

First published 2015
Published in paperback 2017

© Selection and Editorial Material: Anca I. Lasc, Georgina Downey and Mark Taylor, 2015

© Individual Chapters: Their Authors, 2015

Anca I. Lasc, Georgina Downey and Mark Taylor have asserted their right under the Copyright, Designs and Patents Act, 1988, to be identified as Author of this work.

All rights reserved. No part of this publication may be reproduced or transmitted in any form or by any means, electronic or mechanical, including photocopying, recording, or any information storage or retrieval system, without prior permission in writing from the publishers.

No responsibility for loss caused to any individual or organization acting on or refraining from action as a result of the material in this publication can be accepted by Bloomsbury or the author.

**British Library Cataloguing-in-Publication Data**
A catalogue record for this book is available from the British Library.

ISBN: HB: 978-0-8578-5659-3
PB: 978-1-3500-1389-6
ePDF: 978-0-8578-5783-5
ePub: 978-0-8578-5779-8

**Library of Congress Cataloging-in-Publication Data**
A catalogue record for this book is available from the Library of Congress.

Typeset by Integra Software Services Pvt. Ltd.

# CONTENTS

List of Illustrations — vii
List of Contributors — x

**French Connections: The Modern Interior and Mass Media**
Anca I. Lasc, Georgina Downey, and Mark Taylor — 1

**PART I  Sex, Dreams, and Desires: The Perversions of the Modern Interior** — 11

1. Impolite Reading and Erotic Interiors in Eighteenth-Century France
   Georgina Downey and Mark Taylor — 13

2. Intimate Vibrations: Inventing the Dream Bedroom
   Fae Brauer — 29

3. Angels and Rebels: The Obsessions and Transgressions of the Modern Interior
   Anca I. Lasc — 47

4. Machines and Monsters: The Modern Decadent Interior as Spectacle in Huysmans's *À Rebours*
   Emilie Sitzia — 59

5. *La Maison Suspendue*: Imaginary Solutions for an Everyday Domestic Machine
   Peter Olshavsky — 71

**PART II  Aesthetics, Anxiety, and Identity: Reproducing a Decadent Domesticity** — 81

6. The Interiorization of Identity: Portrait Busts and the Politics of Selfhood in Pre- and Early Revolutionary France
   Ronit Milano — 83

7. A Portable Keyhole into the Fictional Apartment Building: The Interiors of Félix Vallotton and Émile Zola
   Karen Stock — 95

8. The *Fin-de-Siècle* Poster: A Healthy Modern Stimulus in the French Interior
   Katherine Brion — 107

9. Mode of a Modern Muse: Fashion and Interior in Édouard Vuillard's Paintings of Misia Natanson
   Jess Berry — 119

10. The Decadent Interior as Modern Lesbian Aesthetic
    Elizabeth Melanson — 131

11. Mallet-Stevens, Modern Design, and French Cinema
    Nieves Fernández Villalobos — 143

Contents

PART III  Intimacy, Longing, and Performance: The Consumption and Display of the Celebrity Home ... 155

12  Staging Domesticity in *La Revue Illustrée*'s Photo-Interviews: *Belle Époque* Celebrity Homes in the Periodical Press
    *Elizabeth Emery* ... 157

13  Hôtel Baronne Salomon de Rothschild 1872–1878: The Imprint of a Legacy
    *Linda D. Stevenson and Susan Tate* ... 167

14  "Un Bel Atelier Moderne:" The Montparnasse Artist at Home
    *Louise Campbell* ... 179

15  Housing the New Dandy: Designing Lifestyle in *Monsieur* Magazine, 1920–1924
    *John Potvin* ... 191

16  "Fashions in Living:" The Duke and Duchess of Windsor, 4, Route du Champs d'Entraînement, Paris
    *Peter McNeil* ... 203

17  "Si Ma Cuisine M'Était Comptée:" *Paris Match* and the *Salon des Arts Ménagers* during the Fourth Republic
    *Guillaume de Syon* ... 217

Index ... 229

# ILLUSTRATIONS

**PART I Sex, Dreams, and Desires: The Perversions of the Modern Interior**

**Chapter 1**

| | | |
|---|---|---|
| 1.1 | *Dangerous Liaisons*, 1988: Valmont enters Cécile's bedroom. | 16 |
| 1.2 | Jean-Honoré Fragonard, *Le Verrou*, 1778. | 16 |
| 1.3 | Pierre Maleuvre, *Le Boudoir*, 1776. | 22 |
| 1.4 | Emmanuel de Ghendt, *Le Midi*, c. 1765. | 24 |

**Chapter 2**

| | | |
|---|---|---|
| 2.1 | Eugène Gaillard, Double bed and wardrobe, *Chambre à coucher, Pavillon de l'Art Nouveau*, Exposition Universelle, 1900. | 31 |
| 2.2 | Eugène Gaillard, Double bed, *Chambre à coucher: Pavillon de l'Art Nouveau*, Exposition Universelle, 1900. | 35 |
| 2.3 | Eugène Gaillard, Chair "Delvincourt" (front view), *Chambre à coucher: Pavillon de l'Art Nouveau*, Exposition Universelle, 1900. | 36 |
| 2.4 | Eugène Gaillard, Chair, "Delvincourt" (profile), *Chambre à coucher: Pavillon de l'Art Nouveau*, Exposition Universelle, 1900. | 37 |
| 2.5 | Eugène Gaillard, Wardrobe, *Chambre à coucher: Pavillon de l'Art Nouveau*, Exposition Universelle, 1900. | 38 |

**Chapter 3**

| | | |
|---|---|---|
| 3.1 | Jacques Wagrez, [Illustration], in *Revue Illustrée*, 1886. | 48 |
| 3.2 | Eugène Prignot, "Panneau de Salon," in Désiré Guilmard, *La Décoration au XIXe siècle*, c. 1872. | 52 |
| 3.3 | P. Brunet, "Boudoir, Salon Louis XVI," in *Le Tapissier décorateur de Paris*, 1878. | 54 |
| 3.4 | P. Brunet, "Fumoir Asiatique," in *Le Tapissier décorateur de Paris*, 1878. | 55 |

**Chapter 5**

| | | |
|---|---|---|
| 5.1 | Paul Nelson, *Suspended House*, Project scale model, 1936–1938. | 71 |
| 5.2 | Kendra Heimes, *Suspended House*, Balcony level plan, 2014. | 73 |

**PART II Aesthetics, Anxiety, and Identity: Reproducing a Decadent Domesticity**

**Chapter 6**

| | | |
|---|---|---|
| 6.1 | Attributed to Anne-Flore Millet, *Portrait of Marie-Antoinette, Queen of France*, c. 1794. | 84 |
| 6.2 | Charles Paul Landon, *Count Bourcet Family*, 1791. | 85 |
| 6.3 | Châteaux de Versailles et de Trianon, *The queen's bedroom with Portrait Bust of Marie-Antoinette*, 1783. | 88 |
| 6.4 | Attributed to Jean-Baptiste Greuze, *Marquis René-Louis de Girardin*, c. 1780. | 90 |

Illustrations

## Chapter 7
7.1 Félix Vallotton, *Apprets de Visite*, 1897. — 98
7.2 Félix Vallotton, *L'Argent*, 1897. — 102
7.3 Félix Vallotton, *La Belle Epingle*, 1897. — 103

## Chapter 8
8.1 Jules Chéret, *Bal du Moulin Rouge Place Blanche*, 1889. — 110
8.2 Jules Chéret, *La Pantomime*, 1891. — 113

## Chapter 9
9.1 Édouard Vuillard, *The Living Room with Three Lamps, Rue Saint-Florentin*, 1899. — 121
9.2 Thadée Natanson and his wife Misia Godebeska in the drawing room of their apartment in the Rue Saint-Florentin, Paris, c. 1899. — 122

## Chapter 10
10.1 Henri Grandpierre, Music room, Hôtel Singer-Polignac, Paris, c. 1904. — 134
10.2 Aubrey Beardsley, *The Peacock Skirt*, in Oscar Wilde, *Salome*, 1907. — 137
10.3 Aubrey Beardsley, *The Dancer's Reward*, in Oscar Wilde, *Salome*, 1907. — 139
10.4 Aubrey Beardsley, *Tailpiece* or *Fin*, in Oscar Wilde, *Salome*, 1907. — 140

## Chapter 11
11.1 *L'Inhumaine*, 1924: Claire Lescot's House and Einar Noorsen's House. — 146
11.2 Villa Noailles, 1924 vs. Claire Lescot's and Einar Noorsen's houses, *L'Inhumaine*, 1923. — 151
11.3 *Les Mystères du Château du Dé*, 1924–1928: Mallet-Stevens's Villa Noailles. — 152

## PART III Intimacy, Longing, and Performance: The Consumption and Display of the Celebrity Home

## Chapter 12
12.1 Photographer unknown, "Le Grand salon," in *Revue Illustrée*, 1892. — 159
12.2 Photographer unknown, "Le Cabinet de travail" and "La Salle à manger," in *Revue Illustrée*, 1893. — 162
12.3 Henri Mairet, "En famille" and "Mme Réjane dans sa loge au Vaudeville," in *Revue Illustrée*, 1894. — 163

## Chapter 13
13.1 A. Cary, *Hôtel Beaujon: Façade sur le jardin*, photograph, before 1891. — 167
13.2 A. Cary, *Hôtel Beaujon: Le Hall (côté de la Galerie)*, photograph, before 1891. — 173
13.3 A. Cary, *Hôtel Beaujon: Salle à manger (côté de la Serre)*, photograph, before 1891. — 175

# Illustrations

**Chapter 14**
- 14.1 Auguste Perret, Studio for Chana Orloff, 1926.   181
- 14.2 Robert Mallet-Stevens, Studio for Tamara de Lempicka, 1931.   183
- 14.3 "Chez Mela Muter," in *L'Architecture d'aujourd'hui*, 1933.   186

**Chapter 15**
- 15.1 Artist unknown, Cover of *Monsieur*, 1923.   195
- 15.2 Artist unknown, "Un cabinet de travail d'homme élégant," in *Monsieur*, 1924.   196
- 15.3 Marc-Luc, "Quel Homme Chic!," in *Monsieur*, 1921.   200

**Chapter 16**
- 16.1 Windsor residence, The entrance hall, in *Country Life*, 1987.   208
- 16.2 Windsor residence, The white and silver salon, in *Country Life*, 1987.   209
- 16.3 Windsor residence, The library, in *Country Life*, 1987.   210
- 16.4 Windsor residence, The Duchess' boudoir, in *Country Life*, 1987.   211
- 16.5 Windsor residence, The Duchess's dressing room, photograph taken for *Country Life*, 1987.   213

**Chapter 17**
- 17.1 Henri Salesse, *Maison de Paris Match* at the Salon des Arts Ménagers, Paris, 1953.   223
- 17.2 Maurice Jarnoux, Household Arts Fair 1954: The wonderful kitchen presented by *Paris Match*.   224

# CONTRIBUTORS

**Jess Berry** is an art history/theory and fashion studies scholar. Her research is concerned with the fashion city, fashion new media, fashion intersections with art, architecture and the interior, and Australian fashion history. Recent articles have appeared in *Journal of Design History*, *Craft + Design Enquiry* and *Catwalk: The Journal of Fashion, Beauty and Style*. She is editor of *Fashion Capital: Style Economies, Sites and Cultures* (Interdisciplinary Press 2012).

**Fae (Fay) Brauer** is Professor of Art and Visual Culture at the University of East London Centre for Cultural Studies Research (CCSR) and Associate Professor in Art History and Cultural Theory at The University of New South Wales National Institute for Experimental Art (NIEA). Her books include *Picturing Evolution and Extinction: Degeneration and Regeneration in Modern Visual Cultures* (2014), *Rivals and Conspirators: The Paris Salons and the Modern Art Centre* (2013), *The Art of Evolution: Darwin, Darwinisms and Visual Culture* (2009), and *Art, Sex and Eugenics, Corpus Delecti* (2008). Presently, she is preparing the books: *Regenerating the Body: French Art and Neo-Lamarckian Biocultures*; *Symbiotic Species: Art, Animals and Transformism in Solidarist France*; *Canvasing Perversion: Picasso, Science and Medicine*; and *Unmasking Masculinity: Imaging Hysterical Men in Republican France*.

**Katherine Brion** is Mellon Postdoctoral Fellow in the Art and Art History Department at Kalamazoo College. She received her doctorate from the University of Michigan, where her dissertation examined the political implications of decorative painting in France, 1890–1914. Some of that research was published as "Paul Signac's Decorative Propaganda of the 1890s," *RIHA Journal* 0044 (July 14, 2012). Other research and teaching interests include representations of race and the role of art in education in the nineteenth and early twentieth centuries. Dr. Brion has been the recipient of an Andrew W. Mellon Curatorial Fellowship at the University of Michigan Museum of Art, a Rackham Predoctoral Fellowship, a Georges Lurcy Foundation Fellowship for Study in France, a Getty Research Institute Library Grant, and a Susan Lipschutz Award.

**Professor Louise Campbell**, of the History of Art Department at Warwick University, is a specialist in late nineteenth- and twentieth-century architecture. She has published widely on British architecture and modernism, public art in the post-war period, and the studio environment in England and France in the late nineteenth and twentieth centuries. She was awarded a Senior Fellowship from the Paul Mellon Centre for Studies in British Art for 2011–2012 for a book on artists' habitats in the twentieth century. She has recently published "Eileen Agar at Home: Domesticity, Surrealism, and Subversion," in *Interiors: Design, Architecture, Culture*, vol. 3 no. 3, pp. 227–246. Her book, *Basil Spence: Buildings and Projects* (coedited with Miles Glendinning and Jane Thomas) was published by the RIBA in 2012.

## Contributors

**Guillaume de Syon** teaches history at Albright College in Reading, PA and is a visiting scholar in history at Franklin & Marshall College. He is the author of *Zeppelin! Germany and the Airship 1900–1939* (Johns Hopkins 2002), of *Science and Technology in Modern European Life* (Greenwood 2008), and of articles on the cultural history of technology. His interest in *Paris Match* stems from the magazine's association with French modernity during the "Trente glorieuses."

**Dr. Georgina Downey** is a Visiting Research Fellow in the Graduate Program in Art History, School of History & Politics at the University of Adelaide. Dr. Downey is a historian of Australian and European art. Her PhD (2005), undertaken in the School of Art, Architecture and Design at the University of South Australia, focused on the work of expatriate woman artists in the modern period and explained how their relocation to the modernist centers of Paris and London in the early twentieth century introduced new subject matter and underscored their exploration of the domestic interior. She has published widely on visual and material cultures around the domestic interior in art, in pursuit of which she has received an Australian Academy of the Humanities Travel Grant (2006) and University of Adelaide small research grants. Her most recent book is *Domestic Interiors: Representing Home from the Victorians to the Moderns* (2013). She is a member of the Art Association of Australia and New Zealand, Museums Australia, the network of the Centre for Studies of Home, and the Edwardian Culture Network.

**Elizabeth Emery** is Professor of French at Montclair State University where she teaches medieval and nineteenth-century French literature and culture. She is the author of books, articles, and essay anthologies related to the reception of medieval art and architecture in nineteenth-century France and America, and has recently published a book exploring the early twentieth-century phenomenon of writers' private homes turned into public museums: *Photojournalism and the Origins of the French Writer House Museum (1881–1914)* (Ashgate Press 2012). *Une Heure chez… Dans l'intimité des célébrités parisiennes de la Belle Époque*, a collection of richly illustrated interviews at the homes of late nineteenth-century celebrities, will be published by the Editions Parigramme in October 2015.

**Nieves Fernández Villalobos** is a Spanish Dr. Architect from the School of Architecture of Valladolid (Spain). Doctoral courses conducted include Modern and Contemporary Architecture, 2001–2002, in the Department of Theory of Architecture and Architectural Design. In 2003, she joined the same department, in the area of Architecture Composition, teaching mainly subjects related to design (Aesthetics and History of Design, Design and Visual Communication, Design Workshops, etc.) and coordinating the Grade of Industrial Design and Project Development. She also coordinates and teaches in the Master of Architectural Research program, on the subject: Architecture, Design and Visual Arts. Her doctoral thesis *The House of the Future. Utopias in Domestic Architecture of Alison and Peter Smithson* (2007), directed by Dario Alvarez, obtained PhD Extraordinary Award of her University (2007–2008). She was also awarded, in 2009, the Seventh Prize for Architecture Thesis by Fundación Caja de Arquitectos. Thanks to this, she has published her book *Utopías Domésticas. La Casa del Futuro de Alison y Peter Smithson* in January 2013. She has recently won the FAD Prize in 2014 in the category of *Thought and Criticism*.

Contributors

**Dr. Anca I. Lasc** is Assistant Professor of History and Theory of Design at Pratt Institute. Her work focuses on the invention and commercialization of the modern French interior and on the development of the profession of interior designer in the nineteenth century. She has published articles in *Interiors: Design, Architecture, Culture*, the *Journal of the History of Collections* and the *Journal of Design History* and has presented at numerous conferences, among which those organized by the College Art Association, the Society of Architectural Historians, and the Society for French Historical Studies. In addition to the modern interior, Anca also studies the art of commercial window dressing in nineteenth-century France and America. Her edited volume, *Visualizing the Nineteenth-Century Home: Modern Art and the Decorative Impulse*, is forthcoming (2015) from Ashgate Publishing.

**Peter McNeil** FAHA is Professor of Design History and Associate Dean, Research, at the University of Technology Sydney and Professor of Fashion Studies at Stockholm University. His research interests are primarily the cultural history of fashion and its interaction with other aspects of art, design and material culture. He has published numerous works on fashion, including the best-selling "Shoes: from Sandals to Sneakers" (with G. Riello, 2006; 2011; Italian translation 2009). Recent book-length projects include the "long" history of luxury, supported by the Leverhulme Trust (with G. Riello for Oxford University Press); and "Fashion Writing and Criticism" (with S. Miller for Bloomsbury). He is also currently working with the Los Angeles County Museum of Art on "Reigning Men," the largest exhibition of men's fashion ever assembled. In June 2014, he was appointed a Distinguished Professor by the Academy of Finland (for Aalto University), in the area of costume.

**Elizabeth Melanson** is Assistant Professor of Art History at Fairmont State University. She earned her PhD at the University of Delaware, where she explored the patronage of modern art by the high society women of France during the Belle Époque. She has presented her research at a number of institutions, including the College Art Association's Annual Conference, the University of Cambridge, the Philadelphia Museum of Art, and the National Gallery of Art. Recent publications have appeared in *Nineteenth-Century Art Worldwide*.

**Ronit Milano** is the author of *The Portrait Bust and Eighteenth-Century French Cultural Politics*. Her publications focus on eighteenth-century French art. In her present project she investigates the intersection between eighteenth-century and contemporary art, through the display of contemporary art in historic sites. She has recently completed her post-doctoral research in the History of Art and Architecture Department at Harvard University, and is a lecturer in the Department of the Arts at Ben-Gurion University of the Negev, in Israel.

**Peter Olshavsky, PhD** is an Assistant Professor of Architecture at the University of Nebraska-Lincoln. Besides UNL, he has taught at McGill, Temple and Philadelphia University and has practiced professionally in Philadelphia, PA. He holds a PhD and MArch II in history and theory from McGill University and B.Arch. from The Pennsylvania State University. Peter's focus is in history, theory and design. He was a recipient of a Canada-US Fulbright Fellowship and his scholarly and design work has been recognized and published internationally. His current research explores architectural machine traditions relative to other disciplines of cultural knowledge.

## Contributors

**Dr. John Potvin** is Associate Professor in the Department of Art History and Director of the PhD Humanities Program at Concordia University, Montreal, where he teaches on the intersections of art, design and fashion. He is the author of *Material and Visual Cultures Beyond Male Bonding* (2008), *Giorgio Armani: Empire of the Senses* (2013) and *Bachelors of a Different Sort: Queer Aesthetics, Material Culture and the Modern Interior in Britain* (2014). He is also editor of *The Places and Spaces of Fashion* (2009) and *Oriental Interiors: Design, Identity, Space* (2015) as well as coeditor of both *Material Cultures, 1740–1920: The Meanings and Pleasures of Collecting* (2010) and *Fashion, Interior Design and the Contours of Modern Identity* (2010). His current project, *Deco Dandy: Modernism, Nationalism and Sexuality in 1920s Paris* explores the fashion, painting, performance and interior design cultures of the much-neglected interwar dandy.

**Emilie Sitzia** is an Associate Professor at Maastricht University (Netherlands) in the Department of Arts and Literature. She holds a PhD in French literature and culture (2005). She was educated in France, Germany and Finland where she followed a double major in Art history and theory and French Literature. Before coming to Maastricht University, Emilie was senior lecturer at the University of Canterbury (Christchurch, New Zealand) (2005–2012) and lecturer at Åbo Akademi University (Turku, Finland) (2001–2004). Her research interests are nineteenth-century Art Literature (such as art novels, art criticism and painters' texts) and Literary Art (paintings, illustrations, portraits of writers) as well as interdisciplinary methodologies and Museum Studies. She recently published a book *Art in Literature, Literature in Art in 19th Century France* (Cambridge Scholars Publishing 2012).

**Linda D. Stevenson**, PhD, is a practicing architect specializing in historic preservation and an adjunct professor in the Historic Preservation program at the University of Florida. She serves as co-director for the Preservation Institute Nantucket. Dr. Stevenson received a PhD with a concentration in historic preservation from the University of Florida. She was named a Richard Morris Hunt Fellow in 1995. She collaborated on the creation of the book *Concorde*, a project directed by Professor Susan Tate, which commemorated the sixtieth anniversary of the Marshall Plan and restoration of the eighteenth-century apartments of the Talleyrand Building in Paris.

**Karen Stock** is an Associate Professor of Art History at Winthrop University, South Carolina. Dr. Stock received her masters and PhD from the Institute of Fine Arts, New York University. Her thesis, "Bonnard, Vuillard, and Vallotton: Masculinity in Question," was completed under the sponsorship of Linda Nochlin. She specializes in French modernism and gender theory but also has research interests in American art of the twentieth century, modern Chinese art, and contemporary art. She has published work on Edgar Degas, Kurt Schwitters and Florine Stettheimer.

**Susan Tate**, AIA specializes in architectural preservation and interior architecture, and is a Registered Architect, consultant in historic building analysis, and Professor Emeritus of the University of Florida. Professor Tate directed a Getty Campus Heritage Grant to develop a Preservation Plan for UF and served as Director of the UF Preservation Institute: Nantucket. For the U.S. Department of State, she directed the commemorative book *Concorde* to celebrate the sixtieth anniversary of the Marshall Plan and the restoration of the eighteenth-century state apartments of the Talleyrand Building in Paris, where the Marshall Plan was administered after the Second World War.

**Mark Taylor** is Professor of Architecture and Associate Dean (Research) at the University of Newcastle, Australia. He has a PhD in Architecture from the University of Queensland, Australia. Mark is an editorial advisor to *Interiors: Design, Architecture, Culture* and regularly reviews papers and book manuscripts for international publishers. His writing on the interior has been widely published in journals and book chapters including editor (with Julieanna Preston) of *Intimus: Interior Design Theory Reader* (Wiley 2006), editor of the four volume collection *Interior Design and Architecture: Critical and Primary Sources* (Bloomsbury 2013) and is currently co-editor of *FLOW: Between Interior and Landscape* (Bloomsbury 2017).

# FRENCH CONNECTIONS: THE MODERN INTERIOR AND MASS MEDIA
*Anca I. Lasc, Georgina Downey, and Mark Taylor*

> It is interesting to an American workman to see who is doing the work in this new palace of the Vanderbilts. All of the decorative work is being executed by Frenchmen— the real imported article at that. Allard & Sons, of this city, who employ nobody but Frenchmen, are doing the color decorations, the hangings, tapestry and furnishings, while about thirty Frenchmen imported especially for the purpose... are doing the plastic and carving work.... (Balch Ingram 1892)

Balch Ingram's observation in *Leslie's Weekly* on the Vanderbilts' employment of French decorators indicates a high regard for these artisans and tradesmen at the end of the nineteenth century. Their employment outside France reflects an ongoing view that since the eighteenth century France has been the wellspring, *nonpareil* of superior taste in interior decoration and design (Craven 2005). The special French expertise for all things "interior" was recognized widely by many cultural producers from all over who flocked to the "art capital of the world." In 1922, for example, Edith Fry, an Australian artist and art correspondent, wrote home to say that South Australian Bessie Davidson's *Portrait de Famille D.*, which is reproduced in the *Salon* catalog, is a charming example of the "interior portrait" of which only artists in Paris "seem to know the secret" (1922: 2). It is perhaps not surprising, therefore, that while Walter Benjamin's *The Arcades Project* (2002 [1927–1940]) dubbed Paris "the capital of the nineteenth century," it could also claim to be "the capital of the modern interior," a status that drew logically upon its preeminence in art and architecture, fashion, and the production of luxury goods for the private home. However, what is less well known is the contribution made by the mass media to spreading new ideas about the French interior. This multiauthor volume addresses the intertwined relationship between media, decoration, and design and focuses on the interiors of one country and one culture, France, because of its central importance to the study of the modern interior.

From the mid-eighteenth century, French talent for defining the modern and comfortable interior transferred gradually from Versailles to both the city of Paris and the country's regional centers. By the nineteenth century, the stylishly modern interior had become somewhat of a national preoccupation for many French citizens, including the aspirational *petite bourgeoisie*, the *demi-mondaines*, the creative classes, and the great, the good, and the modish in all walks of life. The commissioning of living spaces for emerging forms of social interaction inaugurated an unprecedented interest in new building techniques and original fashions for interior decoration, effectively providing the necessary conditions for the emergence of the modern interior. From upholstery and plumbing to running water, flush toilets, and the sofa— the French were at the forefront of modern interior design (DeJean 2009: 1).

France's position as a style leader was achieved gradually and consistently over many centuries. During the *ancien régime*, other European states and countries (what we now identify as England, Germany, and Italy) also had access to luxury exotic raw materials imported from their colonies, which fed into their production centers of excellence. However, the reason why France eventually led the world in designed luxury goods was because of its consistently high-quality standards in terms of materials and craftsmanship (Schleuning 2008: 29). In the nineteenth century, under pressure from their competitors and after the dissolution of guilds, French designers and craftsmen still organized themselves aggressively into a range of professional associations. As decorative arts and design historian Sarah Schleuning notes, these groups "worked collectively to promote French craftsmanship and design by means of international exhibitions, publications and other professional activities" (2008: 29). Moreover, the output of these professionally and politically mobilized design and craft practitioner groups was seen by successive French governments as constituting a keystone of the nation's export economy. Subsequently, policies worked to support and increase the production of luxury goods for both local and foreign markets. Industry protectionism, ample political recognition of the power of craft associations, and state subsidies for design and arts education produced a steady supply of highly skilled workers for the decorative and design arts.

Additionally, a succession of convulsive upheavals in France created the conditions necessary for the emergence of new forms of sociability, class structures, and ways of living. From the attack on Church as State mounted by Enlightenment philosophies through the Revolution and the Terror, dramatic shifts in forms of government, from monarchy to republic to empire to democracy, meant rapid shifts in "outward appearances," with taste becoming a major signifier for power and influence. One important influence was sensationalist theory in philosophy, underscoring décor practices intended to produce powerful, repeatable, and consistent emotional and aesthetic responses. Rooms became highly specialized, and new spatial forms arose (Evans 1989). For example, the increasingly popular activity of reading among both men and women informed the development of both the cabinet and the boudoir. The new needs for intimacy or relaxed, informal social interaction demanded the voyage of furniture from the peripheries of public and official rooms into more central, conversational groupings. In turn, the arrangement of furniture into new groupings freed the walls from geometrical regularity, allowing interiors to adopt a surprising variety of shapes and forms. While new social programs made way for these new room formats, increasingly modern notions of interiority detached the interior from its architectural shell, aligning it more closely with the rapid life cycles of fashion rather than building. Pattern, textile design effects, artworks, and objects created new opportunities for displaying social position, identity, gender, and personality. Alongside these social and cultural developments was an intense shift to bourgeois capitalism, the technological development of photography, film and advertising, and the arrival of dense, highly modern urban environments created by the destruction of old Paris through the process of Haussmannization, and, significantly, the 1880s influx of creative expatriates drawn to the city from all over the world. This influx of foreigners created an unusually strong market for architects, decorators, and other specialists of the modern interior.

Circulating ideas about the French modern interior to the national public and the rest of the world was achieved particularly through publications which benefitted from excellent color and production values. Nineteenth-century advances in photography, coupled with new techniques of color reproduction and photo-mechanical printing processes, served as useful tools for the representation, invention, and circulation of the modern French interior to a wide audience. Traditional architectural drawings were complemented by visual representations of interiors that appeared in many formats including paintings, prints, books, illustrated magazines, department store catalogs, photographs, guidebooks, and films. The variety of media employed in representing the modern private interior since its inception in the eighteenth century have consistently blurred the boundaries between spectacle and privacy, collecting and decorating, the fine and the decorative arts, as well as the domestic and the commercial spheres. As such, they have defined the French domestic interior as an interdisciplinary subject of inquiry par excellence.

The twentieth and the twenty-first centuries further refined and disseminated the image of the modern French interior, crafting for it a firm place in a variety of scholarly disciplines concerned with all things visual, from art and design history, visual and material culture studies, through to media and communication studies. In recent years, there has been an increased interest in the history of the modern interior and its design especially in the Anglo-American world (Sparke et al. 2006; Rice 2007; Schleuning 2008; Muthesius 2009; Sparke et al. 2009). Concurrently, scholars have begun to analyze domestic interiors as representations on paper, in writing, and on canvas in two special issues of the *Journal of Design History* (Lees-Maffei 2003; Aynsley and Berry 2005) as well as in larger publications (Aynsley and Grant 2006; Aynsley and Forde 2007; Downey 2013; Lees-Maffei 2014). Interest in critical and theoretical aspects of the interior has also called for collections of primary reference texts, both historical and contemporary, such as *Interior Design and Architecture: Critical and Primary Sources* (Taylor 2013). In contrast, the equally important but more specific topic of the modern French interior has primarily been treated by historians (Silverman 1989; Walton 1992; Marcus 1999; Tiersten 2001). While these books apply a sociocultural perspective to the development of the domestic French interior and its role in society, they engage little with the plethora of visual imagery associated with the same private interior.

*Designing the French Interior: The Modern Home and Mass Media* has as its primary aim to identify and historicize the singularity of the modern French domestic interior as generator of (reproducible) images, receptor for both highly crafted and mass-produced objects, and the direct result of widely circulated imagery in its own right. The themes that define this book were developed initially through two sessions held at the 58th Annual Meeting of the Society for French Historical Studies in Los Angeles in March 2012 and a subsequent international call for papers. The volume is thus rooted in new, interdisciplinary scholarship that expands traditional notions of architectural representation to embrace the interior through mass media. It investigates the mediated interior, as it was affected by invention, display, and commercialization, as well as advertising, commercial display, and staging through art and media images.

The volume comprises seventeen invited chapters and is organized into three parts with each individual chapter dedicated to the examination of the modern interior's connection to mass media, as explored through a wide perspective. Part I, "Sex, Dreams, and Desires: The Perversions of the Modern Interior" acknowledges the importance of the interior as a safe haven for the family while exploring examples that also invert this convention. The essays included here propose that each interior has a darker side, where one's deepest fears and fantasies are formed and brought into the open. Collectively, they interrogate the role that French media from the late-eighteenth through the mid-twentieth century played in constructing a visual language for the private interior. The media in focus here include books, interior decorating manuals, illustrated magazines, and films read in line with the provocative argument that, in sum, these may have proposed interiors that were less about purity and personal redemption and more about hidden sexuality, repressed desires, and utopian time-travel.

The first chapter in Part I, "Impolite Reading and Erotic Interiors in Eighteenth-Century France," sets up the book's conceptual trajectory by establishing the eighteenth-century interior as progenitively modern. Downey and Taylor explore how erotic texts had a set of effects on the interior. They argue that as erotica became democratized, it was transmitted across several media, from text to illustration to painting and, in the twentieth century, to film. Each transmission functioned as a *translation*, further imbuing interiors with the concept that they may act sensationally upon occupants—sometimes so powerfully that they removed the character's ability to act in any other way than to succumb to erotic sensation. This interaction is explored by reading key erotic moments from Stephen Frears's film *Dangerous Liaisons* (1988), which was based on Pierre Choderlos de Laclos's 1782 novel, and comparing this imaginative construction of erotic space to related spaces in French erotic fiction, architectural advice manuals, and popular engravings of the period.

Fae Brauer shifts the focus of discussion into the late nineteenth century, the time of the post-Haussmann city, whose abrasiveness and pace was felt to overexert the nervous system of the modern individual. Here, the bedroom is positioned very differently and is now in line with the latest in medical and cultural discourse: it is conceived as a "sanctuary," a refuge, and preserve of peace where a person's "interior and exterior [might] become indissolubly fused, reintegrated with nature, … and reenergised by the intimate embrace of its regenerative forms from plant-life to the growth of wood." The "cocoon" bedroom is here exampled by Eugène Gaillard's exquisite *chambre à coucher* for the *Pavillon de l'Art Nouveau* commissioned by Siegfried Bing in 1900, and among others, it serves as *the* space par excellence from where the French nation was to be regenerated.

Anca I. Lasc, in "Angels and Rebels: The Obsessions and Transgressions of the Modern Interior," examines the commercialized private interior available as a two-dimensional image and marketable entity. Lasc explores the designs that the furnishing architect P. Brunet produced in 1878 in parallel with the interiors described by the author Émile Zola in his 1872 novel *The Kill* (*La Curée*). Lasc argues that these interpolated texts offer a fascinating image of the late nineteenth-century *Parisienne* at home, which played on the "forbidden" fantasies of men and women alike and contradicted traditional gender roles at the time. Brunet, she argues, lifted taboos in his playful designs of "fantasy" rooms—whimsies from the Far and the Middle East among others—for *femmes fatales*, and these designs challenged the public image of the proper wife and mother, so prevalent in contemporary Third Republic discourses.

In "Machines and Monsters: The Modern Decadent Interior as Spectacle in Huysmans's *À Rebours*," Emilie Sitzia positions the fictional interior of the Duc Jean Floressas Des Esseintes as a "broken mirror"—a space where occupants can dissolve and disappear. She suggests it is an interior that is "alive" with machines—mechanical fish, digesters and a musical alcohol dispenser—and monsters—the jewel-encrusted tortoise—that suck the life force out of the Decadent occupant, leaving nothing remaining but the interior as spectacle.

## French Connections: The Modern Interior and Mass Media

In "*La Maison Suspendue*: Imaginary Solutions for an Everyday Domestic Machine," Peter Olshavsky explores the visionary unbuilt house in France by the American expatriate architect Paul Nelson. In 1937, Nelson disseminated his ideas for his novel "suspended house" to radicalized readers via a slim, eponymously titled publication that presented the house as a machine for living. While the house embodied the notion of "4D" as developed by US architect and designer Buckminster Fuller, Nelson's concepts also brought into play theories as disparate as that of "Socrates's nest" and Alfred Jarry's concept of "pataphysics." Olshavksy argues that Nelson's machine house offered an even more radical program than Fuller's, with its "suspended room units" hanging literally in an atrium-like space leveraging new technologies while creating a house both poetic and erotic in form.

Part II, "Aesthetics, Anxiety, and Identity: Reproducing a Decadent Domesticity," is dedicated to the variety of artistic media that we have come to associate with the middle-class interior and its decoration. These include portrait busts as early forms of bibelots, posters as affordable ornament, photographs, prints, book illustrations, and early cinema as reflective of and sources of inspiration for domestic life. Together, these essays suggest that the variety of reproductive media that the modern private interior incorporates are as worthy of attention as the spaces which they occupy.

The first chapter in Part II, Ronit Milano's "The Interiorization of Identity: Portrait Busts and the Politics of Selfhood in Pre- and Early Revolutionary France," explains how the correlation between eighteenth-century portrait busts and the interior setting which they occupied reflected the psychological interiority of the busts' owners. Milano focuses on painted portraits at the eve of the French Revolution, which invariably illustrated sitters in their homes, next to decorative portrait busts. She offers a compelling reading of these—often fictive—juxtapositions, where space and mass reproducible three-dimensional objects worked together to illustrate the personality and hidden psychological dimensions of the sitters.

In "A Portable Keyhole into the Fictional Apartment Building: The Interiors of Félix Vallotton and Émile Zola," Karen Stock discusses Vallotton's *Intimités* series in parallel with Émile Zola's novel *Pot-Bouille* (1882). The comparison allows Stock to understand how Vallotton's woodcuts behaved less like visual short stories and more like individual apartments within Baron Haussmann's restructured Paris. Like Zola's fiction, Vallotton's images exposed the hidden secrets of social life to public scrutiny, portraying the petty dramas and intrigues of a middle-class apartment building. The cross-media and cross-disciplinary analysis allows Stock to observe how Zola and Vallotton sought to provide their audience with a surreptitious glimpse into private moments while taking pleasure in mocking, through their fictive spaces, the metaphorical façade of respectability that concealed the moral corruptness of the late nineteenth-century French bourgeoisie.

Through an analysis of the discourse surrounding possible cures to the nervous inflictions brought by modern life, Katherine Brion, in "The *Fin-de-Siècle* Poster: A Healthy Modern Stimulus in the French Interior," inverts our long-held assumption that the late nineteenth-century private interior provided a safe haven and calm refuge from the anxiety of modern life. On the contrary, the combination of sophisticated color effects with the reproducibility and accessibility of a mass medium made the poster an invigorating and welcomed stimulus in private interiors, where, critics argued, it helped prepare the inhabitant to return, with renewed vigor, to the collective fray. As Brion concludes, "if the interior transformed the poster, the poster also helped transform the interior, so that it no longer signified a detachment from public life."

Jess Berry's chapter, "Mode of a Modern Muse: Fashion and Interior in Édouard Vuillard's Paintings of Misia Natanson," explores the body of the Nabis muse, Misia Natanson, as the site where traditional views on women's roles and the discourse surrounding the *femme nouvelle* intersected in *fin-de-siècle* France. While Vuillard's paintings blended Misia's body seamlessly into the organic surrounds of her apartment, keeping her "at home," Berry observes how photographic evidence, including Vuillard's own pictures, portrayed Misia acting upon her interiors and thus challenging the contemporary dominant narrative of female submissiveness to patriarchal authority. By looking at paintings and photographs together, Berry is thus able to observe how the boundaries between the separate realms of domesticity and public life were completely blurred.

Continuing with a discussion of late nineteenth-century gender roles and their expression in the domestic interior, Elizabeth Melanson, in "The Decadent Interior as Modern Lesbian Aesthetic," examines yet another example of a powerful woman who expressed her identity through the private spaces of her home. Using a visual vocabulary adapted from mass media, specifically from Aubrey Beardsley's illustrations for Oscar Wilde's *Salome*, Winnaretta Singer staged elaborate *tableaux vivants* to establish her social position and assert her personality, sexuality, and taste before an audience of elite peers and the popular press. As she adapted a Decadent and Symbolist style in her home to set the stage for her conquest of Parisian high society, Singer made deft use of mass media to get her message across.

Finally, the last chapter in Part II, Nieves Fernández Villalobos's, "Mallet-Stevens, Modern Design and French Cinema," explains how modern design made its film debut through the efforts of French pioneers, who hoped to promote the Modern movement through cinema. Focusing on Marcel L'Herbier's *L'Inhumaine* (1924) and Man Ray's *Les Mystères du Château du Dé* (1929), Fernández Villalobos explains how Mallet-Stevens and other French pioneers demonstrated through cinema that modern design had a great artistic potential both in front and behind film screens. While using cinema to promote modern design, cinema sets themselves helped architects like Mallet-Stevens develop their ideas about real-life architecture and interiors, resulting in spaces such as the Villa Noailles, which itself looked like a film set.

The essays in Part III, "Intimacy, Longing and Performance: The Consumption and Display of the Celebrity Home," explore the fascination the modern public felt toward the houses of the rich, the beautiful, and the famous. The modern interior is here understood as a two-dimensional entity on paper, which could be broken down, montage-style, into a myriad of image-worthy "slices" or frames reconfigured and reassembled by writers, photographers, and illustrators into a new object, to finally be born anew into the houses of "fans" eager to follow in the steps of their role-models. Together, the essays attempt to understand the interconnectedness of celebrity culture and the modern interior as well as the role of the media in cementing this relationship.

The role of magazine photo-interviews to frame homes for public consumption is the subject of Elizabeth Emery's chapter "Staging Domesticity in *La Revue Illustrée*'s Photo-Interviews: *Belle Époque* Celebrity Homes in the Periodical Press." She notes how the most important illustrated magazines of the period provided journalistic reinforcement of the links between interior decorating and identity, which was also evident in contemporary decorating manuals. Analyzing various interviewers' methods of directing the reader's interpretation of the images, Emery observes how the interior could be staged for the public, and how this interpretation is set against the unambiguous photographic documentation of the late-nineteenth century home. While focusing on notable personalities, René Baschet and *La Revue Illustrée* reveal the extent to which the illustrated press participated in promoting interior decoration as an expression of identity.

In "Hôtel Baronne Salomon de Rothschild 1872–1878: The Imprint of a Legacy," Linda Stevenson and Susan Tate trace the history of the baroness's home, its documentation through an album of photographs, and subsequent publication in the *Revue des arts décoratifs* by editor Victor Champier. This lavish home was a collaboration between architects Léon Ohnet and Justin Ponsard and *décorateur* Henri-Antoine-Léopold de Moulignon, who was charged with creating the entire *décor*, ornamentation, decorative paintings, and selection of the fabrics. Stevenson and Tate reconstruct the interior through an examination of the photographs and Champier's text and note that alongside the minute attention to detail the home is a scenographic expression of drama and spectacle, anticipating the celebrity home as a place to see and be seen.

The shift into modernist interiors of the 1920s is reflected in Louise Campbell's "'Un Bel Atelier Moderne:' The Montparnasse Artist at Home." In this chapter, Campbell traces the commissioning and construction of homes for successful Paris-based artists Chana Orloff, Tamara de Lempicka, and Mela Muter by architects Robert Mallet-Stevens and Auguste Perret. She argues that in the highly competitive art world of the 1920s and 1930s, commissioned studio-homes attracted additional publicity and enabled their occupants to manipulate the media while also serving as a conduit between discussions of art and the assessment of contemporary architecture. However, it is in her examination of the art market following the economic crash that Campbell reveals how French tradition and Modernism were played out in the magazine *L'Architecture d'aujourd'hui* with Perret's studio-house for Muter being valorized for its architectural integrity.

Alongside more general and "women-orientated" magazines were some specifically aimed at men and masculine taste. In "Housing the New Dandy: Designing Lifestyle in *Monsieur* Magazine, 1920–1924," John Potvin examines the lush men's fashion magazine, *Monsieur*, as it negotiated a fine line between masculine respectability and fashionable eccentricity for the *modern* French man. The magazine prominently displayed men as arbiters of interior design, with what Potvin describes as a queer approach to masculinity, and questioned the female consumer and woman decorator as the exclusive arbiters of taste and design. Accompanying the photographs of the actual lived-in interiors of luminary male celebrities were ideal and prescriptive instructions for both fashion and interior design, confirming that the interior was a product of mass media.

In the early 1960s, the writer Valentine Lawford was sent by Diana Vreeland, the editor of *Vogue* magazine, to visit the Duke and Duchess of Windsor in their quasi-exile home on the outskirts of Paris. His careful and erudite article is discussed by Peter McNeil in "'Fashions in Living:' The Duke and Duchess of Windsor, 4, Route du Champs d'Entraînement, Paris," where the Windsors' glamorous set of interiors are also examined relative to modernist elegance.

The "Maison Jansen" designed interior contained both traditional and hybrid spaces, for clients that desired both an eighteenth-century French decorative backdrop and the comforts of twentieth-century living. While the *Vogue* article provided some insight into the Windsors' lives, McNeil notes the hôtel was a major investment in terms of artistic design, funds, and emotional energy, hence also a frame for their "arrested" lives.

In the last chapter of this part, Guillaume de Syon examines how a media empire not only represented contemporary design, household technologies, and room layouts within the pages of its main title, but also commissioned projects that it would later feature. In his essay "'Si Ma Cuisine M'Était Comptée:' *Paris Match* and the *Salon des Arts Ménagers* during the Fourth Republic," de Syon discusses how the internationally popular magazine *Paris Match* promoted a new French identity centered on the home. Importantly, he notes the magazine's role in translating the desires offered through the *Salon des arts ménagers*'s exhibitions into the home. However, despite the magazine's professed broad readership, many of the featured articles on home living and kitchen design (complete with celebrity demonstrators) never questioned gender boundaries and continued to reaffirm middle-class gender ideals that ignored the reality of women's constricted social roles.

By the early twentieth century, all the necessary factors were thus in place to put France in a unique position to promote modern interior decoration and design at a level of taste and style unmatched elsewhere. Hollywood and the world looked to Paris with regard to how to decorate their interiors (Massey 2000). French decorators were hired by US clients, and their firms opened offices everywhere in the world while French antiques and contemporary furniture graced the rooms of the wealthy and chic on a global level. This influence went beyond the 1925 Paris *Exposition Internationale des Arts Décoratifs et Industriels Modernes* and the subsequent development of the Art Deco style—which had paved the way to the formation of the Americanized "jazz modern" via popular film art directors such as Cedric Austin Gibbons (Massey 2000)—and reached all the way into the mid-twentieth century, when the preeminent US modern architect Philip Johnson claimed Le Corbusier's interiors as a source for his famed *Glass House* of 1949 (Friedman 2010).

Given France's role as style leader to the modern world, this volume examines some of the rich and complex relationships between the domestic interior and mass media, as these were specifically possible within French history and culture. Spanning roughly two centuries, from the mid-eighteenth century through the mid-twentieth century, the essays included here understand the term "modern" to refer to not only industrialization and urbanization, but also mediatization. To support this idea, individual authors have largely abstained from attaching stylistic labels to the various forms and shapes taken by the modern French interior in order to better trace the connections between mass media and private space. By adopting such a general framework, the essays demonstrate the role mass media had in either consciously or unconsciously promoting spatial ideas to a wider audience. Whether this was achieved through visiting real celebrity homes or through imagining literary/filmic spaces, the construction of "home" and the interior through the media exposes a complicit relationship between inhabitants and their desires, anxieties, and performed lives. The importance of this position is that architectural histories and theories can no longer remain isolated and outside consumer culture, since the two are inextricably linked.

# References

Aynsley, J. and F. Berry (2005), "Introduction Publishing the Modern Home: Magazines and the Domestic Interior 1870–1965," *Journal of Design History* 18, no. 1: 1–5.

Aynsley, J. and K. Forde (eds) (2007), *Design and the Modern Magazine*, Manchester: Manchester University Press.

Aynsley, J. and C. Grant (eds) (2006), *Imagined Interiors: Representing the Domestic Interior since the Renaissance*, London: V&A Publications.

Balch Ingram, H. (February 27, 1892), "Mr. Vanderbilt's Marble Hall," *Leslie's Weekly*.

Benjamin, W. (2002), *The Arcades Project*, Cambridge, MA and London: Harvard University Press.

Craven, W. (2005), *Stanford White: Decorator in Opulence and Dealer in Antiquities*, New York: Columbia University Press.

DeJean, J. E. (2009), *The Age of Comfort: When Paris Discovered Casual—And the Modern Home Began*, New York: Bloomsbury.

Downey, G. (ed) (2013), *Domestic Interiors: Representing Homes from the Victorians to the Moderns*, London: Bloomsbury.

Evans, R. (1989), "The Developed Surface: An Inquiry into the Brief Life of an Eighteenth-Century Drawing Technique," *9H*, no. 8: 120–147.

Friedman, A. T. (2010), *American Glamour and the Evolution of Modern Architecture*, New Haven, CT: Yale University Press.

Fry, E. M. (1922), "Australian Artists Abroad," *The Home* 3, no. 3: 2

Lees-Maffei, G. (2003), "Introduction Studying Advice: Historiography, Methodology, Commentary, Bibliography," *Journal of Design History* 16, no. 1: 1–14.

Lees-Maffei, G. (2014), *Design at Home: Domestic Advice Books in Britain and the USA since 1945*, Abingdon: Routledge.

Marcus, S. (1999), *Apartment Stories: City and Home in Nineteenth-Century Paris and London*, Berkeley, CA: University of California Press.

Massey, A. (2000), *Hollywood Beyond the Screen: Design and Material Culture*, Oxford and New York: Berg.

Muthesius, S. (2009), *The Poetic Home: Designing the Nineteenth-Century Domestic Interior*, London: Thames & Hudson.

Rice, C. (2007), *The Emergence of the Interior: Architecture, Modernity, Domesticity*. London: Routledge.

Schleuning, S. (2008), *Moderne: Fashioning the French Interior*, New York: Princeton Architectural Press.

Silverman, D. (1989), *Art Nouveau in Fin-de-Siècle France: Politics, Psychology, and Style*, Berkeley, CA: University of California Press.

Sparke, P., Martin B. and T. Keeble (eds) (2006), *The Modern Period Room: The Construction of the Exhibited Interior 1870 to 1950*, Abingdon and New York: Routledge.

Sparke, P., Massey, A., Keeble, T. and B. Martin (eds) (2009), *Designing the Modern Interior: From the Victorians to Today*, Oxford: Berg.

Taylor, M. (ed) (2013), *Interior Design and Architecture: Critical and Primary Sources*, London and New York: Bloomsbury.

Tiersten, L. (2001), *Marianne in the Market: Envisioning Consumer Society in Fin-de-Siècle France*, Berkeley, CA: University of California Press.

Walton, W. (1992), *France at the Crystal Palace: Bourgeois Taste and Artisan Manufacture in the Nineteenth Century*, Berkeley, CA: University of California Press.

PART I
SEX, DREAMS, AND DESIRES: THE PERVERSIONS
OF THE MODERN INTERIOR

# CHAPTER 1
# IMPOLITE READING AND EROTIC INTERIORS IN EIGHTEENTH-CENTURY FRANCE
*Georgina Downey and Mark Taylor*

---

The eighteenth century in France is close enough in time for us to appreciate its exultation of the senses and its single-minded pursuit of pleasure. Yet, it is also far enough away to forget that these pleasures were largely *imagined* through text and image, as part of the program of libertine and materialist philosophies of the period. Toward the end of the century, the literacy rate across the general population rose and might have been anywhere between 40 percent and 93 percent, depending on the area (Schama 1989: 180), and erotica could thus be read by all but the poorest. Yet, while Enlightenment reading cultures were driving production and sale of perfectly legal material, the most explicit examples, what Robert Darnton has called "impolite" readings, still attracted the condemnation of the authorities of Church and State. In France as in other Catholic cultures, sin was considered as wicked in thought and word as in deed, and punishments and fines were common. So, whether participating in the politics of libertinage or simply telling a bawdy tale, erotic images and texts were produced and consumed at a cost. Nevertheless, "the *jouissance* to be found in words" was most explicitly recognized by fashionable and influential writers, readers, and viewers of this period with writer-adventurers such as Giacomo Casanova, John Cleland, and Pierre Choderlos de Laclos being perhaps the best known exemplars (Albano 2007: 140). Further, this "impolite" reading had a specific set of interesting effects on the development of the modern French interior, demanding that it be more immersive and more psychologically co-optive than in the previous century.

Modern cultures of looking and reading began to emerge in the mid to late eighteenth century in France, and these shaped attitudes to the interior, in both its material and affective dimensions. In particular, erotic works, in which the interior was an active agent in creating and sustaining erotic sensation, began to enjoy a more broadly based readership. Erotic novels were quite often illustrated with plates. These printed engravings effectively doubled sensation and pleasure as they translated erotica across media. According to Satish Padiyar, these enabled the libertine erotic imagination to be democratized and "went hand in hand with the increasingly free accessibility of the written word." Further, "French engravers self-consciously catered to a public that soon became familiar with the dynamic interaction between words and images" (Padiyar 2006: 56).

To explore this dynamic interaction and its impact on the legacy of the French interior, this chapter traces the emergence of a sensorial approach to the spaces of inhabitation as practiced by a number of painters, architects, and landscape theorists. The chapter thus examines literary and visual devices that bridged theory and erotics, as these interpolated new ideas about architectural space and interiors in the pornographic literature of the period. In order to reconsider representations of erotic space, we trace these as they were translated from one medium to the next: from architectural treatise to fiction; from fiction to illustrations; and later, from painting to cinema. The aim is to reveal not only how erotica was democratized as it was transmitted across media but also how domestic spaces were increasingly imbued with the modern concept that they may possibly act "sensationally" upon occupants. Throughout the period, we thus see new, more intimate categories of interior space, including boudoirs and bedrooms, developing a psychological depth and agency lacking in earlier modes of dwelling. To make this discussion relevant to contemporary understanding, the paper begins with the "turns" from fiction and painting to cinema, in an examination of Stephen Frears's *Dangerous Liaisons* (1988).

## Cinematic interpretation

Foregrounding this process of cumulative transmission of erotic tales through media, Stephen Frears's *Dangerous Liaisons* (1988), based on Pierre Choderlos de Laclos's libertine novel *Les Liaisons Dangereuses* (1782), is a telling paradigm of how fictive space underwent a process of visualization in the service of erotic narrative.[1] For the 1988 film *Dangerous Liaisons*, significant creative, research, and financial resources were directed toward reconstructing material cultures and objects, and filming occurred in the finest and best conserved villas and *petites maisons*. Built around Paris in increasingly large numbers toward the end of the century, these "little houses for love," according to Nicolas le Camus de Mézières, "anticipated pleasures and voluptuousness"—although they were not "small" by contemporary standards (Young 2008: 60).

We contend that Frears's re*visualization* of eighteenth-century domestic space provides a wealth of hypothetical evidence about how, as Giuliana Bruno puts it, "figures made journeys in space" (2002: 56). Through authentic buildings and interiors, and a fluidly moving camera, Frears's film makes tangible the latent analogies in de Laclos's text between interior space and erotic plot lines. The film has been praised by de Laclos scholars for its fidelity to the text of this famous epistolary novel (Coward 1995: xxi). In its twentieth-century incarnation, *Dangerous Liaisons* had first been adapted by Christopher Hampton as a stage play and then reworked by Hampton for the cinema. In de Laclos's text as well as its later materializations, the story is told through an exchange of letters about a succession of sexual wagers between the Marquise de Merteuil and the Vicomte de Valmont, two arch libertines of their aristocratic circle, and once lovers. Valmont, though he would rather perish than confess to a mawkish sentiment such as love (which might trump pleasure), is still in love with the Marquise and takes up the wagers on his side in order to win a night with her. The Marquise, though a woman, is the "harder" player in games of intrigue and seduction, and she enjoys manipulating the Vicomte.

Between the two, they wager their prowess as seducers of, respectively, the virginal and convent-school educated Cécile des Volanges (Valmont, though he finds this too easy, takes up the challenge of seducing the "unimpeachable" Madame de Tourvel) and the Marquise, Cécile's young music teacher, the Chevalier Danceny. Naturally, these two older, more experienced *roués* both succeed in their wagers, but at the cost of life, in the case of the Vicomte, who allows Danceny to wound him fatally in a duel, and health and social standing, in the case of the Marquise, who is publically exposed as a schemer and contracts smallpox. Through their epistolary reports to each other and other characters in the story, de Laclos makes his point about the limits of libertinism and the vacuousness of aristocratic court life with its endless intrigues and cruelty.

Translating this libertine text across media from fiction into film must have been a persistent challenge since de Lacos's text offers scant indication of the details of the letter writers' precise spatial locations or of their décor.[2] Notwithstanding, readers of the novel are informed early on that the Marquise owns not only a "magnificent villa in Paris" but also a "little house" (*petit maison*) or "temple of love" where she seduces suitors. Consequently, the settings chosen for the film were those *likely* to have been inhabited by people like the Marquise and the Vicomte de Valmont. Among the villas used were the Château de Vincennes in Val-de-Marne (used as royal residence from the twelfth to the eighteenth century), the Château de Champs-sur-Marne (owned by the Duc du *Vallière* between July 1757 and January 1759, at which time it was leased to King Louis XV's mistress, Madame de Pompadour), the Château de Guermantes in Seine-et-Marne (Guermantes was the scene of memorable fêtes and built by Paul Pondres, a financier close to Louis XIV), and the Théâtre Montansier in Versailles. Frears thus literally reembodies a series of *galeries* (*grandes* and *petites*), *salons*, music rooms, *oratoires*, *cabinets en filade*, *appartements* and *piéces des bains* as these form "frames" for various scenes in the film.

To "block," in theatre language, the movement of actors' bodies in and through these real spaces of libertinage, Hampton and Frears drew heavily on the iconography of period literature, paintings, and engravings, including masterpieces in oil by such well-known artists as Boucher and Fragonard.[3] Both these humbly born men had become the greatest artists of their day via the patronage of King Louis XV's official mistresses—Boucher to the Marquise de Pompadour and, later, Fragonard to Mme du Barry. In particular, Fragonard's "fantasy figures" are invoked in many of the film's scenes, particularly the bedroom scenes (Percival 2012: 101–103). These teasing puzzle pictures, representing neither recognizable individuals, abstractions, embodiments of the arts nor expressions of Fragonard's genius, but a mix of all four, are important as they suggest what the most arousing imaginary interior might look like. Certainly, as Melissa Percival points out in particular, Fragonard's erotic *bed* scenes with deliciously puffy pillows, tumbles of satin and perfect white linen were known for their "anthropomorphic voluptuousness … suggestive of [a] … heightened sensuality," and the dressing of beds in the film underscores these visual antecedents (2012: 149).

The transposition of de Laclos's story from literature through painting to cinema is especially evident in *Les Liaisons* scene in which Valmont enters Cécile de Volange's bedroom to take her virginity. We first see the camera lingering while Valmont fumbles through the business of opening her door (Figure 1.1). A second, smaller door leading into Cécile's room suggests the metaphoric leap between Valmont "entering" this antechamber and its analogy with Cécile's body. This act of broaching feminine space is emphasized by Valmont having to juggle both the candle and the key to break into Cécile's room.

**Figure 1.1** Stephen Frears, *Dangerous Liaisons*, 1988: The Vicomte de Valmont enters Cécile Volange's bedroom on the first night of his campaign of seduction, Burbank: Warner Brothers.

In its content, composition, lighting effects, and emotional affect, this scene powerfully evokes Fragonard's *The Bolt* (c. 1778) painted some four years before de Laclos's novel was published. Set in a bedroom and staged at the door, *The Bolt* depicts an analogous event to what the film represents, but from the other side of the door, i.e., the interior of the bedchamber. Here, we see a blonde and voluptuous young girl struggling to get away from the youth who has her firmly pinned with one arm around her waist, while he is about to slide home the door bolt that seals her fate with the other (Figure 1.2). Further allegorical details in the scene suggest "innocence betrayed," evinced by the single, fashionably dressed bed, the apple on the table near the bed (a biblical reference to Eve, temptation, and forbidden knowledge), the crushed roses on the floor to the right (a symbol of love), and the tensely contorted draperies falling in labial folds. To reinforce this message (as if any more were needed) an intertextual connection is made between the "bolt" and "penis" functions

**Figure 1.2** Jean-Honoré Fragonard, *Le Verrou*, [detail] oil on canvas, 1778, Musée du Louvre, Paris, Photo ©RMN-Grand Palais (Musée du Louvre)/Stéphane Maréchalle.

as a lubricious visual pun in the Fragonard painting that is in turn echoed later in the film. In the transfer, a dominant trope of eighteenth-century erotica (male encroachment on feminine space) is translated from painting to cinema, the latter medium reiterating the transformation of the interior of the bedroom from a real space of sleep to an allegorical space of the female body in the novel and painting, while adding a new element of journeys through actual space.

Considering "the place of sex" in eighteenth-century English erotica, Karen Harvey suggests that in these texts and illustrations, the locations where sex was "placed" were metaphorical rather than real. Harvey does not focus particularly on French materials, however, but her findings do cut across ours in interesting ways as they apply to the questions we ask of the represented erotic interior. Harvey has stated that "the places at which erotic encounters were imagined to occur...cannot be read as recording the places in which people had sex...the choice of locations in erotica was much narrower than convenience allowed, which suggests that *cultural factors*—relating to the intellectual and emotional associations of a location—exerted considerable force" (2001: 161) [our italics].

Harvey notes that these sexualized locations share the following qualities: they are shady (interior or exterior, i.e., glades), soft textured, if pastoral, partly enclosed by shrubbery and, if interior, by curtains. Screens were often featured, and these performed a similar discursive function to shrubbery or curtains, and texts and illustrations often contained the "apparently banal inclusion of doors and windows" the better to symbolically underscore the threat of discovery (2001: 167). She proposes that these locations are part-metaphors for the female body. She finds that "the interiors in which encounters occurred were spare, even bare to the modern eye, in line with the fashionable eighteenth-century style, but *opulent in materials*," and cites the proliferation of beds turned into "sweet enclosures" through the use of curtains, canopies, and alcoves (2001: 168).

Harvey singles out the importance of masculine broaching of feminine space, of boudoirs in particular, as a central trope in the erotica of the period—and provides many texts that reveal the male protagonist using force and cunning to assail these spaces. She also notes in accompanying erotic engravings the inclusion of sometimes seemingly arbitrary windows and doors, which are reliable indicators of the structural *potential* in the space for broaching or spying and are thus arousing elements. She underscores, however, that, once the feminine spaces are broached, the male character has to relinquish some of his scopic control and phallocentric power in order to enjoy full immersion in these soft enticing female spaces (2001: 174).

Thus, we can see that as a dramatic erotic encounter is "moved across" from fiction and painting to film, it carries with it many of the original elements, and yet new ones are added: the "before and after" of the static captured moment, and the movement of actors' bodies within the rooms responding to the sensorial qualities of fixtures and décor. We see time and space added to the architectural imagination in a manner that suggests how bodies may have moved through these spaces. Giuliana Bruno describes this process of architectural/filmic promenade as an emotional cartography where "an embodiment, [is invoked]...based on the inscription of an observer in the field—such an observer is not a static contemplator, she is a physical entity, a moving spectator, a body making journeys in space" (2002: 56).

## Architecture and sensation

In the translation from medium to medium, we see how particular interiors multiplied sensation and coded for particular kinds of acts, behaviors, moods, and ideas. We also see the compression of a range of ideas about the interior into *tableaux*, and the drawing upon of current (eighteenth century) décors and textiles to convey notions from the original text. Many of the villas Frears used as settings were decorated during the late eighteenth century when a new form of architectural sensitivity arose, which imagined interiors as expressing an emotional state in both inhabitant and intruder. They followed the sensationalist theories of Étienne Bonnot de Condillac (1714–1780) in his *Treatise on Sensation* (1754), produced at a time when the practice of Enlightenment philosophy opened the body to new forms of spatial awareness.

In the eighteenth century, new theoretical constructs by Leroy and Roger de Piles had set the ground for an individual aesthetic appreciation. Claude-Henri Watlet's *Essai sur les jardins* (1774), for example, offered a shift from the geometrical orderliness of the formal French garden to planting in the "picturesque" style, both of which assisted "the cultivation of the picturesque vision that enabled Leroy and later, Nicolas le Camus de Mézières (1721-1789) to see architecture in a new way" (Middleton 1992: 46). Le Camus's treatise *Le Génie de l'architecture* (1780) emphasized the psychological effects of sensationalist philosophy on the spatial environment (le Camus de Mézières 1992 [1780]). In the introduction, he observed that the expression of character might be through a line or plain contour since an "object possesses a character, proper to it alone," a notion that advanced a new psychological reading of character proper to various rooms.

In regard to the sensually multiplied interior, a further important text is Jean-Francois de Bastide's *La Petite Maison* (1789), which is a combination of two literary genres—the erotic libertine novella and the architectural treatise (el-Khoury 1996). Bastide narrates a plot of seduction between the Marquis de Trémicour and Mélite, who had resisted his advances for some time. In the novel, she concedes to visit the Marquis's *petite maison* not realizing it was tastefully arranged for love, and in the course of the narrative, she is led from one room to another, each more artfully arranged than the one before. Toward the middle of the book, she is overcome by the many wonders, feeling "weak, stifled even, and…forced to sit down" (Bastide 1996 [1789]: 83). Weak at the knees and betraying what Bastide calls a "secret distress" she was clearly aroused and complicit in the seduction.

During the narration, Mélite finds herself in a boudoir, where carnal delight was explicitly played out in the decorative, psychological, and tactile affects:

> The walls of the boudoir were covered with mirrors whose joinery was concealed by carefully sculpted, leafy tree trunks. The trees, arranged to give the illusion of a quincunx, were heavy with flowers and laden with chandeliers. The light from their many candles receded into the opposite mirrors, which had been purposely veiled with hanging gauze. So magical was this optical effect that the boudoir could have been mistaken for a natural wood, lit with the help of art…Mélite could scarcely contain her delight. (de Bastide 1996 [1789]: 75–78)

This account, influenced by le Camus's earlier description of the sleeping space as a grove, was designed to inspire pleasure.[4] Moreover, the strategically positioned mirrors and candles returned the libertine's gaze and, for Trémicour, offered a voyeuristic moment of erotic enjoyment. When standing in front of one mirror, for example, he was able to watch Mélite adjust her hair in the opposite one. The architectural intention of the mirror-lined space was not only to dematerialize the walls but to also offer a means by which sexual encounters could be further enjoyed through watching. Within this mirror-lined boudoir was an *ottomaine* strewn with pillows and set in a niche where "the walls and ceiling were also covered with mirrors" (de Bastide: 76). The boudoir elicits a range of emotions and behaviors in the occupants; and their processural experience of it increases desire and aids seduction. The space Mélite enters does more than simply facilitate the sexual act; it seems to remove [her] ability to act any other way (Young 2008: 345).

Such collusion between seduction in words and architectural detailing illustrate an inseparability that was also witnessed in earlier novellas, including *Le Sopha* (1742), in which the narrator exclaims: "everything radiated sensuality: the adornments, the furniture, the scent of the exquisite perfume that was always burning. Everything brought sensuality to the eye, everything transported it to the soul. This *cabinet* could have been taken for the temple of voluptuousness, for the indisputable seat of pleasure."[5] But, this new sensuality that changed architecture was also disturbing, as Louis-Sébastien Mercier observed in his *Tableau de Paris* (1781):

Architecture, once majestic and unyielding, has succumbed to the licentiousness of our lifestyle and ideas. It anticipates and fulfils all the aims of debauchery and libertinage; secret passages and hidden stairways are in the same vein as novels of the day. Architecture, complicit in our disorders, is no less licentious than our erotic poetry. (quoted in Berrett Brown 2009: 102)

Mercier recognized that there was a mirroring between the new architecture and erotic literature. On the one hand, Bastide's *La Petite Maison* used architecture and decorations to effect a seduction. On the other, Mme Gourdan in *Anecdotes sur Mme la Comtesse du Barry* (1775) had initiated a young Mlle Lançon (Comtesse du Barry) into her brothel by showing her through her apartments and, in particular, "my boudoirs fitted out for lovemaking where everything bespeaks pleasure and seduction... I urged her to examine the engravings that adorned the walls—nudes, suggestive positions, and all sorts of images for the arousal of sexual desire" ( Mairobert in Darnton 1996).[6]

## Seduction and space

For the libertine novel and the erotic painting or illustration to achieve their characteristic frankness and directness of address, stories were set in specific itemized domestic interiors, notably the boudoir and its masculine counterpart, the cabinet. Emerging in the eighteenth century, these were small private bedrooms, sitting rooms, or dressing rooms, usually taking their title from the gender of their occupant, but on some occasions, the terms "boudoir" and "cabinet" were interchanged. The boudoir takes its name from French verb *bouder*, to be sulky or to pout; hence, their use by women for "withdrawing." The cabinet traces its roots to the sixteenth-century *studiolo*, and in its Anglophone incarnation became the "study." Being small and private, these rooms fell somewhat outside of the decoration rules and plans that pertained to more public spaces in châteaux and villas of the period and, as such, could reflect the identity of the occupant rather than create a public image. Named for a mood (sulking) and purposed for retreat and solitude, the boudoir as a category of modern domestic space was one of the first to be set aside purely for the [female] individual, rather than for socializing or serving bodily needs, like the kitchen or bedroom. Often personalized with small curios, comfortable furniture, mirrored panels and sometimes curved walls, these small intimate spaces soon became associated with seduction. These "modern" additions to the standard domestic program often contained a bed, bed linen, and swathes of curtains that framed or revealed the subject. Through the eighteenth century, the boudoir and the cabinet became a meeting point for a number of discourses around reading, viewing, and seduction. Thus sexualized, these spaces played a significant role in supporting and enhancing the *mimetic identification* of reader/audience with story/image (Saint-Amand 2008: 386). Interiors were "pressed into the service of eroticism" and played a crucial role in housing sex, making it real for the reader, adding depth to characters, becoming an actor in the unfolding of the story, and functioning as a critical stimulus to the sexual imagination.

For eighteenth-century men and women, the faculty of imagination was a key area of exploration that lent itself to spatialization, both then and in later analysis. Kathleen Lubey explains how the eighteenth-century English journalist Joseph Addison likened the imagination itself to a delightful room "that housed a singular and celebrated faculty that endowed each object with a self-contained capacity for excitement... it accommodate[d] an interior 'secret' life replete with beautiful spectacles, narrative engagement and the satisfaction of virtual ownership... in all visible things" (2008: 415).

Paul Young notes that in many libertine novels, encounters usually took place in cabinets, "small spaces that offered the opportunity for intimacy, and that were seen as more private than the bedrooms of the period" (2008: 338). Taking cues from Rodolphe El-Khoury's introduction to Bastide's *La Petite Maison*, Young has explicitly linked the architectural interior with the erotic eighteenth-century novel and its accompanying visual imagery. He states that the "smaller and more intimate rooms" heralded a changed architecture, and the *niche, alcove, boudoir,* and *cabinet* became the "mainstays of the libertine text" (2008: 335). That is, although the French libertine *cabinet* lay within the enclave of architecture, it offered a closeness and privacy that resided on the outside of society and its transactions. It offered, so to speak, *dangerous liaisons* and was a space that "commit[ted] itself unapologetically and wholly to pleasure" becoming "a self-conscious aesthetic chamber for sexual intimacy and discovery" (Young 2008: 335).

This suggests that some *cabinets* were aimed at arousing desire prior to libertine seduction, whereas others were there for instructional purposes. In *Thérèse Philosophe* (1748), the narrator Thérèse spies on the deceptive rape of her friend, Eradice, by the lecherous Jesuit, Father Dirrag.[7] Concealed in a *cabinet*, she is able to see Eradice assume an unorthodox prayer position which she believes would allow Father Dirrag to purify her with "the cord of Saint Francis":

> I scurried into the closet.... A hole in the closet door, as big as my hand and covered with an old, threadbare Bergamo tapestry, allowed me to see the entire room easily, without risk of being caught... I was positioned in such a manner as not to miss the slightest

detail of the scene: the windows of the bedroom where this scene took place were directly across from the door of the *cabinet* where I was hidden. (Darnton 1996: 235)

And in another, indeed a final, scene from *Dangerous Liaisons* the movie, Frears offers a slightly different interpretation of the viewing dynamics of the cabinet or boudoir. In this scene (an invention, as there is no counterpart in the novel), Frears provides the cinema audience with an "over the shoulder" view of Marquise de Merteuil as she moves through the space of an antechamber to her mirrored boudoir, where her new suitor awaits; and we observe her reining in grief, or guilt, as the ashes of destroyed lives build up around her. As she approaches this concealed mirrored door, her own reflection is multiplied, and the scene recalls another mirrored décor, the one that had enraptured Mélite in Bastide's novella *La Petite Maison*. Likewise, the scene draws upon the hidden chamber or *cabinet*, belonging to Mme de T—in Vivant Denon's *Point de lendermain* (1777), where mirror-covered walls transformed the interior into "a vast cage of reflective glass."[8] "Cage of seduction," "hall of mirrors," or space of brutal self-revelation, these mirrored rooms all reflect the late eighteenth century's new associations between the interior and psychological depth and agency.

Thus, the relationship between mirrors, bodies, space, concealment, and revelation is significant within the iconography of erotic illustrations that accompanied novels like *Thérèse Philosophe*. In this and related illustrated pornographic texts of the eighteenth century, architectural description was very important. While the stories *appear* to contain only a couple, an onlooker, a bed, a curtain and door, and maybe a picture on the wall (alluding to the occasional implausibility of various encounters), they reference the qualities of Harvey's "places of sex" such as "shady enclosures" and *also* draw on tasteful and "sensual" up-to-the-minute interiors of the day. The décor in the discursive spaces of the illustrations accompanying the novels is thus not from an earlier epoch, but is fashionably contemporary and aristocratic. These discursive spaces may be bare, but they're *opulent*, indicating taste and luxury.

What happens then when the fictional interiors are transmitted to other visual media? While authors might refer to spatial and tactile qualities of interiors in kinds of metonymic shorthand, i.e., "Bergamo tapestry," "vast cage of reflective glass," and may even set the sexual acts in interiors of the century before (i.e., interiors already historic in the eighteenth century), the illustrators had to transfer these cursory descriptions into imagery, retaining not only the sex but often inventing the settings, which were inevitably *contemporary* in style. We will explore these shifts in relation to Moreau Le Jeune's *The Boudoir* (1776 after Sigmund Freudenberg) and Emmanuel de Ghendt's *Le Midi* (c. 1765, after Pierre Antoine Baudouin). These are both well-known engravings, one appearing in album format, the other variously as an illustration in a novel or as a stand-alone print. Both depict female readers in erotic spaces and both also bear close intertextual relations to popular erotic fictions.

Their opulent illustrated spaces are suffused with a new kind of agency that acts upon or is at least imbricated in the behavior of their occupants. In *The Boudoir* (Figure 1.3), the drapery, décor, and interior architecture are all highly allusive. *The Boudoir* appears as the seventh plate of the first twelve of an eventual twenty-six plate album, *Monument du Costume Physique et Moral de la fin du Dix-huitième siècle, ou tableaux de la vie*, engraved after illustrations by Sigimund Freudeberg and "Moreau Le Jeune." The *Monument* has a complex publishing history, which has been of great interest to print historians but does not concern us much here except as to say that *Le Boudoir* appears in all three main editions (1776, 1783, and 1789) while also being issued by some printers on its own and collected thus by private and public collectors. In each edition also, its purpose changed, from being just about fashion and interiors, to displaying decaying aristocratic morals and, later, to illustrating Rousseau's ideas of happy families as played out by a stereotypical, wealthy young couple (Heller-Greenman 2002: 67–75).

**Figure 1.3** Pierre Maleuvre after Sigmund Freudenberger, *Le Boudoir*, etching and engraving, 1776, Musée du Louvre, Paris, Collection Rothschild, Photo ©RMN-Grand Palais (Musée du Louvre)/ Michel Urtado.

Fashion historian Daniel Roche describes it as a "deluxe album portraying the practises, furnishings and clothes in vogue in high society.... [Eventually becoming a] ... history of manners" (1995: 15–16). Roche refers here to the involvement of Rétif de la Bretonne, who, for the third edition, authored a text to accompany the images. The engravings from the series "follow in chronological sequence the activities of the *élégante* during one imaginary day from her early morning rising to her bedtime ritual" (Heller-Greenman 2002: 69). In the prior plates, we see our *élégante* waking up in her fashionable bed canopied "*à la Turque*" (Lee 2013: 126) (*Le Lever*), having her bath (*Le Bain*), then her toilette (*La Toilette*), doing her needlework (*L'Occupation*), receiving her lover (*La Visite Inattendue*), going for a morning walk with a friend (*La Promenade du Matin*), and then finally, in the afternoon, reading in her boudoir.

Here in her boudoir, the walls of the interior actually curve around her like an embrace (soft, rounded shapes were considered ideal for boudoirs), graceful lines, and swooping plaster scroll work behind her form a charming relation to the similarly oval pattern in the tiled floor. The room has the latest accoutrements of the fashionable boudoir: potted flowers, soft textiles, a light graceful sofa upon which she sits, and a caged bird, suggesting perhaps also that her heart is claimed. The French windows are open, and beyond them is a young man courting a servant outside, and who peeps through the windows.

Hanging in suggestive pleats and swaying by a gentle breeze, the curtain both reveals and conceals the faint presences of the courtier and servant at the French windows. Here, draperies exteriorize the sensations that the figured subjects are experiencing and amplify these sensations. They also divide the action and the orchestration of gazes along gender lines—as they fall like an abyss from the top to bottom of the picture, between the reader's feminine space to the left, and the spying male on the right hand side. They also divide private from public space and underscore the *boudoir* as public rather than private, as in this case it has all the privacy of a fish bowl. Even so, the *élégante* is occupying her boudoir at the appropriate time of day for the appropriate activity, reflecting not only the general projections around this space as erotic, but also the increase in function-specific rooms in the period. In terms of spaces of consumption of erotica, Suellen Diaconoff conceives of *l'espace du livre* that brings together book, boudoir, women's reading, and its representation (2005: 3). In *l'espace du livre*, space and occupation play an important role, and the female reader was, as representations reveal, inevitably found *en retraite*, in her boudoir. Diaconoff reiterates that such reading was by necessity private and removed from "the agitation of normal household activities" (2005: 3). This eroticization of the ladies' chamber transformed it into a boudoir, hitherto a space of feminine peace and quiet, now an enticing "morally compromised" space of fantasy and desire.

Additionally, a host of narrative prospects abound—the couple on the right are "making love" or are doing what the young lady has possibly just read about. The gentle teasing tone of the text beneath the illustration (*Enter not ... for your benefit/Can you not, from a distance, at your leisure enjoy/At least leave to your works/The happy gift to lull to sleep*) and the allusiveness of the image suggest that readings may satisfactorily be left somewhat open. But, on a host of different levels, we see the compression of a range of ideas, achieved via the fashionable current interior, as it relates back to texts, giving them material form and multiplying their meaning.[9]

Emmanuel de Ghendt's *Le Midi* [c. 1765], made after a gouache by P.A. Baudouin (Figure 1.4) depicts an image of a small enclosed garden at midday, occupied by a young woman who appears to be at the point of orgasm. One hand points to a book that has slipped from her grasp, while the other is otherwise occupied in the folds of her dress. Like the young woman in the Moreau Le Jeune print, she has also succumbed to the pages from an erotic novel. The scenario here references a similar moment in the life of Thérèse, the main character in the well-known eponymous erotic novel *Thérèse Philosophe* (1748). Toward the culmination of her sexual education, the narrator of the tale, Thérèse,

**Figure 1.4** Emmanuel Jean Népomucène de Ghendt after Pierre-Antoine Baudouin, *Le Midi*, etching and engraving, c. 1765, Musée du Louvre, Paris, Collection Rothschild, Photo ©RMN-Grand Palais (Musée du Louvre)/Michel Urtado.

becomes particularly concerned about pregnancy. Her frustrated lover [referred to throughout merely as "the Count"] sends away to Paris for his library of erotic books and pictures, to be brought forthwith, and he wagers Thérèse that after reading these, she will not be able to last two weeks without "touching that part of your body which should, by rights today be within my domain" (Darnton 1996: 297). On day five, Thérèse confides to us, *her* readers, that after an hour of *The Love Affair of Venus and Mars*, "I fell into a kind of ecstasy...I set myself to imitate all the postures that I saw....Mechanically, my hand ventured where that of the man was placed..." (Cusset 1999: 111).

We observe here that this time the "Thérèsian" scene, when transposed from text to image, occurs in a secluded, shady, bushy garden, pleasantly analogous to the boudoir. Once again, this pictorial space was imagined in the absence of information in the text about exactly where the real Thérèse's reading occurred. It is an unabashedly feminine space, this garden, with its centrally placed bust of a woman, and its attractive decorative lattice work wall. Here it is a good complement to the previous image with the fresh potted roses in the *élégante's* boudoir, and the floral, vegetal plasterwork. *Le Midi*, too, concentrates contemporary ideas about the interior *as* an intimate walled garden through multiple intertextual touch points—we have the libertine female reader in a libertine feminine space, an element of instruction, places of sex as feminine and floral, the invasion of the reader's privacy (by us, the viewers of this latter image), and finally, we likewise have the materialization of places of sex in ways that reflect both fashionable taste and sensationalist theory. In particular, the garden in *Le Midi* is planted in the picturesque style, and thus references Claude-Henri Watlet's ideas on the picturesque garden in his *Essai sur les jardins*.

The boudoir's furnishings in *Le Boudoir* (1776) and the picturesquely fashionable garden in *Le Midi* (1748) are not old but innovative, based on libertine and sensationalist philosophies, while also incorporating the latest tasteful Parisian interiors. This process of translating settings for erotic stories across mediums contributed much to the progress of the modern French interior.

## Conclusion

The texts and illustrations explored here are purely imaginary. In the case of the illustrations, they extended from other media (fiction, in most cases), their purpose as illustrations being to create a dynamic interaction between words and images that doubled pleasure. While readers of fiction could imagine complex interplays between body and space, artists and illustrators needed to fix these characters in "erotically fitting" domestic spaces. We have shown here how these transmissions from media to media were to the advantage of the interior, as in each shift the imagined modern interior became a powerful discursive agent, evoking an aesthetic realm with as much claim on our pleasure as clearly on its inhabitants. The relationship between erotic text and image shifts our understanding of the cabinet or boudoir from a static space of seclusion and repose to one invigorated by imagined sensorial participation.

The ability of architecture to express the emotional states of their inhabitants was tested out in the sensationalist approach of eighteenth-century French architectural theory. Through the sustained theoretical consideration of Nicolas le Camus de Mézières as well as his libertine fellow travellers, imitators and interlocutors, architectural character has been seen here to be employed to produce emotional responses and behaviors in the inhabiting subject, offering a new appreciation of architecture and the interior's part in shaping new, more modern identities.

Architectural theory itself becomes subject to fictional transposition, as we have seen with the mirrored room scenes in *La Petite Maison* and *Point de Lendemain*. It is likely that these particular fictional scenes were not subject to transposition into illustration since they were already "sensationalist" and already modern in the manner in which they drew upon contemporary design theory and philosophy; there was nothing an engraving might add to the pure sensation of their descriptive passages. Moreover, our discussion of the film *Dangerous Liaisons* offers a twentieth-century example of how the process of transmission from medium to medium worked to the advantage of the interior by demanding the imaginative repopulation and reoccupation of historical rooms by mobile bodies and authentic furnishing. These imaginative reshapings in the shift from text to moving pictures, hark back to the original manner in which such transpositions contributed to the modern French interior as both an expression of and a tool for affecting various psychological states of being.

## Notes

1. The libertine novel was an eighteenth-century literary genre that blended eroticism and rationalism, but which is increasingly regarded as titillating or pornographic literature. As a genre, it offered explicit depictions of sexuality, often incorporated theatrical elements, and provided a narrative that was both arousing and instructional. Authors include Jean-Baptiste de Boyer, the Marquis d'Argens (*Thérèse philosophe*, 1748), Denis Diderot (*Les Bijoux Indiscrets*, 1748), Vivant Denon (*Point de Lendemain*, 1777), Choderlos de Laclos (*Les Liaisons Dangereuses*, 1782), and the Marquis de Sade (*La Philosophie dans le Boudoir*, 1795).
2. A drawing room is mentioned twice, but its interiors, though "splendid," remain mysterious; an ottoman, the place of Mme de Tourval's final capitulation to Valmont is mentioned once.
3. These two immensely successful court artists, Boucher and Fragonard, both operated at the pinnacle of the contemporary visual cultures of the period, and in their iconography they drew on the languages of the Classical, the mythological and the pastoral. Boucher's *Diana Leaving the Bath* (1742) and Fragonard's *The Swing* (1767) are examples of the Classical and the pastoral respectively; both works are also replete with allegorical allusions and they feature contemporary persons, fashions, gardens, interiors, and court festivities.
4. Le Camus de Mézières describes a boudoir in which the bed recess was lined with "looking glasses," and joints were concealed with carved tree trunks. There was a niche that also contained an ottoman and was decorated with looking glasses on all sides and on the ceiling (1992 [1780]: 116–117).
5. Claude-Prosper Jolyot de Crébillon, *Le Sopha* [1742] (Editions Slatkine, 1996), 333, cited in Berrett Brown (2009: 102).
6. Mathieu-François Pidanset de Mairobert, *Anecdotes sur Mme la Comtesse du Barry*, 1775. This version of the text is from an abridged translation in Darnton, *Forbidden Best-Sellers*, 345.
7. According to Robert Darnton, the "whore biography" *Thérèse Philosophe* is "as close as possible to 'pure' pornography." He argues that although the term *pornographe* hardly existed in eighteenth-century France, some books celebrated reading as a "stimulus of sexual pleasure and sometimes recommended works that provided it" (Darnton 1996: 89). Catherine Cusset argues that while

seeming to serve male sexual fantasy in an objectifying form, novels like *Thérèse Philosophe* featured female narrators with self-agency and complex subjectivities and an awakening interest in sex. We are referring here to ideas about pornography expressed by Catherine MacKinnon (1988) and Andrea Dworkin (1981 and 1987). Reading against contemporary theorists such as Andrea Dworkin and Catherine McKinnon on pornography, Cusset proposes that given the interweaving of the erotic novel and philosophy in the period, "one [can] speak then, of a philosophical or enlightened pornography" (1999: 90). This is a literature that interwove instructional philosophy and sexual arousal, alongside pedagogical and practical advice about sexual health. This combination had great popular impact that was widely absorbed by both sexes, but a certain sophisticated discretion was required. Jean-Jacques Rousseau in *Les Confessions* (1782) confided that "I was more than thirty years old before I looked at any of those dangerous books which a beautiful lady of the world finds inconvenient because, she says, they must be read with a single hand" (Cusset 1999: footnote 2, 184). There are a number of slightly different translations of this passage in the relevant literature.

8. Vivant Denon, *Point de Lendemain*, in Etiemble (1965: 397). Quoted in Cusset (1999: 156).
9. We would like to thank Flore Sivell for this translation.

## References

Albano, C. (2007), "The Pleasures of the Text," in M. Wallace, M. Kemp and J. Bernstein (eds), *Seduced: Art and Sex from Antiquity to Now*, London: Barbican.
Bastide, J -F de, *The Little House: An Architectural Seduction* [*La Petite Maison*, 1789], trans. Rudolph el-Khoury, New York: Princeton University Press.
Berrett Brown, D. (Fall/Winter 2009), "The Female Philosophe in the Closet: The Cabinet and the Senses in French Erotic Novels, 1740–1800," *Journal for Early Modern Cultural Studies* 9, no. 2: 96–123.
Bruno, G. (2002), *Atlas of Emotion: Journeys in Art, Architecture and Film*, New York: Verso.
Coward, D. (1995), "Introduction," in Cholderlos de Laclos (ed), *Le Liaisons Dangereuses* (1782), trans. Douglas Parmee, Oxford and London: Oxford University Press World Classics.
Cusset, C. (1999), *No Tomorrow: The Ethics of Pleasure in the French Enlightenment*, Charlottesville: University of Virginia Press.
Darnton, R. (1996), *Forbidden Best-Sellers of Pre-Revolutionary France*, New York and London: W. W. Norton & Company.
Diaconoff, S. (2005), *Through the Reading Glass: Women Books and Sex in the French Enlightenment*, New York: State University of New York Press.
el-Khoury, R. (1996), "Introduction," in Jean-François de Bastide, *The Little House: An Architectural Seduction* [*La Petite Maison*, 1789], trans. New York: Princeton University Press.
Etiemble, R. (ed), (1965), *Romanciers du XVIIIe siecle*, Paris: Gallimard, Bibliotheque de le Pleiade: 385–402, 397, Vol. 2.
Harvey, K. (2001), "Gender, Space and Modernity in Eighteenth Century England: A Place Called Sex," *History Workshop Journal* 51: 158–179.
Heller-Greenman, B. (2002), "Moreau Le Jeune and the Monument du Costume," *Athanor*, 20: 67–75.
Le Camus de Mézières, N. (1992 [1780]), *The Genius of Architecture; Or, the Analogy of That Art with Our Sensations*, Santa Monica: Getty Centre.
Lee, D. C. (2013), "Between Worlds: The Biography of Madame de Pompadour's Boudoir Turc," *Art and Design Theses* (Georgia State University) Paper: 126.
Lubey, K. (Spring 2008), "Erotic Interiors in Joseph Addison's Imagination," *Eighteenth-Century Fiction* 20, no. 3: 415–444.
Middleton, R. (1992 [1780]), "Introduction," in Nicolas le Camus de Mézières, *The Genius of Architecture; Or, the Analogy of That Art with Our Sensations*, Santa Monica: Getty Centre.

Padiyar, S. (2006), "Introduction," in *The Triumph of Eros: Art and Seduction in 18th-century France*, St Petersburg: State Hermitage Museum/Courtauld Institute.

Percival, M. (2012), *Fragonard and the Fantasy Figure: Painting the Imagination*, Farnham: Ashgate.

Saint-Amand, P. (2008), review of Paul J. Young, "Seducing the Eighteenth-Century French Reader," *Eighteenth Century Fiction* 22, no.: 386–388.

Schama, S. (1989), Citizens: *A Chronicle of the French Revolution*, New York: Vintage Books.

Young, P. J. (2008), "Ce Lieu de délices: Art and Imitation in the French Libertine Cabinet," *Eighteenth-Century Fiction* 20, no. 3: 335–356.

# CHAPTER 2
## INTIMATE VIBRATIONS: INVENTING THE DREAM BEDROOM
Fae Brauer

---

Ours is a society racked ceaselessly by nervous erythrism. We are sickened by our industrial progress, by science; we live in a fever, and we like to dig deeper into our sores.... Everything suffers and complains in the works of our time. Nature herself is linked to our suffering, and being tears itself apart, exposes itself in its nudity. (Zola 1896: 546; Silverman 1992: 80)

Owing to the abrasiveness of the modernized city, the invasiveness of new technologies, and sensory overstimulation by the mass media, by 1896 Émile Zola regarded the modern subject as subsumed by fever (1896). Even before this time France had become, according to Italian criminologist Cesare Lombroso, the most degenerate of all Western nations, his study of *Criminal Man* revealing that it had the highest rate of criminals in any European state (1876).[1] The 385 percent increase in suicide documented by Émile Durkheim (1897), together with the rapid rise in hysteria, neurasthenia, epilepsy, and alcoholism—the French being the greatest consumers in Europe devouring 27 liters of pure alcohol every year including copious amounts of "the green fairy"–was correlated by Valentin Magnan, as well as Zola, to the increasing prevalence of nervous disorders (Magnan 1871). In a series of articles published in *Revue Scientifique*, Charles Richet, followed by Marie Manacéïne, identified overexertion of the nervous system in the metropolis as one of the chief sources of suicide, hysteria, neurasthenia, and national devitalization (Manacéïne 1890; Richet 1919). The mounting fear of rampant degeneration, escalating depopulation, and devolution to the point of extinction generated a national psychopathology of paranoia, a "queasy, sickening feeling that all was not right, that things were in decay and that one could not fit into one's own surroundings" (Hirst 2004: 24).

"We are afraid," confessed the writer Guy de Maupassant in 1889. "We are afraid of everybody, and everybody is afraid under this regime.... Fear of cities, fear of disease, fear of degeneration, fear of corruption, fear of the electors, fear of majorities, and fear of newspapers and the opinions they voiced" (de Maupassant 1889: 388). Without stable boundaries, modern subjects were in danger of being transformed, according to Georges Valbert, into "agitated" and weary "neuropaths."[2] Within the discourses of neuropsychiatry and *la psychologie nouvelle*, both the sensory overstimulation of the "poisonous city" and the artificiality of mass media were inscribed as agents of degeneration, devitalization, hysteria, and neurasthenia with an impact upon the febrile nervous system equivalent to what Walter Benjamin calls "a shattering of the interior" (1935: 38). Bombarded by mass advertising and overwhelmed with the physiological stress and psychological strains of the city, such "new psychologists" as Maurice Rollinat pointed out that both males and females sought an escape from their overwrought nerves and the danger of contracting what Jean-Martin Charcot called *les maladies nerveuses* (Rollinat 1883). Consistent with Henri Bergson's doctoral thesis, *Time and Free Will*, they longed for a sanctuary safe from the feverish pace and fracturing flux of metropolitan life in which intimate relationships, psychological intuition, imagination, and "felt experiences" triggered by memory and empathy could be embraced (Bergson 1889).

With the "sick city" identified by theorists and sensationalized by the mass media as an agent of alcoholism, criminality, suicide, cholera, tuberculosis, syphilis, hysteria, and neurasthenia, by the *fin-de-siècle* the French interior was transformed into a refuge able to fortify the physiology of city dwellers and to nurture their psychology. Following *la psychologie nouvelle*, their psychology was revealed as sensitive, nervous, susceptible to exhaustion and prone to imagistic suggestion and projection. To be able to nurture their psychological interiority, particularly their phantasies and dreams, the French interior became inscribed as a domestic haven of peace and security, imagination and relaxation able to foster the intimacy of close personal and sexual relationships. Within this haven, the French bedroom became valorized as the most precious place for relaxing the body, releasing the unconscious, exploring creativity, enhancing dreams and achieving intimacy, as epitomized by its sanctification by Marcel Proust (1909–1922).[3] Within *la psychologie nouvelle*, the *boudoir* for woman and the *chambre à coucher* with its *lit conjugal* took on new roles as a soothing anesthetizer not just of a citizen's overwrought nerves but that of the conjugal couple. Reconceived as a metaphor for the mind itself, what Jules Bois called a "*chambre mentale*" (1900: 29), the interior space of the *boudoir* and the *chambre à coucher* also became inscribed within Neo-Lamarckian evolutionary theory as a recuperative place to recharge the cerebral and psychological energy required for "creative evolution" in order to attain what Bergson termed *l'élan vital*: "The vital life force" (1907: 88–99). Not only could French citizens seek refuge from the sensory barrage of the metropolis within this "*chambre mentale*" but they could also find intimate vibratory reanimation, as this chapter will reveal, particularly through a dynamic and intimate interaction between interior decoration and their psychological exploration. No more intimate refuge and energizing space existed for this to ensue than the *fin-de-siècle* bedroom.

Reconceived within the interdiscursivity of Symbolist Decadence, *la psychologie nouvelle* and Neuropsychiatry as the site of dreams, memories, felt experiences, and intimate relationships, as well as organic reunification, the *fin-de-siècle* bedroom became the locus for exploration by artists, architects, and interior decorators associated with the Nabis, École de Nancy, *L'Art dans tous*, and *L'Art Nouveau*. This is demonstrated not only by the prevalence of paintings of the intimate interior from Pierre Bonnard to Félix Vallotton but also by the spate of new bed designs ranging from Louis Majorelle's 1900 *chambre à coucher* with its *Lit et table de chevet* (Janneau 1966: 30), Georges Rémon's 1900 *Projet de chambre à coucher*, Émile André's 1902 *Lit de bout à décor de tulipe*, Émile Gallé's 1904 *Lit Aube et Crépuscule*, André Vallin's 1907 *Chambre à coucher*, Henri Bellery Desfontaines's 1907 *Lit et Psyche*, the *chamber à coucher* designed by Charles Plumet and Tony Selmersheim, Frank Brangwyn's *chambre à coucher* commissioned for Mr. and Mrs. Davis, as well as the twin beds designed by Claude Delvincourt for *l'Art Nouveau Bing* in Turin in 1902. Yet, as this chapter will reveal, no more vivid reconception of its new role as the arbor of organic regeneration and the cocoon of unconscious vivification was created for the 1900 *Exposition Universelle* than Eugène Gaillard's *chambre à coucher* commissioned by Siegfried Bing for his *Pavillon de l'Art Nouveau* (Figure 2.1). Only in Gaillard's "dream bedroom" could the psychological interior and physiological exterior become indissolubly fused, reintegrated with nature, reconnected with living species, and reenergized by the intimate embrace of its regenerative forms from plant-life to the growth of wood.

## Organic reunification and *ineluctable evolution*: Gaillard's regenerative bedroom

By comparison to France's wrought-iron monuments to engineering, industrialism, and virility at the 1889 *Exposition Universelle*, the 1900 *Exposition Universelle* represented what Debora Silverman calls a "retreat to an ornamental fantasy in the organicized private interior" (1992: 85). Replacing the public iron monument with the private organic ornament, domestic ensembles of nature and interiority were celebrated in *Art Nouveau*. Interiors with decorations infused with plants, insects, and animals in the process of seasonal renewal were seminal in instilling the Neo-Lamarckian concept of evolutionary regeneration. Termed *Transformism*, after Jean-Baptiste Lamarck, evolutionary regeneration was pursued by many zoologists, one of the most influential being Edmond Perrier. Appointed Director of the Muséum National d'Histoire Naturelle in 1900, Perrier was instrumental in revealing ways in which interspecies interrelationships,

**Figure 2.1** Eugène Gaillard, Double bed and wardrobe, *Chambre à coucher, Pavillon de l'Art Nouveau*, Exposition Universelle, 1900, pearwood with ash paneling, Bibliothèque des arts décoratifs, Paris (no 253 Lit Exposition par E. Gaillard).

lost with industrialization, could be reanimated to revivify the physiology and psychology of the modern subject (1888). These animalized interiors were also integral to the anti-anthropocentricism of modernists who rejected the binaristic demarcation of Homo sapiens and animals in favor of the inseparability of human subjects from nature (Brauer 2009; 2015). As geographer, Elisée Reclus explained:

> Man does not only live upon the surface of the soil, he has also sprung from it; he is its son, as we learn from the mythologies of all nations. We are an arrangement of dust, water and air. (Reclus 1868: 434)

Not until the last minute does Bing appear to have been officially invited to construct a pavilion with such interiors, which may explain why it did not appear in any of the official catalogs. Yet, with the Porte Binet and other installations embodying the evolutionary aesthetic of *Transformism*, it seemed serendipitous to construct *Art Nouveau Bing*. Early in 1900, Bing and his assistant Louis Bonnier drew up plans for this pavilion comprising six model interiors in a modern house or apartment on the French side of the Esplanade for the *Exposition Universelle* (Picard 1903: 273; Brauer 2013: 255).[4] Having already hired Gaillard as the first new architect-designer for his workshops in 1897, Bing commissioned him to design its *salle à manger*, vestibule, and *chambre à coucher* with the assistance of Georges de Feure and Edouard Colonna, on the understanding that everything in the pavilion was to be originally manufactured (Vandam 1985). While de Feure was commissioned to do the *boudoir* and dressing room, as well as the exterior glass panels featuring *la femme nouvelle*, Colonna was responsible for the drawing room colored in golds and blues. This new house was designed to be, as Julius Meier-Graefe surmized, "neither a museum nor a department store but a place of peace for the eye and the nerves ... and an intimate space in which to live, work, think and to dream" (1900: 206–212). With "dream-like" rooms accentuated by the use of colored-glass panels, commissioned from de Feure, *Art Nouveau Pavillon Bing* was commended for evoking thought, memory and dreams. Yet, no place within Bing's "new house" captured this more so than Gaillard's *chambre à coucher*, created in collaboration with de Feure. There, buds, flowers, stems, roots, and vegetables seemed to flourish and intertwine in a profusion of glowing colors and phantasmagorical configurations.

Reunification with nature invigorated with the new methods of hygiene became seminal to designing the healthy domestic interior, particularly the new bedroom, capable of regenerating the nation. As Alfred Fouillée explained: "France needs ... better physical hygiene, capable of counterbalancing the affect of our intellectual overexertion ... and a vigorous reaction against our abandonment of the countryside for the city" (Fouillée 1892: 143–144). Design of the domestic interior then became invested with nourishing the physiological and psychological health of French citizens and regenerating the French nation. This is most clearly demonstrated by Henry Havard's *Art in the House*, first published in 1884 and circulated by the government through schools and teaching training centers in 1891 as the *Manuel* for interior design (Havard 1884; 1891; Brauer 2013: 197–208).

Owing to fear of infection from toxic domestic interiors, as much as from the pre-industrial city infested by plague, in his treatise, Havard highlighted the problems that had been generated by a generation of paranoid hygienists who had insisted upon reducing design, particularly that of the bedroom, to its bare essentials:

> A bedroom had to be absolutely naked without hangings, paperless with white washed walls and floors painted in oil, painted and washed with plenty of water at least once a week. The bed, according to these doctors, had to be reduced to a simple couchette, made of metal, with no curtains, and garnished with a mattress topped by horsehair. As for furniture [these doctors] would barely admit a vase or two—only accepting the most indispensable table and chair and that is all. Why this bareness? Fear of miasma. (Havard 1884: 383)

Yet, paradoxically, this Spartan bedroom had proven no more hygienic than any other, particularly as Havard pointed out that the common cold had managed to kill more people than the plague (1884: 385). At the same time, he was aware that his colleague, Gabriel Mourey, regarded the *chambres à coucher modern style*, designed by those obsessed with modern hygiene—*L'Art dans tout chambre à coucher* of Charles Plumet and Tony Selmersheim—as not much better, being likened to torture chambers of the Inquisition (1900: 268). Historically, Havard traced the rupture and transformation in this design to the exploration of emotional sensations during the Baroque and "the birth of intimacy" when a distinction became clearly drawn between design of the *chambre à coucher*, *boudoir*, and *cabinet de travail* (Havard 1884; Cheng 2011).

From the advent of technologized modernity, Havard considered how the *boudoir* had increasingly become an "essentially feminine" psychological space for female self-fashioning and an emblematic room for women to be alone, to dream and enhance their imagination (Havard 1884: 411; 417; Delon 1999). The *cabinet de travail* for men acted more as "a place where one loves to be locked-in, to meditate, to reflect, a kind of intimate refuge, a blessed port which allowed us to gain possession of ourselves" (Havard 1884: 431). Yet, like others, Havard was aware that, as the culture of intimacy between married couples had changed, so had the articulation of their conjugal bedroom and the significance assigned to what he called the "lit d'anges:" The marital "bed of angels" (1884: 399). Although he detected that many husbands and wives had slept apart at the beginning of the nineteenth century, by the end of it, as Odile Nouvel-Kammerer points out, they were strongly encouraged to sleep in the same bed granting increasing significance to *le lit conjugal* and to the *chambre à coucher* (1995: 102). This was not just symptomatic of the vigorous campaign fought by French theologians against what they called *l'onanisme conjugal*, according to Alain Corbin, but of the French depopulation crisis (2008: 270–276).[5]

With France's escalating depopulation constantly exposed by demographers from inception of the Third Republic to the *fin-de-siècle*, the need for French couples to sleep together in order to procreate regularly was constantly emphasized by State demographer Jacques Bertillon, and by the natalist lobby spearheaded by such Neo-Lamarckian obstetricians and eugenicists as Adolphe Pinard (Brauer 2008). Since depopulation was, in light of Charles Darwin's *The Descent of Man*, aligned with devolution and encroaching extinction, repopulation become such a crucial Republican quest that the single *femme nouvelle* and *Le bachelier* became stigmatized as selfish, decadent, and unpatriotic

(Brauer 2005). The most licit site for repopulation, the conjugal *chambre à coucher* thus became the locus of national attention, although rarely did Havard spell out its imbrication within procreation so explicitly. By contrast to his discrete allusion to its sexual role as "an asylum of mysterious actions, of great and small secrets" (1884: 400), Havard openly stressed its importance in relation to imagination, contemplation, and its function as "the refuge of memories:"

> It is … a sanctuary, and also the fatal place where the most powerful to the most humble find they are alone with themselves, where truth so often betrayed, cutthroat, banned, appears suddenly in its *deshabillé*, sometimes unflattering … where during the night the mind welcomes the vagabond of imagination, reliving the past, evoking vanished images, calculates, speculates, tries to predict, combine, arrange, decide and finally prepare for the future. (Havard 1884: 400–401)

When furnishing their *chambre à coucher*, Havard recommended that the conjugal couple not hesitate to adorn it with paintings, statues, ceramics, and enamels, particularly given "the fortunate influence that art exercises on our imagination and our senses … the contemplation of these beautiful artworks delighting the eyes, lifting the spirit and ennobling our thoughts" (1884: 431). To stimulate the unconscious and to generate healthy energies, Havard also recommended that it be adorned with flowers, particularly a profusion of roses, Japanese and Chinese porcelain, silks and brocaded silks, satins and lacquered woods (1884: 418). "First and foremost," he stressed, "adornment of the *chambre à coucher* must be intimate and contemplative" (1884: 401). These criteria seem to have been heeded by Gaillard when Bing commissioned him in 1899 to design the "dream bedroom."

Directly behind Gaillard's bedhead, a floor-to-ceiling panel was inserted on the wall. Appearing like a bed canopy appropriated and modernized from Rococo designs, it was printed and embroidered with a garland of deep and pale crimson roses (Figure 2.2). Seeming to burst into bloom, this garland echoes the shape of the main bedhead and seems to frame the bed as if it were a bed of roses. Not just appliquéd onto the curtains, but embroidered by Madame Anaïs Favre, as can be glimpsed in the wardrobe mirror of Figure 2.1, these roses were continued onto the chair at the left side of the bed, as can be seen in Figure 2.2, where they appear in a small rosebud pattern printed on velveteen. These roses seeming to burst into full bloom also appear on the tapestry of the armchair on the other side of the bed, as can be seen clearly in Figure 2.3, where they seem to be entwined on both sides of the backrest, as well as across the headrest. As they also appear to have been interwoven into the garland design of the wallpaper, as can be seen in Figure 2.2, *le lit conjugal* seems to be enmeshed in roses. Yet, instead of being literally represented, following Gaillard's emphasis upon the need to be inspired by evocations of flowers, plants, and vegetables found in nature, they are suggested (1900: 107). Rather than rarefying particular flowers, earthworms, algae, insects, dragonflies, or irises and thistles as the essential steps of modern evolution and treating them in the École de Nancy manner as emotive objects, Gaillard stressed the importance of transcending them and transfiguring nature into "haunting" new constellations able to permeate the unconscious (1900: 107; 1906: 34). This transfiguration entailed, in his words:

**Figure 2.2** Eugène Gaillard, Double bed, *Chambre à coucher: Pavillon de l'Art Nouveau*, Exposition Universelle, 1900, pearwood bed-frame with ash panelling, mignonette green silk bed coverlet embroidered with plant stems and vegetable forms, and flat bed canopy on the wall embroidered with a garland of roses, from *The Art Journal* feature on The Paris Exhibition of 1900, London, England, 1901, Photo © Victoria and Albert Museum, London.

> To see forever the same flower in wood, never faded, the same animal—fixed in wood—always in its familiar pose; the insect without a pin in its back, poised there in place so securely that not even a metal disk could dislodge it: By incorporating such realities, our familiar furniture immediately becomes haunting. (Gaillard 1906: 60)

Yet, despite Gaillard's stress upon both capturing and transcending nature by working in wood, particularly by being able to transfix the essence of a flower, animal, or insect, the writer Gustave Soulier pointed out that Gaillard did not necessarily practice what he preached. His innumerable studies of various parts of plants, particularly of stems, leaves, vegetables, and flowers, were rendered so minutely, according to Soulier, that they seemed to be viewed through a microscope (1902: 25). Readily Gaillard admitted to deploying a microscope, although he also confessed to the frustration of discovering with its help so many thousands of diverse elements intertwined in nature, that he could never satisfactorily fathom exactly where they led (1906: 63).

Attuned to Gaillard's concern with tracing organic interrelationships rather than representing organic species, Soulier examined how Gaillard's in-depth scrutiny of vegetable structures revealed their "constant communion" with one another and their interdependence (1902: 26). In being able to discover the movements of what Soulier called "spontaneous grace" alongside the "splaying of nervous forms," he considered Gaillard's studies had proven infinitely precious: the *fibers* that Gaillard was able to reveal, observed Soulier, "deliver all the richness hidden at the heart of the material. The memories, flames, speckles, pearlescent agents, gems and waves seem to succeed one another by very clear lines that have been smoothed into satin by his tool" (1902: 27). At the same time, Soulier considered that Gaillard never seemed to forget how the diverse elements of a tree and plant growing normally are intimately part of the same organic "body" and "seamlessly attached to one another" (1902: 27). Not only does this seamless growth appear in the carved arms-rests of Gaillard's armchair, as can be seen in Figure 2.3, but also in its legs and feet, as can be seen in Figure 2.4. It is continued not only

**Figure 2.3** Eugène Gaillard, Chair "Delvincourt" (front view), *Chambre à coucher: Pavillon de l'Art Nouveau*, Exposition Universelle, 1900, Bibliothèque des arts décoratifs, Paris.

**Figure 2.4** Eugène Gaillard, Chair, "Delvincourt" (profile), *Chambre à coucher: Pavillon de l'Art Nouveau*, Exposition Universelle, 1900, Bibliothèque des arts décoratifs, Paris.

in the framing, legs, and handles of the wardrobe, as can be seen in Figure 2.5, but also in the carved bedheads in which four main vegetable *fibers* seem to flow out from a central stem and seamlessly coil around one another with two of the coils meeting around the center.

Soulier also considered how what he called Gaillard's "naturalistic style" and "skeletal model," emanating from the study of vegetable forms, was illustrated by the way in which the leaves fanned out from the rods at the foot of the bed (Figure 2.2) (1902: 27). For Gaillard, this was seminal to his vision of "*L'Évolution inéluctable*" (1906: 63). By immersing the conjugal couple within this profusion of evolving forms in nature, Gaillard presumed that they would feel not only unified with nature but also vivified by its "ineluctable" energies of regeneration. At this optimum moment, following the *Transformist* dimension of Gaillard's *chambre à coucher*, they would be ready to perform what Pinard called "*procréation rationnelle*"—sex conducted in a rejuvenated state of mind and body to produce the healthiest possible progeny (Brauer 2008: 117–120). Since internal protoplasm was, following Neo-Lamarckian obstetrics, considered to interact with external parasites during conception of the embryo, the "ineluctable evolution"

**Figure 2.5** Eugène Gaillard, Wardrobe, *Chambre à coucher: Pavillon de l'Art Nouveau*, Exposition Universelle, 1900, Bibliothèque des arts décoratifs, Paris.

inherent to Gaillard's design of the *chambre à coucher* may then be ultimately aligned with the Radical Republican policy of repopulation and national regeneration (Giard 1876; 1888). Drawing upon *la nouvelle psychologie*, Gaillard's *chambre à coucher* was also meant to regenerate the unconscious by functioning as a "dream bedroom," as highlighted by critics and the art media.

### Suggestion, hypnosis, and *la nouvelle psychologie*: The dream bedroom

For the Symbolists, as Silverman succinctly surmises, "the interior was no longer a refuge from but a replacement for the external world" (1992: 77). The house was reconceived as not merely, in her words, "a passive receiver of imported technologies but an active producer of new instruments of psychospatial intervention" (1992: 77). Yet, for this production to be able to happen, an understanding of the relationship of the unconscious to the environment was required alongside what Silverman calls "the psychological consequences of space" (1992: 77). This was highlighted by Count Robert de Montesquiou-Fezensac, the model for Huysmans's Des Esseintes, who organized his apartment so that individual objects could dissolve into a field of suggestive visual energy (Huysmans 1884; Chaleyssin 1992). Linking interior decoration with psychological interiority, the Goncourt brothers, Edmond and Jules, also envisaged the interior as activator of both visual suggestion and nervous vibration (de Goncourt 1889). The dialogue between the narrator and his décor, particularly the nervous vibrations they stimulated to the point of transfiguring fevers, was captured in *À la recherche du temps perdu* by Proust, as epitomized by the whirling room in *Swann's Way* in which all the furnishings appear trapped in the centrifuge of the psyche (1913). This linkage between psychological association and interior decoration was corroborated by *la psychologie nouvelle*.

Modern conceptions of the social and psychological significance of interior space were the results of new medical theories on the powers of suggestion and the relationship between external stimuli and mental health. While Théodore Ribot, appointed the first chair in Experimental and Comparative Psychology at the Collège de France in 1888, was one of the pioneers of the new *psychologie scientifique française*, it was at the Salpêtrière where most experiments in the psychology of space were conducted by Jean-Martin Charcot, Pierre Janet, Gilles de la Tourette, Alfred Binet, Charles Féré, and Joseph Babinski. At the Salpêtrière, Charcot and his "Charcoterie" demonstrated that female patients suffering from traumatic or epileptic hysteria and male patients suffering from what Charcot called "virile hysteria," which Gilles de la Tourette also termed "neurasthenia," were susceptible to hypnosis, particularly conducted by animal magnetism (Binet and Féré 1887; 1888). Under hypnosis, various forms of suggestion were found to trigger specific emotional and behavioral reactions, particularly such visual stimuli as colored images, discs, and signs to the extent that specific colors could be correlated with emotional states (Charcot 1888; Didi-Huberman 2003; Hustvedt 2011). Even Charcot's Tuesday performances demonstrated the affective powers of visual suggestion on the nervously febrile (Charcot 1888–1889). At the same time, at the École de Nancy, Hippolyte Bernheim disputed that hysteria and other forms of nervous pathology made patients more prone to suggestion than normal subjects, particularly given the instability of boundaries between subjective and objective reality and the power of the environment to influence thought, feeling, and actions.

Without resorting to hypnosis, Bernheim discovered that he was able to alter patients' behavior by using only visual and verbal suggestion (2014 [1884]). In fact, as Bernheim's experiments revealed, the mechanisms of suggestion and hypnosis could be used just as effectively on subjects not suffering any form of pathological disorder. Rather than imagistic suggestion and the externalization of visual material being confined to nervous pathology, Bernheim reported that they were just as potent in "normal" subjects. In his 1884 treatise, *De la suggestion dans l'état hypnotique et dans l'état de veille*, he diagnosed how visual images penetrated the unconscious, the very thought process transforming ideas into images: "One should not consider the transformation of an idea into an image as a morbid operation but rather a normal property of the brain" (2004 [1884]: 52). He elaborated this transformation by focusing upon ways in which suggestion triggered images:

> Suggestion, that is the penetration of the subject's brain by the idea of the phenomenon through a word, a gesture, a view, or an imitation, seems to me the key to all the hypnotic phenomena that I have observed.... Suggestibility is such that, in the waking state, an idea accepted by the brain becomes... an image.... We are all suggestible and can experience hallucinations by our own or other people's impressions. (Bernheim 1884: 53)

Since "sensorial hallucinations" were a condition of normal sleep when relaxation of judgment and verification released unconscious images, which he called "cerebral automatism," Bernheim concluded that "sensorial hallucinations" form "a great part of our lives" (2004 [1884]: 54).

The discovery that the interior of the human organism was a sensitive nervous mechanism, prone to suggestion, visual thinking, and imagistic projection in dreams as well as everyday life, altered the meaning of interior decoration in the *fin-de-siècle*. Domestic interior decoration became invested with the healing powers of the new psychologist, hypnotically easing French citizens out of metropolitan frenzy and fractured decadence into wholesome subjecthood and nation regeneration. Hence, the domestic interior was invested with a major role on which the psychological health of the modern subject and the nation depended. This specifically French version of psychological interiority provided the intellectual vehicle for the transformation of the domestic interior from a place on display as a historical anchorage to one that was able to express personal feeling, evoke memory, suggest emotional states, and trigger intimate vibrations. With this new medical evidence showing that the built environment could both positively and negatively affect physiological and psychological states, interior decoration became invested with the task of facilitating the mental health of the citizens of France suffering the debilitating physical and mental effects of modern life. Art, particularly that reconnecting the urban subject with nature, was a prime medium for doing so, as explained by Émile Gallé:

> Behold our ideal is achieved: furniture treated like the nude, ornamented with the equilibrium of its own structure, of its internal parts opening out like those of an animal or a plant, in their nerves, in their flesh, fur and feathers, tissues, membranes, bark, in their budding, flowering, fruitfulness; behold the labour of a sculptor, a work of intellect, of truth, of liberty—a work of delicacy, difficult, lasting and beautiful—that we advocate as our own and last efforts. (Gallé 1998 [1884–1889]: 275)

Following *la psychologie nouvelle*, the enterprise of interior decoration also became invested with new significations that entailed transfusing eighteenth-century associations of modernity, intimacy, and interiority with nervous vibration, spatial self-fashioning, and unconscious projection. Inspired by the Rococo, new interior spaces became necessary, according to Alain Mérot for the playing out of dreams (1990: 20). Reality and fantasy oscillated within interiors creating, according to Jean Starobinksi, "a self-contained world in which life can be lived as a representation" (1964: 74–75). Just as Symbolist literature was designed to trigger emotional states in the reader, so the new interiors were designed to trigger these states in the beholder. Through the suggestive power of line, color, texture, odor and shape, interior space became the domain of psychological self-exploration, self-projection, and self-fashioning, particularly as a dream room. That Gaillard's *chambre à coucher* was perceived in this way was affirmed in decorative art reviews, particularly by the critic Gabriel Mourey.

"First of all the eye is charmed," wrote Mourey of Gaillard's *chambre à coucher*. "It is a true visual delight. Some panels of gray-blue silk and gray-mauve and gray-green, like glass lit by moonlight, decorate the walls of a blooming dream" (1900: 266). Yet, while Gaillard may have subdued his panels and wallpaper, as indicated in Figures 2.1 and 2.2 by no means did he apparently modify the color of other parts of his *chambre à coucher*, let alone modulate the texture and composition of his fabrics. Although difficult to discern from Figure 2.2, his bed coverlet was of mignonette green silk and apparently embroidered with plant stems and vegetable forms that seemed to weave their way through the bedhead, the canopy, the curtain, chairs, and the garland design of the wallpaper. The dream-like quality he was able to conjure was consistent with the way in which Bing's *Pavillon* was critically received overall by the art media:

> The minutely wrought metal follows almost voluptuously the moulding and panels of furniture of a solid elegance; their lines suggest, without actually imitation, the finest models of the eighteenth century…. The furniture is soft to touch, like silk, and has the shimmering hues of sumptuous damasks; the finish of the details, the preciosity of the chased copper, like so many jewels, make each item a collector's piece, a rare object, and—a delightful thing—it all blends into the whole…. On the walls, in dream-like rosettes, the same dawn and twilight shades, of which de Feure seems to have discovered the secret, adorn the shimmering waters of a lake. (Silverman 1992: 287)

Its organic wallpapers, curved bedheads, optically charged panels, silken covers in "twilight hues" shimmering, according to this critic, like the water of a lake and its garlands of rosettes enfolding the bed in roses made it feel like a dream (Silverman 1992: 288). "He created a room which was soft, delicate and caressing," concluded Mourey, "without any eccentricity or weakness … with beautiful motifs for thought and for the dream" (1900: 257). However, it was his use of wood that generated other states pertaining to what Gaillard called the "vibrations of nature and human rhythms," as illustrated by Figures 2.1 and 2.2.

## *Les vibrations de nature et les rhythmes humanes*: The vibrating bedroom

Gaillard's choice of pearwood with ash-paneling for his bed was medium specific: "The essences of woods are extremely numerous and their variety offers an immense palette," he explained. "Their complete range has tones of exceptional splendour" (1906: 44–46). By no means was wood an "inert material" for Gaillard. It was a living organism capable of opulent growth and continual enrichment even after it had been cut down (1906: 38). Its design qualities were also ingrained within it, as Gaillard explained:

> Woods representing longitudinal fibres are juxtaposed according to the direction of the vertical thrust, that is to say according to their growth in height with the tree. Fibres are joined together laterally depending on the direction of the growth of the tree.... Wood is rigorously stable in the longitudinal sense of fibres. It is unstable in the transverse direction. Under the influence of the temperature and humidity of the air ... remembering the seasons each year and sensitive to the smell of renewal, fibres move laterally.... They keep concentrically positioned around the heart of the tree, bending sometimes... Yet the bundle of fibres ... cut short at both ends, retains its immutable length. (1906: 39)

Not only did these movements represent the physical phenomenon of wood for Gaillard, but also their psychic qualities pertaining to their deracination: "The tree always haunts wood-making," he explained (1906: 44). When all the *fibers* met in a single piece of wood like the richest of palettes, Gaillard dramatically concluded that "they produce the most vibrant and the rarest intensity of vibration" (1906: 45–56). So important was this vibratory quality to decorative art that Gaillard carped that tapestries were unable to generate any. "All its flavour," he said of wood, "resides ... in the boldness of the vibrations or in the softness of the reflections that alone give to wood the hand of the artist" (1906: 51–52). These bold vibrations are epitomized in Gaillard's *chambre à coucher* by the vigorously pulsating wood graining in the wooden panels chosen for the bedhead and bed-end, as can be seen in Figure 2.1 and more clearly in Figure 2.2. Not only do these vibrations seem to be echoed by the electrifying striations in the bed mat but also by the dynamic wood graining in the curved half-panels either side of the mirror on the wardrobe visible in Figure 2.1, appearing like two sides of an acorn as indicated by Figure 2.5. These vibrant optical wood markings were perceived as able to stimulate the unconscious, particularly through their purported facility to generate neurological vibrations and stimulate new energies comparable to radioactivity.

Once the radioactive materials discovered by Marie and Pierre Curie were perceived as offering unlimited sources of new energy, more than ever did regeneration of France seem attainable and devolution improbable. With Wilhelm Rontgen's discovery of X-rays in 1895 and Henri Becquerel's detection of radioactivity and radio-waves in 1896, Joseph John Thomson's identification of the electron in 1897, the invention of wireless telegraphy and the concept of electromagnetic waves vibrating through the ether by Oliver Lodge, the universe began to be understood as a vast network of continuous vibrations of varying frequencies beyond the threshold of human perception (Dalrymple Henderson 2013: 1–27; Enns and Tower 2013: 2–5). Invisible and inaudible extrasensory vibrations were perceived as conveying a dynamic flow of energy and sensation that scientifically explained psychic and occult phenomena. Within this meta-reality of vibrations, energy was charged with emotive, psychic, and regenerative power, as epitomized by the concept of "sympathetic vibrations" theorized by Helmholtz as early as 1848 and retheorized by Edmund Gurney in 1886 when the brain was reconceived as a wireless transmitter. Within this vibratory model of sensory communication, protoplasm was considered to be able to transmit vibrations between the cells of all living beings from plants, animals, insects, and trees to homo sapiens (Brain 2013: 116–117).

Following the amoeboid model of neuronal mobility, neurons were considered to be able to make functional contact through pseudopal movements of the protoplasm of the nerve cells (Brain 2013: 125). Prior to popularization of Santiago Ramón y Cajal's model of the nerve synapse, neuronal transmission was also likened to the behavior of rhizopods and other unicellar organisms (Brain 2013: 126–127). As surmised in *Matter and Memory*, everything in the universal network is physically interconnected and interdependent through continuous vibrations. "Matter...resolves itself into numberless vibrations," he wrote, "all linked together in uninterrupted continuity, all bound up with each other and travelling in every direction like shivers in an immense body" (Bergson 1912 [1896]: 208). Theorizing how the images of matter were determined by vibrations of light acting upon the retina, Bergson explained how these vibrations were able to penetrate the brain and memory: "The qualitative heterogeneity of our successive perceptions of the universe results from the fact that each, in itself, extends over a certain depth of duration and that memory condenses in each an enormous multiplicity of vibrations which appear to us all at once" (1912 [1896]: 77). When propelled by art, he speculated on the impact of these vibrations having the force of a "shell burst" able to stimulate sensibilities and engender a creative evolution—a concept with which Gaillard appeared all too familiar (Bergson 1912 [1896]: 1907).

Stressing that his creativity was bound up with his interdisciplinarity as an architect-decorator, Gaillard's crossing of disciplines seemed to stretch beyond the arts to Bergson's philosophy, the new sciences, as well as the new psychology. This was perhaps why he conceived of the decorative arts, particularly those integrated with nature, as able to unleash a flow of energy and vibrations between their interior designs and its inhabitants that could stimulate their intimate sensibilities. Like Gallé, Gaillard remained constantly concerned that his organic sensuality was able to impart nervous vibrations. "The vibrations of nature and human rhythms amplified" was what Gaillard confessed that ultimately he hoped to achieve by his *chambre à coucher* (1906: 66). These vibrations were posited as an unseen force able to mediate interactions between the interior self and the exterior organic environment in order to induce a trance-like hypnotic state that would release the imagination and enhance dreams, as well as states of hyper-perception (1906: 54). By no means was Gaillard unaware of the neurological potential that this carried, particularly in terms of the evolution of physiology and psychology. "Once our sharpened sensitivity is able to reveal a different universe to us," Gaillard concluded, "we must modify our expressions and speak a different language" (1906: 66).

Hence, ultimately Gaillard's *chambre à coucher* seemed designed to function not just as a sanctuary from the invasiveness of new technologies and the sensory overstimulation by the mass media, but as an instrument of psychospatial intervention in three different but interrelated ways. By transforming *le lit conjugal* into a bed of roses enmeshed in plant stems, tree roots, and vegetable structures, Gaillard signified their "constant communion" with one another in terms of *Transformist* evolutionary theory while reconnecting French citizens with the lost energies of nature. In keeping with the domestic prominence granted to the *chambre à coucher* at this time of chronic depopulation, the organic life with which Gaillard surrounds the conjugal couple is significantly in the process of budding and blooming. At the same time, his *lit conjugal* appears as the site of vivid vibratory energy conveyed by the dazzling optical wood graining in the panels at either ends of the bed, and the ways in which it was echoed in the wardrobe and bed mats. While consistent with what Gaillard terms "ineluctable evolution," these signs seem to signify the prospective function of this *chambre à coucher* as a regenerative space for "*procréation rationnelle*," where sex could be performed in a replenished psychological state of mind and body in order to produce the healthiest possible progeny. Yet, the design of Gaillard's *chambre à coucher* does not seem to be just aligned with national repopulation and regeneration imperatives. Invested with visually suggestive signs consistent with *la psychologie nouvelle*, Gaillard's *chambre à coucher* seems to evoke emotive states able to trigger the imagination in order to nourish the psychological health of those whom Zola called "weary neuropaths" suffering from the debilitating "fever" of modern life (1896: 546). Likened to a "*chambre mentale*," with an impact comparable to hypnosis, Gaillard's *chambre à coucher* appears to signal the possibility of easing French citizens out of fractured subjectivity into wholesome interiority. In exploring this trajectory, most critics and the mass media found that Gaillard had invented the dream bedroom able to embrace intimacy and, through its powers of suggestion, calm unconscious anxieties and lull its dwellers into a dream-state. At the same time, through his use of woods with vibratory power, Gaillard's *chambre à coucher* also seems to signify the possibility of unleashing a flow of energy capable of stimulating neurological vibrations, releasing the unconscious and generating what Jules Bois considered would be a new state of superconsciousness (1900).

## Acknowledgments

All the translations from the original French are my own. Owing to exigencies of space, the original French quotations that I would have preferred to include could not be published. My sincere thanks to Laure Haberschill, Bibliothèque des Arts décoratifs, for her invaluable help in locating Figures 2.1, 2.3–2.5, and to V&A images for supplying Figure 2.2.

## Notes

1. So popular was *L'uomo delinquente* that five editions were published during Lombroso's lifetime with its first French translation as *L'Homme criminel* in 1887. Since criminals were atavistic, according to Lombroso's study of their skulls, this meant that France was the most devolved and degenerate of all Western nations. To Lombroso, this was proven by the soaring levels of crime—particularly inflicted by the terrorist "apache" and the marked influx of insane asylum inmates.
2. Refer to Georges Valbert's articles, *Revue des deux mondes*, 1890–1900.
3. A chronic asthmatic, for the last three years of his life, Proust rarely left the bedroom of his apartment at 102 Boulevard Haussmann. Decorated with velvet curtains, wooden furniture, a piano, and walls encased in panels of cork, it was designed to keep out the noise and to absorb harmful dust. Proust identified it as the site of his creativity, writing much of *À la recherche du temps perdu* from his bed.
4. So late in the day was Bing invited by Alfred Picard to participate that his *Pavillon* did not feature in Picard's official report.
5. While Catholic theologians stigmatized "*l'onanisme conjugal*" as "fraudulent" and "*un état de péché mortal*," Corbin also points out that refusal to participate in "*l'acte conjugale*" was also identified as placing the soul in peril. At the same time, exceptional conditions were devised by these celibate theologians, listed by Corbin, when "*l'épouse*" could legitimately decline to engage. I am grateful for the gift of this book from Justin Fleming.

## References

Benjamin, W. (2002 [1935]), "Paris, Capital of the Nineteenth Century," in P. Bullock and M. W. Jennings (eds), *Gesammelte Schriften: Walter Benjamin, Selected Writings 1935–1938*, Paris and Cambridge, MA: Harvard University Press.
Bergson, H. (1889), *Essai sur les données immédiates de la conscience*, Paris: F. Alcan.
Bergson, H. (1907), *L'Évolution Créatrice*, Paris: Quadrige, Presses Universitaire de France.
Bergson, H. (1912 [1896]), "Matière et mémoire: Essai sur la rélation du corps à l'esprit," in *Matter and Memory*, trans. N. M. Paul and W. Scott Palmer, Paris and London: G. Allen & Co.
Bernheim, H. (2004 [1884]), *De la suggestion dans l'état hypnotique et dans l'état de veille*, Paris: Éditions L'Harmattan.
Bernheim, H. (2014, [1888]), *Suggestive Therapeutics: A Treatise of the Nature and Uses of Hypnotism*, Paris: Nabu Press.
Binet A. and C. Féré (1887; 1888), *Animal Magnetism*, Paris and New York: D. Appleton and Company.
Bois, J. (1900), "Les Guérisons par la pensée," *La Revue*: 35.
Brain, R. M. (2013), "Materialising the Medium: Ectoplasm and the Quest for Supra-Normal Biology in Fin-de-Siècle Science and Art," in A. Enns and S. Tower (eds), *Vibratory Modernism*, London: Palgrave Macmillan.
Brauer, F. (2005), "Flaunting Manliness: Republican Masculinity, Virilized Homosexuality and the Desirable Male Body," *Australian and New Zealand Journal of Art*, "Masculinities" 6, no. 1: 23–42.
Brauer, F. (2008), "Eroticizing Lamarckian Eugenics: The Body Stripped Bare during French Sexual Neoregulation," in F. Brauer and A. Callen (eds), *Art, Sex and Eugenics: Corpus Delicti*, Hampshire and Vermont: Ashgate Publishing: 97–138.
Brauer, F. (2009), "Wild Beasts and Tame Primates: 'Le Douanier' Rousseau's Dream of Darwin's Evolution," in *The Art of Evolution: Darwin, Darwinisms and Visual Culture*, Dartmore: The University Press of New England: 194–225.
Brauer, F. (2013), *Rivals and Conspirators: The Paris Salons and the Modern Art Centre*, Newcastle upon Tyne: Cambridge Scholars Publishing.
Brauer, F. (2015), "Becoming Simian: Devolution as Evolution in Neo-Lamarckian Modernism," in F. Brauer and S. Keshavjee (eds), *Picturing Evolution and Extinction: Degeneration and Regeneration in Modern Visual Culture*, Newcastle upon Tyne: Cambridge Scholars Publishing.
Chaleyssin, P. (1992), *Robert de Montesquiou, mécene et dandy*, Paris: Somogy.
Charcot, J.-M. (1889), *Leçons du mardi à la Salpêtrière, Policlinique 1888–1889*, Paris: E. Lecrosnier & Babé Éditeur.
Charcot, J.-M. (2012 [1888]), *Lectures on the Diseases of the Nervous System*, Paris: General Books.
Cheng, D. (2011), *The History of the Boudoir in the Eighteenth Century*, A thesis submitted to McGill University in partial fulfillment of the requirements of the degree of Doctor of Philosophy in Architecture.
Corbin, A. (2008), *L'Harmonie des plaisirs: Les manières de jouir du siècle des Lumières à l'avènement de la sexologie*, Paris: Perrin.
Dalrymple Henderson, L. (2013), "Reintroduction: The View from the Twenty-First Century," *The Fourth Dimension and Non-Euclidean Geometry in Modern Art*, Cambridge, MA: The MIT Press.
de Goncourt, E. and J. (1889), *Journal: Mémoires de la vie littéraire, II—1866–1886*, Paris: Robert Laffont.
de Maupassant, G. (December 23, 1889), "Danger Public," *Le Gaulois*, Paris.
Delon, M. (1999) *L'Invention du Boudoir*, Paris: Zulma.
Didi-Huberman, G. (2003), *Invention of Hysteria: Charcot and the Photographic Iconography of the Salpêtrière*, Cambridge, MA: The MIT Press.
Durkheim, É. (1897), *Le Suicide. Étude de sociologie*, Paris: Félix Alcan.
Enns, A. and S. Tower (2013), "Introduction," in *Vibratory Modernism*, London: Palgrave Macmillan.
Fouillée, A. (1892), "L'Art et le programme municipal," *La Lorraine-artiste*: 10.
Gaillard, E. (1900), *Mobilier moderne à l'Exposition de 1900*, Paris: Chez E. Floury, Librairie.
Gaillard, E. (1906), *Nos Arts-Appliqués modernes. À-propos du Mobilier: Opinions d'Avant-garde, Technique Fondamentale l'évolution*, Paris: Chez E. Floury, Librairie.

Gallé, É. (1998 [1884–1889]), *Écrits pour l'Art Floriculture—Art Décoratif—Notice d'Exposition (1884–1889)*, Marseilles: Lafitte Reprints.

Giard, A. (1876), "L'œuf et les débuts de l'évolution," *Bulletin Scientifique* 20, no. 22: 44.

Giard, A. (1888), *L'évolution des êtres organisés* (Leçon inaugurale prononcée le 22 novembre).

Havard, H. (1884; 1891), *L'Art dans la Maison (Grammaire de l'ameublement)*, Paris: Ed. Rouveyre et G. Blond.

Hirst, S. L. (2004), *Symbolism and Modern Urban Society*, Cambridge: Cambridge University Press.

Hustvedt, A. (2011), *Medical Muses: Hysteria in Nineteenth-Century Paris*, New York: W. W. Norton & Company.

Huysmans, J.-K. (1884), *À Rebours*, Paris: Charpentier.

Janneau, G. (1966), "Ébénistes et menuisiers français: L'École de Nancy," *Journal de l'ameublement, meubles et décors* no. 810: 27–38.

Lombroso, C. (1876), *L'uomo delinquente: studiato in rapporto alla antropologia, alla Medicina legale ed alle discipline carcerarie*, Milano: Ulrico Hoefli.

Magnan, V. (1871), *Étude expérimentale et clinique sur l'alcoolisme: alcool et absinthe, épilepsie absinthe*, Paris: Typographie de Renou et Maulde.

Manacéine, M. (1890), *Le Surmenage mental dans la civilisation moderne: effets, causes, remèdes*, Préface: Charles Richet, Paris: G. Masson.

Meier-Graefe, J. (May 1900), "Beiträge zu einer modernen Aesthetik," *Die Insel*: 1.

Mérot, A. (1990), *Retraites mondaines: Aspects de la décoration intérieure à Paris, au XVIIe siècle*, Paris: Le Promeneur.

Mourey, G. (1900), "L'Art Nouveau de M. Bing à l'Exposition Universelle," *Revue des arts décoratifs*.

Nouvel-Kammerer, O. (1995), "La création de la chambre conjugale," *Rêves d'alcoves: La chambre au cours des siècles*, Paris: Réunion des Musées Nationaux.

Picard, A. (1903), *Exposition universelle internationale de 1900 à Paris: Rapport général administratif et technique*, t. I, Paris: Imprimerie Nationale: 273.

Perrier, E. (1888), *Le Transformisme*, Paris: Librairie J. B. Baillière et Fils.

Proust, M. (1913), *À la recherche du temps perdu: Du côté de chez Swann*, Paris: Grasset.

Proust, M. (1913–1937), *À la recherche du temps perdu*, written 1909–1922, Paris: Grasset.

Reclus, É. (1868), "La Terre et l'Humanité," *Nouvelles annales des voyages*, Paris: E. Thunot, Vol. III.

Richet, C. (1919), *La Selection Humaine*, Paris: F. Alcan.

Rollinat, M. (1883), *Les névroses: les âmes, les luxures, les refuges, les spectres, les ténèbres*, Paris: G. Charpentier.

Silverman, D. (1992), *Art Nouveau in Fin-de-Siècle France: Politics, Psychology and Style*, Berkeley and Los Angeles, CA: University of California Press.

Soulier, G. (January 11, 1902), "Quelques meubles d'Eugène Gaillard," *Art et Décoration*: 20–27.

Starobinski, J. (1964), *The Invention of Liberty, 1700–1789*, trans. B. Swift, Geneva: Editions d'Art Abert Skira.

Vandam, P. (1985), *Dossier, Eugène Gaillard: Eugène Gaillard working in the l'Art Nouveau Workshops, c. 1899/1900*, Amsterdam, unpaginated.

Zola, É. (August 8, 1896), "Souvenirs des Goncourts," *La Revue encyclopédique* no. 153, as translated and quoted by D. Silverman (1992).

# CHAPTER 3
## ANGELS AND REBELS: THE OBSESSIONS AND TRANSGRESSIONS OF THE MODERN INTERIOR
*Anca I. Lasc*

The second half of the nineteenth century witnessed the proliferation of a variety of services that helped people consume for the home. French upholsterers, cabinet-makers, and architects offered interior decorating services and competed against each other as well as against the newly rising department stores for securing commissions. The private interior, commercialized as a coherent, two-dimensional image in their pattern books, illustrated magazines, trade manuals, and catalogs became a marketable entity in and of itself. This chapter examines the interior decoration designs that the "furnishing architect" (*architecte d'ameublement*) P. Brunet proposed in 1878 in parallel with the interiors described by the author Émile Zola in his 1872 novel *The Kill* (*La Curée*). It argues that Brunet's designs, which circulated as etchings collected in a pattern book, responded to a particular image of the private interior that popular media such as illustrated newspapers and works of fiction propagated at the time. As such, they both reflected and further influenced contemporary interiors. To enhance Brunet's reputation and potentially attract clients, they offered a fascinating image of the late nineteenth-century *Parisienne* at home, which played on the "forbidden" fantasies of men and women alike and contradicted traditional gender roles at the time. Unlike the morally respectable women responsible for their children's education or the art aficionados tastefully redecorating their homes, the ladies that populated Brunet's designs adopted a range of personas that identified them rather as adventurous libertines or *femmes fatales* upon the acquisition of appropriate furniture, upholstery, and bibelots. The message that Brunet promoted through his book was clear: you chose your furnishings; yet your furnishings defined and transformed you.

Pretending to be someone else or to live in a different world or historical era was common in nineteenth-century France as people enacted their fantasies at home through both elaborate historical costume and matching interiors. Attending costumed balls had been a favorite pastime of French aristocracy since the Renaissance (Rosasco 1989). The masked ball at the Paris *Opéra*, for example, in existence since 1716 and popularized in the nineteenth century through Édouard Manet's paintings, had enabled the high classes to meet and socialize in disguise with their inferiors under the pretense of celebrating the carnival (Martin-Fugier 1990: 134). The postrevolutionary bourgeoisie, eager to adopt the habits of the old nobility, reenacted costumed revelries at home. As early as 1820s, the Faubourg Saint-Honoré witnessed themed balls as Madame Adélaïde de La Briche's "rustic baptism" party, while the banker James de Rothschild, among the richest man in France under Louis-Philippe, went as far as hiring an architect to design themed celebrations in his Renaissance *hôtel particulier* on the Chaussée d'Antin (Martin-Fugier 1990: 129). Following their lead, the colonel Herman Thorn held in 1841 a *fête* mimicking court life under Louis XIV, requiring his guests to visit the new museum at Versailles in order to "study the costumes of the grand siècle" for his masquerade (Martin-Fugier 1990: 113). Similar events were held throughout the second half of the nineteenth century and later, including editor Georges Charpentier's 1878 *fête japonaise* with food from the Japanese restaurant at the *Expositon universelle* of the same year, writer Pierre Loti's 1888 Louis XI dinner in his medieval dining room, and couturier Paul Poiret's 1911 "Thousand and Second Night" fantasy party based on *The Arabian Nights*. Poiret is known to have required his more than 300 guests to dress in "Oriental" costumes or else to be outfitted "on the spot" with Persian-style clothes that he himself had designed after "authentic documents" (Troy 2003: 101–102; Stefani 2006: 36; Vajda 2008: 140).

The costumes needed to animate such parties came in no short supply as the gossip columns of various journals at the time made clear. By the 1880s, newspapers amply illustrated Egyptian, Venetian Renaissance, Assyrian, Louis XIII and Louis XVI gowns, which fashionable *Parisiennes* could study and recreate as needed (Figure 3.1). An article signed "Le Masque de Velours," for example, published in the *Vie mondaine* section of Ludovic Baschet's biweekly magazine *La Revue Illustrée*, described Ancient Egyptian attire, while thanking the Academy for helping teach nineteenth-century "fashionistas" how to transform themselves into "daughters of Ramses or Thutmose, should they desire so ... for a lovely carnival evening—or ... behind closed doors, in the privacy of their summer abode" (1886: 494). The illustration that accompanied the article, signed by Jacques Wagrez, gave visual form to the historical data, providing examples of not only what Ancient Egyptian clothing might have looked like but also what Ancient Egyptian matrons might have chosen for jewelry, hair accessories, and walking gear. Thus,

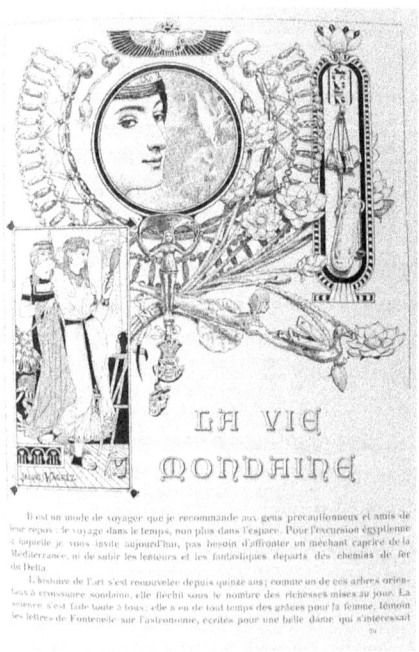

**Figure 3.1** Jacques Wagrez, [Illustration], in Le Masque de Velours, "La Vie mondaine," from *La Revue Illustrée* 2, no. 14, June–December 1886.

nineteenth-century *Parisiennes* could commission "accurate" and complete costumes from their personal couturiers, who were well-versed in meeting such requirements.

Themed balls animated the lavish mansions or apartments that hosted them, which were themselves often themed and arranged so as to imitate the architecture and interior decoration of past centuries or foreign lands (Lasc 2013). By the end of the nineteenth century, the vogue for rooms decorated in historical revival styles was such that Edmond de Goncourt wrote in his autobiographical novel *La Maison d'un artiste* that his bedroom gave him the impression of waking up "not in my own time, which I do not like, but in a time that was the object of my studies and my life's passions: in a room of a castle belonging to a Sleeping Beauty from the time of Louis XV, spared by the Revolution and the fashion for mahogany." It was the room itself that enacted this transformation, permitting imaginary travel to a bygone time. As Edmond confessed, "the confinement of this bed, these furnishings, these bronzes, these porcelains within four walls of white background upholstery" completed the illusion (de Goncourt 1881: 200). Elizabeth Emery explains how the house so themed and decorated was credited with transforming the inhabitant himself into a "superior and multivalent artist from an aristocratic French past" (2012: 12). Furniture and interior décor in nineteenth-century France thus seemed to have had the power to change inhabitants and visitors alike, who adopted the same characteristics as the inanimate objects.

The quest for self-transformation through furniture and décor traversed class and gender boundaries, permeating the nineteenth-century French society at both its high and low ends. Such feats of the imagination were carried beyond the homes of rich collectors and into *fin-de-siècle* brothels, which, as Gena Greene has demonstrated, displayed rooms extravagantly decorated so as to suggest a Turkish boudoir, a Chinese salon, or a Louis XV bedroom with copies after Boucher paintings. Aided by "multi-sensory erotic performances complete with costumes, music, fragrance, and female bodies," the male visitors could "unhinge…from the pressures of modernity, from the restrictive bourgeois moral code, and from the limits of his own fixed persona, and to transform himself into something *other*" (Greene 2008). Men and women alike enjoyed such games and reenacted them as often as possible in public spaces of entertainment such as cafés, cabarets, theatres, and public brothels, as well as in the private seclusion of their homes.

The literature from the second half of the nineteenth century is also filled with accounts of imaginary makeovers inspired by objects, which allowed bourgeois characters to inhabit different personas upon moving from one room to the next. Scholars have already demonstrated how women in the nineteenth century treated furniture and interior decoration as extensions of themselves, dressing furniture items with ruffles, and choosing for their walls hues that best suited their countenance and hair color in order to present themselves in the best possible light (Taylor 2006; Sparke 2008). Taste advisors recommended that blondes surround themselves with blue and brunettes with various shades of yellow interspersed with violet tints (Cardon 1884: 29). However, as design historian Beverly Gordon suggests, the "conceptual conflation of women and interiors" went even further, nineteenth-century novels describing "fictional female characters who came to share physical traits with their houses, or who changed themselves to suit those houses" (Gordon 1996: 282). These ladies not only thought about color schemes and decorative items as personal accessories but also imagined themselves anew in the vicinity of specific furnishings.

Renée Saccard, the chief heroine of Émile Zola's 1872 novel *The Kill*, provides an example. Indeed, the decoration of Renée's bedroom and dressing room in her fashionable Second Empire home on the Right Bank (located in the up-and-coming district near the Parc Monceau, an area much-coveted by the newly risen bourgeoisie) echoed her body. Using the house to promote and expand his new status in Parisian society, the real estate speculator Aristide Saccard, Renée's husband, spared no expense when it came to his home's fitting. He spent little under two million francs for the house and its furniture, an outrageously large sum of money at a time when a coachman earned no more than 1,250 francs per year (Baguley 2000: 203). But it was all worth it, since the house and its rooms were to be a reflection—albeit misleading—of Saccard's fortune and his claim to a spot of honor in the most fashionable Parisian circles. The building generated much interest, and people spoke of "beautiful Mme Saccard's dressing room" as the star of the house and "the room that had all Paris talking." They compared it with "the Gallery of Mirrors at Versailles" (Zola 2005 [1872]: 167). Equally well known as its owner, Renée's pinkish-white dressing room sported a matching pink bathtub, pink tables, and pink basins, all set against pink silk and muslin lining whose folds formed a large, round indoor tent covering the ceiling and the walls. The ensemble reflected the young woman's naked flesh: "The pink bathtub, tables, and basins, and the muslin covering the ceiling and walls beneath which one could imagine a reddish flow of blood, took on the roundness of flesh, of shoulders and breasts, and … it all resembled the snowy white of skin of a child or the warm flesh of a woman. It was nakedness writ large." As such, the room took after Renée, reflecting the scent of her soap or perfume, "suffused with … a fragrance of moist young flesh" (Zola 2005 [1872]: 168).

The furniture in Renée's bedroom also echoed the mistress's body. Taking up half of the room was a bed that "resembled a woman's gown," with an "ample curtain, swelling out like a skirt." Suggesting "a great lady in love—leaning back, swooning, almost collapsing onto the pillows," the bed's upholstery displayed the same decoration as the walls, the latter of which featured enormous bouquets of roses, white lilac, and buttercup flowers set against a pinkish-gray background. The marble fireplace avoided any "glint of metal or bright flash of gold" that might interrupt "the dreamy melody of pink and gray" and distinguished itself instead through simple ornaments—mirror frame, clock, small candelabra—lined with Sèvres porcelain rather than gilt bronze (Zola 2005 [1872]: 116). Complete harmony was thus found in the room's furniture, decoration, and upholstery, which was reminiscent of the eighteenth-century bedrooms of ladies in favor at the king's court. The entire space reeked of "a big bed still warm and moist … upon which lay in dreamy slumber the lovely shape of a thirty-year old Parisienne" (Zola 2005 [1872]: 166–167).

But, if the rooms took after Renée, Renée herself altered her personality and physical appearance according to the rooms (Berthier 1987: 115). Thus, the conservatory of the Parc Monceau house became an Indian jungle or a monstrous temple when Renée and Maxime—Renée's adopted son and illicit paramour—made love. Crouched in the center of the glass enclosure and mimicking the "black marble sphinx" that guarded the room, Renée herself became a "huge cat, its back arched and paws tense," shoulders and waist standing out with "feline sharpness" (Zola 2005 [1872]: 177). As the greenhouse evoked far-away territories or imaginary pasts, Renée and Maxime, too, assumed legendary guises. Driven by visions of distant, almost mythical lands, where palms and ferns were guilty of "reproduction on a gigantic scale," the incest reached its apogee as Renée and Maxime switched genders (Zola 2005 [1872]: 176). While the "pretty, fair-haired, neutered boy" recalling the "slender grace of a Roman ephebe" became a "strapping girl," Renée, now the man, "assumed the posture and the smile of that monster with a woman's head, and with her petticoats undone she looked like that black god's white sister" (Zola 2005 [1872]: 177).

According to Zola, "each room, with its own peculiar fragrance, its own hangings, its own special life, yielded a different sort of tenderness and made Renée a different kind of lover" (Zola 2005 [1872]: 173). Incited by desire, the adulteress morphed into a "grand dame" in the "aristocratic," eighteenth-century bedroom, a "carnal whore" in the "flesh-coloured tent" of the dressing room, or a "blonde Diana" and faithful reincarnation of the pagan goddess in the classicizing parlor. The parlor (*petit salon*), with its buttercup satin and sun-colored silks playing "a symphony in yellow minor," followed the Louis XVI style, likely touched by the simplicity of ancient Roman interiors (Zola 2005 [1872]: 34). It thus naturally invoked dreams of ancient gods and goddesses, chief among whom was Diana, the goddess of the hunt, the moon, and childbirth in ancient Roman mythology. Renée's postures here—revealing "noble lines and an antique grace" with "naked arms in chaste poses" (Zola 2005 [1872]: 173)—mirrored those of virtuous Diana, who, although as beautiful as Venus, had remained a virgin.

Émile Zola must have been aware of contemporary trends in interior decoration and design when contriving the rooms of Aristide and Renée Saccard. Indeed, around the same time that Zola was writing his novel, illustrators and interior decorators were keen to provide visual guidelines for the arrangement of private interiors. The market for such illustrations reached an all-time apogee as techniques of image reproduction such as halftone printing processes and the photogravure were just being developed. Interior decorating schemes inspired by Classical Antiquity, the Renaissance, or the French eighteenth century were popular in pattern books, taste manuals, and illustrated magazines. These schemes often included copies of artworks of undisputed notoriety such as the *Venus de Milo* or Paul Dubois's nineteenth-century *Florentine Singer*, which visually matched the period that an interior attempted to recreate (Lasc 2013: 6). Painted or sculpted reproductions of statues or busts of Diana (Figure 3.2)—with her unmistakable attributes: the crescent moon or the crossbow—were no exception, gracing interior decorating schemes for Renaissance bedrooms as well as Louis XVI drawing rooms (Guilmard c. 1872: 37; Bajot c. 1889: 21). The Louvre museum itself was selling by 1883 plaster casts after its famous ancient sculpture *Diana the Huntress, with Her Doe*. At prices ranging from 300 for a full-size copy to two francs for one of the sculpture's detached members, be that an arm or a leg, such casts made it possible for Parisians to bring the illustrated schemes reproduced in the public press or advice literature to life within their private interiors (*Catalogue des moulages* 1883). It would thus have been easy for a nineteenth-century "fashionista" like Renée to conjure an image of Diana in relation to a classicizing interior—from the Renaissance or the Neoclassical/Louis XVI eras—just as it would have been equally simple to reinvent herself as an eighteenth-century "grande dame" in a Rococo/Louis XV apartment.

**Figure 3.2** Eugène Prignot, "Panneau de Salon: Sculptures et peintures—genre Louis XVI," lithograph by A. Collette, from Désiré Guilmard, *La Décoration au XIXe siècle: Décor intérieur des habitations, composé, dessiné ou exécuté par les principaux artistes décorateurs de Paris* (Paris: Bureau du journal *Le Garde-Meuble*), pl. no. 37, c. 1872.

Yet, Renée's behavior within her Second Empire interiors ran counter to what moralizing Republican men of state recommended after the novel's publication. Zola's readers in the 1870s would undoubtedly have identified Renée with the new generation of rebellious *Parisiennes* determined to redefine their role in the modern society. *La Curée*, available in serial form through the newspaper *La Cloche* beginning in September 1871, preceded the first International Congress on Women's Rights by seventeen years, the Camille Sée Law, which guaranteed state-sponsored education for young women, by eight years, and the new decrees that allowed French women to initiate divorce proceedings by twelve (Silverman 1989: 63; 66).[1] The novel came in the early years of the Third Republic, the moment when the *femme nouvelle* (the New Woman) began to rise as a figure worthy of the attention of almost every newspaper and man of state, inciting most of the male population to proclaim her a "socially subversive" threat to the well-being of the French nation. In the eyes of French Republican men, the "proper" lady of the Third Republic was to renounce any claim to political representation, sexual gratification, birth control, and even bicycling or gymnastics. Instead, she was expected to enjoy her "natural" role as a "vessel of motherhood," moral educator, and home decorator (Accampo 2006). The men of the Third Republic, therefore, attempted to reduce the fears projected by these "new" women by relegating them to the interior. Unlike Renée, as historian Lisa Tiersten has demonstrated, the *mère de famille* was to purchase goods solely in the interest of her family and the nation so that the "civilizing influence of taste" would regulate the "unrestrained individualism and dangerous desires" ascribed to the female consumer (Tiersten 2001: 2). Decorators responded to this trend, and Third Republic taste manuals, department store catalogs, and interior decorating advice books targeted a female population whose main purpose in life should have been the bearing and rearing of children and the tasteful arrangement of private interiors. Images of mothers with their children either shopping for proper items with which to decorate their homes or enjoying their newly created interiors embellished the pages of both advice manuals and store catalogs.

Still, a more detailed analysis of interior decoration designs from the time reveals that not *all* decorators followed this fashion. Zola's fictive interiors—like the accounts of masquerade parties in the popular press—appear to have had a different impact on contemporary interior designs. In 1878, the publishing house Ch. Juliot issued a collection of sixty interior decoration designs for window arrangements and complete rooms designed by the "furnishing architect" P. Brunet, an industrial designer (*dessinateur industriel*) listed in commercial almanacs at the time at 18, rue Tournelles in Paris (Lasc 2011: 299).[2] The collection, titled *Le Tapissier Décorateur de Paris* (*The Upholster Decorator of Paris*), appears to have won a silver medal at the 1879 International exhibition of sciences applied to industry (Claesen c. 1882). Among its designs, it proposed a set of interiors with inhabitants attired in historic or exotic costumes that matched the furniture and interior decoration of the rooms. Thus, for example, a "Boudoir, Salon Louis XVI" showed a highly decorated interior in the Louis XVI style, with the straight-legged furniture and decorative features characteristic of the Neoclassical era (Figure 3.3). The interior, etched by Charles Delfosse after Brunet's drawing, was to display matching gray or gold draperies and harmonizing seating furniture (Brunet c. 1878). But in addition to these details and the Ionic columns punctuating the walls and reflected in the large-scale mirror, the historical feel of the room was enhanced by the presence of a lady dressed in eighteenth-century garb, who, in front of her own looking glass, seemed the perfect reincarnation of an aristocrat preparing for her appearance at the court. Brunet had replaced here the conscientious mother occupied with the rearing of children and betterment of her home with a self-indulgent, vain matron obsessed by her look. Like Renée, inspired by the furnishings that surrounded her, this woman affected the behavior of a lady from the eighteenth century and not just that period's dressing style.

**Figure 3.3** P. Brunet, "Boudoir, Salon Louis XVI," etching by Ch. Delfosse, from *Le Tapissier décorateur de Paris* (Paris: Ch. Juliot), pl. no. 27, c. 1878.

Similarly, an "Asian Smoking-Room" from the same series presented a group of languid women in exotic garb, eroticized odalisques that seemed to have just stepped out from an Ingres or a Delacroix painting (Figure 3.4). Instead of refined gentlemen in black frocks, the usual occupants of the nineteenth-century *fumoir*—a "masculine" room that women often avoided—Brunet conjured for this interior scheme a group of four female beauties that cannot be missed as a reference to the world of high art and especially Orientalist paintings.[3] Lying down in lethargic poses, in rapture over languorous music and dream-inducing smoke, with breasts half exposed, Brunet's reclining figures occupy a space that follows closely the preestablished formula of such works, including traditional "harem accoutrements" and Eastern *bric-à-brac* such as the pipe and the coffee, the lute and its music, low sofas, and colorful silks and fans (DelPlato 2002: 111; 134). Etched by A. de Beaupré after Brunet's design, the image shows the women taking after the material culture and interior decorating scheme, whose "Moorish" arcades and rich decoration also seem to have been inspired by the paintings favored at the time (Brunet c. 1878).

Designers such as Brunet would undoubtedly have used such figures as informal indicators of an object's scale or of the projected social status of those families for whose interiors these illustrations could have served as models. But, as art historian Susan Sidlauskas has argued, "in architectural treatises, manuals on decoration, descriptions of theatrical settings, and novels" of the nineteenth century, "readers/viewers were encouraged to project themselves imaginatively into whatever space was described or represented." Thus, "any figure represented within that space becomes a surrogate for the spectator's own emphatic response" (2000: 3–5). Figures such as Brunet's, therefore,

**Figure 3.4** P. Brunet, "Fumoir Asiatique," etching by A. de Beaupré, from *Le Tapissier décorateur de Paris* (Paris: Ch. Juliot), pl. no. 58, c. 1878.

might have helped nineteenth-century women imagine themselves within similar interiors and surrounded by the objects occupying the space of representation, the latter of which could be commissioned and purchased for their homes. Yet, unlike the morally respectable women responsible for their children's education or the art aficionados shown in the act of redecorating their interiors, Brunet's characters assumed a set of roles that seemed lifted from Parisian fancy dress parties or nineteenth-century novels such as Zola's. Responding to an image of the private interior proliferated through illustrated newspapers and works of fiction, they offered an alternative image of the nineteenth-century *Parisienne*, idle and vain, who could morph into a *femme fatale* and engage in role-playing, possibly to satisfy her man.

Brunet aroused desires that contradicted what was deemed appropriate gender-specific behavior at the time possibly to enhance his reputation as a designer and potential decorator and to thus stimulate the consumption of his designs. While the men of the Third Republic may have seemed eager to ascribe precise roles to their wives, this stood in marked contrast with the image propagated not just by works of fiction such as Zola's but also by interior designs such as Brunet's. Playing on the fantasies of men and women alike, these works suggested for the nineteenth-century *Parisienne* a range of characters that she could adopt with the acquisition of appropriate furniture, upholstery, or bibelots.

As a "furnishing architect" (*architecte d'ameublement*), Brunet naturally placed furniture and décor at the core of his designs. Thus, in a design for a "Renaissance Stairway," he situated a large dresser in the center of the composition. In a "Louis XV Dining Room," he chose an elaborate console to draw the viewer's eye. In a "Japanese Interior," he allowed a large-canopied bed to take up most of the designed space. Yet, in moving from one image to the next, an observer immediately notices figures galore that populate these spaces, from Renaissance courtiers to tantalizing lovers and Japanese geishas, who do not quite seem to fit within the nineteenth-century interior landscapes. A contemporary observer might have understood such figures as the "natural" influence of Brunet's designed objects, which had the potential to imaginatively transform people and change their behavior as described in contemporary mass media. You chose your furnishings, yet your furnishings defined and transformed you in an age where, as historian Michelle Perrot has shown, interior decoration was less about "feathering a nest" and more about "creating an image" (Perrot 1990: 175).

Brunet thus used ideas about the interior from popular media as a selling device for his designs, and the latter's further circulation suggests that he had a responsive audience. His illustrations of interiors appear to have been successful at the time, if not immediately obvious as sources of inspiration for the objects and decorative schemes that the late nineteenth-century French bourgeoisie commissioned for their private interiors, at least as visual imagery that proposed "model rooms" for an audience thirsty for interior decorating advice. Indeed, Juliot's sixty-plate pattern book with designs by Brunet was available for purchase not only through Juliot's or Brunet's offices but also through those of other Parisian architects, who, one may assume, would have been able to recreate them upon request (Brunet c. 1878). Further, by 1882, Juliot's book was issued as a reprint and sold by the publishing house of Charles Claesen. Whoever had not been able to purchase an earlier Juliot edition or see the book at the International exhibition could, for the price of fifty-five francs, own a second edition by Claesen (c. 1882). A reprint seems unlikely without an audience. So, one can thus safely assume that contemporary Parisians found the decorators' designs and the transformations they promised appealing, a fact also potentially explaining how in 1888 and as late as 1911 celebrities such as Pierre Loti and Paul Poiret could count on a large number of attendees at their themed parties.

The second half of the nineteenth century witnessed a proliferation of sources that talked about the transformative nature of the private interior, which had the capacity to alter the behavior and even the appearance of its inhabitants. The themed balls and fancy parties of the rich or the famous were largely covered in the popular press, illustrated journals further propagating the idea of self-transformation down the social scale and fixing it into the public imagination. Now part of daily life, historicist décor encouraged the idea of imaginary travel to a different time or remote place, and decorators seemed keen on taking up these ideas in their work to promote their commercial interests. As works of fiction such as Émile Zola's *La Curée* imagined whimsical personas for their female heroines, designers such as Brunet suggested fanciful environments for contemporary Parisians where they, too, could live the life of their role models from the world of literature or the popular press. Often contradicting the public image of the proper wife and mother, prevalent in the Third Republic discourse at the time, these interiors promised the nineteenth-century *Parisienne* a mode of life that seemed lifted from an Arabian dream or aristocratic past where contemporary taboos were momentarily lifted. With Brunet's furniture designs, the modern interior had the potential to become a transgressive terrain where nineteenth-century bourgeois men and women could live out their obsessions to the fullest.

## Notes

1. The censors suppressed the serial publication of *La Curée* in November of 1871, but the book would be published in its entirety a few months later, in 1872.
2. Plates from this publication were registered with the *dépôt légal* of the French National Library in 1878.
3. Juliet Kinchin labels the hall, the library, the business office, the billiard, and the smoking room as "masculine" due to the sober and dark-toned atmosphere that she sees predominating there, while designating the boudoir, the music room, the bedroom, and the drawing room as "feminine" due to their lighter, more colorful and "decorative" appearance (Kinchin 1996: 12–13).

## References

Accampo, E. A. (2006), *Blessed Motherhood, Bitter Fruit: Nelly Roussel and the Politics of Female Pain in Third Republic France*, Baltimore: Johns Hopkins University Press.

Baguley, D. (2000), *Napoleon III and His Regime: An Extravaganza*, Baton Rouge: Louisiana State University Press.

Bajot, É. (c. 1889), *Les Styles dans la maison française: Ornementation et décoration du XVe au XIXe siècle, à l'usage des architectes et décorateurs, tapissiers, fabricants, artistes et amateurs*, Paris: Édouard Rouveyre.

Berthier, P. (1987), "Hôtel Saccard: État des lieux," in D. Baguley (ed), *La Curée de Zola ou "la vie à outrance,"* Paris: SEDES: 107–117.

Brunet, P. (c. 1878), *Le Tapissier décorateur de Paris*, Paris: Ch. Juliot.

Cardon, É. (1884), *L'Art au Foyer Domestique (La Décoration de l'appartement)*, Paris: Librairie Renouard.

*Catalogue des moulages en vente au palais du Louvre* (1883), Paris: Imprimerie nationale.

Claesen, Ch. (c. 1882), *Catalogue général d. tentures, ébénisterie, menuiserie, décoration intérieure*, Paris, Liège and Bruxelles: Ch. Claesen.

de Goncourt, E. (1881), *La Maison d'un artiste*, Paris: G. Charpentier, Vol. 2.

DelPlato, J. (2002), *Multiple Wives, Multiple Pleasures: Representing the Harem, 1800–1875*, Madison and London: Fairleigh Dickinson University and Associated University Press.

Emery, E. (2012), *Photojournalism and the Origins of the French Writer House Museum (1881–1914): Privacy, Publicity, and Personality*, Farnham and Burlington, VT: Ashgate Publishing.

Gordon, B. (1996), "Woman's Domestic Body: The Conceptual Conflation of Women and Interiors in the Industrial Age," *Winterthur Portfolio* 31, no. 4: 281–301.

Greene, G. (Spring 2008), "Reflections of Desire: Masculinity and Fantasy in the Fin-de-Siècle Luxury Brothel," *Nineteenth-Century Art Worldwide* 7, no. 1: http://www.19thc-artworldwide.org/spring08/108-reflections-of-desire-masculinity-and-fantasy-in-the-fin-de-siecle-luxury-brothel

Guilmard, D. (c. 1872), *La Décoration au XIXe siècle: Décor intérieur des habitations, composé, dessiné ou exécuté par les principaux artistes décorateurs de Paris*, Paris: Bureau du journal Le Garde-Meuble.

Kinchin, J. (1996), "Interiors: Nineteenth-Century Essays on the 'Masculine' and the 'Feminine' Room," in P. Kirkham (ed), *The Gendered Object*, Manchester: Manchester University Press: 12–29.

Lasc, A. I. (November 2011), "*Le Juste Milieu*: Alexandre Sandier, Theming, and Eclecticism in French Interiors of the Nineteenth Century," *Interiors: Design, Architecture, Culture* 2, no. 3: 277–306.

Lasc, A. I. (February 2013), "Interior Decorating in the Age of Historicism: Popular Advice Manuals and the Pattern Books of Édouard Bajot," *Journal of Design History* 26, no. 1: 1–24.

Le Masque de Velours (June–December 1886), "La Vie mondaine," *Revue illustrée* 2, no. 14: 493–496.

Martin-Fugier, A. (1990), *La Vie élégante ou la formation du tout-Paris, 1815–1848*, Paris: Fayard.

Perrot, M. (1990), "Roles and Characters," in M. Perrot (ed), *A History of Private Life IV: From the Fires of Revolution to the Great War*, Cambridge, MA and London: The Belknap Press of Harvard University Press: 167–260.

Rosasco, B. (Summer 1989), "Masquerade and Enigma at the Court of Louis XIV," *Art Journal* 48, no. 2: 144–149.

Sidlauskas, S. (2000), *Body, Place, and Self in Nineteenth-Century Painting*, Cambridge: Cambridge University Press.

Silverman, D. (1989), *Art Nouveau in Fin-de-siècle France*, Berkeley and Los Angeles: University of California Press.

Sparke, P. (2008), "Interior Design and Haute Couture: Links between the Developments of the Two Professions in France and the USA in the Late Nineteenth and Early Twentieth Centuries—A Historiographical Analysis," *Journal of Design History* 21, no. 1: 101–107.

Stefani, C. (2006), "La Maison qui n'est plus," in S. Thierry and J. Godeau (eds), *Pierre Loti: Fantômes d'Orient*, exhibition catalogue, Musée de la Vie Romantique, Paris: Paris Musées.

Taylor, M. (2006), "'Furniture Is a Kind of Dress:' Interiors as Projection of Self," in J. R. Stephens (ed), *Contested Terrains: XIII Annual Conference of the Society of Architectural Historians, Australia and New Zealand*, Fremantle: Society of Architectural Historians: 530–535.

Tiersten, L. (2001), *Marianne in the Market: Envisioning Consumer Society in Fin-De-Siècle France*, Berkeley: University of California Press.

Troy, N. J. (2003), *Couture Culture: A Study in Modern Art and Fashion*, Cambridge, MA: MIT Press.

Vajda, J. (Septembre 2008), "Fêtes et Distractions Mondaines de La Société Cosmopolite Parisienne, 1880–1930," *Paris et Ile-de-France, Mémoires* 59: 129–146.

Zola, É. (2005 [1872]), *The Kill*, trans. A. Goldhammer, New York: Modern Library.

# CHAPTER 4
# MACHINES AND MONSTERS: THE MODERN DECADENT INTERIOR AS SPECTACLE IN HUYSMANS'S *À REBOURS*

Emilie Sitzia

In the nineteenth century, mass media—such as novels, newspapers, and illustrated magazines—took an increasing interest in the display and analysis of interiors. French realist fiction in particular gave interiors a significant role. Realist novels used the characters' environments to help define their personality; Didier Maleuvre calls interiors of *La Comédie Humaine* "indoor landscapes" (1999: 124). Interiors and the objects inhabiting them took on a new significance for writers and readers alike: they became a projection of modern dreams and desires. The importance of the interior went hand in hand with an increasing materialism. For example, Honoré de Balzac lists each object in his house according to its specific location within the interior in his furniture inventory, *L'Inventaire de l'Hôtel de la rue Fortunée* (Maleuvre 1999: 124). But, this increased interest in the life of objects is best represented by Edmond de Goncourt's preface to the poetic inventory of his house in *La Maison d'un artiste*: "why wouldn't we write the memoires of the objects among which the life of a man was lived?" (1898: n.p.). Objects came to life, gained historical importance, and were curated in the home to convey the personality and the life of the house's inhabitants. Interiors were increasingly regarded as personal museums; and de Goncourt's 600-page presentation of his house reads like an extensive museum catalog.

The nineteenth century also saw the identification of interior decoration with developing concepts of individuality. Domestic interiors became "a new topos of subjective interiority" (Rice 2007: 2). The Romantic notion of the expression of the artist's or the sitter's self through landscapes, as found in romantic portrait painting for example, was, by the end of the nineteenth century, transferred to the expression of the individual through interior decoration. As Walter Benjamin emphasized: "the interior is not just the universe of the private individual; it is also his étui … the traces of its inhabitant are moulded into the interior" (2002 [1939]: 20).

By the end of the nineteenth century and the beginning of the twentieth century, the modern French interior was at the international forefront. French culture, and literature in particular, was instrumental in the popularization of the modern interior throughout Europe. Novels such as Joris-Karl Huysmans's *À Rebours* (1884) played a significant role in that positioning. This novel reveals the dreams and desires of an entire generation of modern Decadent dwellers, whose individuality was directly expressed through their interiors. At that period, the interior had become the domain of the Aesthete, both as an allegiance to a distinctive style and as a set of values around "Art for Art's sake." At the same time, its darker relative, Decadence, was similarly expressed in the media primarily as a particular set of tastes in interior design but also in theater, poetry, fiction, and visual arts as an "unbalanced state of mind." The use of the word "Decadence" dates back to the Middle Ages and comes from the Latin *decadere* in its present participle form: falling or drowning. It was used to qualify the aesthetic of a society seen as corrupt and engaged in a process of degeneration. It also was used to designate the mental state of the modern man afflicted by the Baudelairean "Spleen," the melancholic condition of the modern city dweller. Charles Baudelaire transformed the negative term Decadent into a honorific one in 1857 in his "Notes nouvelles sur Edgar Poe" (St John 1999: 84). There, Baudelaire defines Decadent literature as "a poem or a novel that has all its parts skillfully arranged to create surprises, that has a magnificently ornate style, where all the resources of language and prose are used with an impeccable hand" (1990 [1857]: 619). In literary criticism, this term oscillated between negative and positive connotations (Calinescu 1987: 157). Developed and popularized by philosophers such as Arthur Schopenhauer and Friedrich Nietzsche, the notion of Decadence associated pessimism and idealism and elitism and dandyism. It focused on the rise of the notion of individualism and the end of the idea of progress that dominated European thought since the Enlightenment. Paul Bourget, one of the first theoreticians of Decadence, in his "Théorie de la Decadence" published in *La Nouvelle revue* (1881) and in his *Essai de psychologie contemporaine* (1883), defined Decadence in the following way: "by the word of Decadence, one designates willingly the state of a society that produces in too great a number individuals that are unsuited to the work of common life" (1879: 412). The Decadent individual preferred artifice to nature and rejected contemporary society's established norms. He/she objected to the rational world of the bourgeoisie and put art as the only aim of life. The Decadent refused to take part in the bourgeois mass consumption culture and industrial society and denounced its mediocrity, preferring a more exclusive, quasi-fetishist relationship with objects. For the Decadent, the interior became a statement of opposition, a battleground against both nature and bourgeois values.

Huysmans's novel *À Rebours* (1884) was dubbed the "Bible" of Decadence and went on to influence generations of artists and writers. The quasi plotless novel follows the inner struggles and presents the multifarious tastes of the main character Duc Jean Floressas Des Esseintes. Des Esseintes embodies the Decadent posture, contemplative and rebellious, toward the modern world. His frail health, his quest for artificial gratification, and his rejection of the natural world and society exemplify Decadent precepts. After leaving Paris and taking retreat from the world, Des Esseintes designs the interiors of his house as an artificial heaven, a perpetual work in progress, and a personal war against nature.

As early-nineteenth-century realist writers regularly used the character's environment to define it, by the end of the nineteenth century, the motif of the artist's studio in art novels had become a cliché, a necessary means by which the writer could identify the personality of the artists as well as their artistic ideologies. As Philippe Hamon highlights, "the studio has an instant metaphorical, or allegorical or meta- (or auto) referential vocation" (1993: 127). Toward the end of the century, the art novel moved away from the artist's studio to the aesthete's house: art had become a lifestyle and a spectacle (Melmoux-Montaubin 1999). This shift is exemplified by Huysmans's detailed description of the series of interiors created by Des Esseintes. In this aesthete's interiors, Huysmans blends spectacle, Decadent aesthetics, and modern fashion to convey the *fin-de-siècle* quest for sensation at all cost. More than Benjamin's "étui," in this novel, the interiors become the mirror of the modern man, what Jean Baudrillard identifies in *The System of Objects* (1996) as the anthropomorphic homology between dweller and dwelling.

It is this homology between dweller and dwelling that is at stake in *À Rebours*. The modern Decadent man, Des Esseintes, transforms his interiors in private spectacles using machines and monsters in various ways. The aim of this chapter is to uncover what modern dreams and desires are expressed through Des Esseintes's interiors and explore the role of machines and monsters within these intimate spectacles. First, this chapter will investigate the machines presented by Huysmans as the descendants of theatrical machinery that were used to create formidable stage set effects. It will examine how the idea of the machine as catalyst to the creation of an artificial environment has been updated in the novel to embrace the heritage of Baudelaire and create an *invitation au voyage immobile*, a life composed of a series of simulacra. Second, this chapter will consider these machines as simultaneously machines of war and of medicine. The modern man used these machines both to combat his neurosis through sensation overload and to heal his body. This chapter will uncover how those machines transformed the disease of Des Esseintes into a spectacle of its own. Third, the machines will be contrasted with the monsters living in the house as they embody the modern attempt to control and modify nature.

## The Decadent interior as spectacle

The nineteenth century witnessed the growing importance of machines. Scholars and the public took an increasing interest in their history (Dolza and Verin 2004: 7), and they became a symbol of the technical and industrial mastery of modern man, the latter of which allowed for the completion of colossal building projects such as the Statue of Liberty, the Suez Canal, and the Eiffel tower (Grimaldo Grigsby 2012). Machines signified modern man's control over his environment.

When considering the relationship between machines and spectacle, one has to make a distinction between the *théâtres de machines* and *machines de théâtre*. The *théâtres de machines* were illustrated books of machines—mostly Italian and French—that were particularly popular between 1570 and 1670 (Dolza and Verin 2004: 9). These illustrations constituted the first signs of the potential for machines to entertain by their intrinsic nature. These books exposed the ingenuity of the machines' creators and displayed a faith in ongoing technological progress. While there was a certain level of criticism (Dolza and Verin 2004: 12) arising from this mechanical experimentation, the principal aim of these books and the machines they presented was to entertain.

On the other hand, the *machines de théâtre* were used to create illusion-based stage effects and were part of theatrical technology from its beginnings. In ancient Greek theater, machines were created for lowering actors playing gods onto the stage. In the Renaissance, as scenography developed, movable sceneries and traps became more common. In seventeenth- and eighteenth-century Europe, the refinement of theatrical illusion reached a high point due to an intense development of new machines of theater (Corvin 1995: 559). These were specifically designed to create a particular aesthetic effect such as dawn, sea, or rain. Machines of theater had a double function of servicing scenography and offering entertainment. But, most of all, they were an essential component in the creation of illusions that in turn increased the impact of spectacle on the viewer.

In the nineteenth century, machines shifted from theater to more popular spectacles such as magic shows, where illusions resided in machine tricks, mirrors, and trap doors. Illusionist spectacles became at the time extremely popular throughout Europe. Furthermore, the end of the nineteenth century saw the birth of special effects in cinema with pioneers such as Georges Méliès. During this period, entertainment, illusion, spectacle, and artificiality were intimately linked to each other.

In *À Rebours*, Huysmans turned the representation of the home into a spectacle. But, as the home was a dwelling space, a space of "desocialization" (Maleuvre 1999: 121) where there was a lack of social surveillance, the spectacle became an artificial private escape from the world and from others. As Matei Calinescu emphasizes, the voyages in *À Rebours* are more than an escape to/from nature. Rather, they are a "perpetual violation of nature" itself (1987: 172). The dining room and its theatrical setup is a good example of this violation. The dining room, a room within a room, is equipped to evoke sea travel allowing Des Esseintes to travel without the inconvenience of human contact. The windows are covered with aquariums; the water's shades of color can be artificially altered by adding "some drops of coloured essences, thus creating for himself, at his own pleasure, the various shades displayed by real rivers, green or greyish, opaline or silvery" (Huysmans 1998 [1884]: 17). The room itself is set up like a stage, with props such as compasses, binoculars, fishing rods, and nets (Huysmans 1998 [1884]: 18). In the living room, machines are an integral part of the creation of illusion and of the *invitation au voyage immobile*. The mechanical fishes, the only moving elements in this particular *mise en scène*, reinforce the illusion of life, creating moving life and ongoing entertainment: "he would then imagine he was between-decks in a brig, and would watch with great interest as marvellous mechanical fish, driven by clockwork, swam past the porthole window and became entangled in imitation seaweed" (Huysmans 1998 [1884]: 18). The mechanical fish are presented as marvels and as such are fascinating visual objects. The intricacy of their mechanism is implied by the comparison with clock-making. It is this hybridity between the technical mastery and visual attraction that creates the spectacle. The reader's attention here is directed skilfully between disbelief in the sophistication of the machines and sensual contemplation in the proposed illusion (of being "at sea" for example) requiring a suspension of belief. The mechanical fish in Huysmans's text are both *machines de théâtre* (creating an illusion) and *théâtres de machines* (the machines themselves are the spectacle). The fish contribute and reinforce the illusion, they are part of the theater set constructed by Des Esseintes, and as such, they are *machines de théâtre*. But they are also fascinating technical objects, the display of their elaborate mechanism associating them then more closely to the *théâtres de machines*.

To complete the illusion beyond the visual realm, an aroma of tar is blown into the room by a machine: "inhaling the smell of tar which had been pumped into the room before he came in, he would examine some coloured engravings hanging on the wall that depicted … vessels bound for Valparaiso and the river Plate" (Huysmans 1998 [1884]: 18).

This machine, contributing to the creation of the spectacle, is a *machine de théâtre*. In this way, the imagination of the spectator/dweller is stimulated through all the senses. Didier Maleuvre emphasizes that Huysmans built Des Esseintes's interior "as a camera obscura," and "a place of fantasy" (1999: 147). But the illusion is more than a visual trick as the activation of the sense of smell reinforces the belief in the artificial environment and allows the spectator/dweller to be immersed in this imaginary escape. The dwelling becomes a place of immersive spectacle. This reinforces the paradox of escaping in the dwelling. Escape from modernity is no longer a physical escape out of the world but an escape within that world itself. The immersion and the engagement of the spectator/dweller are essential to the functioning of the illusion: "the secret is to know how to go about it, to know how to concentrate the mind on one single detail, to know how to dissociate oneself sufficiently to produce the hallucination and thus substitute the vision of reality for reality itself. Des Esseintes considered, furthermore, that artifice was the distinguishing characteristic of human genius" (Huysmans 1998 [1884]: 20). The interior's role, then, was to provide enough stimuli using machines as catalysts of sensations to create a series of simulacra.

Baudrillard distinguishes three orders of simulacra: the natural simulacra aiming for "the restitution or the ideal restitution of nature made in God's image," the productivist simulacra with "a promethean aim of a continuous globalization and expansion," and the simulacra of simulation that has the "aim of total control" (1994: 121). It seems that Huysmans's Decadent series of simulacra goes beyond Baudrillard's first order, as the natural world is perceived by the character as insufficient: "As he was wont to remark, Nature has had her day; she has finally exhausted, through the nauseating uniformity of her landscapes and her skies, the sedulous patience of men of refined taste. Essentially what triteness Nature displays …" (Huysmans 1998 [1884]: 20). According to Decadent principles, nature, even in its ideal form, was to be improved by human genius. However, it seems that the series of Decadent simulacra presented in the novel are not of the productive order either, as the Decadent philosophy is very much anchored in an ideology against productivity. The third order of simulacra, with its aim of total control, seems much closer to the ideals of the modern Decadent dweller. This prevalence given to artificiality and control in this particular type of simulacra reinforces the central role of machines in these interiors. Malin Zimm goes beyond the idea of Baudrillard's simulacra, proposing that Des Esseintes's house acted as an *excitoir*, that is, "an interior enabling the invention of other interiors, both material and imagined" (2004: 305). She explores the generative potential of these interiors as they function as departure points for further development of interiors that stimulate a sense of creative restlessness, such as that of Des Esseintes and indirectly of Huysmans himself (2004: 308).

This rapid succession of artificial worlds within textual descriptions of the interior seems to lead to the dematerialization of the exterior environment. For example, the architecture of the house itself is elided almost completely, and the house instead becomes a series of décors. The architecture, that is to say the physical presence of the house, disappears (Maleuvre 1999: 149). The artificial interiors invite the dweller to nomadic dreams; they aim to create artificial places within neutral spaces, to transport the dweller, in Baudelaire's term, "Any Where Out of the World" (1987 [1867]: 178–179).

## The diseased industrial man at home

Within Des Esseintes's interiors, the entertainment role of the machines as *machines de théâtre* and *théâtres de machines* is sometimes completed or superseded by their function as medical machines. Des Esseintes's neurosis, an essential part of his character and what indicates the physical decadence of society for Huysmans, is also presented as a form of spectacle. In regard to his disease, machines have two main roles to play: both intimate and functional. They simultaneously provide an escape from the body through an overload of the senses, and they care for the sick figure. Their role expresses the tension in the relationship of the dweller to his body: the body becomes the tool allowing escape and an inconvenience to be rescued from at the same time. It is the machines themselves stimulating the body as escape and rescuing the sick body that turn Des Esseintes's neurosis into a spectacle for the reader rather than a medical condition. Des Esseintes is therefore both a spectator and an active participant in the Decadent spectacle offered by his interior machines.

At the time, the Decadent mind was generally seen as diseased. In the nineteenth century, the work of neurologists such as Jean-Martin Charcot popularized neurosis and hysteria. These diseases of the mind were seen as consequences of the modern lifestyle that created so much sensual and intellectual stimulation that the modern man's body and mind simply could not cope. This popularization was not without criticism, as voiced by Guy de Maupassant who called Charcot an "indoor hysterics breeder" (1882). However, Charcot's work was extremely popular in literary circles and was used as the scientific grounding for many fictional literary characters, for example Émile Zola's Rougon-Macquart family. Finney (1986) shows parallels in the scientific literature on disease, heredity, and environment, between competing schools of Naturalism and Decadence and notes that both movements saw French society as "on its last legs" (1986: 73). Furthermore, Georges Didi-Huberman showed in his seminal book *Invention de l'hystérie: Charcot et l'iconographie photographique de la Salpêtrière* that a lot of the imagery linked to hysteria was very precisely constructed and was very much part of creating "the disease spectacle" (1982: 113). The nineteenth century was fond of those human displays and Huysmans's use of the body stimulated or cured by machines is part of this prevalent culture.

Huysmans presents us with new types of the diseased modern mind. From the Decadent viewpoint presented by Des Esseintes, there were only three types of modern personalities that were recognizable mainly by their tastes in colors for interior decoration: the coarse-blend bourgeois (favoring blue and its derivatives such as mauve and gray), the "full-blooded" impulsive (preferring yellow and red hues), and the "weak and nervous" individual (fond of orange) (Huysmans 1998 [1884]: 13–14). According to Calinescu, in Huysmans's book, psychopathology and the aesthetics of Decadence were merged (Calinescu 1987: 172). Huysmans transforms this modern diseased mind into a literary spectacle.

The functional machines of the Decadent interior, in particular the synesthetic devices, played an essential role in turning Des Esseintes's neurosis into a spectacle for Des Esseintes himself and the reader. For Baudelaire, modernity and Decadence are intimately linked since one of the characteristics of modern art was the "desire to encroach upon neighbouring arts" (Baudelaire cited in Calinescu 1987: 166), which is also one of the essential features of the Decadent movement. Going back to the idea of a Wagnerian *Gesamtkunstwerk*, Decadent desire can only be satisfied through an enhancement of one sense through the others. Furthermore, the essence of Decadence, according to Nietzche, is a lack of will, a surrendering to stimuli and impulses. The Decadent machines within the interior presented by Huysmans precisely fulfill these functions by creating a perfect synesthetic/trans-sensual experience and constructing an overload of stimuli and impulses.

For example, the mouth organ, a "collection of casks of liqueur" (Huysmans 1998 [1884]: 39), exemplifies this machine-led sensual overload. With taps and little labeled stops, this machine allows Des Esseintes to compose drinks based on musical principles. A specific taste is associated with each sound. The *Orgue à bouche* is not a technological novelty or a fantasy; it actually references a real eighteenth-century machine (Lambert 1925). But Huysmans's presentation of the machine is deeply associated with Baudelaire's theory of *correspondence* (Baudelaire 1868: 92; Brunel 2007). Pierre Brunel shows that the main principles of the creation of musical alcoholic tastes of Huysmans's machine (analogy, mixture, imagination, composition, and even virtuosity) are similar to Baudelaire's own creative poetic processes (2007: 150). Des Esseintes either composes drinks based on existing musical pieces or composes his own melodies. The machine's synesthetic effects become a way to overload the senses and to provide Des Esseintes with an escape from the world and his neurosis. But, it is also a way for Huysmans to turn synesthesia and Des Esseintes's neurosis into a spectacle.

Similarly, vaporizers allow Des Esseintes to compose landscapes and scenes through smells (Huysmans 1998 [1884]: 97). The vaporizer also relies on synesthetic effects and on the theory of correspondences. Des Esseintes starts using it to combat smell "hallucinations" that are a symptom of his neurosis. He chooses controlled illusion rather than letting the disease's hallucinations overtake him. There, again, a spectacle is created through smell's evocative power and is intended to help the reader picture Des Esseintes's attempts at controlling the symptoms of his neurosis. Maleuvre wonders here whether "the escape from dwelling is also an escape from being" (1999: 146), which is an essential question for the diseased modern mind. Thus, these machines open up the interior as a place of escape beyond reality, beyond illness and transform the Decadent disease into a spectacle both for Des Esseintes and for the reader.

Some machines in Des Esseintes's interior have a different role: they are medical machines meant to protect the body. Neurosis causes Des Esseintes to have eating and digestive disorders. Des Esseintes therefore acquires a "digester" that extracts from food a "nourishing extract" (Huysmans 1998 [1884]: 144) so that the body is maintained and slowly restored. Based on a sixteenth-century design by Ambroise Paré, and refined in the second half of the nineteenth century, the digester is still present in the medical world and is mostly used for recovering patients (Renner 2006: 94).

The subject's body is not perceived here as a receiver/producer of sensation but as an ineffective and malfunctioning mechanism that can be improved through a mechanically aided process. Baudrillard argues that contained within automatism "is the dream of a dominated world, of a formally perfected technicity that serves an inert and dreamy humanity" (1996 [1968]: 110). This is very much the case for the digester, as "thanks to this device, the progress of his neurosis was arrested" (Huysmans 1998 [1884]: 144), and Des Esseintes is left to his literary reflections.

Both these functional machines in the dwelling seem to work toward the disappearance of the owner or rather the dweller becoming object-machine, lost in sensations and stimuli, detached from his bodily functions. Minsoo Kang in *Sublime Dreams of Living Machines* argues that beyond the economic discourse, living machines were the embodiment of Modernism (2011: 235). Des Esseintes's description of steam trains certainly shows that in his Decadent mind the beauty of machines is superior to human beauty (Kang 2011: 239). The machines in the interiors emphasize the complex relationship between Des Esseintes as an active participant and as a viewer of his own spectacle. One could argue that Des Esseintes's machines exist as automatons, as well as functional machines. It is in this hybrid manner that machines start to populate the modern literary interior at the end of the nineteenth century. They uncover the desire of modern dwellers to be entertained and served, to escape reality while being firmly in control.

## Monsters in the home: The decadent scientist's control

David Weir notes that there are two routes for Decadent beings to escape nature in his publication *Decadence and the Making of Modernism*. One is to get away from nature as much as possible and embrace artificiality. The other is to escape nature through nature, manipulating and adjusting the natural until it becomes unnatural (1995: 92–93). This chapter would like to argue that those two routes are represented in *À Rebours* in the realm of the home by the presence and creation of machines (artificiality embraced) and monsters (nature manipulated). The monsters present another layer of control, that of nature. As Marshall Berman argues, modernity poses man as god (1990 [1982]: 15–19), and it is this godlike function that allows the Decadent interior to be populated by man-made monsters. The monsters and their roles in the Decadent interior also express the tensions between the realm of science and the realm of dreams.

The dwelling as an individual space creates an absolute independence from the world's moral and social rules, an environment necessary to the creation of monsters. In Des Esseintes's interior, monsters go through a process of transformation from authentic to inauthentic, a process one could call "bibelotization" (Maleuvre 1999: 144). As Maleuvre points out, "the bibelot is the consummate homeless, or inauthentic, object: indifferent and untrue to its origins ... the bibelot's main character lies in derivation." (1999: 119) This is precisely what the monsters in the interior are: objects, animal, plants that are denying their own being, origin and identity to become pretense of otherness.

For example, authentic flowers are acquired by Des Esseintes specifically because they appear inauthentic and monstrous: "his object had been achieved; not one appeared real; cloth, paper, porcelain, metal, seemed to have been lent by man to Nature to enable her to create monstrosities" (Huysmans 1998 [1884]: 76–77). Denying their natural origins, these flowers look artificial and nature is manipulated by horticulturalists out of reality, into artificiality. Des Esseintes emphasizes the power of horticulturalists, their control and overtaking of nature: "man is able to bring about in a few years a range of choice that slothful Nature can only produce after several centuries, unquestionably, as matters stand today, the only artists, the real artists, are the horticulturalists" (Huysmans 1998 [1884]: 78). The role played by plants in the interiors expresses this will of absolute control over nature, of finding a way into decadence through nature rather than against it—as with the machines.

The interior is then presented as a spectacle of "bibelotized" nature, an aspect that is reinforced by the writing style of Huysmans that focuses on paradoxes and parody: the literary expression of monstrosity. Michael Riffaterre emphasizes that the heart of Decadent writing is the "rhetoric of the paradox" (1992: 220–233) that expresses tensions and contradictions. Evanghelia Stead explains that Huysmans's description of flowers poses itself between a parody of painting and diseases (2004: 261) and shows how these paradoxes and parodies are central to the creation of monsters, or the perception of regular objects as monstrous by the reader.

Beyond the vegetal realm, Des Esseintes constructs a live monster himself: the tortoise. For Des Esseintes, the animal needs to exalt the personality of the owner like the objects in a collection. It is the symbol, as Maleuvre puts it, of the extreme end point of "bibelotization of life" (1999: 144). In the process, the tortoise loses its animality and its life. The tortoise is to bring movement and contrast to the carpet; it is to become a moving object. First covered by a layer of gold and then incrusted with jewels, its sole purpose is to satisfy its creator: "He felt perfectly happy; his eyes were intoxicated by those resplendent corollas blazing on a golden ground" (Huysmans 1998 [1884]: 38). This "bibelotized" tortoise is objectified and becomes an integral part of the interior, an interior that swallows life to be sustained or rather to sustain its spectacle.

Further, Redon's pictorial monsters, exhibited in Des Esseintes's vestibule, reiterate the message of man's absolute control over nature that the plants and the tortoise represent. The pictorial monsters embody the modern attempt at controlling and modifying nature. Redon's creative process uses the possibility of science as a departure point for the imagination, as a ground for the creation of monsters. Huysmans himself presents Redon's topics as taken from the "nightmarish dreams of science" (1998 [1884]: 52). Furthermore, the pictorial monsters illustrate the part nature still has to play in the modern spectacular interior as a freak show and as the display of a Decadent mad man in control of his world.

Huysmans was certainly influenced by contemporary mass media culture—films, spectacles, newspaper, and written descriptions and illustrations of all sorts—to create his interiors. He also took inspiration from existing interiors of contemporary Decadents such as Comte Robert de Montesquiou-Fézensac; and, while he borrowed details from Montesquiou's "Palais de Scaurus," Antoine Bertrand demonstrated that Huysmans's interiors were very much in the "air du temps" (1996: 116–118). In return, his book went on to influence a number of writers such as Oscar Wilde, Paul Valery, and artists such as Belgian Fernand Khnopff whose "luxurious personal refuge" may be drawing inspiration from *À Rebours* (Facos 2011: 353).

The modern home is a mirror, as the gathering of objects is a "process of narcissistic projection," as Baudrillard suggests (1996 [1968]: 91). However, in *À Rebours*, the individual mirrored in the interiors keeps shifting, as it is not a single interior but multiple interiors that are presented. The succession of interiors presents a never-ending spectacle demonstrating the insatiable desires of Des Esseintes. Huysmans's Decadent interiors are a broken mirror reflecting the fluid, multiple, and fractured modern man.

Des Esseintes's desires of entertainment, health, escape, and control are expressed in the interiors through the diverse machines and monsters he created. As the creatures come to life, they absorb the creator in the spectacle he orchestrated. In the "adorable Babel du bibelot" (de Montesquiou cited in Maleuvre 1999: 127), a man is dissolved and disappears;

he becomes part of the spectacle and of the interior. Huysmans, in a process by which "the object has superseded the subject" (Maleuvre 1999: 143), gives life to the interior, albeit a monstrous and machine-like life that vampirizes the Decadent man of his life force.

## References

Baudelaire, C. (1868), "Correspondances," in *Les Fleurs du mal*, Paris: Lévy.
Baudelaire, C. (1987 [1867]), "Any Where Out of the World," in *Le Spleen de Paris*, Paris: Flammarion.
Baudelaire, C. (1990 [1857]), "Notes nouvelles sur Edgar Poe," in *Curiosités esthétiques, L'Art romantique*, Paris: Bordas.
Baudrillard, J. (1994), *Simulacra and Simulations*, Ann Arbor, MI: University of Michigan Press.
Baudrillard, J. (1996 [1968]), *The System of Objects*, London: Verso.
Benjamin, W. (2002), "Paris, Capital of the Nineteenth Century (Exposé of 1939)," in *The Arcades Project*, Cambridge, MA: Harvard University Press.
Berman, M. (1990 [1982]), *All That Is Solid Melts into Air: The Experience of Modernity*, London: Verso.
Bertrand, A. (1996), *Les Curiosités esthétiques de Robert de Montesquiou*, Geneva: Droz.
Bourget, P. (1879), "Psychologie contemporaine; Notes et Portraits: Charles Baudelaire," *La Nouvelle revue* 13: 398–416.
Brunel, P. (2007), "Musique des sens, de Baudelaire à Huysmans," *Revista de Filología Románica* V: 143–151.
Calinescu, M. (1987), *Five Faces of Modernity: Modernism, Avant-Garde, Decadence, Kitsch, Postmodernism*, Durham: Duke University Press.
Corvin, M. (1995), *Dictionnaire encyclopédique du théâtre*, Paris: Bordas.
de Goncourt, E. (1898), *La Maison d'un artiste*, Paris: Bibliothèque Charpentier.
Didi-Huberman, G. (1982), *Invention de l'hystérie: Charcot et l'iconographie photographique de la Salpêtrière*, Paris: Macula.
Dolza, L. and H. Vérin (April–June 2004), "Figurer la mécanique: l'énigme des théatres de machines de la Renaissance," *Revue d'histoire moderne et contemporaine* 51, no. 2: 7–37.
Facos, M. (2011), *An Introduction to Nineteenth-Century Art*, London: Routledge.
Finney, G. (Spring 1986), "In the Naturalist Grain: Huysmans' À Rebours' Viewed through the Lens of Zola's 'Germinal'", *Modern Language Studies* 16, no. 2: 71–77.
Grimaldo Grigsby, D. (2012) *Colossal: Engineering Modernity—Suez Canal, Statue of Liberty, Eiffel Tower, and Panama Canal: Transcontinental Ambition in France and the United States during the Long Nineteenth Century*, Pittsburgh, PA: Periscope; New York: Prestel Pub.
Hamon, P. (1993), "Le Topos de l'atelier," in R. Demoris (ed), *L'Artiste en représentation*, Paris: Édition Desjonquières.
Huysmans, J.-K. (1998), *Against Nature*, Oxford: Oxford University Press.
Kang, M. (2011), *Sublime Dreams of Living Machines: The Automaton in the European Imagination*, Cambridge, MA: Harvard University Press.
Lambert, P. (December 15, 1925), "Un Précurseur de Des Esseintes ou l'orgue à bouche au XVIIIe siècle," *Mercure de France*.
Maleuvre, D. (1999), *Museum Memories: History, Technology, Art*, Stanford: Stanford University Press.
Maupassant, G. (August 16, 1882), "Une femme," *Gil Blas*.
Melmoux-Montaubin, M. F. (1999), *Le Roman d'art dans la seconde moitié du XIXe siècle*, Paris: Klincksieck.
Renner, C. (2006), "A propos des pots à bouillon d'étains," *Histoire des Sciences médicales*, XLX: 1.
Rice, C. (2007), *The Emergence of the Interior: Architecture, Modernity, Domesticity*, London: Routledge.
Riffaterre, M. (1992), "Paradoxes décadents," in M. Shaw and F. Cornilliat (eds), *Rhétorique Fin de siècle*, Paris: Christian Bourgois.

St John, M. (ed) (1999), *Romancing Decay: Ideas of Decadence in European Culture*, Brookfield: Ashgate.

Stead, E. (2004), *Le Monstre, le singe et le fœtus: tératogonie et décadence dans l'Europe fin-de-siècle*, Geneva: Droz.

Weir, D. (1995), *Decadence and the Making of Modernism*, Amherst, MA: University of Massachusetts Press.

Zimm, M. (2004), "Writers in Residence: Goncourt and Huysmans at Home without a Plot," *Journal of Architecture* 9, no. 3: 305–314.

# CHAPTER 5
## *LA MAISON SUSPENDUE*: IMAGINARY SOLUTIONS FOR AN EVERYDAY DOMESTIC MACHINE
*Peter Olshavsky*

---

Known as an American architect in France and a French architect in America, Paul Nelson (1895–1979) was well born, educated, and connected. While spending much of the 1920s studying at the École des Beaux-Arts and in Auguste Perret's *atelier* in Paris, he established a wide social circle that assisted his design career on both continents. Until recently, history has been unkind to him in part because he fell outside of the modernist canon. Yet, he was one of the most well-known and respected designers of his generation. During his career, he created a diverse oeuvre, including a modernist set for the Hollywood film *What a Widow!*, a personal theater for Joseph P. Kennedy, Sr., a house for Georges Braque and several hospitals in France.

From 1936 to 1938, a seminal period of his career, he pursued architectural research in collaboration with the artists Joan Miró, Jean Arp, and Fernand Léger. This research culminated in an unbuilt work (Figure 5.1), which he titled *La Maison Suspendue* (*The Suspended House*).

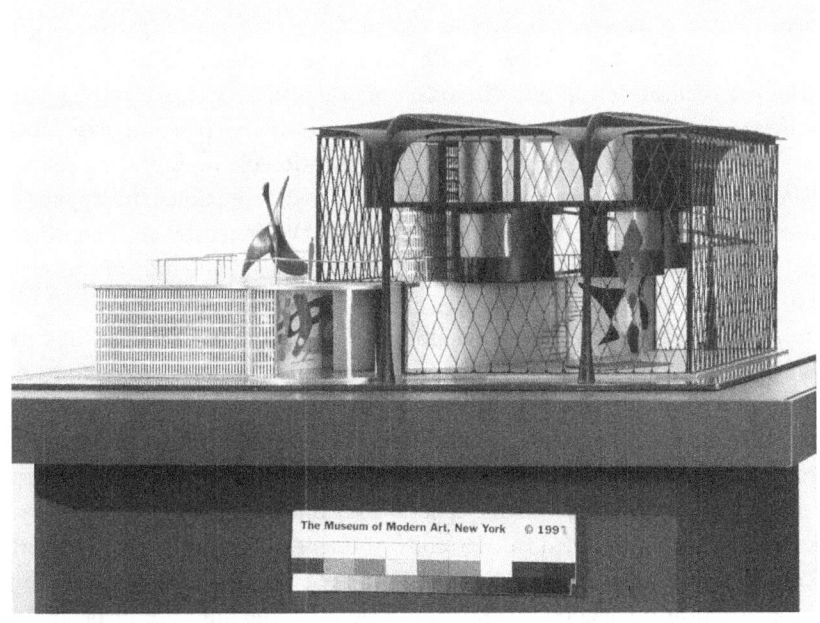

**Figure 5.1** Paul Nelson, *Suspended House,* Project scale model, 1936–1938, Acrylic, metal, paint, stone, textile, wood, Gift of the Advisory Committee (MC 14), Digital image © The Museum of Modern Art/Licenced by Scala/Art Resource, NY.

## Designing the French Interior

Adopting the "machine house" metaphor common to modern architecture, Nelson attempted to synthesize and enrich the metaphor's implied concern with prefabrication, mass production, new functional and spatial organizations, new materials, and formal abstraction. He described this research in a small publication, *La Maison Suspendue: Recherche de Paul Nelson* (1937). This publication simultaneously and quite paradoxically embraced the impact of machines while trying to resist their intrusions into everyday life.

Similar to other newspapers, magazines, and books, Nelson's publication attempted to mobilize public opinion in support of a view that blurred the modernist polarity in architecture between the French bourgeois interior of popular culture expressed in printed mass media and the avant-garde "machine house." This can be unpacked by studying the *Maison Suspendue* as a complex multivalent site of reconciliation between divergent positions. On the one hand, Nelson's work was indebted to Buckminster Fuller's avant-garde concept of 4D, defined as a time-based approach to design and production. On the other, it was a direct response to Alfred Jarry's science of "pataphysics," which was a poetic science of "imaginary solutions" that the author first brought to public attention through his fictional character Père Ubu in a short play dated to 1893. By bridging these two seemingly different approaches to modern architecture, Nelson's work was a distinct call for understanding, arranging, and living in a French society where one could leverage machine technologies to construct an eroticized interior for the sake of an imagined community. To understand Nelson's project, it is critical to examine products disseminated by the mass media, specifically printed texts. These products, as we will see, shaped his conception and design of the *Maison Suspendue*.

## *La Maison Suspendue* and 4D design

Comprised of two constituent structural elements, the *Maison Suspendue*, as imagined in Nelson's publication, has a lower plinth with a gestural profile in plan that is offset from an upper rectilinear volume. The offset between these forms creates a terrace and internal mezzanine. The plinth, constructed of reinforced concrete and glass block, is unfenestrated. Its materiality grounds the house compositionally by appearing solid from the outside. An exposed and expressive structural steel skeleton defines the upper volume of the house, which leaves the interior free of columns. Wrapped by an inboard rhombus-patterned "cage," the upper volume was designed for transparent and translucent glass or opaque panels.

Organizationally, the lower plinth contains the service spaces, including the garages, the servants' quarters, and the kitchen, while the bedrooms are in the upper volume, nearest to the roof. Entry to the latter spaces is gained by two means of circulation: the first is a direct spiral stair that efficiently connects all of the house's levels, while the second is an arabesque ramp that begins on the second level. This ramp also engages units held in-between the lower service areas and the upper living spaces. The units are suspended in space at varying distances from the mezzanine dedicated to entertainment and media (Figure 5.2). Articulated as self-contained forms, these units hang from unseen supports. This organization allows the interior to appear open and gives the impression that the units are suspended in space. Arguably, these suspended units are the most radical elements of the home since they give the house its name.

*La Maison Suspendue*

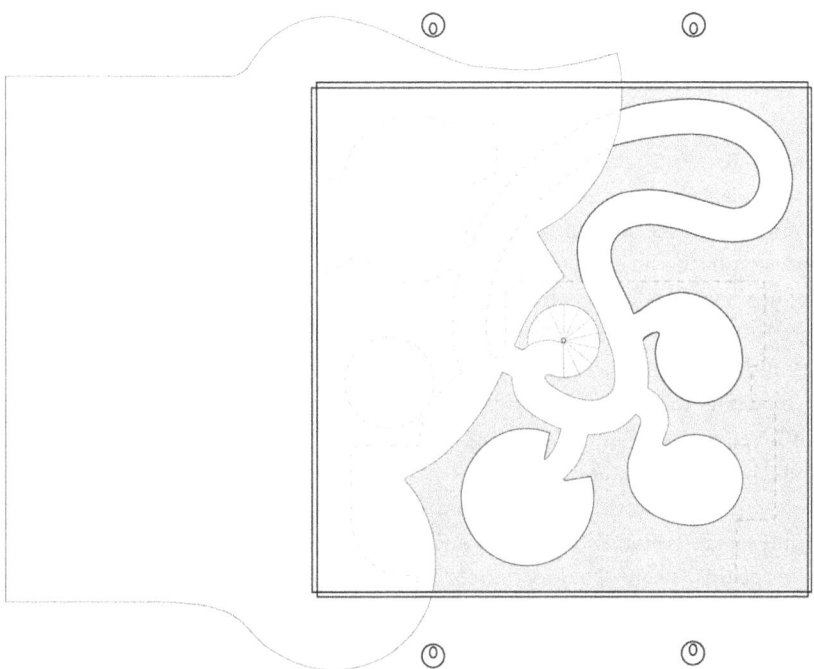

**Figure 5.2** Paul Nelson, *La Maison Suspendue*: Plan at Balcony Level, drawn by Kendra Heimes © 2014.

The *Maison Suspendue* ostensibly embodies what the American inventor and designer Buckminster Fuller (1895–1983) dubbed as four-dimensional thinking or "4D." In contrast to "cubistic" or three-dimensional architecture that focused primarily on an end product, 4D was critical of established architectural traditions. Like other designers trying to articulate what it meant to be modern, Fuller's 4D argued that mechanized industry in the manner of Ford's motor car factories ushered in a new sensibility toward making. Whether this sensibility was directed toward an industrially produced vehicle, interior, or, more broadly, a "new industry," what was obvious for Fuller was that machine processes could and should change how designers construed and constructed their works.

Similar to other popular commodities intended for mass consumption that could be advertised through the media and bought and sold, Fuller thought that housing should also follow suit. For Fuller, 4D was a manner of thinking and making that embraced the popular beliefs associated with machine technologies—efficiency, optimization, and control—that secured the "maximum human advantage...from the minimum use of energy and materials" (Pawley 1990: 39). Practices informed by mechanization, he suggested, offered predictable relief from the uncertainty of an impending future because the gap between conception and realization was diminished. Far from a bottom-up design practice targeting a specific socioeconomic class, Fuller's concept, like mass media, took the majority of social classes as its target audiences. Further, by seeking popular distribution to the masses, Fuller thought that 4D would have "consequences for humanity instead of only immediate personal gain" (Pawley 1990: 39).

While understood as an ideology based on literal and symbolic efficacies of machine technologies, Fuller's 4D was also focused on temporality. Time "represented...the *new* dimension" (Pawley 1990: 39). Thus, Fuller believed that time required "four-dimensional thinking," which Martin Pawley argues, was a form of "thinking in time instead of only in space" (1990: 39). This form of thinking translated into specific design aspirations. For example, Fuller desired to increase the speed of housing production and extend the longevity of materials. He even suggested that 4D design could help people discover higher dimensions of time and space (Lorance 2009: 83–84).

Many of Fuller's mechanistic beliefs were already part and parcel of a popular worldview widely present in the media. Still, Fuller saw himself as the wellspring of 4D in design and a direct influence on the latter's potential. He noted in a letter that Nelson "was introduced [by Fuller] to the 4D idea" prior to leaving on one of his many trips to France (2001: 80). 4D was "the very link," he continued, "that Nelson had been waiting for" and which had imparted to him "the chart for the space between aesthetic modern design and economic necessity" (2001: 80). Setting aside Fuller's self-promoting interests, this "chart" is not the whole story behind the *Maison Suspendue*.

Fuller's letter-writing campaign promoting 4D design's influence on Nelson glosses over crucial differences between these men and their respective approaches to architecture and design. To see this, we need to look more carefully at Fuller's intentions in his writings on the "machine house." On one hand, he thought that the extension of the machine's optimizing logic might lead to a house's functional economy. On the other, he found that the adoption of mass-produced building materials or components would reshape a building's aesthetics. In short, the space between "aesthetic modern design and economic necessity" resulted in an "architectural machine" that combined the functioning of a mechanical device with its looks. Though couched in transcendent rhetoric, he reduced the "machine house" to the forced poles of function and form. Fuller's dualistic thesis narrowed the influence of machines on design to simple mimesis. While aspects of Fuller's 4D theory—especially where it concerned the use and the influence of machines on design—were important to Nelson, and undoubtedly impacted some aspects of the *Maison Suspendue*, the two architects' positions on the "machine house" should not be conflated.

## Nelson and 4D design

Nelson certainly intended elements of the *Maison Suspendue* to be direct expressions of 4D. Setting aside Fuller's notion that 4D design can reveal transcendent dimensions in space-time, Nelson wanted the suspended units to be prefabricated and plugged into their predetermined locations within the house's interior. With new demands from changing circumstances or popular trends, a new unit could be designed, fabricated, and exchanged with an existing one (Nelson 1937). As a consumer product, each suspended unit would then remain relevant to the owners' lives and their changing domestic circumstances.

However, Nelson's suspended units had other aspects that made them complex. As Nelson himself noted, the units were comparable to Socrates' "nest" (Applegate and Nelson 1971: 102). Though seemingly innocuous, this analogy should not be pushed aside as verbiage inessential to understanding his "machine house." Rather, the analogy shows Nelson opening possibilities of inhabitation beyond form and function. His reference was to Aristophanes's character Socrates and the latter's nest from the comic play *The Clouds* (423 BCE). In the ancient Greek work, the philosopher is depicted as a fraud and a Sophist. At first, this seems like an odd choice for a comparison, but Socrates' nest actually hung on a *mechane*, an ancient theatrical machine. *Mechanes* denoted "devices or things that allow one to do or work out something" (Cuomo 2007: 151). They were contentious mechanisms because they were often used to lower a god into a scene to artificially resolve conflict in a theatrical drama. The phrase *deus ex machina* derives from this hackneyed use. By placing Socrates, an ostensible Sophist, within the nest, Aristophanes implies a comparison between the machine's ability to make the weak stronger—through the god's intervention and the Sophist's identical capacity to make weaker arguments appear true. Sophists were derided by some in classical times as frauds whose rhetorical abilities enabled them to argue either side of an argument. This meant that they could persuade others without taking a stand, thus neglecting what Plato felt proper ethical virtue should be (Plato 1986: 455–459). In short, the deployment of a Sophist's mechanisms was not motivated by the virtue of philosophic positioning and appropriate judgment.

It is important to remember that in the age of the Greeks, the bearing of a *mechane* was more metaphysical than physical, with functional or aesthetic values only of secondary concern (Olshavsky 2011). Shifting to a modernist context in which life was increasingly enmeshed in the functional and aesthetic aspects of machines, Nelson's reference should be read as a veiled criticism of 4D's potential sophism. More specifically, fourth-dimensional thinking bent on mere mechanization could easily lapse into an ethically suspect practice and result in what Nelson derided as "rational" architecture. While he clearly understood the positive contribution of 4D to design, instead of adopting it wholesale, he struggled to reconcile it with a more imaginative approach to the conception, deployment, and use of machines.

### The suspended house and its symbolist context

The *Maison Suspendue*'s "essential point," Nelson argued, was concerned with "the spiritual needs of man" (1937: n. p.). This shows that there were alternatives to the canonical architectural machine in Modernism as defined by Fuller and Le Corbusier that moved it beyond a simple mimesis of form and function. "Since the invention of the bicycle established an epoch," Nelson argued, "man has extended the amplification of his powers through mechanical means: the telephone, the telegraph and the automobile are all conquests in two dimensions, while the airplane, the radio and the television are conquests in three." The house, too, he confessed, "must then be a machine which amplifies our sensation of life" (1933: 9).

Amplification in Nelson's quote above should be understood as a process of mechanical intensification through an appeal to travel and the use of mass media. The inhabitants of the machine house were encouraged to take the arabesque-ramped ascent into the upper volume where they could then be willfully isolated within one of the suspended units immediately adjacent to the entertainment and media area on the mezzanine. Programmatically, the units were a library and two individual study rooms that enabled the inhabitants to be alone and continue traveling in mental space. "Suspension in space," Nelson argued, "heightens the sense of isolation from the outside world," which was no doubt helpful for studying and reading (1937: n. p.). However, by looking at earlier conceptions of interiority in *fin-de-siècle* France, Nelson's desire to isolate an inhabitant can be further and better understood.

A discussion of continuity in Euro-American Modernism seems like an oxymoron because Modernism's popular narratives are predicated on change and faith in all things new (Kearney 1998). But overlooking this continuity eliminates the richness from Nelson's appeal for isolation, which echoes an earlier, Symbolist aspiration. As Sharon Hirsh has argued, "Symbolist enshrining of domestic indoor spaces…established a new metaphor for personal interiorization that continued into the work of numerous early Modernists who inherited not only Symbolist theories but also the Symbolists' search for solace from the city" (2004: 233). Bourgeois life during the Third Republic became increasingly identified with an expanding media. A host of favorable conditions led to this situation, among them the 1881 Law on the Freedom of the Press and improvements in printing technologies and transportation infrastructure (Kuhn 1995: 16–20). As Vanessa Schwartz quips, "Paris [during this period] did not merely host exhibitions, it had become one" (1998: 1). The Symbolist need for solace was framed as a way of removing inner life from the contempt in which it was held in the popular press. This was achieved through extravagant interiors, Patricia Matthews argues, that promoted the "grandeur of unnecessary things" over and against utility (1999: 21). Such an interior established a space for the imagination and even elicited "empyreal meditation" (Hirsh 2004: 238). Walter Benjamin, in his well-known essay on nineteenth-century Paris, describes this privatization and its alliance with the bourgeoisie and the culture of the mass media:

> For the private person, living space becomes, for the first time, antithetical to the place of work…. The private person…demands that the interior be maintained in his illusions…. From this springs the phantasmagorias of the interior. For the private individual the private environment represents the universe. In it he gathers remote places and the past. His drawing room is a box in the theatre of the world. (1978: 154)

Nelson's suspended units are clearly heirs to this tradition. They were designed to encourage "every degree of intimacy and reclusion" for the betterment of the inhabitant. But, his effort was not about escape from social life, as Benjamin feared when noting that a person seeking solace in the private interior "has no intention of extending his commercial considerations into social ones" (1978: 154). Rather, the isolation for "recreation and study" enabled by the machine house, Nelson believed, would bring about "a whole unit of culture favourable to the renewal and regeneration of the individual" (1937: n. p.). Similar to the role newspapers (mass media) played in creating nationalism, according to Benedict Anderson, the "machine house" employed "technical means for re-presenting…[a] kind of imagined community" (1991: 25). The social construction of Nelson's imagined community is clearly utopian (and likely upper-middle class) but who constitutes it he does not say. What he makes clear, however, is that an individual who finds solace in the *Maison Suspendue* might even "increase his potential contribution towards the community" (1937: n. p.).

Nelson's adaptation of the Symbolists' conception of interiority demonstrates that he was trying to translate their intentions into a post-Loosian design discourse in which ornament was synonymous with cultural degeneration (Loos 1998: 233). This starts with his rejection of the house's "traditional" frontage and continues in the interior where the phantasmagoria of consumer artefacts, which Benjamin saw in Paris's arcades and fashionable department stores like Le Bon Marché, was de-emphasized. Instead, emphasis is placed on a radicalized interior and the artful grandeur of the sectional space. The *Maison Suspendue*, Nelson contends, is "a new space that one can call 'useless' in comparison to a purely functional space of material needs" (1937: n. p.).

## The everyday pataphysical machine

According to Nelson, the basic structure of everyday life had not changed much since Roman times (1971: 102). Even as the forms and arrangements of design had mutated on a deep level, a certain stability in human activities has allowed them to transcend history. This is another way of saying that, when stripped of sociocultural specificity and symbolic networks, domestic spaces still oblige everyday human requirements of embodiment like gravity, eating, or going to the bathroom. A house silently supports these conditions for its inhabitants, and by carefully designing this support, designers can help shape an inhabitant's reality. However, as Reinhold Martin suggests, one should not commit "the elementary mistake of assuming that reality...is entirely real" (2005: 4). This is a crucial observation because it shows that reality can be reimagined. In the case of the *Maison Suspendue*, Nelson theorized imaginative aspects of inhabitation that went beyond the house's physicality and which could best be described as pataphysical.

Pataphysics is a poetic science articulated by the French writer and dramaturge Alfred Jarry (1873–1907). By the 1930s, Jarry was a mythical figure among the artistic circles—Cubist, Dadaist, and Surrealist—that Nelson frequented. Picasso, for instance, went as far as collecting Jarry's manuscripts and purchasing his infamous revolver. Jarry's play *Ubu enchaîné* (*Ubu Enslaved*), directed by Sylvain Itkine with sets by Max Ernst, was staged in 1937 for the first time for the Paris International Exposition Dedicated to Art and Technology in Modern Life. For the Catalan artist and Nelson's friend, Joan Miró, Jarry was one of the "pure poets" and "avowed heroes" during Miró's collaboration with Nelson (1992: 136). While Nelson himself never made a direct reference to Jarry in his writings on the house, it is likely that, through his friends, he was quite familiar with the science of pataphysics, which can, therefore, offer a lens to better understand the imaginative dimensions of his *Maison Suspendue*.

According to Père Ubu, Jarry's main character in *Ubu cocu*, pataphysics was a science "that we have personally invented, and for which a great desire has been widely felt" (1972: 497). But, the term "pataphysics" itself had been coined during Jarry's school days and likely was not Jarry's sole invention. Jarry used the word "pataphysics" publicly for the first time in an episode involving Père Ubu and his Conscience in the short play *Guignol*, published in the April 28, 1893 issue of *L'Écho de Paris littéraire illustré*. The following year, Jarry published his first book, *Les Minutes de Sable Mémorial*, in which the introduction refers to a future book on this science, titled *Elements of Pataphysics*. However, the book never materialized in that form. Instead, it was incorporated and incarnated in the book *Gestes et Opinions du Docteur Faustroll, Pataphysicien*, a work that Jarry completed in 1898 but did not publish in its entirety until 1911.

Through Dr Faustroll's narrative, we learn that pataphysics is a science of the "particular" and "accidental" that seeks "the laws governing exceptions." It "will explain the universe supplementary to this one," Jarry says, "or less ambitiously, will describe a universe which can be—and perhaps should be—envisaged in the place of the traditional one" (1972: 668). In short, through pataphysics, Jarry proposed that there were other ways of understanding, ordering and perhaps living in society. While we do not have enough space to fully unpack all of Jarry's nuance and humor, suffice to say that, according to Gilles Deleuze, pataphysics is "inseparable from phenomenology" (1997: 92). In Jarry's case, his form of phenomenology is a way of studying embodied experience that goes beyond mere experientialism, becoming a manner of participating in and shaping a society increasingly mediated by machine technologies.

In an early definition, Jarry described pataphysics as the "science of these present and future beings and contrivances, along with the Power their Use confers" (1972: 341). To explore the realm of pataphysics, Jarry invented a series of ingenious machines that appear in many of his major written works. These include a painting machine (*la machine à peindre*), Ubu's debraining machine (*machine à décerveler*), Dr Faustroll's time machine (*la machine à explorer le temps*), and an array of others, including Père Ubu himself. The literary scholar Michel Carrouges argues that these are "improbable" contrivances because they are not governed by mechanics or conventional utility (1975). But, it makes little difference, I contend, whether they were materially feasible or not. By suspending the purely functional aim of mechanics, pataphysical machines may seem "useless," but they present instead "the semblance of machinery, of the kind seen in dreams, at the theatre, at the cinema" (Carrouges 1975: 21). Carrouges, however, does not notice that these machines are also architectural and revive an older understanding of machines. Machines from antiquity, according to Lewis Mumford, who wrote two years before Nelson's research commenced, were crucial to premodern society's "goal" of "a greater intensification of life: colour, perfume, images, music, sexual ecstasy, as well as…thought and exploration" (1934: 149). Like the machines of Hero of Alexandria, their conception and deployment were tied to wonder and other perceived needs that were simultaneously physical and imaginary. This is also an apt description of the nature of Jarry's pataphysical machines as well as of Nelson's "machine house."

According to Jarry, "pataphysics is the science of imaginary solutions which symbolically attributes the properties of objects, described by their virtuality, to their lineaments" (1972: 669). In other words, a pataphysician transforms the quotidian through symbolic attributions. To Joan Miró, the *Maison Suspendue*'s interior had the qualities of a landscape (Nelson 1937). He further made the unusual request to paint portions of Nelson's model to draw out these relationships. He chose to paint the ramp red like a "flower," the underside of a suspended unit blue as the "sky," the ground plane green like the "earth." Miró also painted white circular forms above, "as an expression of the universe" (Nelson 1937: n. p.). The intensified attributes linked the interior with the land and cosmos, a pataphysical process, which connected realities once distant from each other based on an object's existing or implied lineaments, both visible and invisible. Miró's work on the model for the *Maison Suspendue* revealed these links and the project's connection to pataphysics.

Further, Nelson, like Jarry, also attempted to give impetus to the imagination by creating erotic tension within his work. The *Maison Suspendue*, he said, offered "complex and non-simplistic" spaces with "contradictions," including "order and disorder" and "constraint and freedom" (Nelson 1937: n. p.). It equally accounted for "material needs and spiritual, practical and speculative, mechanic and poetic" needs (Nelson 1937: n. p.). As Jarry had also stated: "Human Truth is what a man seeks: a desire" (1972: 950). These competing desires were materialized in the machine house's unique spatial organization.

A rationalist approach to spatial organization can take two forms. In one, form perfectly suits function like a hand and a glove. In the other, an open plan is allowed to accommodate many activities. The *Maison Suspendue* does not belong to either of these two categories. Instead, it reconciles the formal enclosure of articulated units hung within an open floor plan by means of a "free" section. Such an ambivalent hybrid, Nelson hoped, would retain the "mystery" of the interior space (1937: n. p.). Moving away from these two rationalist approaches, Nelson felt that the "whole" of an interior should not be entirely transparent to an inhabitant's gaze. This coincides with what Alberto Pérez-Gómez has termed "the fundamental nature of ... [erotic] space," and it "is *lack* rather than the possession of plenitude" that characterizes architectural eroticism (2008: 64–65). This opens the term "suspended" to an alternative definition meaning "delay" or "lack," which is another way of saying "erotic."

## Conclusion

The *Maison Suspendue* and Nelson's subsequent publication displayed for the public a contradictory, subtly eroticized interior, which relished the tension between the actual and the imaginative aspects of inhabitation. The gains of machine technologies during modernity did not necessitate the reduction of the machine dwelling to a simple mimesis of form and function. Rather, Nelson and his collaborators offered ways of leveraging these technologies to construct a distinct understanding of what an interior arrangement could do for living imaginatively.

As the *Maison Suspendue* shows, the modern French interior in the 1930s was a complex, multivalent site where designers could explore and reconcile divergent approaches while attempting to answer the question of what it meant to be modern in an age increasingly intertwined with mass media. Though it was never built, the *Maison Suspendue* achieved public exposure primarily through the medium of print. Equally, printed sources disseminated in the media—Jarry's and Aristophanes' plays, Symbolist novels, and various architectural writings—no doubt shaped Nelson's conception of the "machine house." This compelling and paradoxical project clearly shows that products of the mass media are crucial to a richer understanding of modern Euro-American architecture and design.

## References

Anderson, B. (1991), *Imagined Communities*, London: Verso.
Applegate, J. and P. Nelson (1971), "Paul Nelson: An Interview," *Perspecta* 13: 75–129.
Benjamin, W. (1978), *Reflections*, trans. Edmund Jephcott, New York and London: Harcourt Brace Jovanovich.
Carrouges, M. (1975), "Directions for Use," in Harald Szeemann (ed), *Le macchine celibi/The Bachelor Machines*, New York: Rizzoli.
Cuomo, S. (2007), *Technology and Culture in Greek and Roman Antiquity*, New York: Cambridge University Press.

Deleuze, G. (1997), *Essays Critical and Clinical*, trans. Daniel W. Smith and Michael A. Greco, Minneapolis, MN: University of Minnesota Press.
Fuller, B. (2001), *Your Private Sky: Discourse R. Buckminster Fuller*, in Joachim Krausse and Claude Lichtenstein (eds), Zurich: Lars Müller Publishers.
Hirsh, S. L. (2004), *Symbolism and Modern Urban Society*, Cambridge: Cambridge University Press.
Jarry, A. (1972), *Oeuvres Completes*, in Michel Arrivé, Henri Bordillon, Patrick Besnier and Bernard Le Doze (eds), Paris: Gallimard, Bibliothèque de la Pléiade.
Kearney, R. (1998), *The Wake of the Imagination: Toward a Postmodern Culture*, Oxon: Routledge.
Kuhn, R. (1995), *The Media in France*, New York and London: Routledge.
Loos, A. (1998), *Ornament and Crime: Selected Essays*, trans. Michael Michell, Riverside, CA: Ariadne Press.
Lorance, L. (2009), *Becoming Bucky Fuller*, Cambridge, MA: MIT Press.
Martin, R. (2005), "Critical of What?: Toward a Utopian Realism," *Harvard Design Magazine* 22: 1–5.
Mathews, P. (1999), *Passionate Discontent: Creativity, Gender, and French Symbolist Art*, Chicago: University of Chicago Press.
Miró, J. (1992), *Joan Miró: Selected Writings and Interviews*, in Margit Rowell (ed), New York: Da Capo Press.
Mumford, L. (1934), *Technics and Civilization*, New York: Harcourt, Brace & Company.
Nelson, P. (November–December 9, 1933), "La Maison de la rue St. Guillaume," *L'Architecture d'aujourd'hui*.
Nelson, P. (1937), *La Maison Suspendue: Recherche de Paul Nelson*. Paris: Editions Albert Morancé.
Olshavsky, P. (2011), "Situating Pataphysical Machines: A History of Architectural Machinations," *Chora: Intervals in the Philosophy of Architecture*, Montreal: McGill-Queen's University Press: 6.
Pawley, M. (1990), *Buckminster Fuller*, London: Trefoil Publications.
Pérez-Gómez, A. (2008), *Built Upon Love: Architectural Longing after Ethics and Aesthetics*, Cambridge, MA: MIT Press.
Plato (1986), *The Sophist*, trans. Harold North Fowler, Cambridge, MA: Harvard University Press.
Schwartz, V. R. (1998), *Spectacular Realities: Early Mass Culture in Fin-de-Siècle Paris*, Berkeley and Los Angeles, CA: University of California Press.

PART II
AESTHETICS, ANXIETY, AND IDENTITY:
REPRODUCING A DECADENT DOMESTICITY

# CHAPTER 6
# THE INTERIORIZATION OF IDENTITY: PORTRAIT BUSTS AND THE POLITICS OF SELFHOOD IN PRE- AND EARLY REVOLUTIONARY FRANCE

Ronit Milano

In Anne-Flore Millet's portrait of Marie-Antoinette awaiting her execution in the Conciergerie, the queen is seated, in a nearly-monochromatic interior, in front of a grated prison-like window and next to a grisailles-painted sculptural portrait of her husband, King Louis XVI (Figure 6.1). Although this representational formula of a sitter next to a bust on a table was common in eighteenth-century imagery, in reality, portrait busts rarely stood on tables within French interiors. This chapter seeks to explore the motivation and aims of the artists using this formula, which communicated a familiar yet imaginary setting. The main argument is that portrait busts in pre- and early Revolutionary France functioned as reflections of certain selfhoods and that, when placed in an interior setting, the bust emblematized mental interiority. By implication, the chapter will attempt to illuminate the constitutive role that reproducible objects intended for broad circulation such as busts or biographic books (which offer a literary portrait) played in the virtual construction of an interior and, consequently, in the conceptualization of the self.

Available in various sizes and materials, in the private and public spheres, as originals and as reproductions—Paris was awash with portrait busts. They were placed above fireplaces and armoires, lined corridors, and flanked doorways and thus functioned as agents of political and cultural agendas (Baker 2001; Scherf 2007: 29–30). The growing public demand for small-scale artworks for the purpose of interior decoration and the rise of a new type of connoisseur throughout the eighteenth century promoted the reproduction of busts, often in materials cheaper than marble, as a modern artistic practice (Baker 2006; 2008). The Parisian bourgeoisie, which commissioned portrait busts both for the purpose of self-promotion and as a form of interior decoration, became a new class of art patrons. The wealthy, upper-class owners of such busts also used them as indicators of their status, political allegiance, and intellectual interests. By virtue of the reproducibility of the medium, portrait busts were thus exposed to a large number of viewers. Although the discussion of publicly displayed busts is beyond the scope of this study, their powerful ideological agency within French culture of the eighteenth century, like that of biographical books, can be comprehended by recalling the destructive reaction of the masses toward them at the break of the Revolution.

In an interior space, most decorative elements were displayed for the purpose of proclaiming social standing. The portrait bust, however, embedded additional qualities, one of which was to endow the physical interior with a pseudo human presence. This presence not only symbolized various allegiances and invoked political, social, and epistemic ideas but also functioned as a simulacrum of a social encounter. The person or group observing the

**Figure 6.1** Attributed to Anne-Flore Millet, Marquise de Bréhan, *Portrait of Marie-Antoinette, Queen of France*, oil on canvas, c. 1794, Private Collection, Photo © Christie's Images Limited 2015.

bust was conceptually conversing with it, the bust thus operating as an open platform for French contemporary identity. It stood, synchronically, for the particular subject that the bust represented, as much as for its owner, the observer, and, finally, a collective form of identity associated with society. It was a reflective medium that, by virtue of its reproducible character for multiple audiences, constituted a simulacrum of the idea of contemporary persons and society. In other words, the portrait bust represented not only a specific person (and yet not a generic image) but rather *an idea of a particular person*—an image that any viewer who wished to do so could identify with. In an ambience that celebrated the rise of the modern self and the formation of a public identity and an individuated society, the portrait bust was thus deployed within a particular interior as a manifestation of self-exploration and self-constitution.

This function is clearly conveyed in the 1791 group painting by Charles Paul Landon, depicting the family of Count Pierre-Jean de Bourcet seated in an interior setting (Figure 6.2). On the left, portrait busts of Louis XVI and his wife are placed on a draped table, accompanied by a vase with a white lily—the symbol of the monarchy and presumably an allusion to the Dauphin. The count was the *Officier de Maison* for the household of the Dauphin, and in this portrait, the immediate purpose of the busts was to declare the royalist loyalties of the couple to the imprisoned king and queen. Another lily, which lies dying upon the table, possibly represents the elder son of the royal couple, the first Dauphin, who perished just before the fall of the Bastille in July 1789 and whose portrait hangs prominently on the wall. At the foot of the table lays a framed portrait of the count's brother. The pair of marble busts of the king and queen are replicas of those by Louis-Simon Boizot, who designed official portraits of the royal couple for reproduction and distribution.

The type of room chosen by Landon for this scene is difficult to identify. The small coffee table on the right, the cradle and stool, the books and notebooks in the lower left corner of the composition, and the *toilette*-like table on which the busts are placed, all engender an imaginary or symbolic interior space that combines the various functions of the private house into the conceptual essence of a family. The curtain in the top left corner is hung in a nonrealistic manner, suggesting the idea of unveiling, of momentarily exposing a private scene to the eye of the viewer. In this constructed interior, the busts are placed where, in reality, a mirror would have stood on the *toilette*. Thus, the images of the king and queen can be construed as reflections of M. and Mme Bourcet, conveying an allegiance so strong that the selfhoods of the count and the countess are united with those of the royal couple. Various levels of interiority are communicated through this composition: on the explicit level, there is the

**Figure 6.2** Charles Paul Landon, *Le Comte Pierre-Jean de Bourcet et sa famille*, oil on canvas, 1791, Photo © Musée de Grenoble.

physical interior setting in which the family is represented; on the implicit one, the imaginary, constructed setting symbolizes the sitters' psychological interiority—their selfhoods. In the context of the family, their selfhoods reveal a devoted mother and wife with her young children, and a sensitive and intellectual father hugging his son while looking at the image of his brother, thereby conveying his responsibility to introduce his son into the masculine social circles of Paris.

The scene, as a whole, also offers another kind of allusion to French society. The two women, the queen and the countess, frame the composition, as if manifesting the importance of the Rousseauian woman in the construction of the family and her supportive role within the societal order. The king and the count are positioned next to one another, separated only by the vase with the lily that symbolizes the Dauphin, a generic idea of potential male power and leadership. Indeed, the count embraces his older son, who seems just old enough to enter male circles. As a whole, this interior composition parallels the French collective consciousness before and during the Revolution, in terms of gender, familial, and social orders. Indeed, the connection between the private-familial order and the public-social one was already pointed out in 1762 by Jean-Jacques Rousseau in *Du Contrat social ou Principes du droit politique*: "The most ancient of all societies, and the only one that is natural, is the family" (1950 book I: 2). If the scene somehow evokes a sense of mental imprisonment, it undoubtedly echoes the physical state of the imprisoned royal couple at that time.

The reflection of both physical and mental interiority here resonates with the painted portrait of Marie-Antoinette made by Anne-Flore Millet. Following the execution of Louis XVI in January 1793, the queen was moved from the tower of the Temple fortress to the Conciergerie after being separated from her children. She was to spend little more than two months there before she was guillotined on October 16, 1793. The Marquise de Bréhan, previously a lady-in-waiting to the queen, probably completed the commemorative portrait while in exile in Berlin. In this painting, Millet emphasized the physical and mental state of the imprisoned queen by using a monochromatic palette, dark tones, and an emptiness of the room. Despite the private nature of the scene, the grated window at the top left corner of the composition—similarly to the curtain in the Bourcet family portrait—suggests the idea of self-revelation. In this portrait, too, physical and psychological interiority intersects, and a portrait bust represents psychological selfhood or interiority, rather than a true form of interior decoration. In Millet's painting, the queen, mourning her husband, is dressed in black, echoing the immediate darkness of the room that surrounds her. She is holding the book *The Life of Mary, Queen of Scots*, recounting the tragic life of another executed queen. On the draped table rests the testament of December 23, 1792, the touching document written by her husband in anticipation of his death. On her chest is a profile portrait of the Dauphin, painted in grisailles to imitate a bas-relief. Also in grisailles is the portrait bust of Louis XVI, placed on the *toilette*-like table. The overt message of these objects centers on the queen's loyalty and devotion to her family. Yet, there is more in the subtext: the sitter's pose and the composition of the picture resonate with portraits of women seated at their *toilette*, a common theme in French art of the second half of the eighteenth century. The queen is positioned at the center, with her body turned toward her *toilette*. However, the portrait bust of her husband stands there instead of a mirror. This is neither a lavish nor a monumental bust. Rather, the sculpted image is life-size, designed simply and naturalistically, with a round cut and a bare chest. As was argued elsewhere, the bare-chested bust during this period was not intended merely to invoke the glory of the ancients, but the physical exposure could also have been construed as a symbol of subjectivity and an act of psychological self-exposure (Milano 2015). The king's sculptural portrait may be viewed as a mirror or reflection of the queen. Together with the portrait of her son, which lies on the imaginary place of her heart, the painting offers an extended portrait in which the interior and its elements transform into a visualization of the sitter's self, in this case enhancing the perception of Marie-Antoinette's selfhood as embodying that of her husband and son.

The interiorization process conveyed by portrait busts is also evident in contemporary writing. During the eighteenth century, the literary genre of autobiography flourished and letter-writing and reading became a common practice. Such writings were subjected for publication as "correspondence" and numerous personal and subjective accounts were thus made available. As such, these works became part of the mass-media alignment and propagated, similarly to portrait busts, the ideology of self-exploration. Books, just like portrait busts, were objects usually used and displayed in an interior physical space and the visualization of an interior setting enhanced the invocation of a mental concept of interiority. For instance, in 1794, the book *Voyage autour de ma chambre* was first published (de Maistre 1854). The author, Count Xavier de Maistre, was a young Savoyard officer who, in 1790, was sentenced to forty-two days of house arrest for fighting a duel. The book, imitating the format of a travel book, is an account of the count's forced interiorization and reflects how autobiographical accounts, whether parodical or serious, formed part of a modern conceptualization of individuated selfhoods.[1] As in the case of de Maistre, for whom the written description of physical surroundings transforms into a narrative of self-revelation, where the self is confronted with its *doppelgänger*, the painted interior in which Marie-Antoinette is positioned next to a bust of Louis XVI also constitutes a subjective space. The portrait bust here—allegedly a merely decorative item—functions as a reflection of the sitter's *other* self.

Paintings such as Anne-Flore Millet's and Landon's reveal the manner in which a portrait bust operated within an interior setting. In a real (rather than painted) situation, the subject standing in front of the bust was actually the viewer, who became a part of the interior space. Portrait busts were usually placed above fireplaces or armoires, many times at the beholder's eye-level. One may consider, for example, the marble bust of Marie-Antoinette produced by Félix Lecomte in 1783 (Figure 6.3); the bust was (and still is) placed in the queen's bedroom in the Palace of Versailles, on the mantelpiece above the hearth. Behind it, on the wall, a mirror hung following the contemporary style in interior design. This room was an important space in the palace and in French culture and heritage as a whole. It was in this room that the queen slept, sometimes accompanied by the king; in it the official ritual of the morning *toilette* was held; and above all, in it the royal births took place. Its essence was therefore associated with a variety of selfhoods: one represented the queen; another, more generic, represented the feminine image in this era; while a third, collective one, invoked the perception of French selfhood and consciousness. For a viewer standing in this room during that time, whether a lady in-waiting or a guest, these selfhoods collided and were united with that of himself or herself. Looking at the portrait bust of Marie-Antoinette thus resembled the act of looking at a mirror, an idea that was enhanced by the actual mirror behind the bust, with the portrait functioning as a reflection of the viewer. This operation

**Figure 6.3** Châteaux de Versailles et de Trianon, The queen's bedroom, Versailles, with *Portrait Bust of Queen Marie-Antoinette* by Félix Lecomte on the fireplace, marble, 1783, Photo @ Ronit Milano.

suggested the embedding of the queen's image in the personal selfhood of the French contemporary beholder. On an extended level, a portrait bust of a celebrated contemporary figure—whether a famous philosopher, a king, or a queen—served as an index of a cultural, historical, and epistemological state and thus symbolized a part of the actual person looking at it. An interior setting enhanced this theme as it prompted notions of a private and personal space and of psychological interiorization. The portrait bust neither functioned as a merely decorative element, nor was it simply an index of cultural agendas; rather, in an interior space, it operated as a reflection of the beholder, forming part of his or her own selfhood and consciousness.

This interiorizing function of the portrait bust was further enhanced when the bust was of a celebrated philosopher, as this situation also invoked the intellectual body of knowledge associated with the bust. Such was the case, for instance, of the portrait busts of Jean-Jacques Rousseau, one of the most prominent advocates of individuality during this period, whose *Confessions* was one of the first autobiographies referring to an individual's worldly experiences and personal emotions. Although not published in his lifetime, Rousseau read his autobiography (written between 1765 and 1769) publicly in leading salons and various other meeting places. Rousseau himself defined this work as a self-portrait, reflecting the increasing focus in this period on subjectivity and introspection, and opened it with the words: "I have entered upon a performance which is without example, whose accomplishment will have no imitator. I mean to present my fellow-mortals with a man in all the integrity of nature; and this man shall be myself" (1903 book I: 8). Rousseau's literary portrayal emphasized the importance of psychological interiorization, sincerity, and self-revelation. As he further wrote:

"Such as I was, I have declared myself; sometimes vile and despicable, at others, virtuous, generous and sublime...let each in his turn expose with equal sincerity the failings, the wanderings of his heart" (1903 book I: 8).

Portrait busts of Rousseau were in great demand in pre-Revolutionary France and were presented in dozens of private houses of the Parisian bourgeoisie. Immediately following Rousseau's death in 1778, the prominent sculptor Jean-Antoine Houdon made a death mask of the revered philosopher. In one of his letters, Houdon wrote that he "received at midnight...an express letter from M. de Girardan [sic], who sent it to me, knowing of my admiration for the great man, and his constant refusal during his lifetime to allow his bust to be made" (Houdon in Poulet 2003: 167). Based on this mask, he created, as was customary in the case of philosophers, three versions of portrait busts that were later replicated: one presented the philosopher wearing a wig and dressed à la française (Poulet 2003: 166–170); the second displayed him in the image of an ancient philosopher, dressed à l'antique and wearing a headband (Bresc-Bautier and Scherf 2009: 484–485); and the third, executed à l'antique, depicted him with his chest bared, featuring a rounded cut (Scherf 2006: 86–89). All busts displayed an extraordinary liveliness and an intelligent, sensitive expression in the eyes. Upon inviting Houdon to create the mask, René-Louis de Girardin, Marquis of Vauvray and Rousseau's close friend and protector, asked Houdon for a copy of the à la française sculptural portrait of Rousseau. Girardin, a highly cultivated gentleman, had offered Rousseau a place to live on his estate at Ermenonville, north of Paris, where he had created "natural" gardens inspired by the philosopher's writings. A plaster portrait of Rousseau à la française was indeed sent to the Marquis on July 5, 1779. Girardin, who was obviously pleased with Houdon's sculpture, had his own portrait painted with this bust of Rousseau beside him (Figure 6.4).

Unlike the bare-chested bust of Louis XVI situated in front of Marie-Antoinette in the example mentioned above, Rousseau's figure is dressed. Since an owner used a bust as a projection of his or her own image, Girardin's presentation of himself as a man of nature, erudite, and fashionably dressed, yet tender and smiling, was underscored by the bust of Rousseau looking at him, bestowing upon him the virtuous nature of the admired philosopher himself. However, if the bust is to be read as a reflection of the sitter or as a visualization of interiority as suggested above, why was a dressed bust used instead of a bare-chested bust that could be interpreted as a symbol of self-exposure? The answer to this question is rooted in the type of busts usually preferred for an interior versus an exterior setting. The following passages aim to offer such a distinction to further construe the interior as a conceptual space of selfhood.

Since it is not always exactly known where portrait busts were placed, an examination of small-scale porcelain portraits facilitates a more accurate examination of the domestic sphere, as they were almost exclusively displayed inside houses, typically on mantelpieces or commodes. Porcelain busts usually portrayed celebrated public figures—contemporary philosophers, the king, and the queen—images that would be produced in multiple copies. Scrutinizing such busts reveals that, in contrast to foreign connoisseurs who frequently preferred the severe à l'antique format, or to royal functionaries who commissioned the à l'antique bust for public spaces and purposes, the majority of small-scale porcelain busts displayed in French domestic interiors featured clothed figures dressed à la française. In 1767, the royal porcelain factory in Sèvres produced its first bust of Voltaire (London, The

**Figure 6.4** [Jean-Baptiste Greuze], *Portrait du Marquis de Girardin*, oil on canvas, c. 1780, Musée de l'abbaye royale, Châalis, Photo @ RMN-Grand Palais/Agence Bulloz.

British Museum). This portrait, modeled in 1767 after a bust by Jean-Claude-François Rosset, presented Voltaire as a relatively old person: the sitter appears bareheaded, with a highly realistic expression and facial features, and wearing contemporary clothes, including a slightly open shirt attributed to Enlightenment philosophers. This version was especially popular in Paris, and Voltaire himself regarded it as the "best bust" made in his image (Taylor 1974: 30). Around the same time, the royal porcelain factory also produced a portrait bust of Diderot, one of which can now be found in a private collection (Becker 2006: 58–63). It was created after Marie-Anne Collot's original life-size portrait, which was also highly praised by the sitter. Similarly to Rosset's bust of Voltaire, Collot portrayed Diderot wearing an open shirt and sporting his natural hair, thus emphasizing the ideals of naturalism and self-revelation. The choice of contemporary attire, in this context, attests to a preference for truthfulness, modernity (including the modern perception of the self), and the concept of the "here and now" over the ideal and remote aura that characterized the *à l'antique* versions. Designated for an interior space, the private preference for draped busts (not only in porcelain, which was used exclusively in the interior, but also in other materials) can be tied to the selfhood-related idea of the "here and now" but also to the interrelations between a physical interior and mental interiority. It is therefore not surprising that this type of bust was more common in painted depictions, as conveyed both in the portrait of the Bourcet family and in the portrait of Girardin.

The preference for draped busts for interior settings resulted in their association with contemporary selfhood. Houdon's *à la française* bust of Rousseau, which is depicted in Girardin's portrait, bespeaks this preference and was chosen for this painting for the sake of suggesting a closer connection between Girardin and Rousseau than the one that would have been implied through a bare-chested bust. Elevated on a marble pedestal, the bust shows Rousseau wearing a short, tightly curled wig, a coat of a plain material with three large round buttons, a vest, and a cravat and jabot. The possession of portraits of philosophers, as mentioned above, embedded the transferal of the sitter's aura onto the bust's owner. Resemblance between the philosopher and the owner of the bust enhanced the accessibility of the bust and the correlation that was virtually generated between the two personas. Therefore, the owner of the bust would have wanted the image of the sculpted figure to be accessible and to resemble him, to the greatest possible extent. This preference for a more accessible type of bust led to the substantial prevalence of the *à la française* type of portraits within the private sphere. In this context, it is also important to acknowledge the significance of the use of death masks: the process transformed the surface of the bust into an embodiment of the real skin, thereby creating a tactile experience that placed the viewer in a form of direct contact with the sitter. Stanislas de Girardin, son of the Marquis de Girardin, praised his father's plaster portrait of Rousseau by Houdon:

> the resemblance of which is striking, especially when looking at it in profile; a smile of merriment is on his mouth; he is the first artist who makes a cavity for the eyes and indicates the pupils, which gives his portraits a feeling of life that is frightening when looking at them a long time. (Girardin in Poulet 2003: 168)

In the painted portrait of the Marquis de Girardin, Rousseau, with his gaze directed at the Marquis, seems even more human and direct than in the actual sculpture. On one level, Rousseau's bust, as a piece of art commissioned by the Marquis and joined by other attributes, the roses, the book, the hunting dog, and the high-fashioned clothes, alludes to Girardin's social standing, intellectual status, and virtue; on another level, through this juxtaposition, Rousseau's philosophical perception of selfhood, self-exploration and individuality was united with the selfhood of the Marquis.

In addition to this juxtaposition, another distinction between the portrait of Girardin and that of Marie-Antoinette by Anne-Flore Millet is that the former is set in an ambiguous space: it includes elements that identify it as an open, exterior space, and others which imply that the sitter is placed in an interior space. This portrait and its composition—the seated Marquis, his body turned in the direction of the bust, and the sculpted portrait facing the sitter—recall the *toilette*-like scenes, exemplified by paintings such as Anne-Flore Millet's and Landon's. But, instead of a table, Rousseau's bust is placed on a pedestal and, instead of an interior space, the scene is installed in a non-conclusive type of space. The natural background, including the tree behind the marquis and the roses, suggests an outdoor scene. However, the elaborate seat and the composition as a whole resonate with traditional Renaissance and Baroque portraits, in which the subject sat on a veranda—part of the interior setting of the house—with a view to an open landscape that attested to the lands in the sitter's possession and, hence, to his social status. In the case of the Marquis de Girardin, the aim of representing landscape was hardly to offer a manifestation of economic power. Girardin was the author of *De la composition des paysages* (1777), which had been inspired by Rousseau's ideas, and which was to strongly influence the modern French landscape garden. The main goal of presenting this natural landscape was thus related to the sitter's self-perception as a Man of Nature, a term propagated by and later attributed to Rousseau (Rousseau 1762). The invocation of a veranda defines the scene as located in an interior space, in which the landscape functions as a visualization of the Marquis's psychological interiority, revealing his natural self, intellectual accomplishments, and manly virtues born through his connection to nature. Within this imaginary setting, Rousseau's bust operated as a part of the Marquis's selfhood, presenting a visualization of a new epistemological state centered on the concept of interiorization.

As in the case of Marie-Antoinette's portrait, where she was painted near the bust of Louis XVI, this complex representation of the Marquis with the bust of Rousseau epitomizes the use of portrait busts in the French pre- and early Revolutionary era, when they operated as indices of inner selfhoods, extending their immediate function as interior decoration items toward a means of transforming a physical interior space into a psychological one. The medium of sculptural portraiture, with its mass-reproducible quality, offers a platform that is also paralleled by other mass reproducible media such as books that conveyed literary portraits. Such seemingly disparate forms of biographical or autobiographical practices are interlinked to the formulation of selfhood during the eighteenth century. Their incorporation within the idea of a physical interior prompts a conceptualization of mental interiority. In the eighteenth century, the physical form of an interior setting was shaped by portrait busts, which invoked a conceptualization of the self, whether present in the room or perceived as a generic or collective entity. The design of the busts in a realistic style enhanced their correlation with the contemporary idea of the self and redefined the interior as a representation of a persona rather than of an ideal sense of social status. Painted portraits that featured portrait busts also attested to these dynamics, and, by deploying an aesthetic formula that resonated with the function of the portrait bust as a conceptual mirror, they underscored the reflective and constitutive quality of the bust. They suggested that the physical interior was a means through which identities could be created and shaped, presenting their viewers with a simulacrum of these processes and reflecting the exchangeability of interior and interiority at the same time.

## Notes

1. Lajer-Burcharth (2010) extends this discussion, focusing on the contemporary medium of video.

## References

Baker, M. (2001), "'A Sort of Corporate Company:' The Portrait Bust and Its Setting," in P. Curtis, P. Funnell and N. Kalinsky (eds), *Return to Life: A New Look at the Portrait Bust*, London: National Portrait Gallery: 20–35.

Baker, M. (2006), "Reconsidering the Economy of the Eighteenth-Century Portrait Bust: Roubiliac and Houdon," in R. Kanz (ed), *Pygmalions Aufklärung: Eropäische Skulptur im 18. Jahrhundert*, München: Deutscher Kunstverlag: 132–145.

Baker, M. (2008), "Replication, Repetition and Reproduction in Eighteenth-Century French Sculpture," in S. M. Bennett and C. Sargentson (eds), *French Art of the Eighteenth Century at The Huntington*, New Haven and London: Yale University Press: 443–452.

Becker, M-L. (2006), "Le buste de Diderot, de Collot à Houdon," *L'Estampille: L'Objet d'art* 412: 58–63.

Bresc-Bautier, G. and G. Scherf (eds) (2009), *Cast in Bronze: French Sculpture from Renaissance to Revolution*, Paris: Musée du Louvre Éditions: Somogy Art Publishers.

de Maistre, X. (1854), "Voyage autour de ma chambre," in *Oeuvres completes du comte Xavier de Maistre*, Paris: G. Charpentier.

Lajer-Burcharth, E. (2010), "Interior and Interiority: Chantal Akerman's *La Bas*," *31: das Magazin des Instituts für Theorie der Gestaltung und Kunst, Zürich* 14/15: 139–146.

Milano, R. (2015), *The Portrait Bust and French Cultural Politics in the Eighteenth Century*, Leiden: Brill.

Poulet, A. L. (ed) (2003), *Jean-Antoine Houdon: Sculptor of the Enlightenment*, Washington, DC: National Gallery of Art and University of Chicago Press.

Rousseau, J-J. (1762), *Émile, ou De l'éducation*, Amsterdam: Jean Néaulme.

Rousseau, J-J. (1903), *The Confessions of Jean Jacques Rousseau*, trans. S. W. Orson, London: Privately printed for members of the Aldus Society. Available on-line through Project Gutenberg, last accessed June 15, 2014, http://www.gutenberg.org/files/3913/3913-h/3913-h.htm.

Rousseau, J-J. (1950), *The Social Contract and Discourses*, trans. G. D. H. Cole, New York: E.P. Dutton and Company Inc.

Scherf, G. (2006), *Houdon, 1741–1828: Statues, Portraits Sculptés*, Paris: Musée du Louvre.

Scherf, G. (2007), "Sculpted Portraits, 1770–1830: 'Real Presences,'" in S. Allard (ed), *Citizens and Kings: Portraits in the Age of Revolution, 1760–1830*, London and New York: Royal Academy of Arts: 25–36.

Taylor, S. (1974), "Artists and *Philosophes* as Mirrored by Sèvres and Wedgwood," in F. Haskell, A. Levi and R. Shackleton (eds), *The Artist and the Writer in France: Essays in Honour of Jean Seznec*, Oxford: Clarendon Press.

# CHAPTER 7
# A PORTABLE KEYHOLE INTO THE FICTIONAL APARTMENT BUILDING: THE INTERIORS OF FÉLIX VALLOTTON AND ÉMILE ZOLA
*Karen Stock*

Félix Vallotton was a Swiss artist who is remembered today for his paintings and his association with the Nabis, an avant-garde group active in Paris in the 1890s. However, Vallotton had his most consistent success not in the arena of high art, but in the liminal media of the woodcut print which, at this time, was being elevated from its origins as mere illustration. The *Intimités* series of 1898 can be considered his masterpiece, due to both the elegance of the formal elements and the way the content captured the contemporary fascination with and anxiety surrounding the subject of the interior. The ten woodcuts that compose the series depict the bourgeois interior as an iniquitous space where couples go to hide their lust, petty cruelty, infidelity, and greed. Through Vallotton's depictions, the viewer is granted an exclusive peek as if through a keyhole to glimpse couples at their most emotionally vulnerable. These messy emotional scenes are rendered with a caustic elegance and are characterized by broad patches of rich black and luminous white.

This chapter discusses Vallotton's series in the context of the reemergence of the woodcut in the nineteenth century as a medium that bridged the divide between mass media, such as posters and journals, and high art. Through a comparison with Émile Zola's 1882 novel *Pot-Bouille*, it suggests that the *Intimités* series behaves less like visual short stories, which has been proposed by previous authors, such as Richard S. Field, and more like individual apartments within Baron Haussmann's restructured Paris. Indeed, contemporary with Vallotton's *Intimités* series was Haussmann's radical transformation of Paris. In the dramatic alteration of the topography of Paris, there was a corollary restructuring of home, family, and gender as men and women negotiated their shifting roles. The apartment building became the dominant form of housing in Paris, and this architectural structure was considered, by architectural critics and public health reformers, a negative influence on the family and the tenants' health. They argued that the apartment allowed cross contamination on both physical and moral levels. Like the prints in Vallotton's *Intimités* series, the rooms revealed through Zola's novel detail the petty dramas and intrigues of a middle-class apartment building. Thus, both Zola and Vallotton appear to have taken pleasure in mocking the metaphorical façade of respectability that concealed the moral corruptness of the bourgeoisie and sought to provide their audience with a surreptitious glimpse into private moments. In order to provide a richer context, it is necessary to undertake a nuanced cross-media and cross-disciplinary analysis that expands our understanding not only of the areas where *Pot-Bouille* and *Intimités* intersect but also of the *fin-de-siècle* urban, specifically Parisian, bourgeois interior.

French Modernism as expressed in art, literature, and theater contains the twin impulses of celebrating the sanctity of the interior and the desire to penetrate the secrets of that space. The Goncourt brothers famously claimed in 1861 that "the interior is going to die" and many of their contemporaries as well as subsequent scholars agreed that the public spectacle of Paris was sapping the life from the interior (Marcus 1999: 137). However, Sharon Marcus argues that the interior was not dying in this period; rather, the interior was now more rigidly demarcated from the exterior and was glorified as a space of tradition/family that was being threatened by modernity (1999: 139). As the interior became more guarded in the latter half of the nineteenth century, so the compulsion to see behind closed doors was also increased. Travel books from this era both praise and are frustrated by the new modesty of the Haussmann-style apartment buildings. Edmond Texier's *Tableau de Paris* (1852) describes a character who "strolls through the streets in vain, no hospitable breach exposes the houses' varied ramparts to his gaze or gives passage to his curiosity; in vain he … contemplates this immense and teeming hive of rooftops …. Hoping that a helpful genie will come to unhat all these impenetrable sanctuaries of private life; nothing of the sort! Paris modestly conserves her domiciles" (Marcus 1999: 146). Communication between different buildings or between the street and the interior had been a common occurrence before the Third Republic; however, by the *fin-de-siècle* one could not witness anything of the sort. The new interiors mostly consisted of isolated, insular domestic units meant to preserve the integrity of the families living within. Zola and Vallotton's work responded to the desire to peer into these Parisian abodes by imaginatively stripping away their architectural façades. There was a deep nostalgia for the home of the past, which seemed more honest and transparent. However, both Zola and Vallotton saw the late-nineteenth-century interior as a space not so much for familial harmony as for the commission of adultery, the infliction of petty emotional wounds, and the disintegration of the public face of moral righteousness—a view almost too consistent with the reception of Haussmann's apartment buildings at the time.

Ten woodcuts compose the *Intimités* series: *The Lie*, *Money*, *The Triumph*, *5 O'clock*, *Preparing for a Visit*, *Extreme Measures*, *The Irreparable*, *The Fine Pin*, *The Other's Health*, and *The Cogent Reason*. The works were published by the *Revue Blanche*, a prominent avant-garde journal that patronized many of the Nabis. But, rather than published in the journal, the prints had an exclusive run of only thirty copies on fine paper. The physicality of viewing the series thus differed greatly from seeing the woodcuts that Vallotton produced for the popular press that were linked to current events. Many of Vallotton's woodcuts appeared in periodicals, but the *Intimités* series was created for the collector. As Peter Parshall has observed, "prints were the defining art of privacy" (2009: 5). A connoisseur was encouraged to keep his prints in a portfolio rather than displaying them on the wall in order to heighten the pleasure of selecting a print for private viewing in an intimate space. Prints were also perceived as a "mode of confession" for the artist and viewing them should, in the words of Charles Baudelaire, be "savoured … as one would a confidence" (Parshall 2009: 7). Vallotton's *Intimités* effectively exploited this confessional nature of the medium itself and thus became ideally suited to satisfy this solitary pleasure. Both the print and the novel were primarily enjoyed alone and held in the hand of the reader/viewer, making them uniquely personal experiences.

## Reinventing the woodcut

Vallotton was arguably the most instrumental artist in elevating the woodcut into the realm of high art. He moved to Paris from Switzerland when the woodcut was reaching the zenith of being transformed from a subservient role in mass media to a loftier position in the hierarchy of the arts. The woodcut in the early 1800s was a cheap method of providing illustration for current events and literature so the craftsman had little choice in what and how the scene was depicted. The redefinition of the woodcut began in the 1850s and culminated in the 1890s when wood engraving was revived as a vehicle for personal artistic expression rather than illustration (Baas 1984: 14). In 1892, Octave Uzanne published the first article on the revival of the woodcut, which exclusively celebrated Vallotton's work, especially the artist's feeling for the medium and his acute social observations (Baas 1984: 86).

During the 1890s, Vallotton's woodcuts were printed in French periodicals more than anyone else's, influencing the work of many prominent artists. Early in his career, Vallotton had mastered a visual vocabulary that borrowed from caricature, shadow theater, music halls, and cabarets. His formal language thus retained the nonacademic and nonmechanized association that had made woodcuts so appealing in the age of industrialization while maintaining the works' modernity. He used side-grain blocks, which were associated with the traditional method of the woodcut, rather than end-grain blocks, which were used commercially and could be engraved with fine detail (Baas 1984: 15). Further, Vallotton was not interested in subtle tonal variations; rather, his images emphasized the inherent qualities of the black ink and the white paper in a method that also echoed the most current trends in painting. For example, Paul Gauguin, among other postimpressionist artists, rejected delicate shading in his painting in favor of broad patches of color.

Vallotton's ability to borrow elements from popular culture and transform them into works that appealed to aesthetes was the element that made his woodcuts such a success with both the general public and the artistic elite. Richard Field observes that "Vallotton was able to formulate his images in accordance with a variety of *fin-de-siècle* pictorial tastes: those of the mass readership of the popular press, the literati of the small publications, and the print collectors with their fastidious expectations of printmaking" (1991: 44).

His prints recognized the popular fascination with peeking behind closed doors and the pleasure in laughing at or being shocked by another's misconduct. Thadée Natanson, a friend and patron of Vallotton, summarized *Intimités* in the following way:

> Ten times a man and a woman meet in all of the attitudes in which the mishaps, the stages of sentimental life are fixed. They express every imaginable aspect, the naïve and the ridiculous, the hypocrisy and the lies, the cruelty and the taste for death that is in all of our conception of love. One laughs, one trembles, one is moved, one is shocked, one shudders. The delicious, disquieting spectacle. (Newman 1991: 141)

The viewer of the prints may consider himself an aesthete but Vallotton nudges him instead into the position of a voyeur. The scenes depicted may momentarily give him a sense of superiority over the couples or provide a condescending chuckle. However, the artist's particular type of humor "makes laughter die on our lips," in the words of Meier-Graefe, as the viewer realizes that what he or she is looking at might very well be a mirrored reflection of one's private life

(Vallotton 1972: xiii). Human nature is thus explored in the woodcuts with a cynical gravity that raises caricature to the highest levels of art. The *Intimités* series contains a variety of Parisian types, but ultimately, the works ruthlessly mock the sanctity of the interior and the faux respectability specific to the middle classes themselves.

According to nineteenth-century commentators, the profligate apartment was threatening the integrity of the home and the family. There was a growing concern that men were becoming effeminate in the modern era and in order to "save the fatherland" it was necessary to "regenerate men at home" (Marcus 1999: 139). Vallotton's works provided visual proof of the moral degradation of the home and the slipping power of the patriarchy. He presented a neatly framed gallery of emasculated men and manipulative women who threatened the very foundations of French society.

Vallotton exploited the tremendous popularity of the domestic interior, a subject often brought up in literature and plays. But, the cynicism of his message and the visual brevity of the woodcuts created a uniquely biting satire on the French home. In *The Triumph*, for example, a woodcut from the series, a woman sits sedately on a sofa while a man buries his face in his handkerchief and weeps at the dining room table, exhibiting a shameful release of emotion. The woman's sidelong glance is the only acknowledgment of his distress and her victory. Conversely, in *Extreme Measures*, a woman uses her own tears to illicit sympathy—and likely much more—from her male companion, who gets up from the dining room table with napkin in hand to comfort her. In *The Irreparable*, a man and woman sit on opposite ends of a small sofa. Their bodies are lost against the dark fabric with only their faces and hands distinguishing them from the furniture. They appear moribund in the interior as much as in their emotional stalemate. The woman in *Preparing for a Visit* (Figure 7.1), on the other

**Figure 7.1** Félix Vallotton, *Apprets de Visite (Preparing for a Visit)*, woodcut, 1897, The Art Institute of Chicago, Gift of the Print and Drawing Club, 1948.3.8.

hand, smiles into her vanity mirror and gains obvious satisfaction from the scowl of the man who sits behind her as she sprays on perfume. These couples provide only a small sample of the emotional bribery displayed in *Intimités*, which seemed to shift control of the interior into the hands of women.

With this series, Vallotton achieved a level of success that was unparalleled in his career. Thadée Natanson even granted him honorary French citizenship, stating that this series "nationalises him a Frenchman" (Newman 1991: 142). The artist was able to condense the fascinations and fears of the public, satisfying their hunger to pry into the interior and translating the bitter message into a visual form that was highly palatable.

## Misogyny and the interior

According to numerous contemporary commentators, the nineteenth-century French home was under threat as dramatic changes in the urban landscape led to a destabilization of patriarchal authority both in the form of the landlord, who was meant to look after the entire apartment building, and the father, who was supposed to monitor his family (Marcus 1999: 137). By the middle of the nineteenth century, both male figures of authority were seen as lacking a proper paternal concern and control over the apartment building and the family. A possible cure for this masculine fallibility was the tender ministration of the woman who could cleanse her home both physically and morally while also making an appealing retreat from public life that would entice the man back home. Émile Cardon wrote in 1884 that it is the "woman, the guardian angel of the home … who can do the most to give us back the cult of the home and of the daily arts that our fathers had" (Marcus 1999: 158). There were, however, consequences when the woman was unwilling or unable to perform her designated role. The "guardian angel" had a darker twin, the *femme fatale*, and in this way the category of "woman" in this period was polarized, with the latter potentially the destroyer of the foyer through the emasculation of her husband within the home and/or her sexual exploits outside of the home.

Vallotton himself was a particularly acerbic misogynist. He once wrote in his journal: "What great evil has man committed that he deserves this terrifying partner called woman? With such violently contradictory thoughts and so clearly opposed impulses, the only possible relationship between the sexes is that of victor and vanquished" (Newman 1991: 74). The "battle of the sexes" was a common metaphor during this time. For example, Armand Charpentier's article "Love in Marriage," published in the *Revue Blanche*, cynically discusses the impossibility of monogamy where "the peace of the foyer is transformed into a state of perpetual war" (1898: 38). Vallotton's series illustrates the various stratagems in the fight for control of the home and, by extension, of society, with the common bourgeois interior of *fin-de-siècle* France as the modern battlefield between the sexes, a *mêlée* in which no blood was spilt, but words, emotions, and sex were the weapons.

*Intimités* shows a variety of spaces that have been compromised and corrupted by infidelity. *5 O'clock* represents an illicit assignation with a partially unclothed couple locked rapturously in a tangle of limbs. Likewise, *The Other's Health* exposes half-naked lovers on a rumpled bed. *The Lie* pictures a man and woman embracing passionately. Her striped dress creates a sinuous line as she presses herself against her male companion. His eyes are closed as he receives her affection. Her face is unseen and disturbingly truncated as it melts into the deep shadow of his profile. The title indicates a deception on her part, either through her body or her words. Each of these works depicts an intimate space that is not the home but an ersatz domestic space. The series is both cautionary and titillating. The intended viewer, likely a bourgeois man, may enjoy witnessing an afternoon rendezvous but is also warned against becoming the cuckolded husband. Vallotton purposely chose to create spaces that the viewer wished to glimpse but never to inhabit. He was well aware of the discourse around the well-appointed interior and satirized it as a space of privacy, stability, and domestic pleasure.

The misogynistic tone of *Intimités* reflects the architectural discourse that held the woman responsible for the man's neglect of the home and also used the feminine as a metaphor for the environment of deceit within the new apartment buildings. Alexandre Weill, in 1860, likened the cheap façades of the buildings to the duplicity of women: "All these petticoated houses are covered with makeup…But as a result the interior is…dishonest…Nowhere is there an honest row of large square rooms, with vast courtyards, as the architects of our forefathers used to make them" (Marcus 1999: 138). Weill uses a common metaphor of the feminine, associated with ornamentation and modernity, while linking the masculine to honesty and tradition.

## Vallotton and Zola

Both Vallotton and Zola did their utmost to strip away the metaphorical petticoats and scrub off the makeup of pretences, thus revealing the ugliness of the bourgeois interior. They used caricatural types to expose mercenary, vicious, and petty inhabitants of the interior. The characters in *Pot-Bouille* are one-dimensional, and the setting of the apartment building "seems to be mere cardboard scenery" (Nelson 1983: 142). The figures are a literary echo of Vallotton's figures who are "flat" both formally and metaphorically. But, if Vallotton's satire was an end in itself, Zola claimed that he had a didactic purpose at the foundation of his satirical novel. In his notes, he stated: "A new bourgeois building…show the bourgeoisie in naked form…and show it to be more abominable, since it calls itself order and honesty" (Solomon 1985: 255). Zola thus aimed to reveal the "nakedness" of the bourgeois class by stripping away the façade of the building and granting the reader access to the inner sanctum. He exploited the prevalent idea that apartment buildings bred promiscuity and the exterior elements of the architecture were deceitful, laying bare "the speciousness of the conjoined social, economic and moral assumptions of the building's design" (Solomon 1985: 255). The building in his novel appears luxurious but is actually poorly built; the public spaces have a silent gravity but the gilt and stucco cannot entirely hide the financial distress and moral turpitude of the residents.

*Pot-Bouille* follows the exploits of Octave Mouret as he takes up residence in a bourgeois apartment building. The various people he meets and the women he seduces are types that Zola ruthlessly parodies in order to expose the hypocrisy of the bourgeois class. The characters are emblematic of the moral wasteland of bourgeois life. *Pot-Bouille* is not a true Realist novel; it is instead a "bitter burlesque of bourgeois life [and] a deliberate distortion of reality in the creation of satiric fantasy" (Solomon 1985: 255). Mouret is an antihero who remains detached from the concerns of the other tenants. He wears various masks of sympathy or affection but is essentially untouched. The characters inspire sympathy neither among themselves nor in the reader. As White observes, those "characters in the know appear quite malevolent and those in the dark appear fairly dim" (1999: 26). Similarly, the couples pictured in Vallotton's series inspire no empathy and leave the viewer gratefully distant from their travails. Many of the viewing angles, with their smooth surfaces and diagonal perspectives, "remove the artist/viewer from the scene [thereby] constructing an observer rather than a participant" (Field 1991: 60).

In *Pot-Bouille*, Mouret is witness to much of the activity in the novel, but the building itself is the true protagonist (Nelson 1983: 131) and provides the dominant unifying feature of the setting, as only a few episodes take place beyond its walls. The building is self-contained, and the female inhabitants are likewise expected to be strictly contained vessels. Female characters are protected from even breathing the air of the street and are complicit with their imprisonment in the suffocating rooms of the apartment building. This fictional sequestering is a parody of the real fears at the time that the interior would somehow be drained by a too accessible conduit to the exterior. The absurdity of this idea "suggests the extent to which the opposition of interior and exterior was a matter of metaphor, not physical reality" (Marcus 1999: 147). The potential meaning of a space exists, not in its physical properties, but in the metaphorical meaning that is created by the inhabitant or in the case of Zola and Vallotton by the reader/viewer.

Like Zola's heroines, the figures in *Intimités* also exist in closed off and slightly claustrophobic spaces. In several works, the saturated blacks seem to threaten to envelop the figures, and the darkness takes on the weight of a presence rather than indicating an absence. There are rare glimmers of light and few indications of an arena beyond the battlefield of the interior. In *Money* (Figure 7.2), a woman stands next to an open window and gazes toward the light. The scrollwork of the balcony provides the only decorative element in this spartan composition. A man speaks to her, but his profile emerges only in contrast to the luminous woman, with his moustache and goatee finely outlined against her white neck. The title *Money* taints the woman's décolletage with unsavory insinuations and perhaps ties her to this space. She seems unlikely to escape the darkness that fills most of the composition and from which the man emerges. *Preparing for a Visit* shows a woman getting ready to leave the questionable security of her apartment for the intrigue of the outside world. The slumped posture and angry expression of the man on the sofa make clear his feelings regarding her departure. Between the couple, the viewer can glimpse the doorknob to an open door. This door is a divisive element both formally and conceptually. Vallotton creates a deliberate sense of ambiguity: does this portal lead out of the room or to the folded linens stacked on shelves? Both figures are potentially trapped in this shallow space.

As in *Intimités*, Zola's characters, too, are caught in a cycle of deceit, greed, and sex. The plot of the novel is "built around detachable, self-enclosed scenes" with the characters moving through the various sets with the "jerky movements of a silent film" (Nelson 1983: 145). The structure of the novel therefore mimics both the structure of the apartment building and the series of prints. Each apartment and each print is distinct from one another; however, each provides a piece of a larger structure, which makes the isolation imperfect.

**Figure 7.2** Félix Vallotton, *L'Argent (Money)*, woodcut, 1897, The Art Institute of Chicago, Gift of the Print and Drawing Club, 1948.3.5.

### The promiscuous interior

According to historian Sharon Marcus, "hygienists often criticized apartment buildings for their *promiscuité*, a word that denoted crowding but also connoted sexual misconduct" (1999: 156). Apartment buildings were considered dangerous both physically, in the transfer of disease and dirt, and morally, in the transfer of bad social behavior. There were concerns of "miasmic commerce" that would be the inevitable result of cohabitation. Both Zola's novel and Vallotton's series artistically reproduce the cycle of contagion and promiscuity of the apartment building. The roaming Mouret provides a thread of continuity and a vehicle for contagion throughout the building. The viewer of the *Intimités* series similarly provides unity as the gaze traverses the "rooms" of the series becoming the active element that links image to image as well as title to image and thereby building a web of expectations and assumptions that make the ten woodcuts a single structure.

Zola expresses the dangers of the promiscuous apartment building through the metaphor of a foul interior courtyard, used exclusively by the servants. All the kitchen windows open onto one fetid courtyard, which is the repository of food waste and malicious gossip. Zola describes that "during the thaw ... a stench rose from the dark little courtyard, all the hidden decay of the stories seemed to melt and exhale itself through this sewer of the house" (Marcus 1999: 178). The hateful words transmute into a miasma that is potentially more corrupting than any literal waste. Whether the residents are aware of it or not, they are affected by this unhealthy stench. They are, however, acutely aware of the need to maintain appearances since a scandal in one apartment taints the entire building, creating a spectacle for the neighborhood. An example of this occurs when the character Valérie Vabres is caught by her husband in Mouret's apartment. She flees in hysterics, running through the hallways in her chemise, unable to get back into her own apartment and shut out by her neighbors. Even though she is an adulteress, she poses no moral threat as long as she remains behind closed doors but her headlong rush through the corridors forces her immorality into plain view.

Valérie Vabres and Mouret are among the most active agents of "miasmic commerce" in Zola's *Pot-Bouille*, but in Vallotton's *Intimités*, the viewer carries the contagion from one image to the next. The viewer must complete the circuit of interpretation since even the titles of *Intimités* are deliberately equivocal. Removed from their context, the titles are benign (*5 O'Clock, Preparing for a Visit*). Rather than choose obvious titles such as *Infidelity* or *Jealousy*, Vallotton expects the viewer to understand that *5 O'Clock* is not merely a time of day, but the moment of sexual transgression. The moral turpitude and misogyny inherent in the works infects the interpretations of the most banal scenes. For example, *The Fine Pin* (Figure 7.3) shows a man embracing a woman as they stand near a bed and away from a heavily curtained window. Her eyes are cast down, likely admiring the titular jewellery. This could easily be viewed as a scene of conjugal happiness; however, happily married couples have no place in this series. Within the context of *Intimités*, it can be assumed that this man and woman are lovers rather than spouses. In the study for this print, the relationship between the man and woman is blatant. Sitting together, he is presented as fully dressed, while she dons a chemise with loose hair. She greedily grasps for the pin as he restrains her with gloved hands. In the final image, however, the

**Figure 7.3** Félix Vallotton, *La Belle Epingle (The Fine Pin)*, woodcut, 1897, The Art Institute of Chicago, Gift of the Print and Drawing Club, 1948.3.3.

woman's greed is contained beneath a demure veneer. Vallotton subtly coaxes the viewer to witness both the sin and the attempt to conceal it.

The spaces of *Pot-Bouille* and *Intimités* are thus saturated with the nebulous but palpable miasma of immorality and deceit. Zola's desire to show "the bourgeoisie in naked form" was meant to release and cleanse some of this infection. For Vallotton, on the other hand, this was simply the human condition. Women were the most egregious offenders but men also had a part in the disintegrating integrity of the home. The bourgeois interior condenses the innate characteristics of lust, duplicity, and selfishness.

## Conclusion

Walter Benjamin, in his discussion of nineteenth-century domesticity, observes that the "private citizen who in the office took reality into account, required of the interior that it should support him in his illusions" (1973: 167). Vallotton shines a harsh light on these illusions and, using an austere contrast of black and white, reveals the dark corners of human nature. Haussmannization created firm barriers between interior and exterior, but these walls could not entirely conceal the moral corruptness of the interior, nor could the new buildings restore the home to its patriarchal bygone glory as revealed in Zola's *Pot-Bouille* and Vallotton's *Intimités* series. Both the novel and the woodcut could physically and psychologically infiltrate the home of the viewer/reader in a way that high art could not. The reproducibility, accessibility, and association with objects of mass culture such as periodicals and newspapers made the bitter satire of the prints and the novel more palatable to the audience. The woodcuts have a visual brevity and interpretive depth that make them a unique expression of *fin-de-siècle* anxiety. As it shifted from mass media to high art, the woodcut was an ideal vehicle to wittily caricature what was considered a very serious situation. The war between genders waged across the social landscape, but the battle within the interior, the home, and the bedroom struck at a particularly vulnerable point in the male psyche. With the *Intimités* series, Vallotton expresses the hypocrisy and insecurities of a generation.

## References

Baas, J. (1984), "The Artistic Revival of the Woodcut in France," in J. Baas and R. Field (eds), *The Artistic Revival of the Woodcut in France 1850–1900*, Ann Arbor, MI: University of Michigan Museum of Art.

Benjamin, W. (1973), *Charles Baudelaire: A Lyric Poet in the Era of High Capitalism*, London: NLB.

Charpentier, A. (1898) "Amour Dans Le Mariage," *Revue Blanche* XVI (May): 38.

Field, R. (1991), "Exteriors and Interiors: Vallotton's Printed Oeuvre," in S. Newman (ed), *Félix Vallotton*, New Haven: Yale University Art Gallery.

Marcus, S. (1999), *Apartment Stories: City and Home in Nineteenth-Century Paris and London*, Berkeley, CA: University of California Press.

Nelson, B. (1983), *Zola and the Bourgeoisie: A Study of Themes and Techniques in Les Rougon-Macquart*, New Jersey: Barnes & Noble Books.

Newman, S. (1991), "'Stages of Sentimental Life' The Nudes and the Interiors," in S. Newman (ed), *Félix Vallotton*, New Haven: Yale University Art Gallery.

Parshall, P. (2009), "A Darker Side of Light: Prints, Privacy, and Possession," in P. Parshall (ed), *The Darker Side of Light: Arts of Privacy, 1850–1900*, Washington: National Gallery of Art.
Solomon, P. (1985), "The Space of Bourgeois Hypocrisy in Zola's *Pot-Bouille*," *Kentucky Romance Quarterly* 32, no. 3: 255–264.
Texier, E. (1852), *Tableau de Paris*, Paris: Paulin et Le Chevalier.
Vallotton, M. and C. Goerg (1972), *Félix Vallotton: Catalogue raisonné de l'oeuvre gravé et lithographié*, Genève: Éditions de Bonvent.
White, N. (1999), *The Family in Crisis in Late Nineteenth-Century French Fiction*, Cambridge: University of Cambridge Press.

# CHAPTER 8
# THE *FIN-DE-SIÈCLE* POSTER: A HEALTHY MODERN STIMULUS IN THE FRENCH INTERIOR
*Katherine Brion*

Initiated by the success of designs by Jules Chéret, the *fin-de-siècle* proliferation of commercial color posters in French (above all, Parisian) streets had, by the 1890s, provoked *affichomanie* (poster mania).[1] Posters were hailed as the essential, artistic elements of a "plein-air museum" or "salon de la rue," accessible to everyone in the public space of the street but also worthy of private collection and contemplation. They became visible signs of the possibilities, for good or for ill, opened up by the liberal economic and media policies of the Third Republic, and by modernity *tout court*.

Yet by the end of the decade, poster advocate Ernest de Crauzat was lamenting the death of the artistic, public posters that had first attracted collectors, and thus the end of the utopian hopes they had inspired. According to de Crauzat, the poster's public and artistic character had split: rather than elevating taste in the public realm, the "artistic" poster had bypassed the street for "the narrow surfaces of the interior," where it had obediently attenuated its aesthetic; the city's boulevards and palisades were relegated to an increasingly mediocre imagery notable only for its quantity (1899: 251).[2] Scholars have largely followed de Crauzat in viewing the poster's entry into the interior as a betrayal or weakening of its aesthetic and democratic potential.[3] The trajectory of the commercial lithographic poster thus appears an exemplary illustration of an oft-repeated narrative of *fin-de-siècle* French modernity, in which the subversive potential of modern forms, subject matter and technologies ultimately cede to the private and/or antimodern impulses epitomized by psychological interiority, "decorative" art, and Art Nouveau organicism, preoccupations that privileged the interior as a refuge—albeit dogged by anxiety—from modern life.[4] As Katherine Kuenzli and Joyce Henri Robinson have highlighted, critics and artists associated the interior and its contents with soothing relief, as in Henri Matisse's 1908 promotion of "an art of balance, of purity, and serenity, devoid of troubling or depressing subject matter, an art that could be…a soothing, calming influence on the mind, something like a good armchair that provides relaxation from fatigue."[5]

Yet here I will suggest another reading of the poster's entry into the interior, as a symptom of, and participant in, the destabilization of the opposition—assumed by the *fin-de-siècle* narrative described above—between public modernity and private retreat.[6] If in the street the poster was seen as rupturing Haussmannian monotony with its picturesque beauty, in the interior it represented a modern stimulant and thus an impediment to a dull or decadent isolation. In other words, the medium constituted an antidote to each space's ailments. The same qualities that allowed the poster to challenge the established hierarchies of artistic practice—its combination of sophisticated color effects with the reproducibility and accessibility of a mass medium—made it a promising vector for a shared aesthetic that was simultaneously public and private, eminently appropriate to a vibrant liberal democracy. And if the democratic aspirations of this aesthetic were never truly realized, it did help reframe the interior and interior decoration as potential sources of an invigorating stimulation different from, yet on a continuum with, that provided by the outside world.

## J.-K. Huysmans and the poster

Joris-Karl Huysmans is perhaps the best-known chronicler of the desire to make the interior a refuge from the trials of modern society. His 1884 novel *À Rebours* (*Against the Grain*) recounted the efforts of Jean Des Esseintes, the sole-surviving member of an aristocratic family, to create just such a retreat from the *ennui* and inanity of the metropolis. Having failed, with Parisian debauches, to assuage either his boredom or the increasing enervation and eventual lethargy of his senses (symptoms that bore a number of affinities with neurasthenia, the nervous condition particularly associated with the stresses and hyperstimulation of modern life (Silverman 1989: 77–79; Forth 2001: 331), Des Esseintes sought out subtler pleasures in the isolation of a provincial home. His careful orchestration of sensation in this interior—through the choice of, for example, his servants' clothing, the color schemes in his rooms, and the texts and artworks to be enjoyed—avoided any evocation of the modern, instead seeking sensual refinement in fantasy or in the past. But what is less often recalled is how this plan backfires: Des Esseintes suffers a return of his debilitating lassitude, and the novel ends as he reluctantly prepares to return to Paris's "communal life" (Huysmans 2004: 240).[7] This ending suggests an ambivalence toward what has been seen as all at once a regressive and absolutely modern feature of the *fin-de-siècle*: a heightened, Decadent sensibility turned as much, or more, inward as outward, its terrain of predilection the fragmented self (Bourget 1891: 24–29).[8] Des Esseintes's interior proved as D/decadent and noxious, as his Parisian lifestyle: his doctor's "verdict—confirmed, moreover, by all diagnosticians of neurosis—was that only distraction, amusement and joy could have an effect on [his] sickness, whose spiritual element eluded the potent chemistry of medication" (Huysmans 2004: 240–241).[9] Yet Des Esseintes wonders where he is to find that joy, disgusted as he is by both the enfeebled, decadent aristocracy and the vulgar materialism of the bourgeoisie.

Outside the confines of the novel, Des Esseintes's creator had suggested a possible solution (or at least the beginnings of a solution). In reviews of the Salons of 1879 and 1880, Huysmans portrayed the poster as a healthy, stimulating element of visual culture, presenting Chéret's "chromos" as an antidote to the "lugubrious" works dominating those exhibitions (2008: 51).[10] His 1880 text ended with this recommendation: "Homeopathically, I can only…advise those disgusted, like myself, by this insolent display of prints and canvases, to cleanse their eyes outside, through a prolonged stop in front of those palisades where Chéret's astonishing fantasies burst forth, coloured fantasies so energetically drawn and so vividly painted" (2008: 160).[11] Huysmans, who so often condemned adulterated, muddied colors and oozing eruptions of paint (Dupont 1987), must have reveled in Chéret's emphatic forms and flat, contrasting expanses of color—a far cry from Des Esseintes's subtle refinements.

In a later, more extensive essay, Huysmans associated the poster with some of the pathologies (Carter 2012–2013: 130–133) haunting Des Esseintes and his interior. Yet he ultimately suggested that Chéret's work provided a remedy for this and other forms of *fin-de-siècle* excess. Huysmans opened the text by describing how Chéret's posters alleviated the hyperrational regularity of Haussmannian urbanization: "the sudden intrusion of their joy" disturbed the gray monotony of the city's "rectilinear streets" and façades, making up for the loss of its "intimate spaces [coins]" (2008: 271). Second, these colorful advertisements took the sting out of another, more Baudelairean, manifestation of modern life: the feverish pace and "demented, nearly explosive joy" of the Parisian pleasures they themselves depicted (2008: 273).[12] "In distilling the essence of Paris," Huysmans wrote, "[Chéret] abandons the vile dregs, leaves behind the elixir itself, so corrosive and bitter, gathering only its gaseous effervescence, the bubbles fizzing at the surface" (2008: 275). Finally, in isolating and distilling the joyous energy buried in Parisian frivolity, Chéret's work provided an aesthetic therapy for another of the excesses on display in *À Rebours*: the vigorous, yet purified, jolt of his posters inoculated the viewer against the hyperstimulation associated with modern urban life, precluding the need for the equally destructive refinements—arising from the similarly modern, heightened sensibility of the Decadent—invented by Des Esseintes to revive his flagging senses.[13] This interpretation was already embedded in Huysmans's use of the term "homeopathically" to introduce his 1880 discussion of Chéret: in doing so he invoked the treatment of sickness with small doses (in this case, modern stimulus) of the very substances that would have produced analogous symptoms in healthy individuals. In other words, Chéret had extracted just the right, invigorating, dose of Paris's "distraction, amusement and joy," distributing it in the concise visual form of his posters.

It should also be noted that, by the time of Huysmans's second essay, the belief in the salutary or deleterious effects of visual form had a much wider purchase. Avant-garde artistic circles were conversant, for example, with the psychophysics of Charles Henry's "scientific aesthetic," which postulated that pleasurable or painful colors, lines, and forms alternately energized (dynamogenized) or inhibited the viewer.[14] In 1888, the critic Félix Fénéon suggested that Chéret would do well to take these psychophysical findings into account, including the notion that painful visual stimuli could be used to attract the viewer's attention (1970: 117). Whether the poster artist took such an admonition seriously, or whether these ideas were simply in the air, beginning in the late 1880s, Chéret's central motifs (generally a female figure and the product or company name) were increasingly arranged along ascendant (and thus dynamogenous) lines, sporting dynamogenous reds and yellows, and set against inhibitory/complementary blues or violets (Bargiel and Le Men 2010: 61; 74, n 36). Examine, for example, the 1889 *Bal du Moulin Rouge* (Figure 8.1), which contains all the elements—including the flirtatious, vaguely Rococo female type that came to be labeled the "Chérette"—that defined the "gaiety" of Chéret's mature aesthetic (Collins 1980: 106–131). The text announcing the attraction arcs upward to the right, its vibrant red (repeated in the central motif of the windmill) offset by a green shadow; this movement is confirmed by the bodies of the two largest female figures, juxtaposed once again with contrasting colors (blue/violet) and movements (the donkey and the angle of the foremost figure's torso).[15] Such vibrant, starkly contrasted primaries and forms would have appeared out of place even in the most eclectic of *fin-de-siècle* interiors. Yet there were those who hoped this might change, and that the poster might revitalize the interior the way it had the street.

**Figure 8.1** Jules Chéret, *Bal du Moulin Rouge Place Blanche*, color lithograph, 1889, Bibliothèque nationale de France, Cabinet des Estampes, reproduction courtesy of the Bibliothèque nationale de France.

### The poster in the interior

In 1888, the writer Maurice de Fleury described a (probably imaginary) "modernist" house dominated by glass, iron, and the light and air consistent with new ideals of hygiene (1888a: 147). Chéret's work figured prominently in the interior alongside works by Impressionists, Neo-Impressionists, and other modern artists: his posters decorated the entryway and de Fleury praised a "healthy" gym room, painted with acrobatic scenes by Chéret and Louis Forain, as perhaps the most successful of the home's spaces (1888b: 150–151). The association of the poster artist's oeuvre with health and hygiene aligned these remarks with those of Huysmans: Chéret's work appears as the aesthetic equivalent of light and air, albeit of a specifically urban vigor. Indeed, de Fleury would go on to write several works emphasizing neurasthenia's ties with heredity rather than modern urban life, which he valued as a source of stimulating sensation and thus, if properly channeled, of energy and action: "Since sensation is our fuel, since it gives us strength, let us cultivate our sensibility" (1898: 257).[16]

Reflections extending the poster's joyous reign beyond the street into the interior became more and more commonplace as Chéret's renown increased. In 1889, his posters were put on display at the *Exposition universelle* and in a solo exhibition (along with pastels) that proclaimed the artistic, as opposed to purely commercial, significance of his work. Huysmans's essay, which had appeared that same year, was explicitly acknowledged by critic and arts administrator Roger Marx in his preface for the catalog of Chéret's solo exhibition. The pathological and psychophysical studies underpinning Huysmans's (and de Fleury's) statements were not much in evidence in Marx's text, but he similarly argued that the poster artist had brought a joyous relief to Haussmannian dreariness, and went even further than Huysmans in highlighting Chéret's transcendence of the other, feverish, modernity that was his posters' principle subject. Above all, Marx insisted on Chéret's "instinctive understanding of decoration," which consisted in satisfying—seemingly without effort—the sometimes competing demands of context, function and harmony (*Exposition Jules Chéret* 1889: iv). In his account, Chéret's texts and images are played against one another so as to capture the eye of the passing viewer but are also harmonized, in part thanks to the poster artist's color modulations. The subject matter, divided amongst "grotesque" male characters and charming female figures, revealed the same dialectical approach:

> A general idea, a system dominates and orders this fantasy, the system of a satirist who wants always to contrast the rough with the delicate, the vulgar with the refined, the crude with the charming. Alongside the sense of "torrential, frenetic" joy so closely analyzed by Huysmans, there exists in Chéret, by antithesis, an equal sense of grace, of voluptuous, fascinating, coquettish grace. (*Exposition Jules Chéret* 1889: v)

In Marx's interpretation, even more than in that of Huysmans, Chéret's "decorative" posters managed to retain but also contain the potential excesses of Parisian modernity. And while Huysmans had reveled in the idea of the poster as a subversive alternative to official (bourgeois) culture, Marx suggested that it should instead be incorporated into that very culture, which he envisioned as more democratic than exclusive. In one of his prefaces for the later *Les Maîtres de l'Affiche* (*The Masters of the Poster*), published from 1896–1900 by Chaix, the printing house with which Chéret had long been associated, Marx argued that the poster had rightfully taken over painting's role both "outside and in the home," providing "the mobile, ephemeral picture demanded by an age captivated by popularization and eager for change" (*Les Maîtres* 1898: iv).[17] He presented the poster's "decorative" aesthetic as an acceptable vehicle of modern energy, and thus as an exemplary model for the collective, national art idealized by the contemporary design reform movement.[18]

## Designing the French Interior

The domestic interior was an important site for this bid to make the poster the basis of a collective modern aesthetic. Already in the 1889 exhibition catalog preface, Marx had marveled that Chéret had not yet received any private commissions for large decorations, and in 1891, he welcomed the poster artist's publication of a set of four large lithographs expressly intended for the domestic interior. Printed with a wider range of color on high-quality paper and without any text, these allegorical depictions of pantomime, music, dance, and comedy were created for a wallpaper merchant and, as Marx emphasized, adapted to the typical spaces of the domestic interior, notably via a more varied, modulated palette. Nevertheless, these works—in which the graceful eroticism of a central female figure, legs parted and skirt afloat, was set against a contrasting background and/or the comic grimaces of male companions or masks (see Figure 8.2 for an example)—displayed many of the same characteristics that Marx had praised in Chéret's commercial posters, and the critic believed that they performed an analogous function.

> On the walls of our apartments, normally so poorly covered that, in terms of sadness, the grey and dreary walls of provincial streets have nothing on them, now, instead of the obsessive, fastidious repetition of a single, dull motif, here we have a bonfire, a bonfire of colour, the evocation of laughing visions that call and respond to one another. (Reproduced in Bargiel and Le Men 2010: 230)[19]

Chéret's four lithographs offered the reproducibility, and thus accessibility, of wallpaper without its absolute repetition. In place of the bleak, but mesmerizing, tedium evoked by Marx, each of the four lithographs offered a different design and the focus of a prominent central figure; they could also be placed in alternate configurations according to the owner's whim.[20] Unlike easel paintings, and in accordance with the unity required of decoration, each figure's pose and associated colors were nevertheless in a dynamic interplay with those of its fellow allegories. In addition to the stimulation of their "bonfire of colour," the works could thus be seen as exciting an analogous, ever-changing movement in the viewer.

## Conclusion

The celebration of the poster's joyous influence in the home presents a useful counterpoint to Joyce Henri Robinson's argument that Pierre Puvis de Chavannes's idyllic paintings best fulfilled the *fin-de-siècle* ideal of a soothing, anti-neurasthenic interior (2002: 122–125). As Robinson has noted, Marx valued Puvis's atemporal idylls as an alternative to the "tormented," worrisome present. Honoring the artist after his death, Marx noted that it was mural painting's "privilege to steal us away from ourselves, away from the present, *anywhere out of the world*; from it we can still learn to scorn the ephemeral, and hope for a temporary relief from fever and anguish" (1899: 1077). On the surface, this conception of Puvis is entirely at odds with Marx's promotion of Chéret for having encapsulated ephemeral Parisian modernity in the poster. Yet according to Huysmans, Marx, and others, Chéret had also presented a "vision of another, better world" (Marx 1899: 1077), a Baudelairean "painting" of modern life that revealed what in modernity was worth preserving, and that was perhaps all the more powerful due to the

**Figure 8.2** Jules Chéret, *La Pantomime*, color lithograph, 1891, Bibliothèque nationale de France, Cabinet des Estampes, reproduction courtesy of the Bibliothèque nationale de France.

contemporary relevance and stimulating potential of its frenetic, yet joyous, rhythms and color.[21] It too had a place in the "soothing" interior, reminding us to be careful with our understanding of that term. Psychophysics, as reported by Fénéon, held that "the unpleasant hyperesthetizes [i.e. hyper-sensitizes]; the pleasant anesthetizes" (Fénéon 1970: 178).[22] But figures like Henry and de Fleury did not believe that pleasure soothed in the sense of putting the viewer to sleep; instead, it made available new reserves of energy. They imagined the possible benefits of this energy when extended to society at large. For de Fleury, these were "joie de vivre and peace on earth" in place of "the feeling of decline and the fatigue of disorder"; for Henry, "the creation of universal harmony" (Henry 1888: 15; Fleury 1898: 461).[23]

The *fin-de-siècle* conjunction of the poster and the interior thus highlight, I argue, the extent to which the latter was increasingly envisioned not as a retreat from modernity and public life so much as a site of rejuvenation, preparing the inhabitant to return, with renewed vigor, to the collective fray. The poster's entry into the interior may not have realized the democratic aspirations—art in everything, art for everyone—inspired by its combination of an invigorating, appealing aesthetic and the easy reproducibility of a mass media, or at least not in a form recognized by its promoters. Later "decorative" or "mural" prints were rarely as poster-like as Chéret's initial foray into the genre (Sainte-Claire 1897: 58–59), and Chéret himself increasingly turned to pastel and painting (Bargiel and Le Men 2010: 126). Yet, if the interior transformed the poster, the poster also helped transform the interior, so that it no longer signified a detachment from public life. While in his 1881 *La Maison d'un artiste* (*The Home of an Artist*) Edmond de Goncourt had contrasted the "exterior" existence of the eighteenth century with his contemporaries' obsession with the interior (1881: 2), by 1908 the writer and critic André Beaunier viewed the prevalence of decorative ensembles (many of them for private residences) in the Salons not as a sign of interiority, but rather of "a time of exterior and collective life" (1908: 362).

## Acknowledgments

I would like to thank the coeditors, Georgina Downey, Mark Taylor, and, above all, Anca Lasc, for their helpful suggestions and editing. Alex Fraser and Cecile Thompson also provided feedback, while conversations with Karen Carter have informed my thinking on the poster. This essay emerged out of research funded by a University of Michigan Rackham Predoctoral Fellowship, a Georges Lurcy Foundation Fellowship for Study in France, and a Susan Lipschutz Award.

## Notes

1. *Affichomanie* was characterized not only by the omnipresence of commercial posters on the street and in public discourse, but also by specialized publications like *L'Estampe et l'affiche*, print publishers and dealers catering directly to collectors, and artists like Henri de Toulouse-Lautrec and Pierre Bonnard looking to benefit from the medium's new cachet. This cachet was largely due to an appreciation for the work of Chéret, who had introduced the color poster as a commercial genre in France (for which he was awarded the Legion of Honor in 1890). His colorful advertisements were the first to indicate that the poster might be worthy of attention for more than its promotional efficacy.
2. All translations are my own unless otherwise noted. The discussion appeared in de Crauzat's regular rubric in *L'Estampe et l'affiche*.
3. Miriam Levin's argument (1993) bears the strongest resemblance to de Crauzat's point of view. More recently, Hazel Hahn has argued that in the street the poster's "artistic" effects were eventually replaced with cheaper, more eye-catching alternatives, while collecting and speculation (both associated with the interior) undermined its democratizing potential (2009: 202–203).

Though she does not discuss the interior, Karen Carter has highlighted an increasing emphasis on individual, as opposed to collective, poster viewing in accounts of the medium's reception in the street, a shift she aligns with the commercial rise and depoliticization of the poster (2012: 13–16).

4. This view is best represented by Debora Silverman (1989), though she also suggested that the image of the interior as refuge was driven by its inability to truly serve as such. Susan Sidlauskas (2000) has gone much farther in highlighting the *fin-de-siècle* interior as a site of anxiety, disorientation, and illegibility. Walter Benjamin is also the obvious reference for the conception of the (Second Empire) interior as an attempt to sustain a bourgeois individuality denied by urban life (2002: 20).

5. Translated and discussed by Kuenzli (2010: 215–216). As Robinson noted, "[w]hile public decoration might be expected to challenge the mind and provoke thought, the decor of the home was intended to calm, rather than excite, the mind and nerves of the city dweller" (2002: 117).

6. This opposition, it should be noted, was never stable in the first place. Scholars such as Sharon Marcus have highlighted the continued permeability of the interior even as it began to be conceived as a distinct, private space (1999: chs. 4 and 5). Kuenzli has also emphasized, invoking Bonnard's poster work in particular, how the Nabis' decorative paintings for domestic interiors were indivisible from their public art ambitions (2010: 33–62). I would add to this argument that Bonnard was able to view the poster as a means of tying together the public and private realm because promoters of the poster were already making this connection.

7. In a departure from this tendency, Rosalind Williams analyzed Huysmans's retreat to Fontenay as a failed attempt to escape the reifying logic of bourgeois culture (1982: 145–149).

8. Paul Bourget displayed a similar ambivalence to the Decadent sensibility he himself helped to codify (notably in the profile of Charles Baudelaire included in *Essais de psychologie contemporaine*, initially published in 1881): while he indicated the creative potential of the Decadent search for ever more refined sensations and the richness of its inward focus, he also suggested that this sensibility undermined the individual's connection to lived experience and to society.

9. Silverman did point to how "[the overstimulated citizen] transported with him the propensity for animating the interior by that very same [overwrought] mechanism of the nerves" (1989: 79); however, this statement still highlighted modern stimulation, coming from the outside, as the root problem.

10. Huysmans briefly referenced Chéret in reviews of the official Salons of 1879, 1880, and 1881, which were all republished in *L'Art moderne* in 1883.

11. Huysmans placed a similar observation in the introduction to his 1879 Salon review (2008: 51–52).

12. Elsewhere in the essay, Huysmans described this feeling as a "frenetic" joy, "une joie que son excès même exhausse, en la rapprochant presque de la douleur" (2008: 272). The text appeared in Huysmans's 1889 *Certains*, a collection of essays on art.

13. Baudelaire was an inspiration for both Decadent subjectivity (via figures like Bourget and Théophile Gautier) and the vision of modernity as a constantly changing array of stimulation (via, for example, his definition of modernity as "the transitory, the fleeting, the contingent" in his 1863 "Le peintre de la vie moderne" (Baudelaire 2009: 20)). Despite these different emphases, both perspectives are in many ways two sides of the same coin, united by a sense of uncertainty, flux, and excess as the mark of modernity. Baudelaire, of course, argued that the modern must be synthesized and thereby fused with the eternal.

14. Robert Herbert ("Parade de cirque and the Scientific Aesthetic of Charles Henry" in Herbert 2001) and Michael F. Zimmermann (1991) are among those who have explored Henry's scientific aesthetic and its implications for the art world.

15. The affinities between Henry's precepts and Chéret's evolving commercial aesthetic were no doubt what led Georges Seurat to align the two in his c. 1890 painting ("Seurat and Jules Chéret" in Le Men 1994: 148; Herbert 2001; Lay 2001: 166–176).

16. De Fleury was still championing urban stimulation as "a bath of vital energy" three decades later, even as Le Corbusier was proposing a radical new vision of Paris (cited in Vidler 2002: 63).
17. Like Marx, poster collector and historian Ernest Maindron identified the poster as both a modern form of fresco painting and as suitable for the interior (1896: 32).
18. For Marx's role in that movement, see Silverman (1989), particularly Chapters 10 and 12. See also Meneux (2006).
19. Marx repeated this sentiment near the end of the decade: "l'intimité de nos demeures ne tarderait pas à se parer, à s'illuminer, elle aussi, de couleur, de joie, et c'en serait fait des habitations mornes et des entours surannés parmi lesquels les jours s'égrènent, un a un, monotones" (*Les Maîtres* 1898: ii).
20. Though the lithographs could conceivably have been placed, like wallpaper, to cover entire walls, they were labeled "decorative panels," indicating that they were to be hung on the wall as a set of isolated yet interrelated elements, as they were in the nondomestic setting of the Chat Noir cabaret (Cate 1978: 28–29).
21. See note 13. Elsewhere, Marx proposed the poster's joy as a modern manifestation of an integral element of the French character: "nous serions vraiment dignes de pitié, si les dons essentiels de la race étaient soudain abolis, et si la grâce, l'élégance, la joie cessaient de trouver des interprètes et des poètes au pays de Watteau, de Fragonard et de Chéret" (*Les Maîtres* 1897: iii–iv).
22. The phrase was used by Fénéon in an 1890 discussion of the practical implications of Henry's ideas, in particular the enhancement of perception through the "ugly." Rae Beth Gordon has discussed the influence of Henry's work, visible in Fénéon's criticism, on the turn-of-the-century avant-garde's increasing focus on the aesthetic benefits of the "ugly" (2009: 106).
23. For Henry, art had a particularly important role to play in this process: "aider le développement normal de l'art c'est favoriser d'autant la réalisation encore lointaine de notre destinée—la création de l'harmonie universelle."

## References

Bargiel, R. and S. Le Men (eds) (2010), *La Belle Époque de Jules Chéret: De l'affiche au décor*, Paris: Les Arts Décoratifs & Bibliothèque nationale de France.
Baudelaire, C. (2009), *Le Peintre de la vie moderne*, in S. Acierno and J. Baquero Cruz (eds), Paris: Éditions du Sandre.
Beaunier, A. (June 1908), "Les Salons de 1908," *Gazette des Beaux-Arts* 1: 377–384.
Benjamin, W. (2002), "Paris, Capital of the Nineteenth Century (Exposé of 1939)," in R. Tiedemann (ed), *The Arcades Project*, trans. H. Eiland and K. McLaughlin, Cambridge, MA: Harvard University Press.
Bourget, P. (1891), *Essais de psychologie contemporaine: Baudelaire, M. Renan, Flaubert, M. Taine, Stendhal*, 7th edn, Paris: Alphonse Lemerre.
Carter, K. L. (March 2012), "The Spectatorship of the *Affiche Illustrée* and the Modern City of Paris, 1880–1900," *Journal of Design History* 25, no. 1: 11–31.
Carter, K. L. (Fall–Winter 2012–2013), "Joris-Karl Huysmans, a *Dénicheur* of Jules Chéret's Posters," *Nineteenth-Century French Studies* 41, no. 1&2: 122–141.
Cate, P. D. & S. H. Hitchings (1978), *Color Revolution: Color Lithography in France 1890–1900*, Brunswick, NJ: Rutgers University Art Gallery.
Collins, B. R. Jr. (1980), "Jules Chéret and the Nineteenth-Century French Poster," PhD thesis, Yale University.
Crauzat, E. de (December 15, 1899), "Murailles," *L'Estampe et l'affiche*: 250–252.
Dupont, J. (1987), "La Couleur dans (presque) tous ses états," in *Huysmans: Une esthétique de la décadence*, Geneva and Paris: Éditions Slatkine.
*Exposition Jules Chéret: Pastels, lithographies, dessins, affiches illustrées (Décembre 1889-Janvier 1890, Galeries du Théatre d'Application, 18 rue Saint-Lazare)* (1889), Paris: Imprimeries Chaix (Succursale Chéret).

Fénéon, F. (1970), *Œuvres plus que complètes*, ed. and trans. J. U. Halperin, (*Chroniques d'art*), Geneva and Paris: Droz, Vol. 1.
Fleury, M. de (September 15, 1888a), "La Maison d'un moderniste: L'Architecture de demain," *Le Figaro (Supplément littéraire du dimanche)* 37: 146–147.
Fleury, M. de (September 22, 1888b), "La Maison d'un moderniste," *Le Figaro (Supplément littéraire du dimanche)* 38: 150–151.
Fleury, M. de (1898), *Introduction à la médecine de l'esprit*, 5th edn, Paris: Félix Alcan.
Forth, C. E. (2001), "Neurasthenia and Manhood in Fin-de-Siècle France," in M. Gijswijt-Hofstra and R. Porter (eds), *Cultures of Neurasthenia from Beard to the First World War*, Amsterdam and New York: Rodopi.
Goncourt, E. de (1881), *La Maison d'un artiste*, Paris: G. Charpentier, Vol. 1.
Gordon, R. B. (2009), "What Is Ugly?" in *Dances with Darwin, 1875–1910: Vernacular Modernity in France*, Burlington, VT: Ashgate.
Hahn, H. H. (2009), *Scenes of Parisian Modernity: Culture and Consumption in the Nineteenth Century*, New York: Palgrave Macmillan.
Henry, C. (1888), *Rapporteur esthétique de M. Charles Henry. Notice sur les applications à l'art industriel, à l'histoire de l'art, à l'interprétation de la méthode graphique, en général à l'étude et à la rectification esthétiques de toutes formes*, Paris: G. Séguin.
Herbert, R. L. (2001), *Seurat, Drawings and Paintings*, New Haven (CT): Yale University Press.
Huysmans, J.-K. (2004), *À Rebours*, Paris: Flammarion.
Huysmans, J.-K. (2008), *Écrits sur l'art*, J. Picon (ed), Paris: Flammarion.
Kuenzli, K. M. (2010), *The Nabis and Intimate Modernism: Painting and the Decorative at the Fin-de-Siècle*, Burlington, VT: Ashgate.
Lay, H. G. (2001), "Pictorial Acrobatics," in G. P. Weisberg (ed), *Montmartre and the Making of Mass Culture*, New Brunswick, NJ: Rutgers University Press.
Le Men, S. (1994), *Seurat and Chéret: Le Peintre, le cirque et l'affiche*, Paris: CNRS éditions.
*Les Maîtres de l'Affiche: Publication mensuelle contenant la reproduction des plus belles Affiches illustrées des grands artistes, français et étrangers* (1897), Paris: Imprimerie Chaix, Vol. 2.
*Les Maîtres de l'Affiche: Publication mensuelle contenant la reproduction des plus belles Affiches illustrées des grands artistes, français et étrangers* (1898), Paris: Imprimerie Chaix, Vol. 3.
Levin, M. R. (Spring 1993), "Democratic Vistas—Democratic Media: Defining a Role for Printed Images in Industrializing France," *French Historical Studies* 18, no. 1: 82–108.
Maindron, E. (1896), *Les Affiches illustrées (1886–1895)*, Paris: G. Boudet.
Marcus, S. (1999), *Apartment Stories: City and Home in Nineteenth-Century Paris and London*, Berkeley: University of California Press.
Marx, R. (December 23, 1899), "Puvis de Chavannes," *Revue encyclopédique* 9, no. 329: 1077–1086.
Meneux, C. et al. (2006), *Roger Marx, un critique aux côtés de Gallé, Monet, Rodin, Gauguin…* Paris: Ville de Nancy and Éditions Artlys.
Robinson, J. H. (2002), "'Hi Honey, I'm Home': Weary (Neurasthenic) Businessmen and the Formulation of a Serenely Modern Aesthetic," in J. Ballantyne (ed), *What Is Architecture?* New York: Routledge.
Sainte-Claire (January 15, 1897), "Chronique d'art," *La Plume*: 56–60.
Sidlauskas, S. (2000), *Body, Place, and Self in Nineteenth-Century Painting*, Cambridge: Cambridge University Press.
Silverman, D. (1989), *Art Nouveau in Fin-de-Siècle France: Politics, Psychology, and Style*, Berkeley: University of California Press.
Vidler, A. (2002), *Warped Space: Art, Architecture, and Anxiety in Modern Culture*, Cambridge, MA: MIT Press.
Williams, R. H. (1982), *Dream Worlds: Mass Consumption in Late Nineteenth-Century France*, Berkeley: University of California Press.
Zimmermann, M. F. (1991), *Les Mondes de Seurat: Son oeuvre et le débat artistique de son temps*, Antwerp: Fonds Mercator.

# CHAPTER 9
# MODE OF A MODERN MUSE: FASHION AND INTERIOR IN ÉDOUARD VUILLARD'S PAINTINGS OF MISIA NATANSON

Jess Berry

In late nineteenth-century France, the Nabis painters and Art Nouveau designers were united in their efforts to redefine the decorative interior through unifying motif and form. The collaboration of Paul Ranson, Édouard Vuillard, and Henry van de Velde for Siegfried Bing's *Maison de l'Art Nouveau* (1895) was the paradigm project, where the aim was to produce a harmonious domestic environment that combined decorative details, furniture, and art objects. While these artists' vision for the role of the decorative in domestic interiors may not have been entirely compatible, their attempts point to larger shared concerns of 1890s Modernism and its social context, in particular, the opposition between public and private spheres; the reconsideration of women's self-identity and roles; and the idea of "interiority"—the emergence of individual persona and its relationship to the interior as a space for self-expression.

The idealized domestic environment of Bing's *Maison de l'Art Nouveau* offers insight into the tensions of the conflation between the feminine and the private sphere that are indicative of the sociocultural and psychological facets of the modern interior at the time. However, as an exhibition display, it cannot give requisite insight into the everyday lived experience of the New Interior and its claim to a "totalizing" effect of visual unity. The New Interior emerged in the years 1890–1914 and manifested as Arts and Crafts design, Art Nouveau, and Jugendstil. Common to their practice was the philosophy of *Gesamtkunstwerk* or "total work of art," a solution to what was seen as the problematic eclecticism of historicist interiors (Sparke 2008: 37).

As such, this chapter will consider how the domestic modern interior of late nineteenth-century France was both conceptually and spatially represented and experienced through the body of the Nabis muse, acclaimed pianist Misia Natanson, as painted and photographed by Édouard Vuillard in her rue Saint-Florentin apartment.[1]

Following from Penny Sparke (2008), this case-study recognizes the complexity of the interior and contextualizes the aesthetic and political project of art and design to generate gendered space in relation to the social, cultural, and psychological formation of female identity. Drawing upon Charles Rice's (2007) concept of the "doubled" interior, the chapter frames these concerns in relation to the interior's significance as both an image—able to convey conceptual space—and as physical, three-dimensional space that inhabitants operated within. In the case of Misia's apartment, I contend that these two types of interiority do not necessarily converge. Vuillard's representations of Misia differ in significant ways both from the image she constructed for herself through her subversion of material space and among each other.

Specifically, I argue that Vuillard's paintings and photographs offer conflicting accounts of Misia's position and role within the interior. His paintings of the musician appear to epitomize the cultural and political campaign to subsume the female body in decoration and contain women in the home. Conversely, his photographs, coupled with historic accounts of the apartment, reveal that Misia's construction of the material space enabled her to embody the characteristics of social mobility, intellectual criticism, and sexual permissiveness thought to typify the *femme nouvelle* (or New Woman). In particular, this analysis depends upon recognizing the crucial link between Misia's identity formed in the interior and represented by her clothing, where her artistic style of dress served to blur boundaries between the separate realms of domesticity and social life and convey her ambition to be recognized as a social and cultural arbitrator of taste.

This chapter contributes to ongoing discourses surrounding the represented room and its function as conceptualized, imagined, and actualized space (Rice 2007; Sparke 2008; Downey 2013). During the late nineteenth century, a variety of visual mediums, including illustration, print, painting, and photography captured and elucidated aspects of a person's self-identity by recording their possessions in modes that were both real and ideal. Through their interpretation and analysis, these images give important insight into how domestic interiors constitute spaces that are both staged and lived, so exposing new gender relations, formulations of individual personas, and reconsiderations of the social sphere, all of which are key sites of contest in the development of modernity.

## Interiorizing the feminine through *fin-de-siècle* art and design

Debora L. Silverman's book *Art Nouveau in Fin-de-Siècle France: Politics, Psychology and Style* (1989) provides important context with which to consider the conflation of women's bodies with interior domestic space. Her comprehensive history of Art Nouveau in relation to political and sociocultural circumstances draws particular attention to Republican politics and the social anxiety that surrounded the figure of the New Woman. As both a cultural image and a sociological phenomenon, the New Woman defied French bourgeois culture of the time and was typically characterized by non-traditional relationships with men and women, employment outside the home, education and economic independence, along with visibility in the public sphere.

In response to the threat of the *femme nouvelle* to bourgeois culture and society, a number of French commentators, writers, and artists undertook a concerted revitalization of the female form, adornment, and the decorative. In particular, many of the Nabis paintings and Art Nouveau interiors sought to enact the social and political project to undermine the New Woman's challenge to the domestic in construing the female body as ornamental form. This view is particularly reflected in the works of Vuillard, whose "Intimist" paintings are much commented upon with regards to how the domestic interior was represented as inseparable from feminine self-identity (Groom 1993; Sidlaukas 2000; Berry 2011). In these works, Vuillard explores interiority as a psychological, conceptual, and representational space; he renders women as decorative equivalents to their interior, seeking refuge in a private world that is socially and culturally familiar to them.[2] Vuillard's articulation of the female body and domestic object as a flattened space of totalizing interior surface reverberates in his portraits of Misia Natanson, where he constrains her body in pattern and decoration.

## Containing the feminine: Vuillard's paintings of Misia in the apartment

During the period 1895 through 1900, Vuillard painted at least thirty portraits and took at least twenty photographs of Misia, in which the implied intimacy between artist and sitter is considered to be a testament to the supposed unrequited love he had for his muse (Easton 1989).[3] Vuillard's paintings portray Misia in her apartment in such a way as to comply with the gendered history of the interior that affirmed women's role as ornamental. However, his photographs of her provide a further layer of nuance in understanding how these representations intersected with sociocultural discourses that encouraged women to fashion both their homes and their bodies in a mode that projected their personality and individuality.

For example, in *Interior with Three Lamps* (1898) (Figure 9.1) Misia is a small, hunched figure, reading or sewing by lamplight. She is almost unnoticeable, since her body blends seamlessly into the chair that she rests upon and the table at which she sits. Only her illuminated white collar indicates her presence in the opulently decorative surrounds. In this instance, she is conveyed as if part of the furniture, visually objectified as decorative form. Vuillard emphasizes the traditionally feminine and submissive qualities of Misia's

**Figure 9.1** Édouard Vuillard, *The Living Room with Three Lamps, Rue Saint-Florentin*, painting, tempera on paper glued on canvas, 1899, Musée d'Orsay, Paris, donation subject to usufruct of Philippe Meyer in 2000, Photo © RMN-Grand Palais (Musée d'Orsay)/Hervé Lewandowski.

body by painting her in a passive position in the corner of the room, with her face obscured. This is in contrast to the two male figures depicted, Thadée Natanson, her then husband, reading on the right, and the playwright Romain Coolus, sitting in reverie in the central rocking chair, both of whom have prominently rendered facial features and recognizable figures.[4]

Interestingly, elements of this painting's interior and composition also feature in a photograph of Thadée and Misia in the Salon, rue Saint-Florentin, most likely taken by the artist between 1897 and 1899 (Figure 9.2).[5] Here, Misia sits in the background, surrounded by a Thonet rocking chair, decorative wallpaper, and ornamental palm. Thadée, reading a newspaper, also provides a V-shape frame for Misia's body. As in Vuillard's painting, Misia's body is small and her face is in profile, but it is clear that she is the focal point of the image and the object of the photographer's gaze. As Easton (1994) explains, the hand-held Kodak used by the artist only had a fixed focus, hence the center of the frame became the object of the composition.

It is likely that this photograph was one of the source images for the *Interior with Three Lamps*, and, importantly, it underlines Vuillard's artistic license to enhance the densely decorated features of the room for symbolic effect. Where his painting overwhelms the viewer with contrasting patterns and colors, the photograph, in its documentation of the material

**Figure 9.2** Thadée Natanson and his wife Misia Godebska in the drawing room of their apartment in the Rue Saint-Florentin, Paris, French photographer, b/w photograph, c. 1899, Collection Annette Valliant, France/Bridgeman Images.

space, renders the interior far less poetic and fluid. Further, as with many other photographs of his muse, Misia's character appears less passive and introspective than Vuillard's paintings would have the viewer believe, her surly gaze to the left of the frame appearing almost defiant at being placed in the background of the composition.

Vuillard depicts a further idealized image of feminine domesticity in *Woman in Blue with Child* (1899), in which his subject plays with her niece, Mimi Godebski. Here he casts Misia in a maternal role and signifies her domestic role by rendering her form as equivalent to the walls and furnishings of the salon. Misia's blue dress, the most distinct aspect of her presence, is in contrast to the golden tones of the surrounding room; however, the dress appears to the viewer as yet another abstract pattern on the singular picture plane overcrowded by form and color. As with the artist's many paintings of his mother, including *The Linen Closet* (1893) and *Madame Vuillard Sewing* (1893), Misia, as the nurturing female figure, is overwhelmed by the interior surfaces that merge with her body and threaten to render her identity indistinguishable.[6]

Vuillard's photograph of Misia Natanson seated on a chaise longue, Rue St. Florentin (c.1898–1899) depicts this same space but with Misia in a different guise. Here, Misia sits coquettishly perched on the chaise wearing a white dress with tightly fitted bodice and low neckline, revealing much of her décolletage. She looks directly at the camera and appears to proposition the photographer. Rather than as a maternal figure, Misia is posed as seductress, where the decorative screen and intimate seating convey a scene more akin to the boudoir than the homely warmth depicted in Vuillard's painting. By visually rearranging the direction of the furniture that is captured in the photograph, Vuillard is able to accentuate the decorative, organic surfaces of his painting, achieving a more tightly confined composition for symbolic effect. Thus, the photograph and the painting together offer insight into the tensions of represented space; where Misia of *Woman in Blue with Child* is a woman contained by her internal world of domestic comfort and family life, Misia of the photograph suggests a woman with sensuous desires that uses the interior to enhance her appearance.

In subsuming Misia's body in a decorative aesthetic that follows traditional discourses of the ideal feminine and domesticity, Vuillard's paintings displace aspects of what appears to be the reality of Misia's self-identity. By her own account, and that of many of her contemporaries, Misia's behavior was more akin to that of the New Woman than the retiring housewife or nurturing mother. While Misia's autobiography, *Misia and the Muses: The Memoirs of Misia Sert* (1953) would appear largely self-mythologizing, we can at least determine how she viewed herself, whether the events portrayed are accurate or not. Misia does not go so far as to declare herself a *femme nouvelle*; however, her life story suggests she desired to experience the emancipated lifestyle that the New Woman symbolized, where, at various times, she had unconventional relationships with men and women, worked to support herself, remained childless, and was cultivated in the arts.

In particular, her ambition to be recognized as a social and cultural arbitrator of taste, which she asserted through her patronage and visibility in the public sphere, underlines her desire to materialize a lifestyle outside the constraints of the bourgeois familial home.[7] As such, Misia appears to engage with what historian Mary Louise Roberts describes as the "disruptive acts" of the New Woman; "a subversive form of performance—an acting that was also an acting up" (2002: 3). I argue that while Vuillard's paintings seem intent on casting his muse as part of the decorative interior, Misia's subversive act was to arrange and decorate the apartment as the background stage upon which to perform her artistic self-identity.

## The annex: Misia's orchestration of space as stage for social mobility

Discourses of the late nineteenth century positioned women as "artists" of their interior, providing many women with a cultivated understanding of art and aesthetics yet also consolidating their role in the home as housewife. As Lisa Tiersten (1996: 32) outlines, "a room decorated by the bourgeois housewife was ultimately not so much her creation as an extension of her inner being… women became the objects, more than the subjects of modern art."

Vuillard's paintings certainly appear to engage with this rhetoric, where his image of Misia is simply an extension of the decorative aesthetic that she creates. However, if we only look at how Misia was represented in the space rather than how she operated within it, we fail to take into account the possibility of Misia's immaterial-psychological understanding of the interior and how it was possible for her to gain agency through it by subverting its functions. This comparison reveals how the "doubled" interior can offer conflicting understandings of interiority.

Misia christened the apartment on the fourth floor, 9 rue Saint-Florentin, "the annex"—an extension to *La Revue Blanche*'s journal offices, where a coterie of artists and writers would meet to discuss their intellectual pursuits. Here, Misia expressly devised frequent informal soirées to converse with the Nabis painters along with Paul Valéry, Romain Coolus, Stéphane Mallarmé, Claude Debussy, and Léon Blum on the diverse topics of poetry, aesthetics, music, politics, and philosophy. Misia's opinion on these matters was well regarded by the circle and culturally influential, as she was often involved in the journal's editorial process (Gold and Fizdale 1980: 47). These gatherings reflected the spirit of the collective avant-garde social structures that had gained momentum in the 1890s and offered Misia the opportunity to disrupt normative bourgeois gendered social behavior.

Misia's gatherings were considered unconventional as she rejected formality and etiquette. This was reinforced by how she organized the apartment. Refusing traditional boundaries, it was arranged in such a way that office, music room, and reception area were integrated in the salon, thus making little distinction between public and private space (Groom 1993: 83). At the time that Misia and Thadée inhabited the apartment, its layout consisted of the large salon adjoined by alcoves dedicated to the kitchen and pantry, dining room, and bedroom. Gloria Groom highlights that the arrangement of space was particularly unusual, arguing that "even Proust… regarded the Natanson's apartment as exotic but forbidden territory" (1993: 70).

The instability of public and private spheres that Misia cultivated in "the annex" transgressed traditional concepts of gendered interior space that was manifested in typical nineteenth-century homes. As Sparke outlines, at the time, dining rooms, studies, and smoking rooms were seen as the masculine domain, while bedrooms, boudoirs, and parlors were feminine. Further, within these spaces, "the codification of the furniture and décor served as an aid to the construction of men's and women's self-identities" (2008: 25). In disrupting the formal conventions of public and private, masculine, and feminine, Misia created a social instability of class and gender that was distinctly modern.

Further, I contend that in subverting the orthodox functions of nineteenth-century rooms through the open arrangement of space and in placing her piano at its core, Misia effectively constructed a stage for the performance of her self-identity. Not only could she perform her talent for music in front of her artistic audience, but she was also able to enact her social mobility by thwarting the customs of domestic behavior that would relegate her to the parlor while men carried on their discussions in the *fumoir* (smoking room) without her. In this way, Misia positioned herself at the center of *La Revue Blanche*'s artistic circle of followers. While she may not have been regarded as an artist in her own right, she was keen to convey to her audience that she had the requisite social and cultural capital to perform as one of them.

Misia's social identity was also on display in the salon through her decorating choices. Vuillard's photographs of the salon coupled with his paintings provide a consistent view of the room's decorations and furnishings.[8] From these sources, it is not entirely clear how separate sections of the salon worked as a whole, but it is possible to piece together an understanding of its decorative features and furnishings. Aside from the piano, which sat in front of a large tapestry, other furnishings included: a Thonet bentwood rocking chair, a chaise longue upholstered in paisley, a three-panel folding screen with textile print, a dark wooden side board with ceramics on display, and a fireplace draped with fabric atop of which a range of pottery and vases was exhibited.[9] Of particular note is the wallpaper of the salon, a unifying feature throughout the room, patterned with a yellow-and-green floral motif similar to William Morris's prints. This backdrop would feature in many of the Nabis paintings but would also serve as the background to many of these same images when the Natansons bought them and put them on display in their home.

According to Groom (1993: 84), Misia applied something of the Morrisian Method to "the annex," a look defined by the decorative wallpaper and complementary patterned textiles and upholstery that would form the backdrop to simple wooden furniture. While Misia may not have strictly adhered to Morris's utopian ideals, her interest in the philosophy of interior design was influenced by her friendship with van de Velde (Sert 1953: 32). The Art Nouveau designer's interest in Arts and Crafts movement's philosophies and personal aim to fashion interiors of interdependent elements that formed a spatial whole may well have filtered into Misia's conception of the open salon as a unified space. Given the collaboration between van de Velde and Vuillard on the Bing *Maison de l'Art Nouveau* (which included the Natansons' five-panel commission of Vuillard's *The Album* [1895]), as well as the fact that Vuillard had designed the offices for *La Revue Blanche* in 1894, it is entirely conceivable that Misia would have been privy to, if not an active participant in, conversations regarding the New Interior's aim of achieving visual unity as defined through the Arts and Crafts and Art Nouveau aesthetics.

It is worth considering the aim of the New Interior to achieve a harmonizing effect through the use of recurring motifs and a singular conception of space in relation to how Misia incorporated Vuillard's paintings into the apartment's décor. The process whereby Vuillard photographs Misia in the interior, reconfigures the room's composition and heightens its decorative features in his paintings, which then go on to be displayed on the same walls that the paintings depict, positions the domestic space as an interactive subject. That is, Vuillard's conception of Misia's character through the symbolic rendering of interior decoration becomes represented in the material space. Her private scenes and experiences of the domestic space, as represented by Vuillard, are put on display in the public space of the salon for her guests to look upon. Misia then, becomes a recurring motif of the room in both represented and material space, both as an image to be looked upon and as a figure who can observe her own image.

The interior of "the annex" was driven by Misia's desire to create an artistic environment that would be the appropriate aesthetic backdrop to her performance. As her biographers Arthur Gold and Robert Fizdale propose (1980: 39), Misia "created interiors which looked like Vuillard's paintings and Vuillard could hardly wait to paint Misia's flat and Misia in it." While Misia's choice of furnishings and decoration may have been considered unconventional for bourgeois tastes, the view that she was "artist of her interior" was part of the cultural turn designed to interiorize women that Vuillard engages with in his paintings. But Misia was able to challenge these assumptions about her role and position in society by orchestrating the space as the stage for her performance as patron to the arts, an image that she further cultivated through dress.

## Performing social mobility through dress: Misia, the artist at home

By the nineteenth century, fashion, like the interior, was considered important to the shaping of modern feminine identity. As design historian Penny Sparke contends, "in their capacity as material and spatial layers around the body, dress and the interior both played a role in the process of 'interiority' through which modern subjects developed a notion of 'themselves'" (2008: 74). This appears true of Misia, whose decoration of her social spaces in the home shares similarities with her self-fashioning at the time.

Misia operated within a society where dress was highly codified and representative of social status; decorative and restrictive dress indicated economic idleness and thus a woman's husband's or father's status and wealth. Just as rules existed for interior spaces in terms of their use, particular forms of dress were deemed appropriate for particular circumstances, with styles dedicated to walking, traveling, visiting, entertaining, and various other social undertakings that were part of the bourgeois woman's lifestyle. Misia appears to have flaunted both sets of dictates through her self-presentation and that of her home.

Photographs from throughout her life attest that Misia followed the fashions particular of the time; for example, she wears a straight-cut, tailored walking suit on the steps of La Croix-des Gardes, Cannes in 1901 (taken by Vuillard); a flapper-style chemise and long pearls in a Cecil Beaton portrait from 1925; and wide-leg pants on the beach in Venice with Gabriel Chanel in 1923. Yet, during the period that she was living at rue Saint-Florentin, Vuillard often documents Misia in his photos wearing an artistic style of dress that defied the sartorial eroticism, ornamentation, and complicated draperies that typified 1890s fashions.

These images include Misia standing with her back facing the camera, her face in profile in front of a fire-place, wearing a heavily draped dress with polka-dots (1897), sitting on a chair in the dining room, wearing a patterned dress with square neckline (1898), and standing alongside Vuillard's *Embroideries* painting in the salon wearing a striped dress with a spotted bow-kerchief tied around her neck (1897). Misia also wears this last dress in the aforementioned image of Thadée and Misia in the Salon, rue Saint-Florentin (Figure 9.2). Each of these garments are high-waisted and loosely structured, with generous flowing sleeves. They are striking in their simplicity and in stark contrast to the prevailing fashionable tight-waisted silhouette of the era achieved through the use of a corset.[10]

Misia's garments in these photographs might be classified as tea-gowns or *robes d'intérieur*, a form of dress worn only in the intimacy of the home. Women often wore such garments for informal entertaining but generally they were picturesque in style and ornamented with lace, ruffles, and bows. With austere geometric patterns, Misia's artistic dress is less overtly feminine and, given her subversion of the interior, it is possible that she is similarly attempting to bridge the separate spheres of domesticity and social life through her clothing by wearing an informal "private" style of dress in company. In particular, her understanding of the Morrisian Method of decoration coupled with her friendship with van de Velde suggests that she may have worn this style of artistic dress for specific purposes of cultural authority.

The English Pre-Raphaelites and the Arts and Crafts movement designers initiated artistic dress reform in the mid-nineteenth-century, where simple style was seen as both analogous to medieval ideals of beauty for women and complicit with their aesthetic aims (Steele 1985). Morris's Aesthetic model for dress continued to be represented in Symbolist paintings and Art Nouveau design, with van de Velde creating the first of his artistic dresses for his wife in 1896. Inspired by Morris, he designed clothes allied with ideals regarding the synthesis of the arts. The dresses, devoid of the constraining undergarment structure and opulent embellishments that were fashionable at the time, were designed to be practical and worn for all occasions. His hope was for women to "recognise the contemptuous and unscrupulous way in which the... masters of haute couture exploit" them (van de Velde cited in Stern 2004: 14). His revolution against fashion was to position dress as a work of art, and, as such, he decorated the garments to echo the organizational motifs of his interior designs.

While it would seem that van de Velde's purpose was to display women as an extension of the interior in their decorative appeal, in reality, much of the artistic dress worn by women were not designed for any specific interior. According to Elizabeth Wilson, artistic dress in the 1890s was associated with a bohemian lifestyle, noting that such clothing was "a symbol of the wearer's tastes and politics" (1985: 218). Less a sign of social class, artistic dress was rather an indicator of identity, a differentiation that made this fashion a "modern" manifestation.

We can only speculate as to why Misia chose an artistic style of dress in Vuillard's photographs. It may simply have been a matter of comfort; however, given her interest in fashioning an image for herself as cultivator of the arts it is conceivable that she was keen to visually align herself to the artistic avant-garde through the symbolic associations of artistic dress. In all likelihood, Misia wears these garments as a form of costume to represent her bohemian lifestyle. It is clear that Vuillard took many of these photographs as studies for his paintings, which he would manipulate into new compositions. Within them, Misia wears the distinctive artistic style of dress in order to provide a contrast between the geometric line of her silhouette and the floral patterning of her decorative surrounds. This, coupled with her deliberate poses and engagement with the camera, implies that Misia may well have been purposely wearing artistic dress in these photographs in order to have some form of visible presence and agency in Vuillard's paintings rather than be subsumed by decorative form. Evidence of this is revealed in Vuillard's painting *Vallotton and Misia in the Dining Room at Rue Saint-Florentin* (1899) in which Misia wears a smock-like dress with check pattern and yellow kerchief around her neck. Here, she does not blend into the wallpaper or the furniture as she might in other instances; her figure and face are clearly defined and she consumes the same space and visual authority as the artist Vallotton in the background.

It is debatable as to whether Misia manipulated her dress to effect the compositions of Vuillard's work; however, significantly, in a letter from Vuillard to Vallotton in October 1897, he comments upon her style: "She is sporting the violent colors that delight you as much as they do me. Perhaps you will come back soon?" (Gold and Fizdale 1980: 70). While this certainly suggests that Vuillard and Vallotton saw Misia's style as inspirational for their work, it also supports the idea that Misia was well aware of her self-fashioning and its appeal to the Nabis painters. Further, she most likely dressed and performed in particular ways to enhance her visual appeal for the purpose of their work.

If this is indeed the case, then Misia was able to orchestrate an image of herself through the fashioning of her body and the arrangement and decoration of the social space of the salon in which she performed. As such, Misia's body becomes the nexus where the "doubled" interior can converge. Through her construction of the interior as material space as much as through her clothes, she asserted her position as tastemaker in avant-garde artistic circles and disrupted bourgeois norms of gendered and social behavior in a mode analogous to that of the New Woman.

In analyzing both Vuillard's paintings and his photographs of Misia in the apartment, it is possible to gain insight into how different mediums were used to represent interior space. Working from observation and photographic sources, Vuillard reconfigured the Natansons' home to heighten its decorative features and enhance its symbolic and psychological effect, recasting Misia as a figure that complied with *his* notions of feminine nurture and domesticity. His photographs provide a more nuanced account of material space, where we witness how Misia was able to create an image of herself through the arrangement of actual space and her place within it. This would in turn influence the representational space of the interior in the Nabis paintings. That many of these paintings would end up on the Natansons' own walls serves to suggest that, in Misia's eyes, these paintings were not so much a representation of her in the interior but rather a back-drop to her performance as muse and artist that would enhance her social standing and artistic credentials.

## Notes

1. Misia Natanson was born Misia Godebska in 1872. An accomplished pianist trained by the composer Gabriel Fauré, Misia married her cousin, Thadée Natanson at age twenty-one and moved to Paris. In 1903, Natanson relinquished Misia to the publisher Alfred Edwards in exchange for money to continue his journal *La Revue Blanche*. Misia was married to Edwards between 1905 and 1909, after which she married her third husband, Spanish painter Jose-Maria Sert. While Misia used the surname Sert until her death in 1950, for the purposes of this paper (given the period under review), I will refer to her as Misia Natanson. For a full account of Misia's biography, see Gold and Fizdale (1980).

2. There is some contradiction in Nabis scholarship regarding Vuillard's representation of women. For Susan Sidlauskas, these images do not "conform to the conventions of feminine display for middle class women of their time" (1997: 85) and possibly subvert conventional readings of domestic comfort by implying psychological anxiety. The counter and more conventional account exemplified by Francesca Berry is that these paintings equate "with dominant domestic ideologies.... That is, as feminine, sometimes specifically maternal, spaces nurturing nostalgic fantasies of masculine retreat" (2011: 67).

3. Misia's claim that Vuillard made a silent declaration of love to her (Sert 1953: 52–53) is partially verified by sentiments expressed in the painter's diaries and letters. For example, on Christmas Eve 1896 he wrote in his journal: "Thadée and his wife a very good time. Tenderness, desires of work, ambitions and sensualities … uncertainty and conflicting desires" (Édouard Vuillard's Journal, 1896, cited in Easton 2011: 194).

4. Kuenzli's (2010: 194) claim that "Vuillard neutralizes the 'masculine' figure's agency by partially hiding it … in order to lessen their dramatic significance" is worthy of consideration given her thesis that Vuillard and the Nabis were attempting to overcome gender categories in order to incorporate both masculine and feminine in unifying decorative rhythms. However, I would assert that in many of his paintings of Misia, her body is often equated with its surrounds while the few men sitters are more frequently portrayed as visibly individualized.

5. According to Easton (2011), Vuillard took more than one thousand photographs, many of which appear to be source images for his paintings, where he might refer to many images in order to combine figures and forms to create a composition. Most of these photographs are in the family's private collection and remain unpublished. For further discussion and examples of Vuillard's photographs, see Elizabeth Easton (1994) and Eik Kahng (1999).

6. See Francesca Berry's observations regarding Vuillard's mother as a recurring decorative motif (2011).

7. Throughout her life Misia was a patron to the arts: she supported many of the Nabis painters, underwrote the Ballets Russes, and financially assisted Stravinski. Aside from the many paintings by Vuillard, she was also frequent muse to Pierre Bonnard, Félix Vallotton, Henri de Toulouse-Lautrec, and Auguste Renoir.

8. As well as the images discussed in this chapter, the apartment at rue Saint-Florentin is also depicted in *Misia at the Piano* (oil on cardboard) (1895), *Cipa Listening to Misia at the Piano* (1897–1898), *The Salon Natanson, Rue Saint-Florentin* (1897–1898), *The Red Dressing Gown* (1898), *In front of a Tapestry, Misia and Thadée Natanson Rue Saint-Florentin* (1898), *Interior with Three People* (1899), and *Misia at the Piano* (oil on panel) (1899).

9. See Gloria Groom (1993) for further description of the salon's decorative features.

10. See Valerie Steele (1985) for a full discussion regarding reform dress and aesthetic costume and its rejection of the corset.

## References

Berry, F. (2011), "Maman Is My Muse: The Maternal as Motif and Metaphor in Edouard Vuillard's Intimisme," *Oxford Art Journal* 34, no. 1: 55–77.

Downey, G. (ed) (2013), *Domestic Interiors: Representing Homes from the Victorians to the Moderns*, London and New York: Bloomsbury.

Easton, E. (1989), *The Intimate Interiors of Edouard Vuillard*, London: Thames and Hudson.

Easton, E. (1994), "Vuillard's Photography: Artistry and Accident," *Apollo*, 138/388: 9–17.

Easton, E. (2011), "Edouard Vuillard's Photography and the Limitations of Truth" in E. Easton (ed), *Snapshot: Painters and Photography, Bonnard to Vuillard*, New Haven and London: Yale University Press.

Gold, A., and R. Fizdale (1980), *Misia: The Life of Misia Sert*, London: Macmillan.

Groom, G. (1993), *Edouard Vuillard Painter Decorator*, New Haven and London: Yale University Press.

Kahng, E. (1999), "Staged Moments in the Art of Edouard Vuillard" in D. Kosinski (ed), *The Artist and the Camera Degas to Picasso*, New Haven and London: Yale University Press.

Kuenzli, K. (2010), *The Nabis and Intimate Modernism: Painting and the Decorative in the Fin-de-Siècle*, Surrey: Ashgate.

Rice, C. (2007), *The Emergence of the Interior: Architecture, Modernity, Domesticity*, London: Routledge.

Roberts, M. L. (2002), *Disruptive Acts: The New Woman in Fin-de-Siècle France*, Chicago: University of Chicago Press.
Sert, M. (1953), *Misia and the Muses: The Memoirs of Misia Sert*, New York: John Day.
Sidlauskas, S. (1997), "Contesting Femininity: Vuillard's Family Pictures," *The Art Bulletin* 79, no. 1: 85–111.
Sidlauskas, S. (2000), *Body, Place and Self in Nineteenth Century Painting*, Cambridge: Cambridge University Press.
Silverman, D. L. (1989), *Art Nouveau in Fin-de-Siècle France: Politics, Psychology and Style*, Berkeley, CA: University of California Press.
Sparke, P. (2008), *The Modern Interior*, London: Reaktion.
Steele, V. (1985), *Fashion and Eroticism: Ideals of Feminine Beauty from the Victorian Age to the Jazz Age*, New York: Oxford University Press.
Stern, R. (2004), *Against Fashion: Clothing as Art 1850–1930*, Cambridge, MA: MIT Press.
Tiersten, L. (1996), "The Chic Interior and the Feminine Modern: Home Decorating as High Art in Turn-of-the-Century Paris," in C. Reed (ed), *Not at Home: The Suppression of Domesticity in Modern Art and Architecture*, New York: Thames and Hudson.
Wilson, E. (1985), *Adorned in Dreams: Fashion and Modernity*, London: Virago Press.

# CHAPTER 10
# THE DECADENT INTERIOR AS MODERN LESBIAN AESTHETIC
*Elizabeth Melanson*

---

When Winnaretta Singer (1865–1943), the American heiress to the Singer Sewing Machine fortune, wished to secure a place for herself in Parisian high society in the late 1880s, she turned to Count Robert de Montesquiou for advice on the decoration of her new Parisian mansion (Singer 1892). Singer, who married the Prince de Polignac in 1893, knew that at the top of the Parisian social hierarchy, the domestic function of the "home" was secondary. For high society women, a house was primarily a public space in which to establish one's social position before an audience of elite peers.

Like many high society women, Singer considered her home a space for the performance of social identity. After the death of her husband in 1901, it became a space for performing sexual identity as she constructed a discourse that justified and celebrated her lesbianism. One of Singer's strategies was to challenge dominant social and sexual ideologies through the appropriation of the art and style of the Decadent dandies of the *fin-de-siècle*. In the first decades of the twentieth century, Singer's interiors and public entertainments were inspired by Decadent literature, particularly the work of Joris-Karl Huysmans and Oscar Wilde and the illustrations of Aubrey Beardsley. She also incorporated *tableaux vivants* in her entertainments. These had become popular among latter-day Symbolists and Wagnerians as well as in avant-garde lesbian circles and in high-end Parisian brothels. This essay examines what it meant for a woman to use Decadent ideals and style in her home in an attempt to (literally) set the stage for her conquest of Parisian high society and justify her lesbian identity in the first decades of the twentieth century.

Singer chose Robert de Montesquiou as her mentor because he was famous for inspiring the character of Jean Des Esseintes in Huysmans's *À Rebours* of 1884. Huysmans's description of Des Esseintes's fantastically imaginative and bizarre domestic interiors became an artistic guidebook for the Decadent movement of the *fin-de-siècle*. Montesquiou's "aesthetic suggestion" to his new protégé was to transform her home into a site for large semi-public spectacles (Montesquiou 1892).

When she remodeled her music room in 1903, Singer had Montesquiou's suggestions in mind. She envisioned this space as a small-scale version of a public concert hall, with the implication that the performances staged there were more significant than the private salon concerts popular in high society at the time (Brooks 1993). Since she purchased her large *hôtel particulier* in the fashionable sixteenth arrondissement in 1887, Singer had become known for featuring the work of avant-garde musicians in her home. Until her death in 1943, Singer's musical patronage was important to the development of musical modernism. She is credited with advancing the careers of Claude Debussy, Igor Stravinsky, Erik Satie, Darius Milhaud, Manuel de Falla, and Francis Poulenc (Kahan 2003).

### Designing the French Interior

In 1908 Singer organized a multimedia performance of works by Aubrey Beardsley in her new music room and private garden. The spectacle, which incorporated music, poetry, and *tableaux vivants* based on the artist's drawings for Wilde's *Salome*, functioned as Singer's "coming out" party after the death of her husband. Few of her guests failed to recognize that Singer appropriated Beardsley's work to assert her lesbian identity. Detailed accounts of the spectacle, with subtle allusions to Singer's sexuality, appeared the next day in Parisian newspapers for the delectation of the public.

### Negotiating high society and homosexuality, elegant style meets iconoclastic substance

Singer was a public figure whose name appeared almost daily in the society columns of the major newspapers of France, America, and England for the majority of her life. Her early years in high society coincided with an explosion of public interest in the socially elite of Paris. In this period, two of the most important French newspapers, *Le Figaro* and *Le Gaulois* added daily society columns. Singer befriended their editors, François Magnard and Gaston Calmette, and invited them to her home frequently (Kahan 2009). The newspapers offered detailed descriptions of the concerts, balls, and spectacles that she hosted and delighted in publishing accounts of her personal affairs, particularly speculations about her sexual orientation. Singer was intensely aware of her public perception and guarded her sexuality from the public. She was surprisingly candid, however, among her close friends, and did not try to hide her homosexuality from fellow members of elite high society.

After 1900, Singer appropriated the ironic, iconoclastic tone and style of the *fin-de-siècle* Decadent dandy (personified by Wilde, Beardsley, Montesquiou, and others) to assert her independence from the social conventions and sexual norms of Parisian high society. This was part of a larger trend among homosexual men and women. Some high society women adopted the dandy's manner of dressing, wearing men's clothing, while others imitated the writing and painting styles of the Decadents and Symbolists. Scholars have explored the appeal of the art and literature of the 1890s to early twentieth-century women, using the term "Sapphic Modernism" to describe the aesthetic espoused by lesbian women (Collecott 1999; Doan and Garrity 2006). These older forms offered women a language with which to construct a new lesbian identity, allowing them to embody difference in a way that was socially recognizable (Elliott and Wallace 1994; Chadwick and Latimer 2003). The ideals associated with nineteenth-century Decadence remained "modern," according to the historians David Weir (1995) and Matei Calinescu (1987), because they closely resembled the ideals associated with other early twentieth-century avant-gardes. The Decadents celebrated individualism and challenged traditional social and art forms through subversion. They attacked conventions like naturalism and mimesis by celebrating artificiality and stylization.

### Reinterpreting the Decadent interior

Robert de Montesquiou was a notorious figure of *fin-de-siècle* France, famous for inspiring Huysmans's Des Esseintes, Marcel Proust's Baron de Charlus, Jean Lorrain's Duc de Freneuse, and Wilde's Dorian Gray. His homes, which he decorated in "a state of drunken delirium," became the prototype for the Decadent interior (Munhall 1995: 47). They were known for their eccentric jumble of Rococo paintings, Empire furniture, Japanese screens, flowers, tapestries, sounds, and scents produced by a perfume machine. What might have appeared to outsiders as a bizarre array of eclectic bric-à-brac was, in fact, a carefully organized ensemble of objects chosen to amplify "sensations and ideas" and to serve as a refuge from the outside world (Carassus 1966: 32). As the visitor moved through Montesquiou's interiors, they were supposed to understand themselves as traveling not through the physical spaces of the real world but through the spaces of the count's mind. This conflation of interior and self was central to Montesquiou's conception of identity. In each room, a series of disconcerting juxtapositions were employed to forcibly remove the room's inhabitant from his habitual behaviors and conventional mind-set so that he might take refuge from the real world. For example, from his fiery red "cave of Ali Baba," one passed into a room decorated entirely in gray. There, even ordinary objects such as furniture, flowers, and rugs became extraordinary when grouped in a monochrome mass.

Above all, Montesquiou believed that his mission was to defend the lost elegance of eighteenth-century aristocratic life. In order to reintroduce Old Regime grace to the modern interior, Montesquiou mixed the extravagance of Decadent style with the elegance of eighteenth-century classicism. His last home, which he called the Palais Rose, was modeled on the Grand Trianon at Versailles and housed a bath once owned by Madame de Montespan. His interior decoration, with its juxtaposition of exotic objects and severe Empire furniture, demonstrated his belief that the truest taste mixed aristocratic elegance with spiritual bohemianism (Core 1984).

In 1904, Singer made extensive renovations to her home. The decoration of her new music room functioned similarly to Montesquiou's interiors. There, she wished to transport her guests to a world away from modern Paris, where they might fully appreciate the music and art that she considered a reflection of her own identity. After seeing the "delightful and very modern house" that he designed for her friend, Jean-Louis Forain, Singer hired the young architect Henri Grand-Pierre for the renovations (Singer-Polignac 1949: 116). Grand-Pierre, who was inspired by the neoclassical architecture of the eighteenth-century architect Alexandre-Théodore Brongniart, designed a Greek revival façade adorned with monumental ionic pilasters for Singer. She appreciated Grand-Pierre's theatricality and his ability to integrate the latest technologies with the restraint of neoclassicism. In addition to her Louis XVI formal rooms, the house also boasted the latest in kitchen appliances, a modern solarium, and a heated indoor pool.

The new music room on the second floor was modeled after the Hall of Mirrors at Versailles and was capable of seating 200 guests and a chamber orchestra (Figure 10.1). Grand-Pierre designed a system of pulleys that allowed the mirrors to act as shutters for the windows. When closed at night, the effect was said to be breathtaking, as the mirrors caught the reflections of two enormous Venetian chandeliers. To decorate the walls, Singer selected the Spanish painter, José-Maria Sert. Later nicknamed "Tiepolo of the Ritz," Sert's style was sumptuous and theatrical. His style does not fit neatly into any category and is most often described as "baroque." Singer felt that he was the only artist with enough originality to differentiate her home from those of her fellow high society Parisians (Fremontier 2008). Painted in black and gold grisaille, in the spirit of Tiepolo's frescoes

**Figure 10.1** Henri Grandpierre, Music room, Hôtel Singer-Polignac, Paris, c. 1904, Fondation Singer-Polignac, Photo © A. Carpentier/FSP.

for the Imperial Hall in Wurtzburg, the mural for Singer's music room was titled *Apollo's Cortege*. One critic compared the work to Japanese lacquer, describing the gold leaf against the black paint as "like the sparkling dust awakened by a ray of sunlight on a summer's day in a darkened room" (Anonymous 1911).

The mural represents Apollo presiding over the Three Graces and eleven muses. The figures are painted broadly in grisaille, the contours of their bodies roughly hatched in red and brown. Apollo is the only male figure among the fourteen life-size female nudes represented in the twelve panels. The subject was appropriate for Singer's music room, which she envisioned as a stage for grand artistic manifestations of all kinds. Looking down on her guests were Euterpe, Polymnie, and Terpsichore—the muses of dance and music—while Caliope, Érato,

Melopomène, and Thalie—the muses of poetry, tragedy, and comedy—presided over the readings, lectures, and plays that took place there.

Sert's treatment of the subject was unique. Compared to paintings of the same subject by, for example, Puvis de Chavannes, Sert's mural is aggressive, powerful, and starkly sexual. It was whispered at the time that the artist was inspired by Singer's "scandalous and Sapphic" reputation (Fremontier 2008: 42). However, it was Sert's Wagnerian conception of art that appealed most to Singer. The artist believed that his murals should be part of total works of art (Studievic 2010). They were painted on wooden panels that obscured the original architecture of the room, and he often designed the furniture and lighting around them. The resulting effect was artificial and theatrical, two virtues that Singer appreciated very much at the height of her involvement with Decadent interior design.

Singer was fascinated with the concept of the Gesamtkunstwerk and the work of Richard Wagner, having taken her first pilgrimage to Beyreuth in 1882. As early as the 1890s, she had attempted to transform her home into a stage for a total work of art. On the advice of Montesquiou, she installed an elaborate electric lighting system that would allow for the performance of sight and sound shows (Singer-Polignac 1998). Proust remembered two of these multi-media spectacles in his famous 1903 article in *Le Figaro*, describing them as "entirely new" for Parisians (Proust as Horatio 1903: 3). In 1895 an orchestra hidden behind a screen, a device favored by Wagner, played while text and musical notations were projected onto the walls. In its program, the event was described as a "sort of visible auditory experience" (Kahan 2003: 93). Three years later, Singer added images projected by a magic lantern to the event. This time, the concert was accompanied by projections of Fra Angelico's *Annunciation* and photographs of a Flemish town at night and a Fontainebleau landscape.

**The Beardsley spectacle**

> The dance Beardsley sees is the dance of gender, the delicacy and permeability of the veil separating masculine from feminine, licit from illicit desire. (Showalter 1990: 151–152)

On June 2, 1908 Singer invited one hundred elite guests to her home to witness an experimental multimedia tribute to the British artist Aubrey Beardsley. When Singer invited *le tout Paris* (a group comprised of aristocrats, wealthy bourgeois financiers, artists, intellectuals and the more discreet representatives of the press) to the spectacle at her home, she was sending a message about her allegiances, tastes and identity. Among the guests were the Princess Murat, the Grand Duchess Vladimir and Proust, whose names were published in *Le Figaro's* account of the evening.

The spectacle was called *Eaux-Fortes* (or "Etchings") and consisted of twelve *tableaux vivants* based on works by Beardsley performed by a troupe of actors. The *tableaux* were accompanied by poems by Julien Ochsé, set to music played by an orchestra hidden behind a partition. To evoke Beardsley's black and white palette, the garden and music room were dimly lit with Venetian lanterns. The rocky walls and black and white tiled floors of the stage, set in the music room, were bordered by black curtains. A giant frame surrounded the stage and was decorated in Beardsleyan style with fruit, flowers, and long tapered candles dripping wax (Gabriac 1908). Black hydrangeas were arranged in parterres, and baskets of fruits and flowers surrounded street lamps. Before the *tableaux* began, large copies of three of Beardsley's illustrations were displayed on the stage. Though it is not indicated in the reports, it is likely that these drawings were projected by magic lantern. When the projections disappeared, the actors appeared, wearing black velvet masks over faces painted white, their hair decorated with ostrich feathers. According to the reports, they wore long coats decorated to look like they were made of butterfly wings, peacock feathers, and rose petals, all in black and white.

It seems that guests were given a printed program that included reproductions of some of the drawings recreated by the twelve *tableaux vivants*. *Le Figaro* published the text of this program without illustrations. Nine of the *tableaux* were pastiches of several of Beardsley's works, but the last three were recognizable as recreations of Beardsley's notorious illustrations for the 1894 English edition of Oscar Wilde's *Salome*.

Even if they were not familiar with his work, Singer's elite guests certainly would have recognized the implications of invoking Beardsley's collaboration with Wilde on *Salome*. Originally published in French in 1893, *Salome* was a great *succès de scandale*. The play was banned from the English stage and premiered in Paris in 1896 amid controversy while Wilde was in prison for "gross indecency." In 1907, Wilde's *Salome* was revived in Paris as an opera composed by Richard Strauss and produced by Gabriel Astruc, a guest at Singer's spectacle. The right-wing press declared the opera, "a beautiful example of the decay of our mores" and "an enterprise in puffism" (Kahan 2003: 151).

The title of Singer's spectacle, *Eaux-Fortes*, indicates that she was self-consciously appropriating and reinterpreting *fin-de-siècle* cultural forms. *Eaux-Fortes* referred, of course, to the Beardsley engravings on which the *tableaux vivants* were based. But it also alluded to a tradition in France of using terms associated with one medium to describe another. A literary genre of *eaux-fortes*, in which pages of text alternated with illustrations, arose in France in the mid-nineteenth century. *Romans à l'eau fort*, as they were called, were so popular during the *fin-de-siècle* that by the early twentieth century, the genre was primarily associated with Symbolism and Decadence in the minds of the French public (Stead 2002). Huysmans, Paul Verlaine, Robert de Montesquiou, and Wilde were among the authors who titled their works *eaux-fortes*, and several reporters compared the experience of Singer's spectacle to reading a *Roman à l'eau forte*. Gabriac (1908: 1) described the evening as an "evocative album" whose pages were turned by an unseen hand, displaying "on one side an engraving, on the other, text." Singer's "album" was made more "tangible," according to Gabriac, because Ochsé's poems, accompanied by music, were "collected" by the ear while the eye absorbed the "engravings."

> Gabriac marveled at how closely the *tableaux* resembled Beardsley's works and remarked on the mysterious quality of the spectacle: From the pages that usually retain and immobilize them, the figures were brought to life for a short while ... [The organizer], with amazing care, interpreted the art of Beardsley as exactly and closely as possible, and captured the smallest details, neglecting nothing .... The actors emerge from the shadows only briefly, and when they return, there is no sense of where they came from or where they are going. Their presence among us is intelligible only by the contours of their bodies against a background of white or black, their shadows against light or their bodies in relief against the night. (1908: 1)

## Decadent Interior as Modern Lesbian Aesthetic

The first of the three Beardsley *Salome* illustrations enacted as a *tableau vivant* was *The Peacock Skirt* (Figure 10.2). This work illustrates a scene early in Wilde's play between Narraboth, a young Syrian officer, and Salome, the object of his infatuation. Salome, on the left, looms menacingly over the smaller male figure. The fact that Narraboth is male is indicated only by his knees and legs. Otherwise, his elaborate hairstyle, draped gown, and effeminate gesture indicate a female figure. In order to imitate Beardsley's illustration, the

**Figure 10.2** Aubrey Beardsley, *The Peacock Skirt*, 1893 lithograph from Oscar Wilde, *Salome*, trans. Alfred, Lord Douglas (London: John Lane, The Bodley Head, 1907).

actors in Singer's *Peacock Skirt tableau* would have had to disguise and manipulate their bodies in ways that were considered unnatural to their genders. The bodies, costumes, and poses of the actors would have indicated the "inverted" (to use the term popular at the time) sexuality of both the masculine woman (Salome) and the effeminate man (Narraboth). Smiling threateningly, Salome bends down to stare into the eyes of Narraboth. His left hand, with its delicate wrist, is raised and extended slightly with his fingers gracefully splayed, as if reaching for a wall to steady himself.

The second *Salome tableau* reenacted *The Dancer's Reward* (Figure 10.3). Here, Salome lifts the head of John the Baptist roughly by the hair, running a finger through the blood pouring from his neck. She is not terrified but fascinated by the severed head, which has become a fetish object for the female protagonist (and viewer). John has delicate features and long hair, suggesting to some art historians that he should be read as female (Fernbach 2001; Heffernan 2006). If John is read as female, then Salome has beheaded the woman she loves, making her a "lesbian fetishist," according to several scholars. Amanda Fernbach (2001: 213) argues that as a "lesbian fetishist," Salome becomes a feminist heroine because she refuses "to internalize the socially sanctioned meanings of sexual difference within a patriarchal order." Thus, Beardsley's drawings and Singer's *tableau* offered the viewer the possibility of taking a variety of subject positions and drawing a multiplicity of conclusions about the gender and sexuality of the characters before them.

Singer's final *tableau* enacted Beardsley's last illustration for *Salome*, called *Design for Tailpiece* or *Fin* (Figure 10.4). Here, Salome has been executed and her naked body is being lowered into a powder box coffin by a Satyr and a masked Pierrot. In the illustration, Salome is nude, her body on full display, and Pierrot smiles blithely as he prepares to inter her. The fanciful scene does not correspond to the text of Wilde's play but was a fitting choice for the finale of Singer's celebration of Aubrey Beardsley. Because *Tailpiece* contains all of the elements of a quintessentially Beardsleyan work, Singer's *tableau* can be read as a celebration of the artist's oeuvre as a whole.

Bringing the *Salome* illustrations to life as *tableaux vivants* was a provocative act. Wilde's *Salome* was notoriously subversive in its attack on bourgeois sexuality and patriarchal society, and Beardsley's illustrations went a subversive step further. The major themes underlying Beardsley's illustrations for *Salome* are gender confusion, androgyny, and homosexuality. Performed in the stately home of a dignified aristocratic woman, Beardsley's strange scenes would have only been more bizarre, their frank sexuality and eroticism heightened when represented in the flesh.

Singer's *tableaux vivants* would have functioned similarly to a performance of Wilde's play, which by 1908 had become overwhelmingly associated with female homosexuality in France. Early twentieth-century female performers and audiences often interpreted Wilde's Salome as a symbol of "the subversion of patriarchal authority and the signification of female power as well as same sex female desire" (Fernbach 2001: 210). For them, Salome became a "modern woman" instead of a *femme fatale*, and the play addressed contemporary women's issues such as feminism and lesbianism. Because of this, performances of *Salome* were often met with disgust, misogyny, and homophobia.

The medium of the *tableau vivant* was also laden with lesbian connotations in the popular imagination of early twentieth-century France. The American expatriate playwright and novelist, Natalie Barney, and her circle were notorious for staging erotic lesbian *tableaux* in their elite gatherings. In addition, lesbian *tableaux* had recently become popular in upscale

**Figure 10.3** Aubrey Beardsley, *The Dancer's Reward*, 1893 lithograph from Oscar Wilde, *Salome*, trans. Alfred, Lord Douglas (London: John Lane, The Bodley Head, 1907).

Parisian brothels, where prostitutes posed together in elaborate static sex-scenes. Alain Corbin has described these nineteenth-century peep shows:

> The inmates, entirely naked, abandoned themselves to homosexual practices on a large black velvet carpet or in rooms hung with black satin to bring out the whiteness of their bodies. (1990: 124)

**Figure 10.4** Aubrey Beardsley, *Tailpiece* or *Fin*, 1893 lithograph from Oscar Wilde, *Salome*, trans. Alfred, Lord Douglas (London: John Lane, The Bodley Head, 1907).

At the turn of the century, the interior decoration of the great Parisian brothels became more extravagant, many featuring Empire style rooms (Corbin 1990). The brothel interiors described in a 1900 government report on prostitution in France are remarkably similar to the decoration of Singer's music room, particularly when it was fitted with the scenery for the Beardsley spectacle:

> A marvelous grotto … is one of the curiosities and one of the mysteries of the establishment…. There are mirrors everywhere, on all the walls and all the ceilings dazzling electric lights everywhere; and everywhere perfumes in this temple of Love, the priestesses of which are naked. (Corbin 1990: 123)

The black backgrounds and white bodies, the electric lights, mirrors, and rocky walls of Singer's *tableaux* very well might have conjured one of the notorious brothel interiors in the minds of her guests, many of whom were known to frequent these establishments. However, when Singer staged *tableaux vivants* for her elite friends, she reinscribed their homosexual connotations with the legitimacy of "art" and the approval of high society.

Performed by actors in Singer's home, Beardsley's illustrations offered themselves for interpretation through any number of subjectivities, including a lesbian viewing position. The *tableaux* allowed an early twentieth-century audience the opportunity to draw their own conclusions about the gender and sexuality of the characters and find their own meaning in the scenes. Some of Singer's guests were unimpressed by the spectacle. The author Marie de Régnier found the affair bleak, muttering to Edmond Jaloux (1942: 51) that it should have been called the *"enterrement pour Cythère."* Jaloux claims de Régnier's comment reflected her distaste for the eighteenth-century decoration of Singer's music room, but it is also possible that she was simply unable or unwilling to adopt a viewing position that would allow her to appreciate Singer's intentions in reviving Decadent art and style.

It was in her new music room that Singer staged the Beardsley spectacle in 1908. In this space, she performed her identity according to Wagnerian and Decadent ideals. The room and spectacle were conceived as spaces of dislocation, refuges from the real world, and sanctuaries where one was shocked out of complacency, much like the Decadent interiors of the *fin-de-siècle*. But unlike Montesquiou's domestic space, which was meant to reflect the psychology of its owner exclusively, Singer's guests were encouraged to project their own subjectivities onto the room and the spectacle.

Singer shared with the men of the *fin-de-siècle* an interest in art and interior design that allowed for the expression of identity. She came to know about these Decadent principles and art forms primarily through the mass media. In Symbolist novels, reproductions of Beardsley's illustrations, photographs of Montesquiou's homes, and even popular press coverage of brothel *tableaux vivants*, she found an aesthetic ripe for appropriation. Her music room, designed on the same principles as Montesquiou's juxtaposition of eighteenth-century, exotic, and bohemian styles, was at once an expression of her interest in the elegant aristocratic past and her embrace of modern life. Because she considered her life as a total work of art, interior design became a performative act, and her home, particularly her new music room, became a public stage where she tested new iterations of her homosexual identity. This stage was made public in the press, where accounts of her concerts and spectacles appeared almost daily in the early twentieth century. In her music room, she appropriated the styles and ideas of the 1890s (personified by Wilde, Beardsley, and Montesquiou) in order to test the boundaries of gender and sexuality in French society.

## References

Anonymous (1911), "Décoration de M. JM Sert," *Revue critique des idées et des livres* 4.
Brooks, J. (1993), "Nadia Boulanger and the Salon of the Princesse de Polignac," *Journal of the American Musicological Society* 46: 416–468.
Calinescu, M. (1987), *Five Faces of Modernity: Modernism, Avant-Garde, Decadence, Kitsch, Postmodernism*, Durham: Duke University Press.
Carassus, É. (1966), *Le Snobisme et les lettres françaises de Paul Bourget à Marcel Proust: 1884–1914*, Paris: A. Colin.
Chadwick, W. and T. True Latimer (2003), *The Modern Woman Revisited: Paris Between the Wars*, New Brunswick, NJ: Rutgers University Press.
Collecott, D. (1999), *H.D. and Sapphic Modernism, 1910–1950*, New York: Cambridge University Press.
Corbin, A. (1990), *Women for Hire: Prostitution and Sexuality in France after 1850*, Cambridge, MA: Harvard University Press.
Core, P. (1984), *The Original Eye: Arbiters of Twentieth Century Taste*, Englewood Cliffs, NJ: Prentice-Hall.
Doan, L. L. and J. Garrity (2006), *Sapphic Modernities: Sexuality, Women, and National Culture*, New York: Palgrave Macmillan.

Elliott, B. and J-A. Wallace (1994), *Women Artists and Writers: Modernist (Im)Positionings*, London and New York: Routledge.

Fernbach, A. (2001), "Wilde's 'Salomé' and the Ambiguous Fetish," *Victorian Literature and Culture* 29, no. 1: 195–218.

Fremontier, J. (2008), *José-Maria Sert: Le Rencontre de l'Extravagance et de la Démesure*, Paris: Les Éditions de l'Amateur.

Gabriac, A. de (June 1, 1908), "La Vie de Paris," *Le Figaro*: 1.

Heffernan, J. A. W. (2006), *Cultivating Picturacy: Visual Art and Verbal Interventions*. Waco, TX: Baylor University Press.

Jaloux, E. (1942), *Les Saisons Littéraires*, Fribourg: Librairie de l'Université.

Kahan, S. (2003), *Music's Modern Muse: A Life of Winnaretta Singer, Princesse De Polignac*, Rochester, NY: University of Rochester Press.

Kahan, S. (2009), *In Search of New Scales: Prince Edmond De Polignac, Octatonic Explorer*, Rochester, NY: University of Rochester Press.

Montesquiou, R. de to W. Singer (May 8, 1892), "Papiers de Robert de Montesquiou: Lettres, Winnaretta Singer," NAF 15122, Bibliothèque nationale de France.

Munhall, E. (1995), *Whistler and Montesquiou: The Butterfly and the Bat*, New York: Frick Collection.

Proust, M. (Horatio) (September 6, 1903), "Le Salon de La Princesse Edmond de Polignac: Music d'aujourd'hui, Échos d'autrefois," *Le Figaro*.

Showalter, E. (1990), *Sexual Anarchy: Gender and Culture at the Fin de Siècle*, Boston: Little, Brown.

Singer-Polignac, W. (1949), "Memoirs of the Late Princesse Edmond de Polignac," *Horizon* 12, no. 68: 137–148.

Singer-Polignac, W. (1998), *Winnaretta Singer-Polignac: Une Amie des Arts et des Sciences: Lettres, 1888–1938*, Paris: Fondation Singer-Polignac.

Stead, E. (2002), "Gravures Textuelles: Un Genre Littéraire," *Romantisme* 32, no. 118: 113–132.

Studievic, H. (2010), *José Maria Sert: Le Titan à l'Oeuvre, 1874–1945*, Paris: Paris-Musées.

Weir, D. (1995), *Decadence and the Making of Modernism*, Amherst: University of Massachusetts Press.

Wilde, O. (1907), *Salome, A Tragedy in One Act: Translated from the French of Oscar Wilde, with Sixteen Drawings by Aubrey Beardsley*, trans. Lord Douglas Alfred, London: John Lane, The Bodley Head.

# CHAPTER 11
## MALLET-STEVENS, MODERN DESIGN, AND FRENCH CINEMA
*Nieves Fernández Villalobos*

After the First World War, as France entered the 1920s, prewar experiments in the arts were taken up with renewed intensity and Paris reclaimed its aesthetic preeminence. Art Nouveau, the Vienna Secessionist style, Futurism, and Expressionism had seen their most fertile years at the end of the war, but when adopted by the cinema, they each contained a number of stylistic features that would eventually coalesce into the distinctive look of Modern architecture, as Donald Albrecht explains in his book *Designing Dreams, Modern Architecture in the Movies* (2000: 35). In 1924, Modern design made its film debut through the efforts of French pioneers, who hoped to promote the Modern movement through the cinema. This chapter will examine two of the key films of the time, *L'Inhumaine* (Marcel L'Herbier, 1924) and *Les Mystères du Château du Dé* (Man Ray, 1929). It will reflect on the ideas and influences of the distinguished French architect, Robert Mallet-Stevens and on the role his set designs played in promoting the Modern movement.

### Mallet Stevens and the Viennese spirit

At the turn of the last century, artistic exchanges between different European cities led to a new environment for creative openness and formal development of refined and pure shapes. The Wiener Werkstätte was founded in 1903 in Vienna by Koloman Moser and Josef Hoffmann, where the latter had marked a new direction in architecture and design, following the orthogonal geometries of the Scottish Arts and Crafts movement and C. R. Mackintosh's style of light rooms with stylized and concentrated decoration. In 1904, with his first public work, the Sanatorium Purkersdorf, Hoffmann anticipated the rational and volumetric architecture of the twenties and, as a student of Otto Wagner, learnt how to bring together all forms of art in the same work, thereby creating *Gesamkunstwerke* or "total works of art." From 1905 to 1914, Hoffmann worked on designs for the Palais Stoclet in Brussels, in which cubic volumes were arranged in ascending order, culminating in a tower and in staggered boxes of white marble framed by bronze stripes. Everything was planned in detail: Hoffmann built the house and designed the interiors, furniture, and Mrs. Stoclet's dresses and jewels. So the Palais became a perfect example of *Gesamtkunstwerk*.

With the strong design lesson of the Stoclet Palace, this Viennese spirit entered Paris via Brussels, resonating immediately among French artists, who soon began to experiment with the *Gesamkunstwerke*. Robert Mallet-Stevens, a nephew of the banker Adolphe Stoclet, was the main transmitter of Hoffmann's work. He had studied architecture at the École Spéciale in Paris that offered a new training method based on Violet-le-Duc's rationalist thinking. By the time his uncle's striking Hoffmann house was built (the building was finished in 1911), Mallet-Stevens had obtained his diploma and acquired some practical experience. He began his career by participating in exhibitions and, although his unyielding character created some initial difficulties, he was soon well-known as an interior designer with several clients in the world of fashion including Jeanne Paquin, Jacques Doucet, and Paul Poiret. The young architect created a new decorative grammar that was embodied in these interior works and in his album *Cité Moderne*, published in 1922. From that date, the architecture of Mallet-Stevens began to acquire a formal balance between Cubist and Neoplastic conceptions; he defined his architecture as smooth surfaces, sharp edges, clean curves, polished materials, and right angles, all of which provided clarity and order.

## The cinema of the seventh art: A publicity tool for Modern architecture

Mallet-Stevens remained closely engaged with the avant-garde movements of his time, and just after the war, in 1920, when aged thirty-four, he met some film-makers and began to design cinema sets. His contribution to the cinematographic art derived from a double desire: firstly to present his research on architecture to a wider audience and secondly to defend the status of cinema as the seventh art. For Mallet-Stevens, the film was an instrument of propaganda much greater than an exhibition or a building, and by bringing new forms and techniques to every corner of the world, it would ensure that Modern architecture would be known and appreciated. But to make this possible, first, cinema had to become aware of its possibilities; it was, as film theorist Ricciotto Canudo, a contemporary of Mallet-Stevens proposed, "a visual tale made with images and painted with brushes of light" (Louis 2005: 147). This critic of Italian origin played a key role in the synthesis of architecture and cinema and Mallet-Stevens's achievements. Canudo, along with Bernard Deschamps and Henri Frescourt, founded the *Club des Amis du Septième Art* (C.A.S.A.) in April 1921, from which branches would be created in major European cities. The C.A.S.A encouraged some admiration for the new cinema with their reinvented sets by pioneering artists like Mallet-Stevens. Mallet-Stevens's book *Le Décor moderne au cinéma* (1928) was the first publication illustrating the aims pursued by the young designers of the French avant-garde cinema. For Mallet-Stevens, the film studio was a factory where all human artistic activities could converge to create a film composed of two parallel elements: the scenery, which was static, and the actors, who were dynamic (Vaillant 1995: 101). But the film set had to evoke a specific atmosphere before the actors entered the stage. Although each period had its own special set, harmony resulted from a total intermingling and meticulous coordination of scenery in every element of production design—in the interior and exterior settings as much as in costume, furniture, and garden designs.

These ideas gradually materialized in the sets for *La Singulière aventure de Neil Hogan, jockey* (dir. Jacques Risen, 1920) and *Jettatura* (dir. Pierre-Gilles Veber, 1921), which were eclectically and richly decorated and were strongly influenced by the Art Deco style. In some of his other films, including *Le Secret de Rosette Lambert* (dir. Raymond Bernard, 1920) and *La Ronde de nuit* (dir. Marcel Silver, 1925), inspired by Canudo, there was an attempt to simplify through sober, pared-back volumes, marked by the Viennese spirit, which culminated in an austerity different from the far more personal aesthetic explored in *L'Inhumaine* (dir. Marcel L'Herbier, 1924) and *Le Vertige* (dir. Marcel L'Herbier, 1926). As will be shown in the following pages, architecture influenced film, which, in its turn, influenced architecture.

## *L'Inhumaine*: French catalog of the early avant-garde

In 1923, Mallet-Stevens was commissioned to design some sets for Marcel L'Herbier's film *L'Inhumaine*. It was a big budget movie, shot in the Plateau Lewinsky in Joinville. The film's credits included the most distinguished names of the "new art:" Pierre MacOrla wrote the script, Mallet-Stevens created the exterior architecture of the buildings and Alberto Cavalcanti designed the interior sets, except for the engineer's laboratory built by Fernand Léger and the winter garden made by Claude Autant-Lara. Pierre Chareau designed the furniture; René Lalique and Jean Puiforcat made objects; Paul Poiret designed costumes and Raymond Templier created the jewellery. Darius Milhaud, also a member of the C.A.S.A., composed his first music for the film. It premiered in Paris at the Cinéma Madeleine on December 12, 1924 amid great excitement, although most viewers were disappointed, as the actor Jaque Catelain passionately described (1950: 76). But despite the great failure among the public, the film has passed into history because, as the director said, "we wanted it to be a sort of summing up, a sort of resumé of everything which made up the research into form in France …" (Deshoulières and Jeanneau 1980: 43).

The movie is about the fascination that a famous opera singer, Claire Lescot (Georgette Leblanc), exerted among men, especially for engineer Einar Noorsen (Jaque Catelain), who managed to seduce her with technological devices from his laboratory. But the originality of the script was not the most important thing in this silent film. Rather, the main focus was its celebration of diverse artistic expressions and its astonishingly modern treatment of the sets (Figure 11.1).

Although the only real location used in the film was the Théâtre des Champs-Élysées, designed by Auguste Perret and opened in 1913, the exterior architecture of the two protagonists' houses, the singer and the engineer, were both designed by Mallet-Stevens to play an active role and reflect the personality of the characters. Thus the size of Claire Lescot's villa attests to her wealth and is accessed by a monumental staircase emphasized by strong side lighting, another perceptible symbol of her luxurious lifestyle. Throughout the film the house is only seen at night, where light plays an essential role: it emphasizes the relief of the various parts and it differentiates volumes through raking light directed from the ground plane, all of which create a dramatic atmosphere through stark oppositions between light and shadow.

As Louis Michel points out (2005: 150), the way this house is discovered, at the beginning of the film, "is a revealing example of the cinematographic approach to the 'modern' architectural object." As if the audience is seated behind the wheel of a car, in the first frames we see two light beams directed onto the main façade of the geometric villa. This radically innovative automobilial point of view, referencing the car itself as a symbol of modernity, also featured in the work of architect Le Corbusier and in films by Pierre Chenal, such as *L'Architecture d'aujourd'hui* (1929), the latter of which was produced to promote

Designing the French Interior

**Figure 11.1** M. L'Herbier, *L'Inhumaine*, 1924: Claire Lescot's House (left side): An exterior view, the main hall and her private room; Einar Noorsen's House (right side): An exterior view, resurrection room, and laboratory, L'Herbier Cinégraphic, Studio Levinsky in Joinville, Paris.

an architectural journal of the same name founded in 1930 by Auguste Perret and Robert Mallet-Stevens. Many years later, actor Jacques Tati in *Mon Oncle* (1958) would also use the car to present a Modern house, the Villa Arpel, with its two circular windows representing eyes. However, in L'Herbier's film, *L'Inhumaine*, the two lighted windows of Claire Lescot's house watch the viewer as the eyes of an immobile anthropomorphic face, in which the nose is suggested by a large vertical hole and the cheeks by two symmetrical light halos surrounding the entrance.

The formal synthesis and rationalist volumes that Mallet-Stevens shows in this piece of theatrical architecture are similar to those presented by his peers' architectural projects. And, like most of them, if ornamentation existed, it was scarce and concentrated, making use of contrasting geometric elements and contributing to the creation of elegant Art Deco accents. So, at the home of Claire Lescot, while the façades are smooth and bare (except for a vertical stripe, a decorative feature in a corner), the entry hall brings all the ornamentation to direct the viewer's gaze to the point where the main action takes place. The door plays with opaque and transparent features in a striking composition of geometric shapes reminiscent of many period textile designs.

If Mallet-Stevens's exterior set for Claire Lescot's house comprises a unique eclectic synthesis of Cubism, Art Deco, and Neoplasticism, the prime interior set, designed by Cavalcanti, was fully in the Art Deco style, promoting through numerous details the exoticism of this movement. The main hall, of unusual dimensions, is emphasized by its eclecticism and its sharp contrasts in black and white. The viewer's gaze converges on a central platform, the floor of which has a geometric pattern with staggered zig-zags and a perimeter pond of oriental design. In the water canal, crossed by two walkways, some swans add a German Romantic note. The floating platform is versatile: servants, with strange Japanese-style masks and dressed in waistcoats with abstract shapes and checkered edging, first serve dinner to dignitaries and foreign ambassadors and later retire tables and chairs with pointed backs to provide a space for different artistic performances. Opposite to the entry area, Claire Lescot's private rooms are accessed between two angled staircases. Huge curtains, in theatrical swathes, frame and underscore with tongue-in-cheek grandiosity the entrance where the singer first appears before her distinguished guests. The other side of the room accommodates a lowered arch, decorated with triangles, forming a stage for the diva. Before it, the font which feeds the canal is placed beside a sofa full of bright, circular cushions and some cuboid armchairs, whose squared lattice recalls the ornamentation of Mackintosh and Hoffman. On the opposite side, on an upper floor, the orchestra plays jazz music at different speeds, as each scene requires.

In *L'Inhumaine*, cinema and interior architecture always work together, and this relationship is highlighted when the camera sweeps around the main hall from above, usually from the front door, in order to fully expose the opulent and exotic space and to emphasize the theatrical tone of the mise-en-scène. Within this eclectic setting, two discordant elements are integrated. On the one hand, short fiction films are montaged, with the fantasies of the engineer's three rivals living a common life with Claire, and on the other, a graphic resource is presented that shows the influence of the most famous of Expressionist films, Robert Wiene's *The Cabinet of Dr. Caligari* (1920). These preface the enigmatic words of Claire Lescot about a mysterious force that could prevent her from undertaking her journey around the world. This sentence is received by Einar Noorsen as real written lines in space, the movie exploiting new special effects in a manner similar to Wiene's *Cabinet of Dr. Caligari*.

Expressionism emerged in the twentieth century as a movement that stressed the subjective and symbolic aspects of objects and spaces, which were often realized as abstract distortions of color and form. Expressionist aesthetics had a great impact on all varieties of art, most notably in Germany. Although Wiene's anti-realist mode of film design never formed the basis for a particularly cohesive school of set decor, its aesthetic and angular repertory would initiate a short-lived series of films that reinterpreted its stylized forms. Thereby, the influence of this masterpiece of German Expressionism would pervade French cinema in some films of Jean Epstein and would also influence the work of L'Herbier in *L'Inhumaine*. The most overt reference to the German classic presented in this film is the obvious artifice of overlapping planes of plants in Claire Lescot's winter garden, created by Claude Autant-Lara, which surrounds a luminous glass pyramid and frames the emotionally desperate Einar Noorsen.

## Designing the French Interior

There is also a cinematic Art Deco treatment of the décor in Claire Lescot's private rooms, which are accessed through floor to ceiling curtains and down three steps. In Claire's boudoir, divans, sofas, cushions, tables and screens are arranged informally in the large space, which is divided into two levels. The furniture pieces, designed mostly by architect Pierre Chareau, show his exquisite and perfectionist style, marked by three main features: honesty of materials, variable transparency of forms and substances and the juxtaposition of industrial and modern elements with more traditional ones. Chareau's furniture of the early 1920s shows a preference for undecorated, rounded forms executed in rich and highly polished woods with elaborate upholstery.

Three designs that he created in 1923 are notable among the pieces presented in this space of the movie: the tulip table in rosewood that had already appeared in the interior of the apartment for Edmond and Madeleine Fleg in Paris; his wooden conical stand with a shade made of four triangular alabaster plaques held together by brass clips, *La Religieuse* (also nicknamed as "The Nun"), which had been exhibited at the *Salon d'Automne*; and the long oval sofa enclosed by a low-level back, which curved at the ends to form armrests. This, as well as the folding screen and the carpet that precedes it, were upholstered in Cubist geometric patterns. The velour and tapestry were designed by Jean Lurçat, the Cubist painter, tapestry designer, and brother of architect André Lurçat, who Chareau had met through Jean Dalsace (his loyal friend and benefactor and owner of the Maison du Verre (1928–1932)), who was a close friend of Lurçat from their school days in Epinal. This sofa is an elegant version of the French *Canapé à confidents* of the nineteenth century, which Pierre Chareau would also use in the sets of *Le Vertigue* (1926), and which would become one of the most distinctive furniture pieces in the Maison du Verre (Wouters 1990: 91–107).

Thus, reflecting his understanding of the *Gesamkunstwerk*, Mallet-Stevens carefully coordinated every single decorative element in his sets for Claire Lescot's house in *L'Inhumaine*. However, the exterior and interior sets for Einar Noorsen's laboratory are even more consistent. Where the combination of horizontal and vertical planes offers a balanced set of volumes to the singer's villa, the vertical surfaces of the engineer's house provide a sense of exaltation to construction. Here, the volumes are broken down into small parallelepipeds, which remind one of some of the utopian contemporary *Architectons* created by the Russian artist Kazimir Malevich. The staggered building seems to take cosmic forces in through the roof, in order to supply power to the underground laboratory. Mallet-Stevens introduced some geometric elements in the upper part of the building, such as the ovoid structure from which several tensioned cables descend vertically along the façade and enter the building above the entrance. To emphasize the vertical composition of this construction, the camera features the house via a panorama that sweeps from top to bottom. The villa is shown at night, illuminated by two side openings and a vertical narrow window, near the entrance. This architecture is more discrete, consistent with the mysterious world that is hidden inside. To accentuate this, the door is opaque and has an asymmetrical abstract composition based on intersecting squares and rectangles.

The interior set design for the Einar Noorsen's laboratory was created by artist Fernand Léger. It appears to have been a three-dimensional recreation of the Cubist universe that Léger had developed in two dimensions between 1918 and 1921. In his *disk paintings*, he had approached Robert and Sonia Delaunay's *Simultaneism*, a concept that expressed the spirit of the dynamic and kaleidoscopic machine age, using shape and color. Léger also enjoyed the machine, and considered that its prodigious power defined the age. In Léger's so-called mechanical period he did not merely copy machines. Rather, he invented a visual language to represent them. His inclusion of eye motifs, turning into engines, turbines and dynamos, suggests the essence of the machine and its assemblage from fragment to complete unit. In paintings produced in the same period as his designs for *L'Inhumaine*, Léger explored flat architectonic forms intersected through repeated juxtapositions between disks and planes of plain colors. This body of work forms a fascinating likeness to his set for the film's laboratory. In addition, the board with the title, which is slid in front of the camera with the inscription "*L'Inhumaine,*" is also a Cubist design by Fernand Léger and refers to the streamlined Modernist style of the film. Apparently, Léger's machine aesthetic extended into a workman-like, hands-on approach to construction. Director L'Herbier stated that "Léger built the set with his own hands; as a true carpenter he arrived at eight o'clock to Joinville and began to work with his spheres, his cubes, his cones, retreating a bit to judge the effect obtained, as if he were painting a still life" (Gorostiza 2007: 21). This simple method of construction belies the sophisticated effects he achieved with the advanced gadgets that fill the space. It is a magic room where the pistons are set in motion and the levels go up and down at increasing speeds and everything begins to come alive under the command of the engineer. Circles, cylinders, cones and spheres alternate their movements contrasting black and white, while the machines emit steam and the assistants, performed by dancers from the *Ballets Suédois* in black overalls and safety helmets, operate the control rods and act as "changeable décors," while Einar Noorsen, dressed in white, orchestrates the event.

Again, the light is everywhere. At the bottom of the laboratory, the aseptic "resurrection" hall, consisting of three staggered prisms, is inspired by the backdrops of *L'Homme et son désir* (1921) by Madame Parr. In this room, the energy descends through a vertical gap and the lateral zig-zag generates prisms of light, which crackle and blink rhythmically across the walls (Le Roy 1995: 117). This pure geometrical approach creates a coherence between the interior and exterior shots. It is completely different to other laboratories usually shown in the cinema of the time. Many of these films, including *Metropolis* (dir. Fritz Lang, 1926) or *Frankenstein* (dir. James Whale, 1931), portray laboratories that are hidden, desolate, dark places full of electrical gadgets (Neumann 1999: 80–83). However, the laboratory of *L'Inhumaine* is a bright, well-lit environment that houses machines composed of simple geometric figures, which have incorporated dynamism by the lighting and physical movement of the forms, features that anticipate Op art and Kinetic art qualities. In this sense, as Donald Albrecht (2000: 47) points out, the film rather echoes the mechanical imagery used in other science fiction sources, including Frederick Kiesler's theater décor for Karel Capek's *W.U.R.* (*Werstand Universal Roborts*) of 1923. Léger opts, therefore, for the mechanical vocabulary typical of the Modern style, and the final assembly also contributes to the feeling of movement. The laboratory, visually constructed as an impossible space, is presented via staccato, montaged sequences, individual frames tinted red, among the latter of which are interspersed stills of pure colors characteristic of Léger's paintings. The frantic final scenes, accompanied by Darius Milhaud's percussion music are so radical (even narrative is sacrificed) that they give the film a whole a new plastic look. In 1924, Léger made a short film, *Ballet Mécanique*, where everyday objects and fragments were the real target. This experimental work closely resembles the final sequence of the *L'Inhumaine*'s laboratory, with a set of oppositions and a frenetic assembly between elements, which, at the time, dazzled even the famed Russian film director Sergei Eisenstein (Verdet 1970: 27).

Most people were not prepared to digest these sophisticated images that were the cinematic equivalent of Cubism. But not all reviews were negative. Adolf Loos, for example, wrote: "It's a stunning poem to modern technique…. The last images of *L'Inhumaine* surpass the imagination. On leaving the theater one has the impression of having witnessed the birth of a new art." And just before, he said: "Tristan's cry has become reality: 'I hear the light!…'" (Louis 1980: 154).

This demonstration of new trends in *L'Inhumaine* seems to have anticipated *The International Exposition of Modern Industrial and Decorative Arts* held in Paris in 1925, but despite its artistic boldness, the film was not selected to be screened at the great exhibition. However, in 1975, it was shown during the opening ceremony for the exposition's fiftieth anniversary. Thus, several years later, the audience itself seemed prepared to admire the visual richness of the film and *hear its light*.

## Mallet-Stevens's Villa Noailles, a cinematographic poetry

Characterized through a simple, unornamented architecture with clean lines and clear contrasts between light and shade, Modern architecture was presented by Mallet-Stevens as indispensable for contemporary cinema scenery. Reciprocally, *L'Inhumaine* would directly influence Mallet-Stevens's first major architectural projects (Figure 11.2). In 1924, while designing key sets for *L'Inhumaine*, he was commissioned by the Viscount Charles de Noailles to design a villa on the French Riviera, on the side of Hyères, in the shadow of the ruins of an ancient castle. Initially, he designed a compact, two-story building with a tower, which he then extended to compose a whole complex that spilled down the hill like a cascade of architectural fragments. He used walls, openings, and terraces to obtain unity between interior and exterior architecture. Following in the footsteps of Hoffmann's Stoclet Palace, and with the aim of creating a total work of art, Mallet-Stevens counted on the participation of various artists, including Piet Mondrian, Pierre Chareau, and Francis Jourdain for interior decoration (Briolle, Fuzibet and Monnier 1990: 35–85). The outdoor garden spaces designed by Gabriel Guevrekian were described by Darío Álvarez in his book *El Jardín de la arquitectura del siglo XX* (2007: 120–122) as the first Cubist garden design.

Not surprisingly, given Mallet-Stevens's close relationship with Modernist cinema, his client, the Viscount, a known patron of Modern art and lover of cinema, decided to take the Villa to the big screen. In 1928, he commissioned a short film from Man Ray, who had expressed his admiration for the Villa Noailles: "Severe and discreet, this building seems to wish to dissimulate the opulence concealed within (…) The *château's* cubic shape makes me think of a poem by Mallarmé, 'Un coup de dés jamais n'abolira le hazard'" (Louis 2005: 156). This poem would inspire the title and development of the film, *Les Mystères du Château du Dé*.

In the enigmatic and captivating poetry of Mallarmé, form takes precedence over intellectual meaning and logic. Similarly, Man Ray created for his film images that were based on the richness of the poetic imagination; he used different angles in each sequence,

Mallet-Stevens, Modern Design, and French Cinema

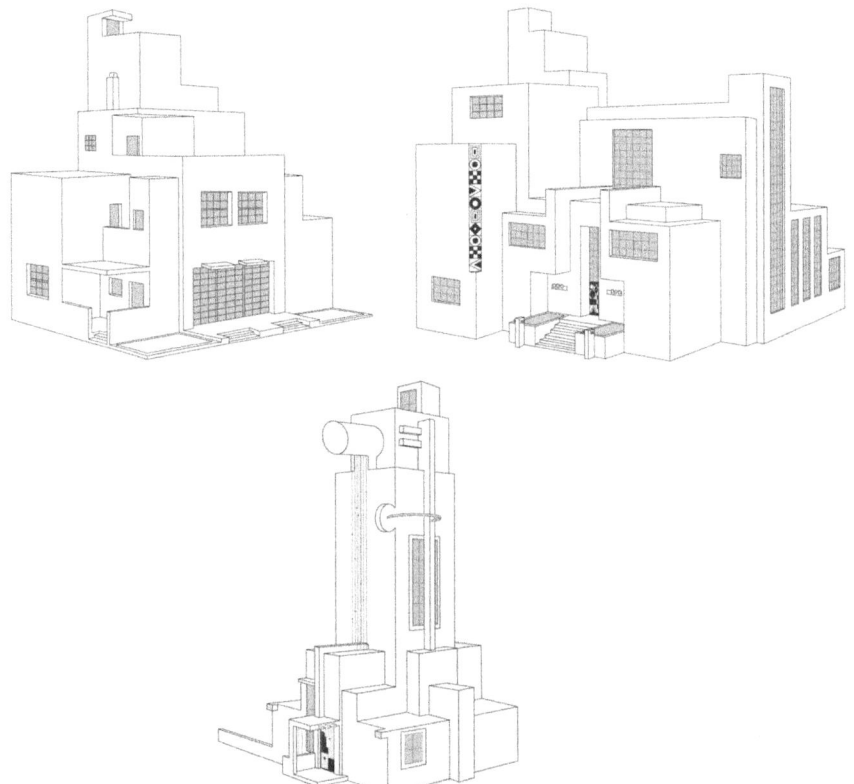

**Figure 11.2** Robert Mallet-Stevens, First project for Villa Noailles, 1924 compared to Claire Lescot's and Einar Noorsen's houses from Marcel L'Herbier's film *L'Inhumaine*, 1923, drawn by Nieves Fernández Villalobos.

mixing frames and inverting the camera. Mallet-Stevens's volumes shape abstract forms on the screen, transforming familiar spaces into something mysterious. Inanimate objects come to life and living things become automatons. As Odile Vaillant suggests (1997: 33), Le Corbusier's *"machine à habiter"* turns into a comfortable house whose volumes have a symbolic function.

In the film, viewers are introduced to the villa by some enigmatic intruders who roll the dice and begin to explore its confines: the entrance door, shown as a Neoplasticist painting composition similar to the one designed for the engineer's house in *L'Inhumaine*; Charles de Noaille's office, featuring Marcel Breuer chairs and Louis Barillet's skylight; the Viscount's painting collection; the terraced garden and the views through its holes; and Guevrekian's triangular garden with the stirring sculpture of Jacques Lipchitz titled *J'aime le movement qui déplace les forms …*. The camera delights in the indoor swimming pool, where actors entertain the audience with various diving and gymnastic movements, including a woman juggling underwater, suggesting that Man Ray filmed not only the building, the interior design and the Viscount's art collection but also a new way of life (Figure 11.3).

Designing the French Interior

**Figure 11.3** Man Ray, *Les Mystères du Château du Dé*, 1928: Exterior and interior views of Mallet-Stevens's Villa Noailles, 1924–1928, Produced by Le Vicomte de Noailles.

## Conclusion: The interaction between Modern architecture and cinema

Cinema sets helped architect Mallet-Stevens develop his own ideas about real-life architecture and interiors, and, as a result, the Villa Noailles itself looked like a film set.

Although the sophisticated cinema designs of Mallet-Stevens, Léger, and this group of great artists, architects, and designers had not excited the masses, other French films such as *Le Vertige* (Marcel L'Herbier, 1926), *Le P'tit Parigot* (René Le Somptier, 1926), *Le Diable au Coeur* (Marcel L'Herbier, 1928), *L'Argent* (Marcel L'Herbier, 1928), *Les nouveaux mesieurs* (Jacques Feyder, 1928), and *À nous la liberté* (René Clair, 1931) also incorporated a similar design iconography and continued to link the Modern movement to cinema. While daringly innovative, Modern film design would not achieve its great triumphs until the next decade. By then, the *Zeitgeist* would shift significantly: the Paris exhibition of 1925 would have generated a great deal of public interest in the Modern movement, and numerous publications confirmed the fact that the movement had been widely accepted. At the same time, the avant-garde architects began to have more real-life commissions, so Modern film sets were left to film design specialists, who followed in the footsteps of Mallet-Stevens and his circle. But what is significant is that Mallet-Stevens and other French pioneers demonstrated through cinema that Modern design had a great artistic potential both in front and behind film screens.

## References

Albrecht, D. (2000), *Designing Dreams: Modern Architecture in the Movies*, Santa Mónica: Hennesey + Ingalls.
Álvarez, D. (2007), *El Jardín de la arquitectura del siglo XX*. Barcelona: Reverté.
Briolle, C., Fuzibet A. and Monnier G. (1990), *La Villa Noailles: Rob Mallet-Stevens*, Marseille: Parenthèses.
Catelain, J. (1950), *Catelain présente Marcel L'Herbier*, Paris: E. Jacques Vautrain.
Deshoulières, D. and Jeanneau, H. (1980), "The Demands of Architecture," in D. Deshoulières and H. Jeanneau (eds), *Rob Mallet-Stevens, Architecte*, Bruxelles: Archives d'Architecture Moderne: 35–61.
Gorostiza, J. (2007), "Proyecciones y utopías de la vanguardia. La arquitectura moderna en el cine fantástico (1920–1950)," in VVAA (Rivera, D. dir.), *Paradigmas: el desarrollo de la modernidad arquitectónica visto a través de la historia del cine*, Madrid: La Fábrica, Fundación Telefónica: 11–37.
Le Roy, E. (1995), "Décoration et cinéma," in VVAA, *France, années 20 et 30. Le cinéma au rendez-vous des arts*, París: Bibliothèque nationale de France: 110–119.
Louis, M. (1980), "Mallet-Stevens and the Cinema, 1919–1929," in D. Deshoulieres and H. Jeanneau (eds), *Rob Mallet-Stevens, Architecte*, Bruxelles: Archives d'Architecture Moderne: 143–159.
Louis, M. (2005), "Mallet-Stevens and the Cinema, 1919–1929," in J. P. Lyonnet (ed), *Rob Mallet Stevens, Architecte*, Paris: Éditions Alternatives.
Mallet-Stevens, R. (1928), *Le Décor moderne au cinéma*, Paris: Charles Meunier.
Neumann, D. (ed) (1999), *Film Architecture: From Metropolis to Blade Runner*, Munich: Prestel.
Vaillant, O. (1995), "Rationalisme et Onirisme: Les architectes et le cinéma," in VVAA, *France, années 20 et 30. Le cinéma au rendez-vous des arts*, París: Bibliothèque nationale de France: 100–109.
Vaillant, O. (1997), "Robert Mallet-Stevens. Architecture, Cinema and Poetics," in F. Penz and M. Thomas (eds), *Cinema and Architecture*, London: British Film Institute: 28–33.
Verdet, A. (1970), *Fernand Léger*, Col. Grandes maestros del siglo XX, Barcelona: Nauta.
Wouters, L. (1990), "Cinema and Architecture," in J. F. Pinchon (ed), *Rob. Mallet Stevens: Architecture, Furniture, Interior Design*, Cambridge, MA: MIT Press: 91–107.

# PART III
# INTIMACY, LONGING, AND PERFORMANCE: THE CONSUMPTION AND DISPLAY OF THE CELEBRITY HOME

# CHAPTER 12
## STAGING DOMESTICITY IN *LA REVUE ILLUSTRÉE*'S PHOTO-INTERVIEWS: *BELLE ÉPOQUE* CELEBRITY HOMES IN THE PERIODICAL PRESS
Elizabeth Emery

René Baschet, director of the lavishly illustrated *Revue Illustrée*, announced in 1891 a photographic initiative allowing his magazine's readers to stroll virtually through the residences of *Belle Époque* celebrities. Consisting of five- to ten-page collaborations between reporters and photographers, the series came to be entitled "Une Heure chez" [An Hour at Home with…]. Over the next decade, Baschet's editorial team would print visual and textual details that opened the doors of some fifty private French homes and offices. This was a radically new idea, made possible by the advent of smokeless flash photography and new innovations in photo-mechanical reproduction. Photographers recorded visual details about modern homes, while reporters situated the photographs in time and space. The resulting photo-interviews, read by subscribers around the world, capture in print a decade of French interior decorating in a number of different styles, from the neo-Gothic and the rococo to classical and Oriental revival. These photo-interviews, published at the height of the nineteenth-century French vogue for collecting and interior decorating as forms of self-expression, were unique in their day and anticipated the modern media treatment of celebrity interiors in such television programs as *Lifestyles of the Rich and Famous*, *MTV Cribs*, and, most recently, HGTV's *Front Door*.

The "Une Heure chez" series presents the homes of writers Émile Zola, Alphonse Daudet, Alexandre Dumas fils, Maurice Maeterlinck, Paul Bourget, and Jules Verne, actresses Jane Hading and Cécile Bartet, musicians Jules Massenet and Augusta Holmès, the directors of l'Opéra Garnier, scientists Camille Flammarion and the Curies, and politician Jules Ferry, among many others.[1] Photographs of such homes were described by readers of the day as "relics of history" (Tissandier 1892: 170), yet the narratives created by these celebrities suggest a less straightforward documentary intent: many used their homes as theatrical sets to perform a private life commensurate with their public persona. Indeed, the fact that flash photography was first used in a theatrical context would not have been lost on contemporaries.[2]

In this essay, we will first evoke *La Revue Illustrée* and the contribution it made to an international appreciation of French domestic interiors, before examining the relationship between text and image in three photo-interviews—those of playwright Victorien Sardou, composer Jules Massenet, and actress Gabrielle Réjane—in order to show how reporters and interviewees chose to frame homes in the service of public relations. These two men and one woman provide complementary insights into journalistic reinforcement of the links between interior decorating and identity posited by decorating manuals such as Henri Havard's *L'Art dans la maison* (1884).

The *Revue Illustrée* was among the most important illustrated magazines of this time (along with *L'Illustration* and *Le Monde Illustré*) and placed, as its title suggests, great emphasis on visual culture (Watelet 1998 I: 256; 303–306). Like its competitors, the biweekly *Revue Illustrée* published literary works and musical compositions, travel narratives, celebrity portraits, recaps of recent plays and social happenings, and a fashion section. But the *Revue Illustrée* considered itself much more "artistic" and "eclectic" than the others, describing itself in its first number as largely unconcerned with current events (December 1885: iv).[3] The emphasis placed on documenting the current art scene was a hallmark of the magazine (each cover contained an original portrait of a leading artist, writer or musician), as was its focus on fashion and domesticity. One of its earliest and longest running essay series (1885–1894), for example, was Alexandre Sandier's *La Maison moderne*, each liberally illustrated chapter of which was dedicated to a specific room of the modern interior ("Le Boudoir," "Le Fumoir," "Le Cabinet de Toilette," "Une Chambre d'homme") and discussed strategies for designing and furnishing it.

The *Revue Illustrée* was read internationally from its inception because of its artistic interest, as indicated in an anonymously authored review in the *Nation*, which singled out Sandier's series (1886 42/1077: 150). It was also identified as a valuable source of information about French music, drama, and interior decoration. The editorial board of the *Revue Illustrée* prided itself on this international reputation and announced, in 1891, a revised strategy to keep up with new technologies and new developments in celebrity culture: a photographed "chronicle" showing famous actresses, theatrical sets, and documenting celebrity life through interviews.[4] The magazine had engaged a photographer to capture "instant" photographs (*instantanés*), thus named because of their near-instant exposure time (November 1, 1891: n. p.). A subsequent letter from the editor was published in the 15 January issue, noting that Henri Mairet would be in charge of this section. Mairet had invented a device that allowed for smokeless indoor photography (earlier flash photography generated a great deal of ash, thus making it impractical for home use) and he would go on to contribute a number of photo-interviews to the *Revue Illustrée* under the pseudonym "Le Photographe."[5]

This new initiative likely stemmed from a desire to capitalize on the popularity of *Nos Contemporains chez eux*, a series of what would go on to be more than 400 photographs of celebrities at home produced by Dornac (Paul Cardon) beginning in 1889. They were sold in photography stores or engraved and printed in *Le Monde Illustré* and licensed to other illustrated periodicals around the world.[6] Dornac used only natural light, thus limiting his photographs to rooms with windows (generally studies and offices) on sunny days; they necessitated a thirty-second pose time (itself an advantage over the weeks of sitting for portrait painting). Mairet's smokeless flash was much more convenient and less invasive than other forms of flash photography: it allowed for any room to be photographed at any time and without a mess, thus inviting a new kind of pairing with reporters, who travelled to private homes to interview celebrities. While Dornac's photographs were devoid of context, the *Revue Illustrée*'s photographs were conceived from the outset as fully embedded within a new kind of multimedia collaboration.

The photo-interviews produced for the *Revue Illustrée* generally contain five to ten pages and nearly as many photographs, which, instead of showing a celebrity in a single room, as had most of Dornac's photographs, lead the reader visually from one room to the next. Alongside the images, the journalist provides a running commentary situating the house or apartment within a neighborhood. The attention given to markers of time and space, coupled with the photographs themselves, creates a remarkable sense of immediacy. The use of direct discourse also reproduces some of the "banter" between reporter and celebrity. The text thus offers temporal and social cues with which to read the photographs, while the photographs visually confirm the authenticity of what is said in the narrative. Together, text and image produce a rich historical and sociological contextualization rare in either stand-alone photographs or interviews.[7]

The 1892 ten-page interview dedicated to the seventeenth-century castle of playwright Victorien Sardou was the third in the series. It contains eight photographs (two full-page) of his opulent residence in Marly, not far from Paris.[8] There are images of the castle's exterior—its façade, its backyard with woods and "lawn-tennis," its elaborate metal grille opening onto a park, Sardou in the park wearing slippers and having a glass of wine—as well as interior pictures—the *grand salon* and corner of the dining room seen in Figure 12.1, an antechamber, and his study. Sardou appears in most of the images thus creating a particularly homey atmosphere beginning with the initial engraving of him wearing slippers at a table on the terrace. Indeed, to see "great men in their slippers" had been a major preoccupation of

**Figure 12.1** Photographer unknown (possibly Henri Mairet), from "Une Heure chez Victorien Sardou" (Le Grand salon), in *La Revue Illustrée* (June 15, 1892).

the late nineteenth-century French press. Eighteenth- and early nineteenth-century students of "great men" had preserved a discrete distance, while the brash *fin-de-siècle* reporter sought to penetrate into the private home in order to "read" it as a mirror of the "real" man behind the public persona (Emery 2012: 48–55).

Sardou was eager to show his home, slippers and all, and he welcomed interviewer Eugène Tardieu, explaining that the castle was entirely his "own work" (*mon oeuvre*). He had arrived in 1863 by chance and completed all the renovations to the 50,000-square meter property himself, clearing scrub, discovering an orchard from the time of Louis XIV, and decorating the interior, spending his entire fortune on the castle and the collection it housed (June 15, 1892: 209–210). Sardou's enthusiasm compels Tardieu to have him photographed in these rooms and the text adds another layer to the black and white images by referring to colors and by identifying the disposition of the rooms.

The photographs speak volumes about Sardou's decorating materials and practices, yet Tardieu directs their interpretation, pulling the reader toward specific elements that emphasize the playwright's interest in history, such as the clock on the mantel of the *grand salon*, which was from Fontainebleau and which once belonged to Louis XVI (211). Tardieu also does not hesitate to criticize certain decorative choices. He notes, for example, that the walls of the *grand salon* are covered by well-preserved eighteenth-century Beauvais tapestries but questions the cutting of these "precious fabrics" just to mask the moldings and frames: "theatrical reminiscence!" (210).

The emphasis on historical and theatrical recreation is reinforced as they visit Sardou's study, lined with rare framed engravings and paintings and packed with valuable papers and letters from the Revolutionary period, which he has used to write his plays (notably the recently opened *Thermidor*). He has also constituted an archive retracing the castle's history (215–216). Sardou regales Tardieu with stories about the historical figures that have frequented the castle and they engage in a debate about contemporary theater and particularly about the remuneration that has made this restoration possible (Sardou was one of the best-paid and internationally acclaimed playwrights of his day). Tardieu questions him on the tremendous expenses he has incurred and Sardou answers in terms of aesthetics: "Marly is better than a museum: it is a rare item in the historical museum of France and its character must be preserved" (216).

While the photographs seem to present an unambiguous scientific recording of the interior and its contents, the stories told by Sardou and repeated by Tardieu reveal how the depiction of such an interior could be staged for the public. While they may have talked about many things during the visit, Tardieu, like any modern journalist, has organized them according to an interesting "hook," in this case, elements of the conversation most associated with Sardou's public identity as the author of historical dramas. Tardieu does not specify whether this is Sardou's primary residence or rather a "museum," as the playwright has described it, nor do they visit any "private" rooms (bedrooms, for example). Instead, Tardieu follows Sardou's lead in presenting the castle as a direct reflection of his work; either his passion for theatrical décor ("theatrical reminiscence!") or his fondness for the past (the motivation for his historical plays). The emphasis Tardieu places on what Pierre Bourdieu called "cultural capital" reinforces Sardou's identity as an artist: he does not write simply to amass a fortune; his writing—like his collecting—stems from a deep interest in the French national patrimony to which he has dedicated his life (and income). Indeed, Tardieu ends the interview by presenting Marly as a symbol, a visible statement of the playwright's social status.

This tendency to reinforce the public persona through a reading of the home is the case for many of the theatrical writers and directors featured in the "Une Heure chez" series, like the director of the Opéra Garnier, Pedro Gailhard, whose extravagant "Mauresque" house in Paris is rationalized in terms of an artist's enhanced aesthetic sensitivity (June–December 1893: 121–128). Most of the other photo-interviews follow a similar pattern: an ostensibly open-door visit leads to a reinforcement of professional persona, the luxurious home decoration a stand-in for bourgeois success, no matter the field. This is the case for Émile Zola, who offered a similar explanation for his own luxurious (and eclectic) home, filled with colors, textures, and patterns so dizzying that interviewer Jules Huret was overwhelmed. "When a man becomes successful," Zola quipped, "he always reproduces the luxury he dreamed of in his youth" (January–June 1892: 349).

The discussion and display of what Thorstein Veblen (1899) would call "conspicuous consumption" only four years later (1888) is as much a hallmark of the *Revue Illustrée*'s photo-interviews as it is of modern television productions such as *Lifestyles of the Rich and Famous* or *MTV Cribs*: the public is fascinated by rags to riches stories and especially by how those who have become wealthy have chosen to display their wealth. This accounts for the preponderance of *nouveau riche* figures in this series. Few aristocrats engage with journalists and impoverished poets without fixed homes (such as Paul Verlaine) do not make the cut. *La Revue Illustrée* thus reinforced the contemporary belief—a commonplace in decorating manuals—that the home was a mirror of the person.

Charles Fromentin's 1893 interview with composer Jules Massenet, known for his operas *Thaïs*, *Manon*, and *Werther* reveals that even non-theatrical celebrities staged the presentation of their homes for the public. Unlike Sardou, Massenet plays down his celebrity, assuring readers that he is a boring homebody (January–June 1893: 117–124). Fromentin sets up the visit to this fourth-floor apartment in a quiet neighborhood on the rue du Général-Foy as an impromptu event in which he supposedly surprises the maid who is busy dusting when he arrives. Eager to interpret Massenet through his surroundings, he seizes on several eccentricities in his decor that suggest that the composer is not as sedate as he claims. Masssenet then reorients the conversation to rationalize even these seemingly odd elements.

This eight-page interview contains five images (two of them are full-page), not all of which were taken in Massenet's home, and the opening photograph of Massenet is credited to the photographer Otto. The visit begins in the luxurious dining room (Figure 12.2; at left), its walls covered with remarkable Gobelin tapestries, cupboards full of brass, silver, fine china, crystal, and a "majestic" grandfather clock. This room opens up to the study (visible in Figure 12.2, through the dining room toward the right), with a work table and bookshelves brimming with literary works, among them Massenet's favorites: Beaumarchais and Jean-Jacques Rousseau. A glass-fronted bookcase contains his own publications, classified in alphabetical order and maintained lovingly by his daughter.

These details confirm his comfortable bourgeois lifestyle, but Fromentin uses this normalcy to reveal an eccentric fact about Massenet: there is no piano in his study and he does not use a piano to compose. This leads to an involved discussion of his composing techniques, which he does entirely in his head, keeping the entire score in his brain until it is finished (a process that sometimes takes two years). He transcribes it ("it sings itself to him") only when finished. In Massenet's telling, this is perfectly normal. During this discussion Fromentin visits Madame Massenet's perfumed Louis XV bedroom (of which there is no

**Figure 12.2** Photographer unknown (possibly Henri Mairet), Two-page spread from "Une Heure chez Massenet" ("Le Cabinet de travail" and "La Salle à manger"), an article published in the periodical *La Revue Illustrée* (January–June 1893).

picture) and the Louis XVI salon full of flower arrangements and family portraits (a full-page photograph). Fromentin's conclusion is that although Massenet has reached the pinnacle of success, he remains the same simple, kind bourgeois family man he has always been, an identity reflected in the comfortable opulence of his apartment.

"Scoops" such as Massenet's missing piano are part of the fun of the "Une Heure chez" series where readers discovered that Senator Jules Ferry was not just a busy politician but also an excellent painter; science fiction writer Jules Verne lives a simple life with his wife in Amiens, eating like a vegetarian while regaling his guests with more substantial fare; and Alexandre Dumas fils spends most of his time collecting the art objects that fill the rooms of his home and entertaining his grandson. While for some celebrities (Zola, Ferry, Verne) this may have meant making a fairly stodgy public image a bit more lively, for others more in the public eye, like Massenet or famous actresses, it meant playing up humdrum family life.

C. de Néronde's 1894 interview of comedian Gabrielle Réjane hinges precisely on this public-private divide (June–December 1894: 56–61). She has given more than 233 straight performances (every night and every Sunday and holiday matinee for nearly eight months straight) of Sardou's play, *Madame Sans-Gêne*, in which a frank-speaking laundress settles scores with Napoleon Bonaparte. Néronde has come to ask about her vacation plans. His "hook," of course, is fatigue, which dominates his narrative: Réjane is not awake when he arrives, he features photographs of her looking exhausted as well as a photograph of her resting in her dressing room, and this despite her specific request that he not say she is tired of playing a role she loves.

This six-page article contains seven images, including one full-page reproduction of a Reutlinger portrait of her as Madame Sans-Gêne. Of those taken in her "vast" apartment on the rue d'Antin just off the Champs-Elysées three of them include her husband, two young children, and domestics (a maid, a governess, and a nurse), and one is her own photograph of their Normandy vacation home, for which her husband, Paul Porel (perhaps foreshadowing their separation in 1905), insists she will have no time because he has arranged for her to take the play on a European tour. Although the article is ostensibly devoted to family time, it doubles back unremittingly to Réjane's professional life by mixing descriptions and photographs of home and theater.

In Figure 12.3, we see a two-page spread juxtaposing home (at left) and work (at right). At home Néronde discovers an Empire style so authentic that he remarks that Madame Sans-Gêne would feel right at home (58). He proposes no details other than to note that Réjane lives here quite "simply" with her husband and two children. Because it is lunchtime, they sit down to eat (Mairet photographs the scene, reproduced in the half-page engraving that opens the article), and Réjane promises to catch up with the reporter during intermission that night at the Vaudeville Theater.

She is true to her word and they discuss her performance before she returns to the stage. Mairet photographs her in her dressing room (reproduced via engraving in Figure 12.3 at

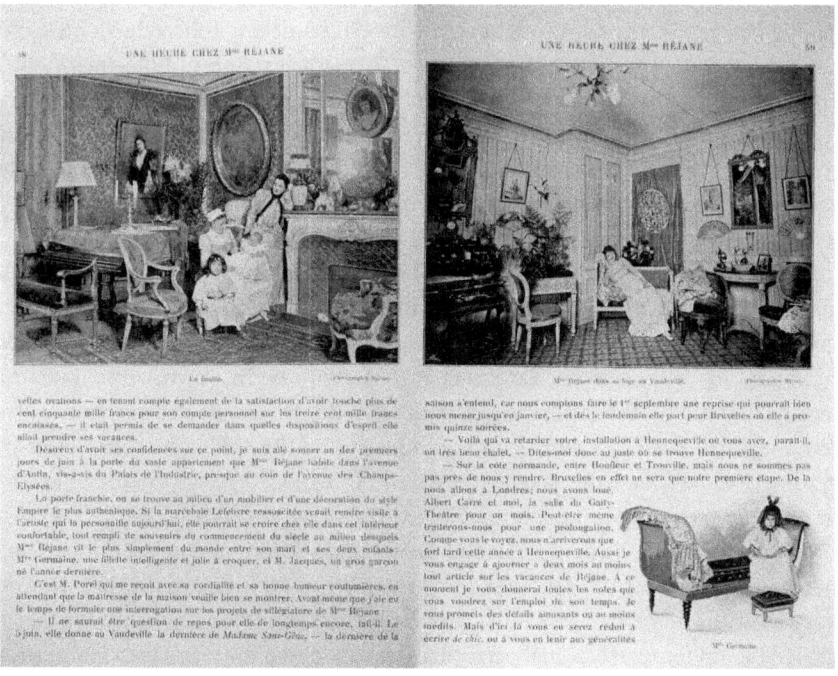

**Figure 12.3** Henri Mairet, Two-page spread from "Une Heure chez Mme Réjane" ("En famille" and "Mme Réjane dans sa loge au Vaudeville"), an article published in the periodical *La Revue Illustrée* (June–December 1894).

right) and Néronde describes colors and shapes: the tasteful "pure Louis XVI" room with its light blue and white striped walls, lattice-work mirrors covering the windows, the green and golden desk, the wicker bed with its half dozen cushions of various shapes, and the fluted ottoman. Not in the picture frame is the *cabinet de toilette* where she changes when there are too many people in her dressing room (59). Thus switching back and forth from work to home life and juxtaposing the two visually through the photographs, Néronde subordinates his visit of both apartment and dressing room to Réjane's actress persona: he may show her family, but she is above all a successful actress who has charmed some 300,000 spectators through her performances, which have netted her 150,000 francs.

Such commentary reveals the series' primary interest today: the interaction between text and image. The dialogue makes the "Une Heure chez" series much more interesting than other illustrated articles about French interiors (government offices, schools, laboratories), which the magazine occasionally covered, but with little information about when and exactly where the photographs were taken. The "Rois chez eux" (Kings at Home) series for the *Figaro Illustré* begun in 1890 is similarly devoid of contextualized information about its photographs. In *La Revue Illustrée*, however, readers find out how Sardou discovered his castle, why Zola needed so much color in his home, why Massenet has no piano, or how Réjane is not like her character.

The interaction between text and image in the *Revue Illustrée*'s photo-interviews thus provides a truly remarkable window into decorating fashions of the affluent bourgeois Parisians of the 1890s. We see trends running the gamut from medieval (Jules Lemaître and Pierre Loti), classical revival (Paul Bourget), and seventeenth- and eighteenth-century (Sardou, Massenet) to Empire (Réjane) and "Oriental" (Pierre Loti, Pedro Gailhard, and Robert de Montesquiou). We also learn why these celebrities chose these styles. Nonetheless, these photo-interviews cannot be considered transparent historical documents. The direct reproduction of photographs in the magazine, for example, depended on perfect contrast, which means that many were copied by engravers. In Figure 12.3, for example, one sees efforts made in the caption to reflect that the engravings signed at bottom left of each image were based on photographs taken by Henri Mairet. Other photographs have been inserted from other contexts, sometimes with a photo credit and sometimes without. Such editorial decisions raise a host of questions related to provenance and alteration of photos or engravings.

Moreover, despite what celebrities say, we do not always know exactly who decorated the homes and for what reasons. Sardou claims Marly to be his "own work," but what does this mean? Did he have the vision and direct the work? Or did he cut out sconces from the eighteenth-century tapestries and sew them himself? By the 1890s, an entire Paris industry (which advertised heavily in the pages of the *Revue Illustrée*) had grown up to support the home decorating trend, working with celebrities, just as stylists do today (Auslander 1998). Although Massenet loves his home, he does not claim to have decorated it and neither does Réjane. Did they own their apartments? Or rent them furnished? Did Réjane design the Empire style of her apartment? Or was this a choice made by her husband as a nod to *Madame Sans-Gêne*, much as he signed her up for international performances to prolong the play's financial success? Was Réjane's dressing room on loan from the theater? Or did she have a hand in its decoration? If not, can we really say these interiors are a reflection of her taste or personality?

We should thus use caution in considering as "relics of history" the elaborate photo-interviews Baschet published to entertain a public fascinated by celebrities and interior decoration. In the *Belle Époque*, fame was already dependent on the press. Staging photo-interviews of private homes satisfied the public's hunger for information about celebrity private life and contemporary domestic interiors, all while keeping real home life safe from prying eyes. Given the popular belief that the home reflected the person, there was nothing easier than designing the public spaces of one's home as one wished to be interpreted. Accordingly, Sardou's drapery becomes "theatrical" and Réjane's orderly apartment and well-dressed children a reflection of her efficiency and reliability as an actress who has not missed a show. These photo-interviews enabled celebrities to perform domesticity by cleaning, arranging furniture and paintings, dressing, and orchestrating activities for the reporter. Is it a coincidence that Massenet's maid has not quite finished dusting when Fromentin arrives? Or rather, is this an affectation of realism like that reproduced in twentieth- and twenty-first-century television series where the guests pretend to open their doors in surprise to interviewers without commenting on the large (invisible to viewers) film crews surrounding them? Nineteenth-century celebrities "staged domesticity" in different ways to achieve different goals, much as celebrities today engage stylists to decorate homes they present as their own.

The *Revue Illustrée*'s photo-interviews document the popular bourgeois styles of the time, but perhaps even more importantly they reveal the extent to which the illustrated press participated in promoting interior decoration as an expression of identity. As well-known figures read one another's interviews and studied photographs of one another's homes they thought about how to place themselves along this continuum of conspicuous consumption. Playwright Ludovic Halévy, for example, begins the tour of his home by warning interviewer Eugène Tardieu not to expect the sumptuous furnishings or clever wit of Émile Zola (January–June 1892: 77–84).

Such comments suggest that *La Revue Illustrée* played an integral role in promoting home decoration as an act of self-expression. Then as now, a public display of domesticity was a way of establishing social relevance and of competing with one's peers. And by publishing photographs and commentary about private homes, Baschet and his reporters made decorating practices accessible not just to friends and colleagues but to readers all over the world, thus allowing viewers to emulate their favorite celebrities. Globalization is often cast as an Internet phenomenon, but the mass illustrated press of the late nineteenth century allowed for an international domestic stage the likes of which had never before been seen.

## Acknowledgments

Research for this project was made possible by a grant from the National Endowment for the Humanities.

## Notes

1. A selection of these photo-interviews will be published in France by the Editions Parigramme in 2015.
2. Paul Boyer, whose photographs make up the bulk of those reproduced in the *Revue Illustrée* until 1891, won a prize at the 1889 World's Fair for his magnesium flash. My use of the terms

"performance" and "posturing" have been inspired by L. Braudy's *Frenzy of Renown* (1986). The concept of writers' "posturing" has been theorized more recently by J. Meizoz (2007).

3. Watelet notes that the magazine employed a remarkable number of artists and illustrators (88), writers (329) and photographers (20) (1988: 303).
4. Interviews may be commonplace in today's world, but when the genre arrived from the United States in the 1870s it completely transformed the French public's relationship to celebrities. See Emery (2012).
5. This device was advertised for sale in numerous issues of the *Revue Illustrée*.
6. They appeared in all illustrated French periodicals as well as a number of British and American ones and were subsequently used to illustrate books. Marie Mallard (1999) provides a list of the Dornac photographs she located in many French magazines (the list is not comprehensive). See Emery (2012: 67–107; 130–150) for an analysis of the photographs and their social context. For reproductions of many of these photographs see the catalogs produced by Piasa for auctions on May 16, 2008, June 29, 2011, and May 24, 2013.
7. Unless photographers keep meticulous records it is difficult to retroactively determine subjects and shooting dates. Even when records are kept (as in the case of Dornac photographs sold at auction in 2008), they are often incorrect, at odds with the date of the legal deposit, for example.
8. The article labels a photograph "Le Château de Marly" and Sardou does nothing to dispel the illusion (he continually refers to his castle as "Marly"), but this is not Louis XIV's castle (torn down after the Revolution) but the Château du Verduron, home of Louis XIV's head valet.

## References

Auslander, L. (1998), *Taste and Power: Furnishing Modern France*, Berkeley: University of California Press.
Braudy, L. (1986), *The Frenzy of Renown*, New York: Vintage.
Emery, E. (2012), *Photojournalism and the Origins of the French Writer House Museum (1881–1914)*, Aldershot: Ashgate.
Havard, H. (1884), *L'Art dans la maison. La Grammaire de l'ameublement*, 2 vols. Paris: E. Rouveyre et G. Blond.
*La Revue Illustrée* (1885–1912), Paris: Librairie Baschet.
Mallard, M. (1999), *Etude de la série de Dornac: Nos contemporain chez eux, 1887–1917*, Unpublished MA thesis, Université Paris IV.
Meizoz, J. (2007), *Postures littéraires. Mises en scène modernes de l'auteur*, Geneva: Slatkine.
*The Nation* (1886), New York: The Evening Post Publishing Company.
Tissandier, G. (1892), "Nos Savants chez eux: M. Pasteur," *La Nature* 168–170.
Veblen, T. (1899), *The Theory of the Leisure Class*, New York: Macmillan.
Watelet, J. (1998), *La Presse Illustrée en France. 1814–1914*. 2 vols. Ph.D. thesis, Université Panthéon-Assas. Paris II.

# CHAPTER 13
# HÔTEL BARONNE SALOMON DE ROTHSCHILD
# 1872–1878: THE IMPRINT OF A LEGACY
*Linda D. Stevenson and Susan Tate*

One might ask why the Hôtel Baronne Salomon de Rothschild had been chosen for the opening feature in the series "L'Habitation Moderne" for the magazine *Revue des arts décoratifs* (1891–1892). Indeed, this was a remarkable mansion, an *hôtel particulier* of the celebrated Rothschild banking empire, which featured spectacular collections. According to the distinguished editor Victor Champier (1851–1929), the selection was of deeper significance as it was inspired by a contribution to a public museum which presented views of a private property for public dissemination. An album of documentary photographs of her significant mansion and collections had been donated to the Musée Carnavalet by the prominent Baroness, Madame la baronne Salomon de Rothschild. In 1891, the publications *Le Figaro* and *Le Rappel* recognized her recent donation of an album of thirty-five "vues photographiques représentant l'hôtel qu'elle habite, 11, rue Berryer Balzac" (*Le Figaro* 1891: 3) (Figure 13.1).

**Figure 13.1** A. Cary, *Hôtel Beaujon: Façade sur le jardin*, photograph, before 1891, © Bibliothèque historique de la Ville de Paris.

## Designing the French Interior

Madame la baronne Salomon de Rothschild (1843–1922) was born Adèle Hannah Charlotte de Rothschild into the Naples branch of the Rothschild dynasty. She married Monsieur le baron Salomon-James de Rothschild (1835–1864) of the Paris branch of the family. In this chapter, the English language translation "the Baroness" will refer to Mme la baronne Salomon de Rothschild.

At the forefront of media dissemination of modern domestic interiors, the contribution by the Baroness of the album of photographic images and their subsequent publication in the *Revue des arts décoratifs* would lift the curtain for a large audience to view, and perhaps to emulate, the lifestyle of a prominent member of Parisian society. Champier extolled her legacy to this public archive and her willingness to allow publication of her mansion and collections. He cited this as an example for other patrons of the arts who more typically shielded their acquisitions in cloaks of privacy (Champier 1891–1892: 65). From the perspective of the Baroness, the publication would recognize the collections of her late husband, the Baron Salomon-James de Rothschild, very likely in fulfillment of her efforts to honor his memory after his early death at age twenty-nine. As a Rothschild descendant in her own right, she could view the Champier media publication as a jewel in the Rothschild crown as sovereigns in Parisian society and the arts.

The holistic design of the site, architecture, décor, and display of collections drew on the widely recognized principles set forth in César Daly's work, *L'Architecture privée au dix-neuvième siècle sous Napoléon III*, published in 1864, to create *l'habitation moderne*. Through the photographic donation and subsequent publications, the mansion and collections of the Baroness would inspire contemporary society and document for future generations the holistic concept of the mansion and collections.

## The media podium

As the Hôtel Baronne Salomon de Rothschild took shape, Paris was emerging from the devastation of the Franco-Prussian War, the short-lived Paris Commune government, and Haussmann's systematic demolition and rebuilding of the city over the previous two decades. Emblematic of the time, the Paris Opéra was inaugurated in January 1875 after a lengthy construction period during these troubled times. The Opéra's spectacular grand staircase set the stage for a society entranced by seeing and being seen. Alongside the contrasts of wealth and poverty, social and political unrest, a new horizon was emerging in the arts, sciences and technology.

As the century progressed, advancing technology spread to the merging media of photography and publication. Early photographic and daguerreotype developments in the 1820s and 1830s led to image reproduction through lithographs and woodcut engraving. Photographic portraits of family members by such celebrated photographers as Nadar became enviable features for domestic interiors. Conversely, the art establishment rained criticism on the demonic photograph and on photographic representations of works of art (Champier 1891–1892: 66; Vidal 1891: 9–10). By the time of the *Exposition Universelle Internationale de 1889* the processes of photography merited an extensive article by Jerome Léon Vidal in *La Photographie á l'Exposition de 1889* (1891: 54), who lauded in particular the process of *photocollographie* or collotype, which employed a coated plate to print high quality copies.

Continued advances in the halftone printing process, patented in 1881, enabled photographs to be screened into dots and printed alongside type for a large number of high quality copies. During the 1890s, the fields of photography and publication joined forces to meet the growing demand and create a new face of publication for mass audiences.

Published in Paris from 1880 to 1902, the *Revue des arts décoratifs*, the official publication of the *Union Centrale des Beaux-Arts Appliqués à l'Industrie*, prevailed as an authoritative review on the arts and a forum for debates on the state of the decorative and the applied arts. Reflecting the booming transatlantic interests in architecture and décor, an abbreviated version of the Champier article from the *Revue* was published in English in the Chicago-based publication *The Decorator and Furnisher* as "The Hotel of Madame Salomon De Rothschild, Paris" (Champier 1893).

The editor of the *Revue des arts décoratifs*, Victor Champier, was a renowned historian and art critic who also wrote for *Le Moniteur* from 1879 to 1887. His passion for the decorative arts and the role of industry enabled him to become secretary for the *Société des Musées des Arts* and one of the founders of the *Union Centrale des Arts Décoratifs* and the school of industrial arts at Roubaix, France. Among his publications was a limited edition art book with extensive photogravure illustrations on the subject of the history and collections of the Palais Royale (Champier and Sandoz 1900). Throughout his writings, Champier grappled with the theme of creating an appropriately modern aesthetic sensibility. The period became a moment of convergence of developments in photographic methods and publication. It was in this setting of social and technological change that the Baroness determined to build a mansion as a stage for her late husband's collections and as a modern expression of the Rothschild style of living.

## A significant site for a modern mansion

For the mansion of the Baroness, a site was selected on rue Berryer, on which an existing house would be demolished. Adding to the drama, the house had belonged to noted novelist Honoré de Balzac. To justify this, the magazine *International* suggested that "the real story" was not that the Baroness had wanted to enlarge her house or expand her garden but rather that the former pavilion of the Folie Beaujon that Balzac had renovated for his house with Mme Hanska was in fact dilapidated and falling into the street (White 1898: 44). To respect Balzac's legacy and recognize the site's heritage, the Baroness erected a "shrine" at the corner of the estate, a small structure that recalled classical tempietto forms, with a circular plan covered by a dome. The Vestibule door came from the bedroom of Balzac's residence and featured painted arabesque forms (DRAC Report 2004). This monument to Balzac was congruent with the persona of the Baroness as a patron of the arts, French literary heritage, and the *patrimoine*. Her homage to Balzac may be further discerned by her contribution of two door panels from the Balzac house which accompanied the album of photographs donated to the Musée Carnavalet (White 1898: 53).

In response to the site constraints, the composition of the spatial sequence of the mansion was particularly inventive. The raised garden terrace above street level was a significant feature of a site that demanded a different design response for each façade of the *hôtel*. The garden side of the building was one level above the entrance court façade, so that the entrance Vestibule lead to sweeping double stairs rising to the upper level principal rooms. Thus, the *grand étage*, with its entertainment rooms flanked by private suites, opened directly onto the garden.

### Designing the mansion

The challenges of the site, the complexities of the collections to be integrated in the interior and the significance of the Rothschild heritage required particular expertise in architectural response. For this, the Baroness selected the architect Léon Ohnet.

The younger generation of Rothschilds (sons of James-Meyer) often used the same architects for their residences and their commercial and industrial projects. Architect Léon Ohnet (1813–1874) established a relationship with the Baron James de Rothschild when collaborating with Lejeune for the *Chemin de Fer du Nord* during the 1850s (Bowie 1987: 105–112). Ohnet had previously worked on residential projects for James de Rothschild, father-in law of the Baroness, and her brother-in-law, Alphonse, in renovating and expanding the Hôtel de Talleyrand at the Place de la Concorde to suit a Second Empire lifestyle (Stevenson 2011: 112–113). Despite Ohnet's death at the beginning of the construction phase, the completed edifice is remarkably faithful to the intent of his design, largely due to Ohnet's student, Justin Ponsard, who continued with the project.

The contribution of the Baroness to the Musée Carnavalet included a collection of thirty-five photographs of the mansion and its interior. The text from the front panel of the album of photographs affirmed the intent of the Baroness to follow Ohnet's plans. Champier himself would later provide an assessment of Ponsard, which suggested that, "as modest as he is full of talent, M. Ponsard knew, while taking inspiration from the ideas and customs of the owner, how to make a remarkable work having a distinctive and sober character in its elegance" (Champier 1891–1892: 72). Construction was completed in 1878.

During the four-year design and construction phase, Ponsard worked in close collaboration with the *décorateur* Henri-Antoine-Léopold de Moulignon (1821–1897). In the *Dictionnaire… des arts et métiers* (1773), Abbé Jaubert described the *décorateur* as one who knows how to use the talent of each artist to best advantage and how to arrange the most elaborate pieces of furniture in an interior. "To excel in this art, which has been born before our eyes," according to Jaubert, "it is necessary to have a good eye, to have a good knowledge of design, and to create an ensemble that will give a pleasing impression" (Verlet 1991: 22).

Moulignon's interior décor for the mansion incorporated classical themes, often with gilded backgrounds. His recurring motifs of birds, flowers, laurel branches set against a blue sky background reflected a pastoral theme which reinforced the period's prevailing interest in nature brought into the interior. Moulignon understood the aspiration of the Baroness to present the décor, furnishings, and art collections to best advantage, and his skill in creating a harmonious interior experience was acknowledged by Champier who praised his ability to create harmony between the furnishings and the choice of colors to a degree rarely seen (Champier 1891–1892: 72).

Charged with creating the entire *décor*, ornamentation, decorative paintings, and selection of the fabrics, Moulignon also administered the interior architectural works, soliciting the bids from the artisans and overseeing their work. Many of the contractors and artisans employed on the project had previously worked on other Rothschild commissions. These companies included Pruchon Martel et Laîné (masonry), Hussent (mirrors), Balastet (carpentry), Haussen (fabrics and upholstery), Dasson (bronze), Gagey (finish carpentry and paneling), Feist (painting), and Lefèbvre et V. Fontaine (sculpture) (Prévost-Marcilhacy 1994: 367). All of these artisans contributed to the holistic design of the site, architecture, décor, and display of collections, which drew on the widely recognized principles set forth by César Daly to create *l'habitation moderne*. Through photographs and descriptions in subsequent publications, the mansion of the Baroness would inspire contemporary society and inform future generations.

## Interior décor and distribution

Since the eighteenth century, the interior of a building was defined by its *distribution*. This term referred to the relationship of interior spaces along with the intent of the *décor* to achieve "an effect of harmony, as well as comfort and grandeur…the choice of appropriate wall-decoration and an assessment of the principal pieces of furniture required" (Verlet 1967: 57).

In 1864, the influential architectural critic and architect César Daly recognized the heritage of the *hôtel particulier* of the *ancien régime* but stated that "the grand, noble and formal *distribution* and function of spaces of the past do not lend themselves readily to the demands and needs of the new style of modern living" (1864: 14). In the case of private architecture, the needs of the domestic life became the driving force in the organization of the plan while robing these more modern conceptions of space in the "clothing" of a rich variety of historical references (Stevenson 2011: 63). This metaphor was used by Daly to describe the role of the modern residence. In his three-volume work, *L'Architecture privée au dix-neuvième siècle sous Napoléon III. Nouvelles maisons de Paris et des environs*, Daly described the modern roles of the *hôtel's* principal spaces and provided a systematic catalog of the characteristics for a new urban mansion. These volumes, which served as a guide to incorporating modern patterns of living into the *hôtel particulier* while reflecting the goals and lifestyles of the client, were commonly available among architects of the period.

Describing the spaces needed for the modern mansion, Daly held that the Vestibule may be monumentally scaled, but it must not create conditions that "cause a chill in the elegant and delicate woman who must walk across this space, or who wishes to stop a moment upon leaving the warm and scented atmosphere of a party" (Daly 1864: 14). Regarding the salon, Daly noted that it was not enough that the space possessed an ornate décor and be richly furnished; the space must also be both warm and well-ventilated. In order to incorporate collections and works of art in the mansion, Daly cited other considerations alongside life style and functions of the *hôtel*. He suggested that "when the client loves the arts, if he owns statues, paintings, the architect should create special features in the gallery space, so that these works are shown in conditions that are especially favorable to display and to lighting" (Daly 1864: 14–16). The *distribution* of the Hôtel Baronne Salomon de Rothschild reflected both the guidelines established in Daly's work and characteristics of earlier Rothschild residences.

Designing the French Interior

## The spaces portrayed by Champier

While Champier describes the mansion façade as *pur style Louis XVI*, it is in the interior *distribution* that the concepts of "*l'habitation moderne*" emerge. Framed by the developing technologies of modern iron and glass structures and enrobed with rich collections and décor, the mansion affords a modern commodious living environment for the owner. The spectacle announced by the entry Vestibule is enhanced along the carefully orchestrated sequence of spaces through the display of collections from past and sometimes exotic sources, all with high quality and good taste or, in the words of Champier, "*de bon aloi*" (1892: 75).

Setting precedent in the Rothschild realm, the scenographic expression of the love of drama and spectacle integral to the *goût Rothschild* and to the era had emerged in 1862 with the inauguration of the Hall at the Château de Ferrières. Designed by the British architect Joseph Paxton in 1859 for Baron James de Rothschild, Ferrières was to be the subject of the third of the four articles in the Champier series "L'Habitation Moderne" for the journal *Revue des arts décoratifs* (Champier 1893: 287–292).

Were it not for the photographs donated to the Musée Carnavalet and the Champier publications, subsequent generations would have had no opportunity to experience the holistic concepts, décor, and collections of the Hôtel Baronne Salomon de Rothschild. In the opening article of the series, Champier leads the reader from the Cour d'Honneur to the interior. The drama opens with the Grand Vestibule. Paired monumental staircases which sweep the visitors up on both sides of the space meet to form a virtual stage for the evolving spectacle of events. Sculptural garlands of carved flowers festoon the overdoor panels and anticipate the décor of the principal spaces. Niches on each side of the stairs and a central pulpit at the upper landing were filled with "magnificent exotic shrubs, whose green foliage forms with red color of the carpet and the white of the stone an agreeable harmony" (Champier 1893: 205). A sense of movement, drama, and spectacle is achieved by manipulating space and light levels from the entry Vestibule through to the entertainment spaces of the *hôtel*. The upper level of the double height Hall is surrounded by a corbeled gallery containing two curved corner balconies that reinforce the theatrical aspect of the space and the spectacle of seeing and being seen. The ceiling is dominated by a glass roof with wrought iron motifs, abstracted floral "jewels" at the edges of each pane, large coved cornice, and a decorative band of Greek key scrollwork. The small inset paintings between the robust brackets of the supporting cornice feature doves on laurel branches set on a gold background that characterize Moulignon's décor. The Hall was furnished in a manner that encouraged the visitor to flow around the space and observe the collections (Champier 1891–1892: 73). Champier remarks on his impressive experience of sitting "on the immense circular sofa" and absorbing the "architectural law of the hall ... the collections, as rich as imposing ... the four high showcases ... of the rarest and most precious among the authentic masterpieces of ceramics, glass working, armory, ivories, enamels among all peoples" (1893: 206) (Figure 13.2).

From the Hall, a doorway leads to the Salon Rouge in which the existing grey paneled walls were originally covered with fabric above the wainscot. The room opens directly to the garden and a pair of doors joins the Red Salon to the Grand Salon. Floral motifs fill the overdoor panels and the medallions in the carved moldings of the ceiling. In keeping with the spirit of integrating artifacts from the earlier structures on site, the Red Salon has a relocated

# Hôtel Baronne Salomon de Rothschild 1872–1878

**Figure 13.2** A. Cary, *Hôtel Beaujon: Le Hall (côté de la Galerie)*, photograph, before 1891, © Bibliothèque historique de la Ville de Paris.

ceiling painted by the eighteenth-century artist Louis-Jean-François Lagrenée. In his ecstatic descriptions of the room, Champier marvels at the collections, which included "more delicate porcelain than we have ever seen in our museums, the most beautiful pieces of the famous table service executed by the Manufacture de Sèvres for Mme. Du Barry… almost a complete set represented by more than 150 pieces… a marvel of elegance and coloration… and of unequaled cost at auction" (1891–1892: 74).

The spatial sequence progresses to the Grand Salon, where the striking feature is the integration into the ceiling of a large eighteenth-century allegorical painting salvaged from the octagonal salon of the Chartreuse de Beaujon that once stood on the property. The painting is signed by Louis-René Bocquet (1717–1814), who was the Inspector-General and chief designer for the *Menus-Plaisirs du Roi*, the royal department charged with creating special events for the court of the *ancien régime* (Gady 1994: 355). Analyzing the Grand Salon, Champier remarks that the space is "vast" and the décor is "rich and of a liveliness made in harmony" (1893: 206). Champier describes the wall décor as composed of painted gilded panels with insets of blue silk fabric embroidered with garlands of flowers. Highlighted furnishings include Beauvais tapestry armchairs executed for Mme du Barry and two game tables in leather marquetry by André Boulle, and he notes that various precious objects were displayed with good taste, "to not shock the eye" (Champier 1891–1892: 74).

From the Grand Salon, the top-lit Galerie acts as a corridor linking four principal rooms. This richly decorated space leads from the Hall and terminates on the central axis of the Dining Room and the attached Winter Garden. The transparency of the Winter Garden (Jardin d'Hiver or Serre) embodies the design counterpoints of visual connectivity and privacy. Reflecting a passion of the era, the glazed Serre serves as a way of bringing nature into the residence and creating an expression of the exotic interests of the time. The counterpoints of transparency and verdant cover of tropical plants suggests the interplay of intrigue and spectacle (Figure 13.3).

The Winter Garden visually extends the Dining Room when seen from the Galerie and Hall. The placement of this space at the end of a major east-west axis of the architectural plan creates a focal point while providing a sense of visual and acoustic privacy. Three bays with clear glazing visually connect the Dining Room with the Winter Garden. The rear wall of the Serre, which completes the line of sight from the Dining Room, was lined with mirrors to reflect the greenery and to create the illusion of greater spatial depth (Champier 1893: 206–207). According to Champier's description published in *The Decorator and Furnisher*, the décor of the Dining Room (Salle à Manger) was intended to create an "illusion of verdure." A window provided a view of the garden and extended the connection to nature introduced by the Serre. Expanding the reflection of nature, the ceiling mural offered an image of a cloudy blue sky viewed through foliated moldings and punctuated by four floral medallions under gilded lattice frames. The décor is noteworthy for the gray Auvergne walnut paneling with insets of eighteenth-century Gobelins tapestries and an elaborate plaster cornice with wood-grain painted to match the walnut paneling.

Of the spaces of the *hôtel*, Champier mainly described the spectacle of the public rooms and the collections but also included the private quarters of the Baroness. This private world was another form of spectacle for the public to view or imitate through photographs published in the media. By locating the private apartments at the garden level, Ohnet breaks the usual pattern of placing the private spaces on the upper level. The historic photographs of A. Cary illustrate the character and décor of these spaces in detail. A grand stair with foliated iron and brass railings sweeps from the Hall to the upper floor, which contains the Salle de Billard, the Oratoire, and the apartments of her only child, her daughter Hélène de Rothschild (1863–1947). While no original plans for the upper floor have been found, the existing layout of the spaces was documented in the 1922 renovation plans to accommodate the Secretariat of the Bibliothèque Doucet (Bois 1922). Notable for its exotic motifs, the Oratoire was located

**Figure 13.3** A. Cary, *Hôtel Beaujon: Salle à manger (côté de la Serre)*, photograph, before 1891, © Bibliothèque historique de la Ville de Paris.

above the bedroom and boudoir of the Baroness. The details of the décor conceived in the "Arab style" were created for Jewish religious ceremonies. The décor of this space has since been removed and the only record of its appearance and design features are recorded in A. Cary's pre-1891 photographs.

## Legacy

Fulfilling the legacy of the great collections became a driving force in the vision of the Baroness for the future of her home and the collections housed within. In memory of her late husband, Baron James-Salomon de Rothschild, she bequeathed her mansion, its contents, and gardens to the French government as a "house of art." Presenting the architecture, interior décor, and collections as a "living place" was very much a part of the Rothschild *savoir-vivre*, of comfortably conducting family and social life within the sumptuous décor and amid the works of art (Stevenson 2011: 110). In 1924, two years after the death of the Baroness, Carle Dreyfuss wrote:

> The Baronne Salomon de Rothschild did not want there to be yet another museum in Paris. The visitors who will penetrate into the vast rooms of the *rez-de-chaussée*, with the tall windows opening on the beautiful garden bordering the avenue de Friedland, will by no means have the impression of visiting a museum. Precious works of art, bequeathed to the State which furnish the display cases within the hôtel, form a magnificent ornament for this beautiful house, that is dedicated, through the will of an intelligent and generous woman, to artists and to friends of the Arts. (Joubin and Dreyfus 1924: 324)

Alas, her will was not to be. Eventually, the distinguished collections were removed to the Louvre and the mansion was transferred through the French government to house the *Bibliothèque Doucet* and later the *Fondation nationale des arts graphiques et plastiques*. Today, the property hosts exhibitions with public access, so that later generations may experience part, but not all, of the story. Absent from the visual record are the exceptional furnishings and collections that were conceived as one with the architecture, formed by the lifetime mission of the Baroness to convey the ensemble to the public.

## Art and memory

In the introduction to his 1891–1892 *Revue des arts décoratifs* article on the Hôtel Baronne Salomon de Rothschild, Victor Champier expounded the value to the nation of the photographic collection held in the archives of the Musée Carnavalet in Paris and the public access afforded through their publication to the mansion and collections of the Baroness. Champier gauged the social impact of the photographic documentation in his opening statement:

> Assuredly, the consideration that inspired the donor is as scholarly as delicate, and one should wish that her example might be followed by many of our presumed patrons of the arts who, for the most part, jealously surround in mystery their treasures of art which embellish their residences… nobles of the past considered it an honor to open the doors of their palaces to artists in quest of original ideas…. These ancestors understood that to cultivate the expansion of good taste was a way to serve the nation and contribute to her glory. Where are the melted snows of yesteryear? The fear of abominable industrial imitations and apprehension of fearsome photography has changed everything. (Champier 1891–1892: 65–66)

The photographic collection and Champier's review of the Hôtel Baronne Salomon de Rothschild not only imprinted the public of its own era but also provided the only comprehensive record of the her lifestyle among the collections in her *hôtel particulier*. Were it not for the photographs donated to the Musée Carnavalet and the Champier publications, subsequent generations would have had no opportunity to experience the holistic concepts, décor, and collections. The legacy of the Baroness, Madame la baronne Salomon de Rothschild, and the Victor Champier publication, with his praise for her contribution, will remain as both tangible record and inspiration for future patrons of the arts to open their collections for the benefit of humanity.

## References

Bois, F., architecte en chef de gouvernement, (October 9, 1922), [Architectural drawings of the Hôtel Baronne Salomon de Rothschild for the Fondation Salomon de Rothschild], Archives Nationale, Paris, file F/21/6032.
Bowie, K. (1987), *Les Grandes Gares Parisiennes*, Paris: La Délégation à l'action artistique de la Ville de Paris.
Champier, V. (1891–1892), "L'Habitation moderne. I. L'hôtel Salomon de Rothschild. L'ancienne folie de Beaujon et la maison de Balzac," *Revue des arts décoratifs* 12, no. 1: 65–75.
Champier, V. (1893), "The Hotel of Madame Solomon De Rothschild, Paris," *The Decorator and Furnisher* 22, no. 6: 205–207.
Champier, V. and G. R. Sandoz (1900), *Le Palais-Royal: D'après des documents inédits, 1629–1900*, Paris: Soc. de propagation des livres d'art, Vol. 1.
Daly, C. (1864), *L'Architecture privée au dix-neuvième siècle sous Napoléon III*, Paris: A. Morel.
DRAC (Direction régionale des Affaires culturelles) Report 2004, Photo from meeting proceedings for the CSMH, November 15, 2004.
Gady, A. (1994), "Folie Beaujon et Chapelle Saint-Nicolas," in B. de Andia and D. Fernandes (eds), *Rue du Faubourg-Saint-Honoré*, Paris: Délégation à l'action artistique de la ville de Paris.
Joubin, A. and C. Dreyfus (1924), "La Fondation Salomon de Rothschild. I. La Bibliothèque d'art et d'archéologie. II. Les Œuvres d'art conserves dans l'hôtel," *Gazette des Beaux-Arts* 752: 317–332.
*Le Figaro* (August 17, 1891): 3.
Prévost-Marcilhacy, P. (1994), "Hôtel Salomon de Rothschild", in B. de Andia and D. Fernandes (eds), *Rue du Faubourg-Saint-Honoré*, Paris: Délégation à l'action artistique de la ville de Paris.
Saint-Amand (1893), "L'Habitation moderne. III. Château de Ferrieres et l'art décoratif," *Revue des arts décoratifs* 14, no. 14: 287–292.
Stevenson, L. 2011, *The Urban Mansion in Nineteenth-Century Paris: Tradition, Invention and Spectacle*, Gainesville, FL: University of Florida. http://purl.fcla.edu/fcla/etd/UFE0043636.
Verlet, P. (1967), *The Eighteenth Century in France: Society, Decoration, Furniture*, trans. G. Savage, Rutland, VT: Charles E. Tuttle.
Verlet, P. (1991), *French Furniture of the Eighteenth Century*, trans. P. Hunter-Stiebel, Charlottesville: University of Virginia Press.
Vidal, J. L. (1891), *La photographie á L'Exposition de 1889*, Imp. Paris: Gauthiers Villards et fils.
White, L. (1898), "Where Balzac Lived," *The International*, 5, July to December. Available from http://books.google.com/books?id=gm4eAQAAMAAJ&pg=PR7&lpg=PR7&dq=the+international+where+balzac+lived+1898&source=bl&ots=17iaiSfcWq&sig=mUng226PDAOg7tlg32bTUhf9Sr8&hl=en&sa=X&ei=HtT7Uo_PHYrE2QW5_YHAAg&ved=0CFQQ6AEwBg#v=onepage&q=the%20international%20where%20balzac%20lived%201898&f=false [accessed February 12, 2014].

# CHAPTER 14
## "UN BEL ATELIER MODERNE:" THE MONTPARNASSE ARTIST AT HOME
*Louise Campbell*

---

In 1925, an article about studio-houses in the rue Cassini, Montparnasse, concluded: "We hear that there are charming things inside, but respectful of the privacy of these 'homes' of artists, we have not spoken of them" (*L'Architecture* 1925: 436). Such restraint—more typical of an architectural journal than of the popular press—did not last long. By the end of the decade, even specialized journals like *L'Architecture* were illustrating the interiors of the homes of artists who had commissioned leading architects to work for them. The journal—published by the Société Centrale des Architectes—was until 1927 dominated by reviews of exhibitions, reports of architectural competitions and congresses, analyses of public buildings and town-planning schemes. After that date, *L'Architecture* grew in size and scope; now supported by the Société des Architectes Diplômés par le Gouvernement and the Association Provinciale des Architectes Français, it included accounts of new buildings alongside historic ones and adopted a more conversational style. Although house interiors were shown devoid of their inhabitants, there was some discussion of the personality and tastes of the clients, rather than simply the architectural character of their homes. By contrast, the drier and more factual journal *L'Architecte* illustrated few interiors and generally identified clients only by their initials.

This informal new tone reflects both the journalistic practices of 1920s and the publicity courted by contemporary artists. It does not merely indicate a dwindling concern for privacy and a merging of the techniques of the mass media with the sober traditions of architectural journalism. It also registers a change in attitude toward artists, who, until the early twentieth century in France, were shown the deference due to public intellectuals. An expanded illustrated press and a bourgeoning entertainment industry meant that the stars of stage and screen began to appear in the pages of general interest magazines. So did artists and the studios which—with greater economic well-being after the First World War—provided them with a stylish domestic environment and enhanced opportunities for display and entertaining as well as working.

This chapter examines the significance of the modern studio space in inter-war Paris and explores the interconnections between celebrity culture, the art market, and the modern studio interior. It considers the ways in which three women—Chana Orloff, Tamara de Lempicka, and Mela Muter—made their way in a highly competitive art world, helped by an adroit manipulation of the media. All three achieved critical success in the 1920s and their choice of leading architects to design their studio-homes served to attract additional publicity. The chapter argues that the volatile economic conditions of the 1920s and 1930s gave studio design an unexpected importance. During the boom years studio-dwellings signaled success, but after the Wall Street Crash of 1929 they were implicated in critiques of the art market and its impact on an old artists' quarter. In the wake of this critique, broader debates about the artist's vocation, the commerce of art and the relationship between French tradition and modernism surfaced.

The French art world of the 1920s was transformed by the boom in the market for contemporary art. By mid-decade, in response to the demand for studio and living space, the area south of the Carrefour Vavin was developed with short cul-de-sacs (known as *impasses, cités* or *villas*) behind principal street frontages. Alice Halicka termed it "an age of gold" which impacted the lives of artists as much as the area of southern Paris containing warren-like studio complexes built on awkward plots of land left over from nineteenth-century urbanisation. With an acid tongue, Halicka wrote: "New streets sprang up in which the artists lived in town houses in the style of Le Corbusier and Mallet-Stevens. The painters carried themselves like *nouveaux-riches*, talked lots about country properties, makes of cars, jewels they'd given their wives … Montparnasse was the cradle of the new over-optimism" (Silver 1985: 45).

It was in one of these new cul-de-sacs that the sculptor Chana Orloff made her home. Orloff (1888–1968), born in Ukraine to an impoverished but well-educated Jewish family, came to Paris in 1910 to work in an *atelier de couture*. After attending classes at the École des Arts Décoratifs and studying sculpture at the Academie Wassilief, she exhibited work at the Salon d'Automne and began to frequent the literary and artistic milieu revolving around the journal *SIC*. Her marriage to the Polish poet Ary Justman was cut short by Justman's death in the influenza epidemic of 1918, leaving her with a one-year old son. By the early 1920s, Orloff began to make her name as a sculptor and wood-engraver and purchased a building plot with a bank loan made possible by these improving prospects. She commissioned the architect Auguste Perret, whose portrait bust she had modeled in 1923, to build her a "workshop" in a newly created street, the villa Seurat (sometimes known as the cité Seurat). Orloff's house, designed and constructed in 1926, provided studio spaces on the ground floor and compact living quarters above. These elements were accommodated behind a well-proportioned tripartite elevation, with a generously windowed studio occupying the lion's share and the living quarters above forming a sort of attic storey beneath a deep concrete cornice (Culot, Peyceré, and Ragot 2000: 152).

Perret took advantage of the capacity for concrete to create generous spans and textured surfaces. Although he did not normally use concrete to create extensively glazed façades, he did so here out of necessity. But in contrast to other modern architects of the period, his design revealed the construction process. The concrete beams and columns which articulated the façade he left un-rendered, providing a contrast in color and texture to the brickwork of the panels separating the street-level doors and the bricks set at an oblique angle to create zig-zag profiles in the upper façade (Culot, Peyceré, and Ragot 2000). Perret's façade composition provided differentiation between structural frame and infill (a feature of almost all his buildings) and gave this sculptor's studio a markedly classical character. This design strategy distinguished Orloff's habitat from the other artists' dwellings in this street, all built during the same period. Mostly designed by André Lurçat, these studios, houses and apartments combined a concrete frame with infill brick walls. But, unlike Perret's, Lurçat's façades were smooth and uniformly rendered, accentuating their cubic character and play of solid to void, recessed terraces and projecting bays (Imbert 1927).

## "Un Bel Atelier Moderne:" The Montparnasse Artist at Home

Orloff's house was ingeniously planned. The ground floor contained two studios. The first had a north-facing street frontage with a mezzanine gallery running around two sides to allow sculpture to be viewed from above, whereas the second studio was a top-lit space to the rear. In practice, the front studio functioned as an exhibition space, through which visitors were routed before entering the working studio. The living quarters included a mezzanine sleeping cubicle for a nursemaid and on the first floor, two small bedrooms, living-dining room, top-lit kitchen and bathroom. "I don't like furniture; I prefer the walls to be furnished," Orloff told the correspondent of *L'Architecture* (Imbert 1927: 111). This remark is borne out by photographs of the interior which show rooms sparingly but stylishly equipped with furniture designed by Orloff's friends the designer Francis Jourdain and architect-designer Pierre Chareau. The bedrooms were described as "cells without austerity, mother's room and child's room, cheerful, neat and sober" (Imbert 1927: 112). Built-in storage cupboards, beds, and mirrors were designed to save space and keep loose furniture to a minimum. Textiles pinned to the walls complemented the robust textures of the plank-marked concrete studio ceiling and beams. Sculpture was displayed on handsome timber plinths (Figure 14.1).

Orloff's success at the 1926 Salon d'Automne followed by an exhibition at the Galerie Druet brought the artist public recognition and articles in *Vogue, Vanity Fair*, and *Paris-Midi*, which featured Orloff side by side with the beauty queen Edmonde Guy as contemporary celebrities (Coutard-Salmon 1980: 48). Both popular and more specialized journals commented on the phenomenon of a woman sculptor practising in a field traditionally

**Figure 14.1** Auguste Perret, Interior of studio for Chana Orloff, 1926, Fonds Perret, CNAM/SIAF/CAPA/Archives d'architecture du XXe siècle/Auguste Perret/UFSE/SAIF-2014, Photo: Chevojon.

dominated by men. Art critics described her sculpture as vigorous, powerful and the sculptor herself as "cette robuste ouvrière" (this sturdy worker) (Charensol 1927: 40). It was an image which Orloff was careful to sustain. At a time when artists were increasingly featured in gossip columns, she steered a judicious course between courting the publicity that artists attracted and maintaining the more anonymous role of the artisan. This was a particularly difficult task for a sculptor who relied on portrait commissions and received both ongoing and prospective sitters at her studio. While maintaining the friendships and prewar Montparnasse's traditions of informal hospitality, Orloff entertained a more worldly and successful crowd (Coutard-Salmon 1980; Silver 1985).

The character of her studio helped to counter both the superficial glamor attached to the modern artist (especially the woman artist) and the identification of Montparnasse as a home for foreign artists. In the light of Perret's image as an architect belonging to the French classical tradition, it is significant that Orloff had at first considered using Lurçat as her architect, but turned instead to Perret in the year before she and her son acquired French citizenship (Campbell 2002). In 1928, a critic writing in *L'Amour de l'Art* referred to Lurçat's house designs as lacking traditional elements of architecture, as "dead-end fantasy." By contrast, he wrote, the Orloff studio nearby "teaches them a lesson, functions as a call to order, to good sense, to good taste ... it is frank, likeable, robust, distinguished. Down-to-earth architecture, up-to the minute architecture, French architecture" (Mayer 1928: 268). Montparnasse was viewed as an increasingly Americanized place dominated by large modern cafés and a spate of "Studio Buildings," a place which was losing its character as a *quartier* (Golan 1995; Renault 2013). By contrast, Orloff's studio, with its bold frame and infill of glass, brick, and timber, referenced the buildings of an older Montparnasse such as the sculptors' workshops around the Avenue de Maine, while employing elements derived from classical architecture.

Tamara de Lempicka's career and studio is in striking contrast to that of Orloff. Lempicka (1898–1980), ten years her junior, was part of a new breed of artists emerging in the 1920s who grasped the opportunities for self-advancement offered by the illustrated magazines and gossip columns. She was born Tamara Gorska in Poland to an affluent professional family and enjoyed a privileged childhood. Stranded in St Petersburg at the outbreak of the First World War, she fled from Russia with her family in 1917. By 1919 she was married to Count de Lempicka and living in Paris where she studied art with André Lhote. In 1922, she exhibited paintings at the Salon d'Automne and regularly showed there until 1938. During this period she painted portraits of aristocrats, rich collectors, family members, and professional models. In 1929, Lempicka purchased an apartment in a new building designed by Mallet-Stevens in the rue Méchain near Montparnasse cemetery, for which her sister Adrienne de Gorska designed some of the furnishings. Described in detail in the sumptuous decorative art journal *Mobilier et Décoration*, this apartment was the setting for private views and glittering social gatherings (Remon 1931). Although Lempicka was a regular exhibitor at the Salons and at FAM (Société des Femmes Artistes Modernes), like Orloff, she did not have a dealer's contract (Birnbaum 2011), and therefore her studio functioned as an important ancillary gallery. This similarity aside, there are significant differences between the character of these two artists' habitats and the ways in which they served to frame the endeavor of their occupants.

## "Un Bel Atelier Moderne:" The Montparnasse Artist at Home

Lempicka's apartment was a duplex, entered via a streamlined spiral staircase with a carpet containing geometrical designs. A lobby with doors of iron, glass and chrome opened into a magnificent double-height studio lit by a north-facing window. An open staircase led to a mezzanine floor which contained a cocktail bar-cum-library and two bedrooms, the smaller of which doubled as a study. Located opposite the staircase, this room (used by the artist's daughter) provided spectacular spatial effects and provided views of the studio below, but not very much privacy. The high gloss of the furniture and fittings (glass, chrome, and steel) contrasted with the smooth texture of the gray-painted walls. Specially designed light fittings threw dramatic shadows across the walls and ceilings, accentuating the highly theatrical nature of this place. A bronze sculpture by Orloff was placed at the foot of the staircase, and a sheet zinc sculpture by the Martel brothers occupied a mirrored niche (Figure 14.2). Although the owner's initials were part of the geometric design for the upholstery in the library, the photographs published in *Mobilier et Décoration* presented surprisingly little evidence of her occupation as an artist (Remon 1931). These photographs showed areas to play cards, drink cocktails, dine, relax, apply make-up, and sleep. Instead of an easel, a bridge table and chairs dominated the foreground of the magnificent space of the studio (Gronberg 2004: 55).

Both Lempicka and Orloff presented themselves in ways which re-defined what it meant to be a woman artist in the modern era. Orloff, speaking to a journalist in 1936, referred to women's traditional concern with affairs of the heart, stressing that her own, rather different, priorities were her work and her child (Coutard-Salmon 1980: 47). De Lempicka, who

**Figure 14.2** Robert Mallet-Stevens, Detail of studio for Tamara de Lempicka showing staircase, bridge table, and corner of the salon, in *Mobilier et Décoration* (January 1931), Courtesy Alain Blondel, Photo: Gravot.

appears at first sight the epitome of frivolity, embodied a distinctively modern femininity, a sexualized, high-earning artist with sophisticated tastes. The 1932 Pathé newsreel, *Un Bel Atelier Moderne*, showed the artist seated at her dressing table laden with an impressive range of beauty products, being served dinner by her man-servant and painting a nude portrait of the night-club singer Suzy Solidor (Gronberg 2004: 52). Lempicka later gave credit to Solidor for the publicity which she herself began to attract: "While she was sitting for the portrait, she brought the newspaper [writers]. And that was the first newspaper that started [to publish] photographs of myself and my studio… It was wonderful publicity for me" (Claridge 2000: 187). Accounts of studio parties now supplemented the architectural descriptions of Lempicka's home. These included the French version of the American cocktail party known as *le 5 à 7* at which guests drank tea or alcohol and artists mixed with the *beau-monde*. Attended by guests displaying their talent, beauty or wealth they underlined the exclusive character of these occasions and echoed reports of glamorous Hollywood parties. They conjured an image of the film-star artist, whose habitat was so closely tailored to her own appearance that the décor was described in terms of fashionable coiffure: "this magnificent studio, all in gray and platinum, the color tones of the latest in hair styling" (*Notre Temps* quoted Blondel 1999: 499). Lempicka's reputation for painting explicitly erotic subjects, suggestive of unstable sexual identities was enhanced by an episode in 1931 when a theater poster based on her painting *Adam and Eve* was banned by the police (Blondel 1999: 236). Such publicity further added to the artist's reputation for being daring and challenging convention.

By 1932 the impact of the 1929 Wall Street Crash began to have a serious effect on the French art market. For the first few years after the Crash, artists like Lempicka continued to sell well, but the 1931 currency restrictions undermined the international art market. Buying contemporary art, which had seemed a good investment for collectors in the 1920s, now appeared riskier. However, Orloff and Lempicka had extended their client base to the United States, and although this provided both artists with some protection, other Montparnasse artists were less fortunate.

On the strength of exhibitions at the Galerie Druet in 1926 and 1928 the Polish-born painter Mela Muter (1876–1967) followed the example of her friend Orloff by commissioning a studio-house from Perret in 1928, the year in which she acquired French citizenship (Silver 1985; Birnbaum 2011). The house Perret built for her was an L-shaped building arranged around a patio on a cramped site in a cul-de-sac off the rue de Vaugirard. The ground floor contained a large exhibition room, a garage, a dining-room and a kitchen, whereas the first floor accommodated a studio, bedroom, and bathroom. The design enabled the house to be adapted for diverse purposes such as making, exhibiting and selling her paintings; holding painting classes; and social events and private views.

Like in Orloff's studio, the design appears to be a studied complement to the character of the occupant's work. Muter was a figurative painter with strong links to the work of the Pont-Aven school and was known for her bold handling of paint and use of strong color. Perret again employed a strongly articulated concrete frame with slightly recessed wall panels. However, the wall surfaces of this house were extremely lively and consisted of red and white brick panels arranged in groups of three, laid alternately horizontally and vertically to create a checkerboard pattern. Squares formed by the horizontally laid bricks were raised and, together with the broad courses of mortar, created a strong relief. The effect was enhanced by curtains with bold stripes hanging at the windows.

## "Un Bel Atelier Moderne:" The Montparnasse Artist at Home

Perret's interest in painting and sculpture and sensitivity to his clients' needs attracted a wide spectrum of artist-clients throughout his career (Campbell 2002). Five years after building Muter's studio, Perret provided her with assistance of a different kind. In 1933, the year in which the French art market hit rock bottom, the journal *L'Architecture d'aujourd'hui* devoted an article to the work of Muter, which was accompanied by two photographs of the artist. One photograph presented the artist in her patio-garden, with her dining room's rustic wooden chairs, woven table covering, and pottery ornaments glimpsed through the open French windows; the other photograph showed her in her studio painting a portrait of Perret (Figure 14.3). The journal, founded in 1930 with the aim of defending modern architecture from its critics, occasionally featured the work of such artists as Chagall and Czaky, as well as illustrating studio-dwellings by architects like Mallet-Stevens. However, this article was unusual in that it showed the artist at home and represented Muter as the innocent victim of circumstance, observing: "in an epoch when bluff often takes the place of talent and when many painters are either the prey or the accomplices of picture-dealers, it is good to note that some artists continue to exercise their profession honestly and courageously" (Bloc 1933: 96). Perret (whose work the journal supported enthusiastically) is here co-opted in order to boost Muter's reputation.

In 1933 the art dealer Berthe Weill, looked back at the preceding boom years and judged the 1920s to have been "disastrous for art, disastrous for commerce, an epoch of speculation, of bluff, an unwholesome epoch" (Klüver and Martin 1994). In a similar vein to Weill, the inference in *L'Architecture d'aujourd'hui* was that the market had collapsed as a result of speculation and dishonesty rather than as an inevitable consequence of the worldwide economic crisis (Gee 1981). Similar claims fueled criticism of both art dealers and artists who in their way of life and their habitats were highly conspicuous 1920s consumers. These critiques served to bring to the fore the vexed issue of artistic integrity and—more significantly for the present chapter—served as a conduit between discussions of art and the assessment of contemporary architecture. The discourse of truth and deception characterized architectural debate in the nineteenth century as new structural materials like iron became available and were accommodated into the existing lexicon of architecture. A similarly moralized discourse acquired new currency in the economic crisis of the 1930s, when during this era of protectionism and xenophobia it was suggested that new buildings in Montparnasse were soulless, badly constructed, and of little architectural value. These emerged in parallel with criticisms of foreign-born artists working in France. A growing preoccupation with questions of ethnic and national difference emerged, and alongside the term "École de Paris," which denoted the rich diversity of both French and foreign artists who worked in the city, the more selective term "École française" came into use (Golan 1985: 80–87).

Orloff, Lempicka and Muter struggled to navigate this altered landscape. Orloff, who had many American clients, had special grounds for concern, but family connections in Mandatory Palestine and a loyal network of patrons in France allowed her to survive (Marcilhac 1991). Her decision to commission the Palestinian architect Zeev Rechter to build three flats, a garage, and another studio beside her original house appears in retrospect rather rash (Tamir, Justman and Birnbaum 2012: 30). However, it provided a useful source of rental income and space to execute large-scale sculptural commissions for the new state of Israel after the Second World War. Lempicka's finances were eased by her alliance with the wealthy Baron Kuffner from about 1928, something which probably made possible the purchase of the studio-apartment in the

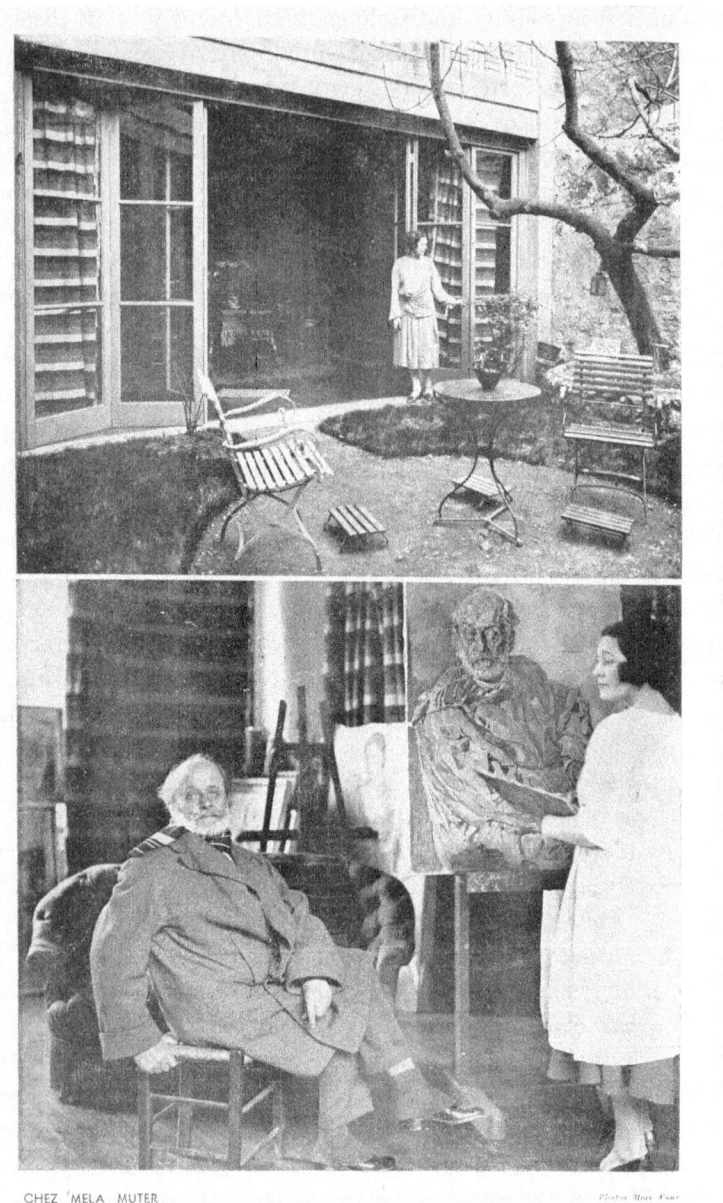

**Figure 14.3** "Chez Mela Muter," *L'Architecture d'aujourd'hui*, April 1933, RIBA Library Books & Periodicals Collection, Photo Marc Vaux.

rue Méchain. She was in New York when the Crash occurred and remained there for several months longer in order to complete commissions. Reputed to have lost money on investments and forced to lower the high prices she had previously asked for paintings, Lempicka appears to have used her apartment and the social events it accommodated as a means to sustain interest in her work during the 1930s (Claridge 2000: 182–183). After suffering a period of depression which affected her style and subject matter and curtailed her output, she and Kuffner immigrated to the United States in 1939 (Blondel 1999: 56–60). The impact on Muter's career was more serious. This was already looking precarious in the late 1920s, when—with abstract art and Surrealism in the ascendant—her brand of figurative painting appeared old-fashioned. Exhibitions in the United States failed to generate the anticipated sales, and her financial predicament obliged her to spend more time teaching and, in 1934, to let her house to tenants. Unfortunately, postwar legislation gave her tenant security of tenure, and Muter was never able to resume occupancy (Nawrocki 1993: 5).

Analyses of inter-war French art have significantly underplayed the effect of the *retour à l'ordre* on architecture (Golan 1995: 23). The buildings of the boom years were unmistakable signs of the affluence, rapid modernization and new ways of living which the 1920s brought to Paris. The blocks of studio-apartments by Henri Astruc in the rue Delambre and Louis Süe in the Boulevard Raspail were conspicuous examples (Delorme and Dubois 1998). The following decade saw a new interest in the vernacular and regional and a resurgence of interest in the classical tradition of French architecture. The private house—a place where tradition and modernity collided—now became the focus of critical debate. In 1933, Camille Mauclair launched an attack on modern architecture criticizing Le Corbusier's journal *L'Esprit Nouveau* for encouraging the machine aesthetic and for promoting an architecture devoid of sensory pleasure or spirituality (Mauclair 1933). The painter Ozenfant responded with a robust defense of his studio-house designed by Le Corbusier, which he described as practical, light, and comfortable: "I work there happily, and I love the cosiness. And I hope, M. Mauclair, that you will one day live in a similar house 'à la française:' you'll see that you can think more clearly there" (Ozenfant 1968: 258). The following year, the critic Waldemar George called for an end to the "modernist exhibitionism" of modern architecture and proposed the eighteenth-century house as the epitome of France's "ethnic and aesthetic reality" (1934: 182).

It was in this context that attitudes to Perret—who until the mid-1920s was regarded as a pioneer modernist—were subtly revised in such a way as to situate him as heir to the classical tradition of French architecture. In 1928 Perret's use of concrete was simply compared favorably with that of Lurçat's, but, by 1929, Marie Dormoy characterized Perret's treatment of concrete as "true" and Lurçat's as "false," the latter having walls prone to discoloration and structural systems obscured by cladding (Dormoy 1929: 132). This moralized discourse (magnified by the economic crisis) helped to shape attitudes to Perret in ways which unexpectedly worked to the advantage of his artist-clients. To the jaundiced eye of the 1930s, Parisian studio-houses had come to be associated with profiteering and the gradual erosion of local and national identity. The glamor of Lempicka's slickly elegant studio evoked Hollywood, conspicuous consumption, and the economic crash. By contrast, Perret's work was described by *L'Architecture d'aujourd'hui* as evidence of a rare architectural integrity and consistency in an era of ephemeral success (Bloc 1932: 1). The architect's commitment to clarity and invention of a form of ornament integral with the wall was explicitly linked with Muter's refusal to modify her style according to fashion. Her solid little house, with its clearly delineated frame and infill, was said to represent a commonsense Modernism, a French alternative to the international language of modernism practiced by Lurçat and Mallet-Stevens. Perret's clients—although not immune from the downturn in the art market—benefited from his reputation as a classicist. The symbols of high culture—majestic cornices, fine proportions, and emphatic frames—with which he endowed their homes, were to afford Orloff and Muter a welcome means of protection in the years when issues of ethnic origin and national identity began to color the criticism of art.

## Acknowledgments

The author gratefully acknowledges Alain Blondel for permission to reproduce Figure 14.2.

## References

Birnbaum, P. (2011), W*omen Artists in Interwar France: Framing Femininities*, Farnham: Ashgate Publishing.
Bloc, A. (1932), "The Question of Ornament," *L'Architecture d'aujourd'hui*, October: 1.
Bloc, A. (1933), "Les Portraits de Mela Muter," *L'Architecture d'aujourd'hui*, April: 94–95.
Blondel, A. (1999), *Tamara de Lempicka: Catalogue raisonné, 1921–79*, Lausanne: Sylvio Acatos.
Campbell, L. (2002), "Perret and his Artist-clients: Architecture in the Age of Gold," *Architectural History*, 45: 409–440.
Charensol, G. (1927), "Les Expositions," *L'Art Vivant*, January: 39–40.
Claridge, L. (2000), *Tamara de Lempicka: A Life of Deco and Decadence*, London: Bloomsbury Publishing.
Coutard-Salmon, G. (1980), *Chana Orloff et son époque*, Paris: Université de Paris, Sorbonne, thèse du IIIe cycle.
Culot, M., D. Peyceré, and G. Ragot (2000), *Les Frères Perret: L'oeuvre complète. Les archives d'Auguste Perret (1874–1954) et Gustave Perret (1876–1952) architectes-entrepreneurs*, Paris: Institut Français d'Architecture.
Delorme, J.-C. and A.-M. Dubois (1998), *Ateliers d'artistes à Paris*, Paris: Editions Parigramme.
Dormoy, M. (1929), "Le Faux béton," *L'Amour de l'art*, April: 128.
Gee, M. (1981), *Dealers, Critics and Collectors of Modern Painting: Aspects of the Parisian Art Market Between 1910 and 1930*, London and New York: Garland Press.
George, W. (1934), "Une Mise en accusation de l'architecture moderne: culture et architecture," *Le Bulletin de l'art ancien et moderne*, May: 181–184.
Golan, R. (1985), "The 'Ecole français' versus the 'Ecole de Paris:' The Debate about Jewish Artists in Paris between the Wars," in K. Silver and R. Golan (eds), *The Circle of Montparnasse: Jewish Artists in Paris 1905–45*, New York: Jewish Museum.
Golan, R. (1995), *Modernity and Nostalgia: Art and Politics in France Between the Wars*, New Haven and London: Yale University Press.
Gronberg, T. (2004), "'Le peintre installé par la femme,' Femininity and the Woman Painter," in *Tamara de Lempicka Art Deco Icon*, London: Royal Academy of Arts.
Imbert, C. (1927), "Le Quartier artistique de Montsouris, la cité Seurat, 101 rue la Tombe Issoire Paris," *L'Architecture*, XL, no. 4: 101–112.
Klüver, B. and J. Martin (1994), *Kiki's Paris: Artists and Lovers 1900–1930*, New York: Harry N. Abrams.
*L'Architecture* (1925), "Deux hôtels particuliers d'artistes-peintres à Paris, 3 et 5 rue Cassini," XXXVIII: 436.
Marcilhac, F. (1991), *Chana Orloff*, Paris: Les Editions de l'Amateur.
Mauclair, C. (1933), *L'Architecture va-t-elle mourir?*, Paris: Nouvelle Revue Critique.
Mayer, M. (1928), "Un Oeuvre classique," *L'Amour de l'art*, July: 267–269.
Nawrocki, B. (1993), "Souvenirs et confidences sur Mela Muter," in *Mela Muter 1876–1967*, Pont Aven: Musée de Pont-Aven.
Ozenfant, A. (1968), *Mémoires 1886–1968*, Paris: Seghers.

Remon, G. (1931), "Architectures modernes: L'Atelier de Mme de Lempicka," *Mobilier et Décoration* 9: 1–10.
Renault, O. (2013), *Montparnasse, les lieux de legende*, Paris: Parigramme.
Silver, K. and R. Golan (eds) (1985), *The Circle of Montparnasse: Jewish Artists in Paris 1905–45*, New York: Jewish Museum.
Tamir, A., E. Justman and P. Birnbaum (2012), *À la rencontre de Chana Orloff*, Paris: Avivre Editions.

# CHAPTER 15
# HOUSING THE NEW DANDY: DESIGNING LIFESTYLE IN *MONSIEUR* MAGAZINE, 1920–1924
*John Potvin*

---

During the five years of its publication (1920–1924), Europe's first men's fashion magazine, *Monsieur*, established itself as *the* uncontested arbiter of sartorial *savoir-faire* and stylish living for the French man. More specifically, the magazine proffered a blueprint for the redesign and re-emergence of the dandy, whose supposed disappearance we have long been led to believe. On its lush covers and within its pages, *Monsieur* propelled itself to the forefront of masculine taste and proposed to establish, what I have identified and labeled elsewhere, the New Dandy (Potvin 2009). He was a decidedly queer figure fascinated with all things elegant and sophisticated whose contours, in the aftermath of war, were defined by a healthy dose of the sporting life and physique culture. Unlike the decadence that characterized the *Belle Époque* dandies that preceded him, within the modern consumer ethos that drove the New Dandy's ambitions, athletics virtuously and seamlessly fused with aesthetics, fashion with rigorous fitness. First and foremost, this modern dandy was a well-informed and refined consumer. In *Monsieur*, fashion—under the edifying auspices of elegance and civilization—was channeled through various cultural outlets to outline what exactly constituted an ideal dandy and more exactly his all-consuming life and style. No other cultural product at the time better understood or shrewdly marketed the ways to fashion one's (dandified) masculine self-image. Paris, after all, remained at once both capital of fashion and culture and personification *par excellence* of stylish living. *Monsieur*, however, provided a much-needed vehicle to advertise men's emerging role in this internationally recognized civic image. As part of the noble and edifying program the magazine set out to establish, the interior served as indexical of the dandy's identity and more expressly its hybrid disposition. In the world of design, a debate raged as to whether, on the one hand, revivalism, pastiche, and traditionalism or, on the other, Modernism were best equipped to furnish the contemporary home and subsequently revitalize national industries and their cultural cachet on the global landscape. This chapter sets out to explore how the magazine advertised a possibly novel way of living for the *modern* French man who, within the pages of *Monsieur*, precariously straddled a fine line between masculine respectability and fashionable eccentricity by adhering to steadfast historical precedents while relishing the forward momentum that Modernism offered.

The largely forgotten monthly magazine is not only an important missing link within the intersecting histories of French masculinity, fashion, and art but is also significant for how it prominently displayed men as arbiters of interior design decades before the "bachelor pad" gained credibility in the USA and UK (a spatial concept noted for its decidedly hetero-masculinist connotations) and in a period when men were supplanted by the emergence of the professional woman decorator. Sandwiched between these two distinct gendered types and temporal moments in the history of interior design, *Monsieur* stands as emblematic of a slightly, if not at times blatant, queer approach to masculinity, design, and the modern interior. As a result, by exploring the notional interior of the New Dandy, this chapter challenges the extant scholarship that has long positioned the female consumer and woman decorator as the exclusive registers of national, industrial, and design debates in the postwar period.

## Making space for *Monsieur*

*Monsieur* was the crowning jewel established and financed by Swedish impresario Rolf de Maré (1888–1964), which, along with *La Danse, Théâtre et Comoedia Illustré*, and *Paris-Journal* was mandated to promote de Maré's interests and those of his select homosexual male coterie. When he founded the magazine, de Maré already had a rather equivocal if not hostile relationship with the press media in Sweden, where his sexuality and his interiors in Skåne (Southern Sweden) were decried for their decadent and degenerate flavor (Potvin 2014). While de Maré himself was not a dandy, his coterie of queer aesthetes influenced the direction his cultural endeavors took. In practice, the magazine's mandate was twofold. First, it was meant to stimulate interest in another of the impresario's cultural endeavors, that of the Ballets Suédois, which he inaugurated in the same year as the magazine. Located in Paris and housed at the Théâtre des Champs Élysées in Avenue Montaigne, the ballet was formed as a creative platform for de Maré's then lover, dancer Jean Börlin (1893–1930) who, at the time, was a struggling member of the Royal Stockholm Opera. Second, *Monsieur* was inaugurated to give voice to a burgeoning male consumer culture following the deprivations of the First World War. Given the symbiotic relationship between the two cultural outlets, de Maré appointed journalist and theater producer Jacques Hébertot (1886–1970) to manage both the ballet and the magazine. In its early days, *Monsieur* also received additional financial backing from couturier Paul Poiret (1879–1944).[1]

To honor the dandy's long-established and esteemed traditions reaching back to its late eighteenth-century English progenitor Beau Brummell, the magazine importantly introduced regular monthly articles recounting the life and style of historical luminary figures that served to chart the legacy and genealogy of the dandy. Among numerous others, Baudelaire, Brummell, Napoleon, Lord Byron, and Edward VII were said to form this select fraternity of high social standing and good breeding; in short, they were responsible for having helped to fashion the codes and values of the modern dandy. Despite the magazine's penchant for the modern, traditional, and historical precedents importantly lent legitimacy, credibility, gravitas, and a sense of safety to its male readers, unsure of the new directions design was taking in the aftermath of the Great War. Given that the magazine concerned itself with the sartorial choices of men and given the sex's conservative disposition since the purported "great masculine renunciation" of the early nineteenth century, the magazine purposefully established a dialog and at times a dialectical relationship between past and present, walking an uncertain path between Modernism and traditionalism. However, contemporary celebrity dandies like Le Comte Boni de Castellane, whose domestic interiors were represented in the magazine, were also featured to advance the idea that the complete lifestyle of the dandy was not only alive but still, importantly, *au courant* among France's intellectual, cultural, and social elite. The magazine attempted to forge a modern aristocracy through both contemporary and respected historical dandies, men of honor for whom elegance was indicative of an unfaltering moral character.

Rhonda Garelick has argued that through mass media and its ever-expanding audience, the female stage star replaced the dandy "as a representative of fashionable modernity" (Breward 1999: 255). As Christopher Breward has asserted, however, Garelick's insistence on the feminization of the public sphere has meant that the dandy has been closeted, of sorts, "relegating his austere visual presence to the private interior which had originally been her domain" (Breward 1999: 255). Garelick's comments, I posit, point to a concern for historiography. The shift in celebrity culture and closeting domesticity she outlines might help to explain, if only in part, the absence of the dandy from the late nineteenth century to the post-1960s period in contemporary scholarship (Irvin and Brewer 2013). Undoubtedly *Monsieur*, as a product of popular media, attempted to bridge the supposed ideal divide, which gendered the public and private spheres and suggestively defied, I posit, Garelick's reading of the dandy's apparent demise. However, within the pages of *Monsieur* the dandy's domestic design came out of the closet and into the cultural media landscape, helping to redefine the figure's celebrity. The dandy, often a *flâneur* consuming the delights of the metropolis as urban bazaar, has, oddly enough, rarely figured within the histories and study of interior design. However, as Elisa Glick notably asserts, the "logic of the dandy *is* the logic of the commodity" (2001: 134). Interior design and the decorative economy were crucial spatial, visual, material, and corporeal registers of this commodity system. Slow to take form, the 1920s witnessed a burgeoning of consumer culture in which Modernism was no longer the purview of an avant-garde elite but rather was transformed into a, if not, *the*, consumer product itself, now made available for consumption to a vast array of publics. Consumerism had become *the* "path to modernity" itself. In *The Gender of Modernity*, Rita Felski also posits that "a view of modernity as driven by the logic of productive forces gives way to a recognition that consumer demand is not simply passive reflections of economic interests, but shaped by a variety of relatively independent cultural and ideological factors, of which gender is one of the most significant" (1995: 60). The New Dandy, in the aftermath of war, was at once both the object and the subject of this consumerist ethos that transformed Modernism into a complete lifestyle on all fronts while adhering to the gendered, if sexually ambiguous, codes and values historical luminaries had provided long before.

### Picturing "furnishing orientations"

Within the pages of the magazine, photographs were only used for the actual, lived-in interiors of luminary male figures, such as for the residences of man of letters Abel Hermant (March 1920), writer Marcel Boulenger à Chantilly, poet Fernand Gregh (January 1920), or so-called "contemporary dandy" Comte Boni de Castellane (March 1922). While the magazine deployed photography as a way to allow its readership to enter into the homes of contemporary celebrities, it used the *pochoir* printed page to fashion ideal and prescriptive blueprints for both fashion and interior design. According to Jeremy Aynsley, "Poiret guided interior designers to think of their work as part of a fashion system" given how he integrated fashionable figures in well decorated, bright, and "intensely patterned" interiors (2008: 11).[2] Not unlike Poiret's ideal female patrons, fashion and interiors were wedded in *Monsieur* toward a synergistic whole. It should be no surprise then that Poiret's, if indirect, influence is present in the pages of *Monsieur*, particularly the pages that deployed the saturated colored and luxurious *pochoir* technique. A reaction to the increasingly mechanized printing processes overwhelming the industry, magazines like the illustrious *Gazette du Bon Ton* and various luxurious interior design portfolios deployed the lush *pochoir* (or stencil) technique at the height of the Art Deco period, elevating their visual culture above that of more quotidian fashion and design magazines of the day. In keeping with the perception of the dandy's luxurious lifestyle, *Monsieur* deployed the printing technique for the cover and various color printed pages.

Art Deco, largely associated with women and the feminine and inseparable from the Modernism of the day, was upheld as a way to reinvigorate the industries of luxury, fashion, and design in the wake of deprivation and devastation following the First World War. While *Monsieur* rarely displayed the dandy within the confines of his domestic interior on its covers, when it did, it imaged the space within a discernibly simplified Art Deco aesthetic (Figure 15.1). *Monsieur* kept within a timely aesthetic of the period, one that conformed to contemporary Art Deco visual standards. Beatriz Colomina has shown how the modern interior was more a mass image than simply a spatial experience or physical expression. As she argues, "modern architecture only becomes modern with its engagement with the media" (1994: 14). As a result, it becomes a product of the avant-garde drive to at once expose and yet render the public over the private domain ever more powerful. Magazines, cinema, photographs, and advertising, among others, make public the very private realm of the domestic and its spaces of intimacy, ever-expanding the space of celebrity. Publicity was not only a way to represent modernity and define taste, but in the case of *Monsieur* it offered a blueprint for the elegance that helped to define the subjectivity and assist the interpolation of the New Dandy into the narrative of Parisian Modernism.

Yet, in order to do so, the interior must importantly signify a clear identity within the collective conscious of the avant-garde as much as within the bourgeois mass, the latter clinging to its importance as a site of protection and comfort. The interior through the mass media of a fashion magazine makes for an uncomfortable space in this instance; one driven by a need to improve, identify with the present, and yet move beyond it, all the while adhering to the rites, rules, and ideals of a historical precedence. The media image—whether fantastical or real, *pochoir* or photograph—exposes the limits, conditions, and contours of the subjective interior. *Monsieur*, I argue, uses this mechanism of exposure not only to advocate an ideal dandified space but also to establish the conditions of a resistance to domestic normativity. The magazine, through the matrices of text, image, furniture, and space, extends the mythology associated with the figure and advertises the more private and intimate aspect of the inhabitant's identity, exposing it to the public domain.

One of the magazine's design critics, Quick, lamented: "[I]f I were fortunate enough, I would totally form my home with modern pieces, contrary to the spirit of the times. For the bourgeois, one must acknowledge, despite his noble tendencies, wrongly follows his furnishing orientations" (1924). At least according to Quick, Modernism was more expressive of the modern dandy lifestyle while traditionalism was a sign of moribund bourgeois tendencies. Quick's use of "furnishing orientations" betrays a desire to move

**Figure 15.1** Artist unknown, Cover, color pochoir print, *Monsieur*, June 1923, Author's collection.

the New Dandy well beyond pre-war styles and bourgeois normativity. The critic tacitly points to the phenomenological imprints of the domestic environment; after all, objects, spaces, and movements inform subjective orientations. In this way, the home is not unlike "sexual orientation" which "might also be a matter of residence, of how we inhabit spaces, and who or what we inhabit spaces with" (Ahmed 2006: 543). Following along from this, it is important to underscore how the magazine suggestively offered a hybrid "furnishing orientation" to its readership.

## Designing the French Interior

### "At home" with the Ancients and the Moderns

In its inaugural issue, the magazine included one of many articles on the domestic design it would publish through the years (Figure 15.2). In this first of the monthly feature, "La Maison," which appeared throughout 1920 and was penned by Roger Boutet de Monvel, the epigram made clear the duplicitous mandate of the magazine's reportage on the interior: "Here it would seem to reopen, in regards to our residences, the quarrel between

**Figure 15.2** Artist unknown, "Un cabinet de travail d'homme élégant" with text by P. Chanlaine, *Monsieur*, March 1924, Author's collection.

the Ancients and the Moderns. 'Monsieur' will take part by opening wide its columns to the most rigid defenders of traditionalism and the propagators of today's styles, of the fantasy of tomorrow" (de Monvel 1920a). From the outset, "le home," as it was referred to, was an integral facet of the New Dandy's cultural and consumer identity. Despite the ambivalence of the magazine's stance, de Monvel made clear that "all the styles, all the types can, sometimes, go together, as long as they form a harmonious whole...responding to your existence, your own character." Along these lines, a proper approach to interior design was always an "affair of tact and measure" (de Monvel 1920a). This, de Monvel believed, ensured a perception that the dandy appeared not only as if, naturally, "at home" in his domestic environment but that the space lent the semblance of always having been like that, seemingly defying the tests of time and vagaries of fashion.

In his articles de Monvel often constructed a dialog between himself and someone else, usually a patron (real or imaginary) searching out the best design from among an endless array of choices Paris had on offer. Within this consumer landscape, de Monvel concluded that previous generations of styles (Directory, Empire, Louis XIV, to cite the most pervasive) were more fitting and appropriate to certain types of spaces. He claimed:

> given that today we hold on to the style of our fathers, I would council you on a few good Louis XIV chairs, few armchairs from the Regency...furniture from de Boule, so long since relegated to backstreet boutiques, these should find with you the place they merit. Heavy? Not at all. But rich, harmonious, virile, worthy of a young man of quality. (de Monvel 1920b)

Noteworthy is how objects from the past are noted for their "virile" disposition, suitable for a young dandy of the present. For critic René Boylesve, however, contemporary notions of elegance consisted of a renunciation of the past. "Elegance of the spirit," according to him, "follows the movement indicated by the evolution of furniture or painting. I heard say to a devotee of the avant-garde schools: 'I don't know if it's beautiful, but in any case it's new'" (Boylesve 1920). In short, at least according to the modernist critic, the debate between the Classicists and the Romanticists (or the Ancients and the Moderns), a debate that has waxed and waned since the seventeenth century, was fundamentally a futile and useless endeavor.

Whether a modernist or traditionalist, simplicity and elegance became the twin pillars of the dandy's interior. In 1924, for example, P. Charlaine was proclaiming:

> Simplicity! A word that expresses the current trend in artistic movements. Finished are complex designs, the actual attitudes; burry the sumptuous and the allegorical! All of this has melted into the contempt of one word: the pompous. We must design simple, execute simple.... Not to live with the times, remain stubbornly in the crumbling past, is suicide. (Charlaine 1924)

However, as Simon Dell has shown, the seemingly novel and purportedly modern quest for simplicity "should be seen as a redefinition of the relation between consumer and commodity [and] facilitated the redefinition of consumption as an individual, expressive practice." For *Monsieur*'s P. Hardy, the contemporary dandy Count Boni Castellane stood as an exemplary model from among those "few enthusiasts of the past, which, in this time of destruction, not only saved many works of art, but also many old hotels, which without them would have been delivered to vandals." Due to "his discerning taste" Castellane "not only restored, but still singularly embellished" his interiors and provided, through his choices, interiors, and collections, a portrait not merely of the modern dandy but also of his subjective personality (Hardy 1922).

In the post-war period, elegance became an antonym to expenditure "in so far as it was the reduction of mere ostentation that would allow the truly personal organization of an ensemble to appear" (Dell 1999: 318). The ensemble then took on the space, image, and disposition of the individual consumer rather than the dictates of the individual (nearly always male) artist-designer. In the May 1920 edition of "La Maison," de Monvel began his discussion by underscoring the fanaticism that invariably follows when one continues to amass an entire interior, furniture, and decorative ensemble premised on one period. What exactly was being created, or "reconstituted," in a period room? As the critic points out:

> when you have spent insane sums of money, when everything has been completed, each piece of furniture, each object well placed and forming an impeccable ensemble, then you will have the distinct impression of being condemned for the rest of your life to live in a theatre decoration. Our grandparents had the taste for bric-à-brac and interiors encumbered by chinoiseries, of turqueries and bibelots of all styles and all periods. This was not of the best effect… All this to say that in a modern home, logically, modern furniture is required. (de Monvel 1920b)

The critic made clear that although the modern style was relatively poor and weak, he hoped its improvement would allow for a combination of ensembles of different styles. After all, the combination of ensembles was "a question of tact and moderation." This alternative use of ensembles could prove to be a novel way to attend to the question of historical versus contemporary design for the interior.[3] Certainly for critic Quick, who longed to live in a completely modern interior, a combination of styles and the work of various designer-artists was the ideal way to furnish the home. An ensemble was not to be guaranteed through the work of one solitary artist-designer (or *ensemblier*) but rather through the various seductive propositions of numerous designers, which would, nevertheless, work harmoniously for the home as a whole. As part of his wish list, for example, he would choose a bathroom from Mr Matet, for the critic preferred "a bathtub, athletic, and devoid of the effeminacy of the past," as well as "a sink equally virile." A virile body, it stood to reason, required a virile and masculine space and "furnishing orientation." Importantly, this space of hygiene should contain "a low table, two chairs, a low, round stool and an indispensable sofa used for after physical culture whose exercises demonstrates rude discipline" (Quick 1924). The critic was quick to remind his readers that *monsieur* dandy was not only interested in elegance of design, but so too was he invested in the physical well-being of his body to support the fashions of the day. For Quick, the past (and likely the moribund perceptions of the nineteenth-century dandy) suggested an undesirable effeminacy, while the future was at once virile, modern, and eclectic by design.

## A space of one's own

Despite the dialectical environment the magazine established at its debut, the overarching program was to respect the past and invigorate the present, to spark debate and interest in an industry that was at once both crucial to the national well-being as much as to the New Dandy's subjective positioning in the expanding landscape of cultural consumption. From its inception, as a fashion and lifestyle magazine, the interior was represented as a product of mass media. Not unlike fashion's duplicitous nature, *Monsieur* characterized the post-war masculine interior as driven by the needs of the two faces of Janus, seduced by the novelty of the continuous present while forever charmed by the treasures and legacies of the past. Modernity and Modernism indeed embody this duplicitous experience, for it provided "an environment that promises us adventure, power, joy, growth, transformation of ourselves and the world—and, at the same time, that threatens to destroy everything we have, everything we know, everything we are" (Winning 2006: 18–19). However, as de Monvel repeatedly invoked, the interior of the New Dandy must be the result of both tact and moderation. Here the twining of Modernism and traditionalism revitalized while assuaged fears of an ever-shifting cultural geography. *Monsieur* was forward looking while providing its male readership with a sense of comfort. In the magazine's managing editor's office, Jacques Hébertot managed to achieve the balance tacitly proposed by *Monsieur*'s various critics by having a table by famed contemporary designer Francis Jourdain while on his hearth a fountain from the Directory period (Marsan 1922).

In its own highly unique way, *Monsieur* served as a microcosm for the study of the post-war interior as one of conflict, flux, evolution, and historical friction. The first five years of the 1920s saw an increase in the debate over how best to generate renewal and growth faced with a devastating past and an uncertain and yet hopeful future. However, the modern interior, after all, was not always so "modern" but a product of give and take with historical objects and forces that collided to provide a unique environment, design, and perhaps more suggestively orientation. Furthermore, the magazine advertised the very debates ensconced in design and decoration within and beyond the periodical press, that of historical versus modern. *Monsieur* did not take up a definitive position but attempted to work through these problems with its readers, opening up its constituency of male followers to feel comfort in the knowledge that what *Monsieur* was ultimately advocating was not novelty for novelty's sake but objects, spaces, and certainly fashions befitting the New Dandy. Whether photographs of prominent literary figures and cultural impresarios or *pochoir* prints of the ideal scenarios of *ensembliers* like Jourdain, Dominique, or Atelier Martine, the landscape the magazine fashioned was that of a lifestyle distinctly male and a subtle though tacit masculine acceptance of consumer culture.

Unlike his illustrious predecessors, the New Dandy, much like his domestic environment, was the product of a hybridity uniquely modern, in which fashion/fitness, past/present, connoisseurship/consumerism, and traditionalism/Modernism formed a unique though seemingly ambivalent masculine orientation, meant in large part to stave off any feminizing inferences. In this way, the domestic interior became a vital space through which to advertise the New Dandy as much as to provide an acceptable environment for homosociability as well as for the unadulterated pleasure of fashion, consumption, and elegant living (Figure 15.3). The semiology of the dandy that *Monsieur* engendered was that of a man of good breeding,

**Figure 15.3** Marc-Luc, "Quel Homme Chic!," Fashion spread featuring models from M. Omer, color pochoir print, *Monsieur*, March 1921, Author's collection.

fashioned through connoisseurial knowledge, while actively engaged in the world that surrounded him inside as well as outside his home.

## Notes

1. It is worth mentioning that in the 1990s the magazine has since been revived by luxury magazine publisher Montaigne publications. On their website, both Poiret and Hébertot are listed as the originators of the periodical, while no mention is made of de Maré, a recurring theme in the mention of the magazine in various French outlets.
2. All translations from French to English are author's own.
3. For a similar, though not identical discussion regarding the late nineteenth century, see Lasc (2011).

## References

Ahmed, S. (2006), "Orientations: Toward a Queer Phenomenology," *GLQ: A Journal of Lesbian and Gay Studies* 12, no. 4: 543–574.

Aynsley, J. (2008), "Pochoir Prints: Publishing the Designed Interior," in S. Schleuning (ed), *Moderne: Fashioning the French Interior*, New York: Princeton University Press.

Boylesve, R. (1920), "De l'élégance de l'esprit: querelle des anciens et des modernes," *Monsieur*, June.

Breward, C. (1999), *The Hidden Consumer: Masculinities, Fashion and City Life 1860–1914*, Manchester: Manchester University Press.

Chanlaine, P. (1924), "Un cabinet de travail d'homme élégant," *Monsieur*, March.

Colomina, B. (1994), *Privacy and Publicity: Modern Architecture as Mass Media*, Cambridge, MA: MIT Press.

de Monvel, R. B. (1920a), "La Maison," *Monsieur*, January.
de Monvel, R. B. (1920b), "La Maison," *Monsieur*, May.
Dell, S. (1999), "The Consumer and the Making of the *Exposition Internationale des Arts Décoratifs et Industriels Modernes*, 1907–1925," *Journal of Design History* 12, no. 4: 311–325.
Felski, R. (1995), *The Gender of Modernity*, Cambridge: Harvard University Press.
Glick, E. (2001), "The Dialectics of Dandyism: Gay Identity and its Secret," *Cultural Critique* 48 (Spring): 129–163.
Hardy, J. (1922), "Un Dandy Contemporain: Le Comte Boni de Castellane," *Monsieur*, March.
Irvin, K. and L. A. Brewer (2013), *Artist/Rebel/Dandy: Men of Fashion*, New Haven and London: Yale University Press.
Lasc, A. I. (2011), "*Le Juste Milieu*: Alexandre Sandier, Theming, and Eclecticism in French Interiors of the Nineteenth Century," *Interiors: Design, Architecture, Culture* 2, no. 3 (November): 277–305.
Marsan, E. (1922), "Dialogue sur les meubles qu'il nous faut," *Monsieur*, November.
Potvin, J. (2009), "The Vaseline Mafia: Rolf de Maré and a Certain *Monsieur*," *Lambda Nordica: Journal for GLBT—Studies* ("Queer Fashion" special issue) 14, no. 3/4: 160–190.
Potvin, J. (2014), "Homosexuality/Modernism/Nationalism: Between Excess and Exile in 1920s Europe," in J. Skelly (ed), *The Uses of Excess in Visual and Material Culture, 1700–2010*, Aldershot and Burlington: Ashgate.
Quick (1924), "Les joies du foyer ou le Salon des Artistes Décorateurs," *Monsieur*, July.
Winning, J. (2006), "The Sapphist in the City: Lesbian Modernist Paris and Sapphic Modernity," in L. Doan and J. Garrity (eds), *Sapphic Modernities: Sexuality, Women and National Culture*, New York: Palgrave Macmillan.

# CHAPTER 16
## "FASHIONS IN LIVING:" THE DUKE AND DUCHESS OF WINDSOR, 4, ROUTE DU CHAMPS D'ENTRAÎNEMENT, PARIS
*Peter McNeil*

The "style politics" of the Duke and Duchess's arrangement of their Paris residence, redecorated from 1953 by the celebrated firm "Jansen," were quite remarkable. Living in a type of quasi-exile, the Duke and Duchess of Windsor were among the most famous figures in the world between the 1930s and 1960s. In 1963, Valentine George Nicholas Lawford [known as "Nicholas" to his friends] and the life partner of the photographer Horst P. Horst visited the Duke and Duchess of Windsor at their home in Paris and filed a report for *Vogue*. *Vogue* had commenced as a society weekly in New York in 1892. Condé Nast had purchased it in 1905 and dramatically improved the quality of its film technology and printing, building his own printing plant in the 1920s, emphasising color, and adding other periodicals to his stable such as *Vogue Pattern Book*, *Vanity Fair*, *House & Garden*, *The American Golfer*, and *Glamour of Hollywood* (later *Glamour*). The *Vogue* headquarters were subdued and elegant, with antique furnishings and a servants' zone; it was not a demotic space.[1] Nast wanted his stable of magazines to reflect on fashions in all things as connected to contemporary writing and ideas, and therein lay a strong part of their innovation. His formidable "lady editors" included Edna Chase, Carmel Snow, and Diana Vreeland. Editors determine the content, layout, and the mood, and the contribution of women to this profession in the twentieth century has been underestimated. The last listed among these—Vreeland—did not deploy a new format—lifestyle recording was common in the late nineteenth and early twentieth centuries illustrated periodical press—but she introduced a new emphasis upon modernist elegance and a refined and economical integration of word and image.[2] One of her innovations was the "fashions in living" series for *Vogue*.

For such a famous figure and leader of fashion, the Duchess has been subject to little sustained academic study, partly because she was not a cultural producer as such; she did not "design" (that we know of, although Lawford wrote that she had designed her Louis XV-style green-blue painted dining-room chairs), she did not write or perform. Rather, she attained her status through her marriage to a former king (Lawford 1964: 1840). Indeed, she is harder to "rehabilitate" than a woman such as her contemporary Elsie de Wolfe, equally style-addicted, but who can be rescripted as a suffragette or a pioneering businesswoman-decorator (McNeil 1994). That the Duchess was blamed by so many people in Britain and the Dominions for the Abdication Crisis (1936) has not helped. Pierre Barillet criticized the royal couple in a memoir: "this depraved Philemon and Baucis were bound together by a legend that was bigger than they were" and described their life as "ultimately futile."[3] He continued: "Their elegance, celebrated in servile fashion by the popular press, was nothing but ostentatious rags to disguise the repellent nature of their souls" (Barillet 2004: 370, cited in Coudert 2010: 45).

The Duchess's principal claim to fame was her choice of *couture* clothing, her sense of *chic*, and her role as a consummate hostess. She was sartorially also very modern, wearing denim in 1966. Nonetheless, the Duchess may also be studied as a patron who was also a type of orchestrator of the home or an *ensemblier*, a French term that exceeds the notion of "decorator" and is sometimes used to refer to the profession of interior decoration.[4]

If we turn to the Duchess's surviving material culture, we note that her garments, private spaces, and jewelry collection contained a great deal of text, literally "writing," on and for the body. Her initials "WW" and quasi-royal cipher were embroidered onto both inner and outer clothing and linen and incorporated into the furnishings and the very structure of the private rooms of her dwelling. This was not widely seen at the time but has emerged since her private collection was dispersed following her death. Although the Duchess was technically not entitled to a cypher until 1972, when agreed to by the College of Arms, she surrounded herself from the 1930s with emblems that indicated quasi-royal status. Style politics gave both the Duke and Duchess pleasure and emitted signals, as royal households have always done. As Terry Castle (1993) has noted, worldliness and modernist aesthetics were promoted by a great many exceptional women between the wars. The Duchess certainly knew some of the socially "present" lesbians, indeed was on close terms with the hostess and columnist Elsa Maxwell and the decorator Elsie de Wolfe. The impact of these women's lifestyle choices, actions, and events was greatly amplified by the advent of mass media, the rise of color printing, and better quality photographic processes. A figure such as the Duchess of Windsor, a well-to-do American who became the wife of a former king of one of the greatest world empires and who lived her life in the media spotlight from the mid-1930s to the 1970s, exemplifies this historical shift.

### Brief biographical account

Prince Edward of York was born on June 23, 1894, to the Duke and Duchess of York and christened Edward Albert Christian George Andrew Patrick David. In 1901, Queen Victoria died and was succeeded by Albert Edward, Prince of Wales, as King Edward VII. On Edward VII's death in May 1910, George, Prince of Wales, ascended the throne as King George V. A month later, the then Prince of York became Edward, Prince of Wales, at his investiture in Windsor. In this period, he became one of the best known men in the world and a central part of popular culture via reportage, photography, and news-reel. It was in 1931 that the prince met Mrs. Wallis Simpson, the wife of an American businessman, and this encounter sparked off a relationship that was to court controversy and to ultimately lead to a constitutional crisis.[5]

As the relationship deepened, Edward discussed the possibility of renouncing his inheritance to the throne in order to marry Mrs. Simpson, but the issue remained unresolved. The situation came to a head when King George V died in January 1936 and Edward acceded to the throne. Nearly a year later, on December 10, 1936, the new King Edward VIII signed the Instrument of Abdication and within six months married Wallis, following her

British divorce, in France. Edward was granted the title of His Royal Highness The Duke of Windsor. The Duchess was denied a royal title but for the rest of her life she styled herself "Son Altesse Royale" (Her Royal Highness). The couple lived for a short time in the South of France and Paris before the war broke out, then for several years in the Bahamas in the Government House, finally settling in Paris and at a small French country weekend "mill" until their health declined. The Duke of Windsor died at home in Paris on May 28, 1972, while the Duchess, also at home, on April 24, 1986.

## "Bright Tweeded Opulence"

From 1953, the Windsors resided in the so-called "Villa Windsor" at 4, Route du Champs d'Entraînement in the Bois de Boulogne on the edge of Paris, a courtesy house of the Paris government that had previously been leased to General de Gaulle. This late nineteenth-century house in a Louis XVI revival style was redecorated for them in the mid-1950s by Stéphane Boudin, President of the famous Paris-based decorating firm "Maison Jansen." The line between the public and the private was sketched differently for the upper classes in the interwar period. People lived with fewer servants and more simply in terms of entertainments, but they did not abandon luxury and a distinction between public and private rooms. The firm of Jansen worked within a range of concepts that had as their backdrop eighteenth-century aesthetics and the idea of *ancien régime* Paris as an *apogée* of domestic civilization.

Bettina Dietz and Thomas Nutz (2006), in an essay on "the aesthetics of curiosity" and collecting in eighteenth-century Paris, point to the significance of the *"art de disposer"*—the matter of disposition—in creating the ensemble of an aristocratic, upper *financier* or elite interior in which "the elements of an artwork [were] to be grouped in such a way that the senses and the spirit of the observer perceived a unity." The relevant theorists of the time included Jean-François Blondel, who worked within an eighteenth-century philosophical aesthetics in which the parts found synthesis in a whole. Such compositions required an audience, and "prestige was created as a momentary triumph in the eyes of the visitor" (Dietz and Nutz 2006: 62). In other words, the arrangement of a house and the objects therein was not a solipsistic but a shared public experience that was essential to the maintenance of social status. Plutocrats and aristocrats during the Windsors' stay in Paris continued to decorate within such a formula. Architectural historian John Cornforth has already argued that the "Villa Windsor" was a theatrical set—a recreation in the 1950s of a 1930s idea of the historical past. Being modern—now defined as driving a Buick, owning contemporary luggage, and sporting the latest sartorial fashions but also living in the past and observing ritual and protocol—colored the Windsors' existence. Stéphane Boudin (who also famously worked for Jacqueline Kennedy at the White House) had a gift of being able "to give expression and form" to the way in which his clients wanted to live. This taste, preferred by the international transatlantic rich, was driven by patrons who wanted an eighteenth-century French decorative backdrop, "tempered by a twentieth-century desire for lightness and ease as well as an insistence on American comfort" (Cornforth 1987: 120–121). Many more such examples are documented in James Abbot Archer's monograph on Jansen but also in the pages of auction catalogs for residences long since dispersed, such as the Mr. and Mrs. Henry J. Heinz II's Manhattan apartment with its extraordinary double-height green velvet *salon* (Property from the Collection of Mr. and Mrs. Henry J. Heinz II 1977).[6]

The Windsors made extensive use of the mass media following the Abdication Crisis to manage their image and serve their own ends. Ryan Linkof (2011) has recently claimed that the Duchess was one of the first media figures to be "hunted" and that the events surrounding the couple's romance constituted the first tabloid frenzy. Permitting photography in the setting of their new Paris home was a fairly regular activity, with a series of photographs being taken for *LIFE* magazine in the 1950s soon after the decoration was completed and the Duchess appearing in American newspapers instructing her chefs in the kitchens. Postwar life suggested that any stylistic choice was available in democratic societies, even older aristocratic forms, and magazines and advice literature, film and later television, showed working and middle-class women how to acquire these looks (Urizzi 2009).

## Sources

The material culture aspect of the couple's life can be followed closely. When the Duke of Windsor died, his effects were retained by the Duchess, possibly as a type of shrine to her husband. As she became ill, most of the household contents ossified; the house was partly closed-up and "moth-balled." But following her death in 1986, the jewels and some of the royal silver now belonging to the Duchess of Windsor were carefully cataloged and sold at auction.

Her most important French furniture was gifted to Versailles, where it has been placed, in perhaps an unintended irony, in the recreated Madame du Barry (a royal mistress of Louis XV) apartment which was formed from a series of empty rooms. The contents of "Villa Windsor" were acquired by the Chairman of Harrods of London, Mohamed Al Fayed, who had them documented and restored and then dispersed at auction at Sotheby's in 1997. The carefully photographed objects range from their monogramed toothbrush cups to their dishes and bed linens, and even the Duchess' fetishistic mink garters. The *refus* of their life, laid out bare for vicarious consumption by an auction house for all to see, is certainly an incredible visual resource.

## Diana Vreeland sends Horst and Lawford to visit the Windsors

Diana Vreeland was the Francophile Paris-born American who possibly did more than anyone to influence Anglo-American fashion culture toward continental taste in the postwar years. Vreeland appears to have been responsible for a new type of editorial format at *Vogue*, where she was editor-in-chief from 1963 to 1971. From her first year at the helm, she commissioned the highest quality color photography fused with lifestyle editorials on fashion figures from Lee Radziwill to Truman Capote, presenting intimate images of their domestic interiors, in which their fashionable persona was co-joined with everyday life. Although husbands appeared sometimes in the images, it was very much presented as the world of women. Magazines had, of course, reported on the lives of high society women since at least the nineteenth century.[7] Vreeland was not an intellectual—she had no higher education—but she loved world culture, atmosphere, and civilization. These she brought together in new combinations of word and images in her magazine work, commissioning great photographers such as Horst P. Horst and erudite writers such as the ex-diplomat Valentine Lawford.

Among Vreeland's innovations was a new layout with text and image arranged in a dynamic manner with photographs of different sizes, sometimes not much larger than a large stamp and other times double-bleed for maximum impact. All of the images and texts were republished on high quality paper in 1963 as *Vogue's Book of Houses, Gardens, People* (1968 [1963]).

Around 1962–1963, Lawford visited the Duke and Duchess of Windsor in Paris and filed his report (1964: 176–187; 190–194). In a brilliant piece of writing linking past and present, Lawford described what was in effect an aesthetic dandyism at work in the "Villa Windsor," created through materials and textures; a series of orchestrated movements through a set of mnemonic spaces; and the suggestion of a "frame" for this semi-marooned couple. He reported: "It is hard to believe that there can ever have been an interior more surpassingly clean—where crystal was more genuinely scintillating and porcelain more luminous, or where wood and leather, polished to the consistency of precious stone, could more truthfully be said to shine" (1964: 187). Here, he refers to the famous clear-water vases of flowers for which the Duchess was famous as well as her large collection of *bibelots* of various materials. His allusion is to the well-worn woollens, lustrous leather, and smooth pearl buttons of the Regency dandy. The villa is entered through the largest room in the house, a double-height entrance hall (Figure 16.1) painted in *trompe l'oeil* marble in contrasting muted shades of yellow, green, and ochre, "opening" to an illusionistic painted Baroque-style parapet and sky. The Duchess was famous for the atmospheric effects she created for her guests, which according to Diana Mosley included the best and most flattering lighting in Paris, concealed perfume burners (that had also been reported by Cecil Beaton in the 1930s), and banks of flowers from her own hothouse. Ahead was a pale white and silver salon, containing a portrait of Queen Mary, the Duke's mother, an Aubusson carpet woven with the Prince of Wales's feathers in pale blue and silver and the best French *ancien régime* furniture in the house (Figure 16.2). To the left of the hall was the dining room, which included old *boiseries* with two minstrel galleries, *Chinoiserie* wall paintings, and electric-blue silk curtains in the eighteenth-century manner. To the right was the Library, whose dominant tone was saffron with contrasting upholstery in crimson and dark-red niches for books. The only other rooms on the ground floor were a pantry to service the dining room and the office where the secretaries worked during the day. Lawford (1964: 192) described the effect of movement through the succession of rooms as "respectively solemn [the hall], brilliant [the salon], light-hearted [the dining-room] and mnemonic [the library, which contained the books concerning the Duke's family history and the famous portrait of the Duchess]."

**Figure 16.1** Duke and Duchess of Windsor residence, 4, Route du Champs d'Entraînement, Paris: The entrance hall, Photographer Alex Starkey, published *Country Life*, June 25, 1987, © *Country Life*.

The library is significant as it included a recessed banquette by Jansen tented with a *lambrequin* in an aristocratic seventeenth-century manner after the upholsterer Daniel Marot (Figure 16.3). Above the fireplace hung the famous Gerald Leslie Brockhurst portrait of the Duchess in a Venetian frame against a mirrored *trumeau*. The oil was central to the composition of the public rooms of the ground floor interior as it was at the end of the *enfilade* and could therefore be viewed from both the center of the dining room and the salon; the *châteleine* of the house was ever apparent, hovering. Painted in 1939, the Duchess wears a simple dark blue Mainbocher blouse and one of her famous Van Cleef and Arpels multicolored gemstone brooches (Brumbach et al. 1993: 14; 20).[8] The painting was widely known as it had been reproduced in color in both the British and American *Vogue* and was heavily criticized when displayed in the United States. It was compared to works of "prettified likeness completely lacking in character or integrity," an indication of the high quality art criticism of the time (No Author 1939: 11). People might have also spotted the erotic dimension. Of Brockhurst's portraits of women generally, Thomas B. Brumbagh (Brumbagh, Ladis, and Phagan 1993: 15) remarks: "Those magisterial females of Dante Gabriel Rossetti and Holman Hunt, their Liliths, Magdalens, Circes and Isabellas, learned in sexual arts, were her immediate ancestry." It is the most successful portrait of the Duchess, as it captures what the philosopher of beauty

**Figure 16.2** Duke and Duchess of Windsor residence, 4, Route du Champs d'Entraînement, Paris: The white and silver salon, Photographer Alex Starkey, published *Country Life*, June 25, 1987, © *Country Life*.

Curt John Ducasse has called "fascination." The work is spatially impressive as it projects the Duchess into another time and space. She sits against a parapet and a limpid sky, heavily reminiscent of an Italian Renaissance scene. The effect of Brockhurst's paintings was frequently compared to one of the most famous pieces of art criticism ever written, by Walter Pater, on the enigmatic mystery of the *Mona Lisa* (Brumbagh, Ladis and Phagan 1993). It also created the sense of an additional window at the end of the *enfilade* making her the focus of the whole ground floor composition. "How many other women could have filled the void where a Kingdom was, and created a substitute for Britain and the British Dominions beyond the seas, out of a Paris house in a miniature park, and an old mill in the Ile-de-France with a rock-garden and a water garden?" asked Lawford for *Vogue*. That "the house is above all a frame for themselves," was his conclusion (1964: 193–194).

Although not very large, the interior was elegant and imposing, with highly distinctive and separate sleeping, bathing, and dressing spaces upstairs for the Duke and the Duchess for the care of their clothes and their bodies. Details of the upper private floor were not revealed in Lawford's report nor was the floor ever reported in the media in detail. Photographers at *Country Life* were also permitted only limited access to photograph the private interiors, once

**Figure 16.3** Duke and Duchess of Windsor residence, 4, Route du Champs d'Entraînement, Paris: The library, Photographer Alex Starkey, published *Country Life*, June 25, 1987, © *Country Life*.

for a story on the Duke's wardrobe and once for a rather melancholy story following the death of the Duchess and the creation of Mohamed al Fayed's quasi-museum therein. Instead, the auction catalog at which the Windsor collection was dispersed prints the plan of the house and reproduces many of the private spaces that might otherwise have remained hidden. The photographs are problematic, however, as many of the finer furnishings had been removed, a reminder of that most ephemeral of cultural acts, the arrangement or the decoration of the domestic interior.

## The Duke and Duchess's private spaces

The Duke and Duchess each had a bedroom, dressing room, adjoining clothing storage, and bathroom. The Duke had a study interconnecting with his bedroom, and the suites were connected with a small private drawing room or boudoir, which led off the Duchess's bedroom and was decorated in a feminine style reminiscent of the taste of Syrie Maugham and Elsie de Wolfe, decorator friends of the Duchess (Figure 16.4). Boudin supplied paneling in pale peach picked out in white with Ionic columns and inset book-shelves covered in

**Figure 16.4** Duke and Duchess of Windsor residence, 4, Route du Champs d'Entraînement, Paris: The Duchess' boudoir adjoining the Duke's suite, Photographer Alex Starkey, published *Country Life*, June 25, 1987, © *Country Life*.

chicken-wire in the eighteenth-century manner. The timber curtain pelmets were carved with the entwined "W's of the Duchess" cypher. This room was intimate; the interconnecting door led directly to the foot of her bed. The plan was also practical in that a landing provided servant access to key rooms such as the Duke and the Duchess's separate dressing rooms. The Duke and Duchess were able to observe guests entering the Hall below and they were in fact frequently photographed doing so, with great effect, as a late-nineteenth century banner with the Arms of the Prince of Wales hung from the upper floor, its presence reinforcing the narrative of the former king. Their bathrooms were nearly as large as their bedrooms and the decoration of the former was more artful than the latter, reflecting perhaps the focus of this couple on the "care of the self."

There do not appear to be photographs taken of the Duke and Duchess in their private suites apart from personal photography, which was published by Hugo Vickers on the request of Mohamed Al Fayed following his taking over the estate. The upper floor therefore remained private until it was photographed following the Duchess' death. A wholly mirrored door next to a *vitrine* of glass-ware crested and engraved with Royal associations led to the Duchess' side of the private quarters on the first floor, a modern gesture emphasizing the different nature from the public floor below. It was typical for men and women of the elites to occupy different bedrooms at this date. The concept dates from the sixteenth century with Leon Battista Alberti, who had recommended separate beds for men and women. The practice had remained part of élite culture ever since (Cavllo 2015).

The Duchess possessed sheets and coverlets embroidered with motifs ranging from crowns to broken or bleeding hearts, which linked her private life to early modern traditions of personal jokes and allegiances reiterated through craft practices and gifting. Many of these artifacts show extensive signs of repair. Victoria Kelly reminds us that, when thinking of material culture, we should look beyond decay and ruin to "maintenance, the often hidden and frequently overlooked assiduous habits of upkeep that were and are used to counter dereliction and to stave off ruin" (2015).

There is clearly a link between the embroidered heart designs found on her sheeting and napery with the fabulous Cartier jewel gifted to her by the Duke in 1957, an emerald, ruby and diamond twentieth-anniversary brooch. These were not simply souvenirs but parts of a public and private narrative concerning a former King and his wife. The meaning of the objects would be determined by people's proximity to the couple; from their intimates to the wider general public who experienced them as a media spectacle. This artifact therefore suggests that we might also consider looking for connections across clothing and accessories, as well as the furnished interior architecture of a dwelling, in order to understand clothing motivations and practices.

The Duke's bedroom was talismanic, containing some of the furniture that he had owned at his favorite English property "Fort Belvedere." His bed was covered with his royal insignia and surmounted by an *appliqué* wall hanging that had hung above his bed at the "Fort" in the 1920s. The furnishings were resolutely English. The Duchess' bedroom was in ice-blue moiré taffeta, in the French eighteenth-century manner with an empire-style bed in a niche, recalling aristocratic precedents. The custom-made furniture supplied by Jansen included a dressing table entirely covered in *moiré* silk and trimmed with a wide *bouillon* fringe, on which the entwined initials "EW" for Edward and Wallis were impressed on the gilded knobs. The *boiseries*, picked out in gold as the bed, included either authentic eighteenth-century or later copies of trophies with attributes of love such as quivers of arrows surmounted by cornucopia. Her dressing room included a rotondo, a circular ceiling "supported" by four columns capped with facetted mirrors that multiplied her dresses and appearance endlessly (Figure 16.5). Colorful red and golden japanned Chinoiserie *etagères* were included for accessories and an adjustable tripartite mirror was available in order to inspect her appearance as was also the case in the Duke's bathroom.

The Duke's exquisite bathroom was crafted with veined white marble, stainless steel fixtures, and brick-red curtains piped in beige scallops. All of the doors were mirrored and it contained several additional pivoting mirrors so that the Duke could inspect every angle of his appearance. It included modern tubular steel framed furniture by PEL Ltd Birmingham and a Chicago "Health-O-Meter" scale. Its walls were decorated with framed prints of regimental dress and its snappy red and white decoration had a military but also rather melancholy air.[9] A Royal Standard was placed near the window, perhaps for purposes of photography, although in the 1930s in the South of France the Duke's bathroom was also photographed for *American Vogue* with military insignia, metal and glass furniture, and even a pair of rubber beach slippers ("flip flops").[10] The Duke's modernity was signalled in his bathing practices: his preference for showers was so extreme that the bathtub was boarded over, becoming a working and storage place for personal photographs and letters detailing the famous romance with his wife.

"Fashions in Living"

**Figure 16.5** Duke and Duchess of Windsor residence, 4, Route du Champs d'Entraînement, Paris: The Duchess's dressing room, Photographer Alex Starkey, taken for *Country Life*, 1987, © *Country Life*.

The Duchess's bathroom was spectacular. Its furnishings included a remarkably luxurious commode, probably by Jansen, in which the top was inset with bird feathers forming a Neoclassical swagged decoration. The room included theatrical paintings by the Russian *émigré* Dimitri Bouchène, the French "Oliver Messel" (Menkes 1987: 46), which recalled the ludic nature of the postwar School of Paris, and its ceiling comprised a blue and white candy-striped tent, both *trompe l'oeil* and three-dimensional metal, forming a canopy and opening to a further illusionistic crystalline and mountain sky. The bath-linens were a high-keyed shade of blue-violet, a color she had worn a great deal when younger. It was rather narcissistic but also nostalgic. A November 1936 Cecil Beaton sketch of the Duchess hung on the mirrored wall above the bath, an image of her as a mistress just before the abdication, not a wife, but with great self-assurance. The toilet and bidet were behind a concealed mirrored door, and although surviving photographs are not comprehensive, its walls were painted with a series of murals incorporating bouquets of flowers, the Swiss Alps, and a blindfolded woman. This painting was within the private toilet cabinet of the Duchess, which means it would be seen by no one else. The image of the blindfolded woman with her hands raised in the air is reminiscent of the dress designs of Schiaparelli as depicted in a famous photograph by Man Ray. One wonders what it meant, this act of not seeing and being seen. Was it about the creation of her self, the interaction of her self and self-creation, something that was secret but that she knew would be seen after her death? Does the painted decoration of her private suite concern the interaction of herself with others or with her very self-creation?[11] The figure might also refer to the allegory of Justice. Regardless, the design is highly unusual and ambiguous in the history of interior decoration.

The creation of a glamorous set of interiors might be construed by some, as is often the case with many views of sartorial fashions, as facile. Nonetheless, we now have more sophisticated ways of reading the modern interior, which ought also to be applied to a more traditional and hybrid space such as the "Villa Windsor." I have previously asserted this for Elsie de Wolfe (Lady Mendl) in "Designing Women" (1994); and work on the relationship between gender, modernity, and domestic life in general has grown apace since 1994. For example, Victoria Rosner's *Modernism and the Architecture of Private Life* (2005) examines the way in which writers such as Virginia Woolf and Lytton Strachey created autobiographical sketches of interiors that "are a means of marking the distance travelled to reach the fluidity and experimentation of their adult lives" (Livesey 2006: 369). The creation of the house at 4, Route du Champs d'Entraînement, Paris, I have argued, was a major investment for the Windsors in terms of artistic design, funds, and emotional energy. As Valentine Lawford explained in his reporting for *Vogue*, in an age of media attention, the house became a literal "frame" for their lives. The appearance of their residence, which some might define as classical elegance, was heavily influenced by twentieth-century art and fashion, and it also reflected the curious stasis of their "arrested" lives.

## Notes

1. *British Vogue* was inaugurated in 1916 to deal with war-time blockade and did not have identical copy, sharing some but not all stories and images. For an excellent summary of Condé Nast's entrepreneurial imagination, see Shawn Waldron, "Horst's World in Colour" (2014).
2. At the time of going to press there appeared Glenn Adamson's "Conversation Pieces: Interiors of Horst and Lawford" (2014). In an imaginative reading, Adamson connects Horst's photography of interiors to traditions ranging from the *vanitas* still-life to the eighteenth-century conversation piece and Susan Sontag's "Notes on Camp" (1964). He indicates Horst's relationship as lover with the film director L. Visconti and the postwar culture of escapist fantasy. Horst had also worked on the Le Corbusier design of the infamous kitsch Paris penthouse of the Comte de Beistegui. Of Horst and Lawford, Adamson writes: "they also knew this world of closed, cosmopolitan refinement was not built to last. At its best, their work captured that fragility" (2014: 269).
3. Philemon and Baucis: literary and mythological figures who were a poor, old married couple who entertained Zeus and Hermes, protected by the Gods and later fled to the mountains as their village was destroyed behind them, first mentioned in Ovid. The connotation is that of desertion.
4. The French concept of a decorator is more expansive than the term in English and exceeds the notion of a tradesman. For example, Émile-Jacques Ruhlmann was an *ensemblier* who also worked with interior architecture and the design of textiles, furnishings, and lighting.
5. For details of this account and on the Prince's image in an age of "mechanical reproduction" see McNeil (2012).

6. *Property from the Collection of Mr. and Mrs. Henry J. Heinz II*, New York, Sotheby Parke Bernet Inc. March 1977, unpaginated insertion at end of catalog illustrating plan and photography of the residence at 450 East 52nd St, New York City.
7. I am yet to read or hear of an eighteenth-century *fashion* periodical that comments on the interior decoration of a real person with a co-joined image of that interior.
8. National Portrait Gallery, London; oil on canvas, 1939
   40 in. × 32 in. (1,016 mm × 813 mm)
9. On the Windsor bathrooms, see acclaimed biographer Hugo Vickers (2008a; 2008b).
10. American *Vogue* also published a photograph of the Duchess's outdoor banqueting table at the Villa La Cröe in the south of France, an enormous elongated "W." Such an extreme decorating feature was not published in British *Vogue* nor were the Duke's modernist glass and steel bathroom furnishings. Different media copy was created for the two marketplaces.
11. See my previous study in *Mode und Bewegung* (2013).

## References

Adamson, G. (2014), "Conversation Pieces: Interiors of Horst and Lawford," in S. Brown (ed), *Horst: Photographer of Style*, London: Victoria & Albert Museum Press: 269–301.

Barillet, P. (2004), *A La Ville comme à la scène*, Paris: Edition de Fallois, cited in T. Coudert (2010), *Café Society, Socialites, Patrons, and Artists: 1920–1960*, Paris: Flammarion.

Brumbagh, T. B., A. Ladis, and P. Phagan (1993), *The Art of Gerald Brockhurst*, Georgia Museum of Art, University of Georgia.

Castle, T. (1993), *The Apparitional Lesbian: Female Homosexuality and Modern Culture* (New York: Columbia University Press).

Cavllo, S. (2015), "Invisible Beds: Health and the Material Culture of Sleep," in A. Gerritsen and G. Riello (eds), *Writing Material Culture History*, New York and London: Bloomsbury.

Cornforth, J. (June 25, 1987), "The Duke and Duchess of Windsor's House in Paris," *Country Life*: 120–125.

Dietz, B. and T. Nutz (Fall 2006), "Collections Curieuses: The Aesthetics of Curiosity and Elite Lifestyle in Eighteenth-Century Paris," *Eighteenth-Century Life* 29, no. 3: 44–75.

Kelley, V. (2015), "Frayed Jacket with One Remaining Button: Time, Wear and Maintenance," in A. Gerritsen and G. Riello (eds), *Writing Material Culture History*, New York and London: Bloomsbury.

Lawford, V. (April 1, 1964), "Fashions in Living: The Duke And Duchess Of Windsor In Paris," *American Vogue* 143, no. 7: 176–187; 190–194.

Lawford, V. (1968 [1963]), *Vogue's Book of Houses, Gardens, People*, New York: Viking Press.

Linkof, R. (Nov. 2011), "'The Photographic Attack on His Royal Highness:' The Prince of Wales, Wallis Simpson and the Prehistory of the Paparazzi," *Photography & Culture* 4, no. 3: 277–292.

Livesey, R. (2006), "Review: Modernism and the Architecture of Private Life: Victoria Rosner," *Journal of Design History* 19, no. 4: 369–371.

McNeil, P. (1994), "Designing Women: Gender, Sexuality and the Interior Decorator, c. 1890–1940," *Art History* 17, no. 4: 631–657.

McNeil, P. (2012), "The Duke of Windsor and the Creation of the 'Soft Look,'" in P. Mears (ed), *Ivy Style: Radical Conformists*, New York, New Haven and London: Yale University Press and Fashion Institute of Technology.

McNeil, P. (2013), "Movement and 'Pep:' Re-animating the Duchess of Windsor's Lifestyle Fashions," in K. Tietze and A-B. Schlittler (eds), *Mode und Bewegung. Beiträge zur Theorie und Geschichte der Kleidung, Textile Studies* 5, Edition Imorde, Berlin, 57–68.

Menkes, S. (1987), *The Windsor Style*, London: Grafton/Collins.

No Author (October 15, 1939), "Emily Genauer Acclaims Farnsworth Portrait," *Art Digest*: 11.
*Property from the Collection of Mr. and Mrs. Henry J. Heinz II*, New York, Sotheby Parke Bernet Inc. March 1977, unpaginated insertion at end of catalog illustrating plan and photography of the residence at 450 East 52nd St, New York City.
Urizzi, M. (2009), "'Jusqu'au bout du rêve:' Neo and Aulic Romanticism in René Gruau's art," in E. Tosi Brandi (ed), *Gruau and Fashion—Illustrating the 20th Century*, Milan: Silvana Editoriale: 126–145.
Vickers, H. (May 2008a), "A Wash with Elegance" (The Duchess of Windsor's Bathroom), *The World of Interiors*.
Vickers, H. (September 2008b), "My Bathroom Is My Castle," *German Architectural Digest*, 176–181.
*Vogue's Book of Houses, Gardens, People. Photographed by Horst, Text by Valentine Lawford, Introduction by Diana Vreeland*, 1968 [1963], London: The Bodley Head, reprinted every year until 1968 by Condé Nast publications.
Waldron, Shawn. (2014), "Horst's World in Colour," in S. Brown (ed), *Horst: Photographer of Style*, London: Victoria & Albert Museum Press: 153–162.

# CHAPTER 17
## "SI MA CUISINE M'ÉTAIT COMPTÉE:"
## *PARIS MATCH* AND THE *SALON DES ARTS MÉNAGERS* DURING THE FOURTH REPUBLIC
Guillaume de Syon

In 1956, the French writer Boris Vian penned a satirical song, *La Complainte du progrès* (*The Lament of Progress*), in which he satirized the popular obsession with the annual *Salon des arts ménagers* (Household show), from now on referred to as *SAM*. The poem suggested that to keep domestic peace and love, words no longer sufficed, having been replaced with a list of household items ranging from kitchen machinery to cupboards (Boggio 1995: 476). Ironically, the song was very well received, for, in its later phase, the French Fourth Republic (1944–1958) witnessed a substantial rise in consumerism associated with reconstruction. That interior decorating and furnishing could become part of French identity was not novel, as earlier iterations of French interior styles made clear. What was novel, however, was the role the media played in fostering the development of "progressive" styles, household technologies and room layouts. While historians have acknowledged the role of women's mass distributed print media in emphasizing the importance of interior furnishings, that of one magazine, *Paris Match*, is often overlooked. In fact, the widely circulated magazine's engagement in promoting the value of new housing and reconstruction contributed to the formation of a new French identity centered around the home, which would grow stronger over the course of three decades but especially during the Fourth Republic.

*Paris Match* was an active purveyor and democratizer of French Modernism at a time when few press titles could claim a readership across class and gender boundaries. In so doing, it not only supported governmental efforts at establishing a French housing agenda, but it resurrected modernist designs from the interwar years by commissioning French artists and architects to work on projects it would show at the *SAM*. To understand this process, and before turning to examples of the magazine's exhibits at the *SAM* during the Fourth Republic, it is necessary to consider briefly the conditions of French interwar design, as these affected both French consumerism after the Second World War and the position of *Paris Match* as a unique, cross-gender media outlet.

### Media actors in the Fourth Republic

Though the Cold War and decolonization were the main crises that shaped the culture and values of the Fourth Republic, few historians have incorporated changes in style and taste in France into narratives of that era. This presents a rich irony, for France became a battleground of ideology and culture between left and right as it moved to recover from the war (Kuysel 1997). Beyond the exclusion of France from scholarly discourse about functional design and its social meaning, Freeman (2004), Crowley and Pavitt (2008), and Oldenziel and Zachmann (2009) subsume the French case to a wider Western European movement when discussing sociocultural developments and their impact on living. All, however, use evidence from neighboring nations to demonstrate the tensions between Americanization and adaptation to new cultural influences.

In fact, the French home was very much a site of contested values and ideals in the postwar period, as the country struggled to recover and deal with a variety of foreign and domestic concerns. As applied to the French habitat, as Nicole Rudolph notes, the new, post-Second World War French home became a site of social engineering, democratization, and modernity. Several other authors join Rudolph in emphasizing facets of this modernization process, including the role of the *SAM* (Leymonerie 2006).

Paradoxically, as France began to recover from the Second World War, the need for technology-driven forms of reconstruction required the resurrection of design ideas from the interwar period. At this intersection appeared the representation of modernist domestic interiors that promoted better living and encouraged new investments in the private sphere. These were achieved through a variety of actors including the French government's reconstruction initiatives, industrial groups eager for investment, and social groups (Ainsley 2006: 209). While urban policies, economic forecasts, and political posturing all played a role in this process, that of the popular general interest media is less covered (Bullock 2008). Yet, as Oldenziel and Zachman, echoing Ruth Schwarz Cowan have pointed out, newspapers and magazines served as mediation junctions between technology and identity in the same way that interiors were consumer junctions (2009: 10).

Feminist scholars have shown the role that women's magazines played in disseminating the notion of modernity. Kristin Ross in particular sees this effort as part of the need to "provide a daily narrative of female existence involving shopping, housekeeping, [and] fashion" (Ross 1995: 81). Several authors mention *Paris Match*, acknowledging that the paper's massive circulation numbers (among the highest for a weekly French magazine in the 1950s) meant that it reached into most homes, thus making the magazine's pages visible to a wide social array. Nick Bullock, focusing on the still surviving women's titles, *Marie Claire* and *Elle*, offers an insightful review of the importance of the collaboration between the *arts ménagers* show planners and the press in "selling" interiors (2010: 140–142). All the authors surveyed make important contributions to tracing, through mass media, the transformation of France into a consumerist society. In so doing, however, they overlook the peculiar place of *Paris Match* as a *unisex* magazine in spreading the word about modernity under the Fourth Republic.

## The interwar incubation of mass interior design

The discourse that existed in the pre-Second World War specialized press regarding kitchen design was not generally circulated for a mass readership. Its main programs, however, originated the echo that would be heard in the 1950s. In 1934, *Arts décoratifs* had lauded a design by Georges Appia that sought to acknowledge limited apartment space as well as the need to combine the luxury, functionality, and comfort required "for the preparation of food and its enjoyment." Appia took into account the "need for light" as well that of introducing a glass and venting separation to protect the room from smells and food spills. The message was that the kitchen should no longer be "dishonorable and unshowable" but required acknowledgment of its own value or even luxury (Migennes 1934: 118). Scientific management thus entered the house—without, however, paying much attention to the specific needs of users (Fijalkov 2011: 102). The design itself projected housewives into a mechanized environment quite contrary to their expectation, thereby exacerbating a tension between an ideology of work and a nascent one of leisure. Generally, most of the feminine press agreed on the need for simplification of household chores but diverged on how to reach such goals. Most commentators on the home in the print media were thus left to discuss the meaning of social and family transformations resulting from the First World War, and very few chose to emphasize the value of new interiors, except when addressing the upper-middle classes (Werner 1984: 61–64). Among these exceptions, *Le Journal de la femme* and *Arts ménagers* each posited the benefits of electrification in the kitchen (Werner 1984: 73–77). All, however, struggled with the tension between novelty and necessity, a tension that would also appear after the Second World War.

## Discovering postwar consumerism

During the 1949 *SAM*, the winner of the show's home economics prize was offered a choice between an electric- or a gas-powered stove. Her home, however, had neither gas nor electricity (Demory 2007: 77). What was on show was but a three-dimensional dream. Making it a reality would require multiple actors, one of which was the media, notably *Paris Match*.

Though *Paris Match* is often assimilated into the realm of women's magazines, it was in fact among the first glossy publications to reach *across* gender lines through the nature of its content. When researchers choose to emphasize the role of *Marie Claire* in promoting the French interior, they overlook the fact that the latter was not published until 1954, five years after *Paris Match* first appeared as a rebirth of a pre-Second World War title. *Paris Match* eventually became the leading weekly until its decline in the 1970s. To understand further its eventual role in promoting the *SAM* alongside women's magazines, it is necessary to consider the immediate postwar era, when attitudes did not evolve much in the direction of consumerism. On the contrary, cost consciousness, exacerbated through the use of food stamps in France until 1948, were reminiscent of conditions three decades earlier. Though fewer men had died than during the First World War, the country's dire economic state slowed down many families' hopes of acquiring a new kitchen or a new interior. What had also not changed was a vision of the *SAM* that, to male observers, matched that of the kitchen: "the quiet discipline of the car show is replaced with a gentle mess where the eye gets lost upon arrival. [...] A slow flux, moving, circumspect, that recognizes its familiar stars: vacuum cleaner, washing machine, and refrigerator" (Calan 1952: 108–110).

The costs associated with bigger investments remained prohibitive, leading to many concerns, including some gendered reactions, as when one spouse commented on an item stating: "I'm convinced, but we need to check with my husband" (Calan 1952: 108–110).

The writer, Madeleine Calan, noted the mix of amazement and skepticism at the various contraptions and wondered how it was that instead of looking at new models, she wanted to see "her" washer, "the one I praise every day." Calan concluded her portrait of tired Parisians by noting how they seemed eager to return home to their "leaky mechanical washer, a dark kitchen, and an old coffee mill." Biting though she was in her descriptions, Calan offered nonetheless an important reflection of the early visions of the *SAM*'s role: a show that offered dreams but no blueprint on how to transform them into home-based reality.

Other publications echoed such frustrations. *Antoinette*, a union-sponsored monthly intended for women, noted acidly that washing machines were saving time for middle-class women who did not work but ignored factory workers dying to own such contraptions (Delaunay 2003: 415). Regardless, the publications landscape discussing interior design and kitchen furnishings was mostly a feminized one, whether it welcomed or attacked the concepts offered. The magazines *Arts ménagers* and *Marie Claire*, for example, came to emphasize the need to mechanize daily chores. In so doing, however, they were preaching to the converted. In an essentially patriarchal society as that of the French Fourth Republic, men did not look at such publications.

In this context, *Paris Match* faced the difficult task of reaching a wide readership that was diverse both class-wise and gender-wise (Frère 191: 198). The watering down of political debates was an established policy in light of its determination to retain a broad-based readership. Though one may be tempted to view it as a female-oriented magazine, the fact that it covered themes likely to appeal to a male readership meant that, regardless of how long people spent reading it, the weekly could serve as a common conversation topic. Politics, royalty, technology, or interior design and fashion would reach the average couple in a manner *Marie Claire* could not. Furthermore, since *Paris Match* was in the business of reflecting a social ideal that normalized relations according to middle-class sensibilities, one might find the magazine in working-class areas as well as in the more well-to-do living rooms. Thus, its coverage and promotion of the *SAM* would gain in both importance and impact.

## The discreet charmlessness of the kitchen

As Martine Segalen and Claire Leymonerie have shown in separate instances, the *SAM*, first inaugurated in 1923, served as a channel to modernity that called for turning a "society of traditions" into a consumerist one (Leymonerie 2006; Segalen 1994). As the French people stopped attending church in droves after the Second World War, the secularization process also caused a sense of abandonment of identity, and pushed toward the adoption of one associated with one's immediate habitat (Astier and Laé 1991: 87).

The support for a new home the *SAM* offered came in the form of a show intended to prove that the combination of aestheticism and functionalism was not contradictory (Rouaud 1993: 21). However, this also meant showing a *possible* private sphere in public. This presented a challenge, both for the *SAM* and for the associated media such as *Paris Match*. As Michel de Certeau and Luce Giard have emphasized, the home was to be protected from the gaze of outsiders for fear that observing it would reveal the personality of its owners. In a sense, the home did not "lie," as it presented its inhabitants' lives "without make up" (Certeau and Giard 1994: 207). As for the kitchen, it was doubly invisible, because the work it necessitated, though essential, lacked finiteness. Three or more times a day, the woman of the house (as opposed to the maid or the cook in earlier decades) was expected to occupy it and feed the family. Added to this invisibility was a certain cultural double standard around the finished product. While French cooking was lauded as a national identifier that associated good food with health and proper childrearing, the actual work was demeaned as monotonous and empty. For instance, there were no dietary training or etiquette formation programs in schools (Certeau and Giard 1994: 221). If the kitchen was to be the place where *Madame* was on standby for anything from the children's snacks to the unannounced arrival of the husband with his work colleagues, how did one reconcile the anonymity of the place with the essential function of the kitchen's main occupant?

### Enter *Paris Match*

*Paris Match*'s role in resurrecting the interwar notion of a "living kitchen" becomes clearer in this context. Offering new ways of building one's surroundings would parry the sense of alienation from the kitchen or so the editors seemed to think. To show what *could* happen in a kitchen and to serve as an intermediary between manufacturers and consumers reflected a kind of advocacy, which served all parties.

In the 1952 *SAM*, *Paris Match* sponsored a model apartment on the grounds of the exhibition and showed a selection of photographs of it in its pages. Squeezed on 74 square meters, and with no expense spared, the place was intended to house a family of four (Bullock 2010: 127–128). Designers Jean Prouvé and Charlotte Perriand were called to create some of the furniture, while several dozen companies were hired to build colorful walls and sliding partitions, one of Perriand's innovations dating from the 1920s (Blondel 2011: 29). Called "the radiant apartment" in connection with the first unit of Marseille's "ville radieuse" constructed that same year, it injected a distinctive French identity into interior design intended for a mass audience, which showed that modernization went beyond Americanization or the import of Scandinavian design already known at the time. The designers' names may have been new to the public, but they were in fact among the most respected in their field. That *Paris Match* chose to cite them in the article, which featured beautiful, color illustrations, was also indicative of a wish to inform and educate that went beyond entertainment.

The response to this model apartment was overwhelmingly positive, to the point where a picture of the main room appeared in the second edition of *L'Art ménager français* in 1963, with further discussion in architectural circles arising partly because of the placement of the kitchen itself (Faucheux 1952; Piqpoq 2009). The emphasis fell on the use of natural lighting for an area that was neither a "laboratory" kitchen nor a grandiose one characteristic of a well-established estate. Rather, the moderately sized area had enough space to allow inhabitants to take meals (presumably breakfast and quick lunches) and to permit the storage of all culinary utensils (Valentin 2013: 15). One should note, however, that the rhetoric employed in the article very much echoed what might be found in women's magazines. Since men leafed through *Paris Match*, the language was clearly *not* entirely one of female emancipation (especially since most writers were men); but the writing did ease some of the imaginary chains that restricted women at the time, with headline stating: "In her mechanical kitchen, the woman is no longer a slave." Though social and historical studies have disproven the rhetoric, the presentation of the ideal kitchen still made sure to not fully challenge traditional gender roles. The mother still worked in the kitchen, but she now did so in comfort, having more space to lay out her wares, find ingredients, or do the dishes. Her function, nevertheless, was clearly reaffirmed, and in no picture was a male model posing as the husband.

Fascinating though the "ideal apartment" was, it remained just that. In the context of the early 1950s, France was in the throes of a housing crisis that necessitated a massive engagement of state planning, private enterprise, and financial backup to support the continued migration of large population groups into urban areas. As if on cue, *Paris Match* echoed this concern in its 1953 iteration of the *SAM* exhibit. Working with the assistance of the Minister for Reconstruction and Urbanism (MRU), the magazine commissioned Marcel Roux, a former collaborator of Le Corbusier, to take the concept of the experimental "radiant apartment" of the preceding year to the working-class town of Fresnes in the Paris suburbs (Newsome 2009: 146). The fact that actual costs were, this time, fully factored into the project from the beginning represented a departure from the quasi-utopian representation of the previous year. The new project also took into account the reality of space shrinkage, as the 1953 model witnessed a reduction of the living space from seventy-four to fifty-four square meters. The parental room was folded into the living area, and multiple closets incorporated into walls were added, thus not counting in the area calculation.

The model appeared at a time when optimism began to affect public perceptions of housing. To prove that it was not simply entertaining its readers with dreams of modernity, *Paris Match* went ahead and bought the land intended for the development of the dwellings, promising that it would guarantee affordable mortgage conditions for young families. In so doing, the weekly extended itself into the realm of a social contract, as if to show that technology (the new housing was essentially a novel form of prefabricated construction), mass media initiative, and public financing could cut across the impossible. The catch came in the form of the location of the proposed apartments, in Fresnes, in the suburbs of Paris, and thus reflected the trend toward dormitory-style suburbs instead of rebuilding in downtown areas. However, at the time, the solution represented the best of both worlds and should not be seen as implicated in the social tensions around urban sprawl that would begin within the next two decades. Instead, the "Résidence de Tourvoie," as the development became known, seemed like a wonderful promise that had real potential and apparent backing (*Paris Match* 1953: 207) (Figure 17.1).

The magazine's commitment to social engineering, however, ended discreetly. The plot of land *Paris Match* had optioned in 1953 and promoted in its pages with Roux's architectural model that same year, rapidly turned into an albatross. Building permits and other bureaucratic bottlenecks had very little to do with selling a magazine. As a former mayor of Fresnes noted, the magazine was only too happy to hand over the project to an association that completed the building process (Villette 1991: 10). In doing so, it ushered in the heyday of affordable and modern housing in the Parisian suburbs. The magazine dropped its commitment to the actual construction of the housing and returned to its primary agenda, which was to introduce readers to the new consumerism associated with novel designs and styles made possible by budding technologies. Whereas 112 families would eventually occupy the housing development at Fresnes, thousands more who were already settled in the suburbs could not expect to relocate to newer buildings. The magazine could not take on such matters that were

"Si Ma Cuisine M'Était Comptée"

**Figure 17.1** Crowds entering the *Maison de Paris Match* at the Salon des Arts Ménagers, Paris, 1953, © Henri Salesse/MEDDE/MLET.

more the remit of the Ministry for Reconstruction. It thus returned to presenting interior design and technology as it had done in the previous year: it would continue to address gender roles directly and to do so in an entertaining manner.

In 1954, *Paris Match* introduced its "Four Marvelous Kitchens" (*Paris Match*: 257) which were described as "fairy tales for housewives" and which went beyond the "Picasso" model of 1954. Referencing the colorful models built in the gardens of the Grand Palais, where the *SAM* was held, the journalists emphasized the fact that the kitchen occupant was no longer isolated: sliding doors or windows made the kitchen into a part of the dining room. The "lab kitchen" was gone. The irony was apparently lost on the public. Here were solutions that the likes of Le Corbusier and Charlotte Perriand had suggested two decades earlier, with the main difference that the discourse surrounding the developments was not about modernity and Americanization, but about the formation of a specifically French identity. By linking the stove to the dining table and even the living room in some models, the new interiors suggested a reaffirmation of "the great farmer's tradition of a common room" (*Paris Match* 1954: 257). Only once this had been emphasized could the notion of modular constructs be introduced, and with good reason. Mass-produced furniture had been so poorly received that some designers abandoned its manufacture altogether (Forest 2010: 53). Diminishing the modern identity in favor of a nationalist one was thus essential, especially as it also reinforced gender roles.

In order to show that these models were in fact real solutions to the problem of housework, each of the four featured kitchens were presented by well-known female personalities. There was only one exception, in the form of a man presenting the single walk-in closet in the entire exhibit. The idealized kitchen presented in Frankfurt, Germany, as part of an American exhibit had also included German women going about their business. However, all these female models were largely unknown. Anonymity in the French case would have glossed over the essential element of cultural identity. Geneviève Page had been pictured in the "Picasso kitchen" of 1954 endorsing a colorful design inspired from Kandinsky, which the public loved no doubt due to its adopted name (Figure 17.2). Similarly, in 1954, *Paris Match* had actress Jeanne Moreau pose in one of the kitchens with her husband and son. In so doing, the editors broke class barriers and symbolically a famous French actress was on her knees, in a "cuisine standard," fetching a pot, while her husband returned home triumphantly with a bottle, cheered by a toddler. The affordability of the kitchen unit, as the columnists stated, was possible thanks to mass production. Though she was still restricted to house work

**Figure 17.2** Maurice Jarnoux, Household Arts Fair 1954: The wonderful kitchen presented by *Paris Match*, © Paris Match Archive/Getty Images.

(at least in the photographs), Mme Moreau could "stay in touch with her family through the open sliding windows between the kitchen and the dining area." Such a notion had in fact taken twenty years to be assimilated into a format that might attract consumers. If she so chose, Madame would not only be in the kitchen but could also participate directly in casual conversation with people in the dining area (Martin 1987: 106). But it was the photograph of a respected actress that was required to communicate such a theme. In another 1954 kitchen, film actress Michèle Morgan, in a perfectly tailored "tailleur," brought drinks to her husband, who was seated in the living area that continued the nearby kitchen bar. This tradition of including celebrities between the fridge and the oven would become a standard, with fantasy and aspirational desires clearly playing a role. It would define *Paris Match*'s presence at the *SAM* the following year.

As Nick Bullock has ably shown, *Paris Match*'s 1955 iteration at the *SAM* not only offered fantasy in the fully electrified house it exhibited, but it did so with one the most famous singers of the period, the young Patachou. Wearing very little as she marveled at the novelties on display, Patachou herself became a sex novelty for the male readers (Bullock 2010: 129). This practice of including female celebrities as actors in model housing units reflected the shift away from the functional toward entertainment. These kitchen displays ended up emphasizing the event itself rather than its meaning. In so doing, they also reflected the fact that France was well on its way to full economic recovery even as it struggled with decolonization.

The 1955 show also suggested another dimension to Modernism. Instead of focusing merely on the functional, *Paris Match*'s pavilion included a commissioned aluminium sculpture by François Stahly (De Staël 2008). Stahly's metal wall pierced with rectangular windows appears to have little to do with a small kitchen. However, it suggested that renewed Modernism had entered French everyday life and that *Paris Match* was there to welcome it. Building a "new" house was indeed an event. By melding cultural statements (murals and sculptures) with new technologies of the interior, the magazine seemed to suggest that a new interior was also part of a modern French identity as much as a French automobile or airplane might be. That same year, French media lauded the arrival of "Caravelle," the first French-built commercial jet. That fall, *Paris Match* went as far as placing an automobile on its cover (a departure from its tradition of placing mostly people) to welcome the stylized Citroën DS (*Paris Match* 1955: 340). Common to all these themes about style, however, was a call for standardization and efficiency, with no concern for the tensions these might cause. *Paris Match*'s pavilion was, after all, an exhibit designed to entertain as much as to inform. The cultural dimension added in the form of a modernist sculpture and Patachou's charms were designed to reach across cultural boundaries and suggest modern beauty in the transformation of the kitchen.

Such domestic utopias (at least from a male point of view) reached their highest point in 1957 when the magazine brought to its readers "Tomorrow's kitchen." Co-sponsored with *Marie Claire* magazine, the futuristic contraption featured self-cleaning ovens, spring-loaded shelves for easy supply management, drying dishwashers, all of which seemed to have been brought home by a magician (*Paris Match* 1957: 416). In this case, the magic was played by the dancer and choreographer Roland Petit who brought wonders to his "petite" wife, the ballerina Zizi Jeanmaire. The irony was not lost on anybody. Jeanmaire was a phenomenal, classically trained dancer, whose early shows as a "cancan" girl at the

Casino de Paris were legendary. Dressed in scant clothing, she posed marveling at what her husband, "the magician," had brought her. The text, the pictures and even the tone were all parodical (Kelly 2000: 85). The technological marvels were not shown as such (for this would have meant acknowledging the American engineering background of such features already in use overseas) but, instead, were "imagined" as future developments. What was not removed, however, was the affirmation of the gender role. The only thing futuristic about Zizi Jeanmaire's appearance was her short hair, a novelty at the time. Otherwise, Jeanmaire's poses were more akin to a Cinderella moment as she watched her Prince Charming bring her a gilded cage. The allegory was obvious. The male head of any family reading the *Paris Match* could become such a magician and rescue his damsel from the horrors of a dreary interior. Boris Vian's satire of 1956, where the key to love came through interior furnishings, had come full circle a year later in the most widely read magazine in France.

The escalating crisis in Algeria that precipitated the end of the Fourth Republic also affected French culture from popular songs to post-structuralist philosophical discourse (Ross 1995: 110; 121). Algeria had been deemed a "piece of France" in the popular psyche, and things were not well in that part of the homeland. The extent of this "internal-external" crisis would also affect editorial priorities in the media. *Paris Match* reacted to the associated state of confusion as it moved to cover events in North Africa and the resulting political crises in France. However, the shift to the Fifth Republic also marked a new high in consumerism that displaced the importance of the *SAM*. The novelty phase of showing kitchens connected to their adjoining living rooms appeared to have ended because private companies now understood better the importance of *prêt-à-meubler* and advertised their own wares independently (Forest 2010). The 1959 *SAM* received its due coverage but without any sponsorship on the part of the magazine (*Paris Match* 1959: 517). *Paris Match*'s concoctions of modern domestic spaces of a few years earlier were no more.

## Conclusion

In 1962, a national survey devoted itself to examining household equipment, notably cooking tools. It noted how, regardless of income and living conditions, "working class families hardly benefited from technological improvements" (*Population* 1963: 387). Madeleine Calan's remarks from a decade before were still pertinent. The beautiful kitchens *Paris Match* had so actively promoted remained for the most part utopian dreams. For example, the "Picasso kitchen" of 1954, "modeled" by actress Geneviève Page, did not find its way into mass production but was taken apart and reassembled as part of a modernist home built in the Vercors region by some of the finest interior artists and architects of the era. It is now on the list of national monuments (Gencey 2014).

However, by opening the household and its associated kitchen spaces to public view and encouraging discussion of what the interior could mean to the average French family, *Paris Match* had offered its readers and visitors to the *SAM* an ethnographic spectacle, one in which readers could examine the solution to several problems at once: where to live, *how* to live, and how to match one's interior to one's identity. *Paris Match*, however, never questioned gender boundaries while doing so, reaffirming middle-class gender ideals and ignoring the reality of women's constricted social roles. The bourgeoisie's charming dullness or the working-classes' financial stress could not enter the realm of the photographs and texts the magazine published: all could only be glamor and novelty when showing a new kitchen or furniture.

By keeping its readership informed yearly of the various developments in household and kitchen design, *Paris Match* made these events comparable in import to the appearance of new technologies, all the while suggesting that what the new interior proposed was not uniquely Parisian but could be adopted nationally. In so doing, then, *Paris Match*, as the most widely distributed weekly in France, played a central role in helping the *arts ménagers* build an *interior* culture of acceptance. If the dining room was a social machine reinforcing the traditions of the French nuclear family (Certeau and Giard 1994: 278), then the kitchen was its engine, and *Paris Match* offered some of the fuel necessary to push French mass culture onto the road to incorporate some of the ideals into modern home life.

## References

Ainsley, J. (2006), "Displaying Designs for the Domestic Interior in Europe and America, 1850–1950," in J. Ainsley and C. Grant (eds), *Imagined Interiors: Representing the Domestic Interior since the Renaissance*, London: V&A: 190–215.

Astier, I. and J.-F. Laé (1991), "La Notion de communauté dans les enquêtes sociales sur l'habitat en France: Le Groupe d'Économie et humanisme, 1940–1955," *Genèses* 5: 81–106.

Blondel, N. (2011), *Un Certain goût français 1920–1980*, Paris: Éditions courtes et longues.

Boggio, R. (1995), *Boris Vian*, Paris: Livre de poche.

Bullock, N. (2008), "'20,000 Dwellings a Month for Forty Years:' France's 'Industrialized Housing Sector' in the 1950s," *Construction History* 23: 59–76.

Bullock, N. (2010), "La Cuisine au Salon: Le Rôle des arts ménagers dans la formation de l'idéal domestique moderne," in D. Voldman (ed), *Désirs de toit: Le Logement entre désir et contrainte depuis la fin du XIXe siècle*, Treillères: Créaphis: 125–155.

Calan, M. de (April–June 1952), "Au Salon de Arts ménagers," *Etudes* 273: 108–110.

Castillo, G. (2008), "Marshall Plan Modernism in Divided Germany," in D. Crowley and J. Pavitt (eds), *Cold War Modern Design 1945–1970*, London: V&A: 65–71.

Certeau, M. de and L. Giard (1994), *L'invention du quotidien*, Paris: Gallimard, Vol. 2.

De Staël, A. (2008), *François Stahly*, http://www.stahly.fr/FRANCOISSTAHLY/ACCUEIL.html [accessed June 2014]

Delaunay, Q. (2003), *Société industrielle et travail domestique. L'électroménager en France (XiXème-Xxème siècle)*, Paris: L'Harmattan.

Demory, J. (2007), *Les arts ménagers*, Boulogne: Du May.

Faucheux, P. (1952), "Appartement Paris-Match présenté par le Salon des arts ménagers et Paris-Match," *L'Architecture d'aujourd'hui* 40: XXII–XXV.

Fijalkov, Y. (2011), *Sociologie du logement*, Paris: La découverte.

Forest, D. (2010), *Mobi Boom. L'explosion du Design en France 1945–1975*, Paris: Arts décoratifs.

Freeman, J. (2004), *The Making of the Modern Kitchen*, Oxford: Berg.

Gencey, P. (2014), "Villa Székely//cuisine merveilleuse," http://art-utile.blogspot.ch/2014/05 [accessed May 2014]

Kelly, M. (2000), "Demystification: A Dialogue between Barthes and Lefebvre," *Yale French Studies* 98: 79–97.

Kuysel, R. (1997), *Seducing the French. The Dilemma of Americanization*, Berkeley: University of California Press.

Leymonerie, C. (2006), "Le Salon des arts ménagers dans les années 1950. Théâtre d'une conversion à la consommation de masse," *Vingtième siècle* 91, no. 3: 43–56.

Martin, M. (1987), "Ménagère, une profession? Les dilemmes de l'entre-deux-guerres," *Le mouvement social* 140: 89–106.

Migennes, P. (March 1934), "Une cuisine-salle à manger de Georges Appia," *Art et décoration*: 118.

Newsome, W. B. (2009), *French Urban Planning 1950-1968: The Construction and Deconstruction of an Authoritarian System*, New York: Peter Lang.

Oldenziel, R. and K. Zachman (2009), *Cold War Kitchen: Americanization, Technology, and European Users*, Cambridge, MA: MIT Press.

*Paris Match* 155 (March 1, 1952) 207 (March 7, 1953) 257 (February 17, 1954) 260 (March 20, 1954) 309 (March 3, 1955) 416 (March 30, 1957) 517 (March 7, 1959).

Piqpoq (2009), "Le point sur la petite chaise dite Gascoin," (March 18), http://vintageforkids.blogspot.ch/2009/03/le-point-sur-la-petite-chaise-dite.html, [accessed May 2014].

*Population* (1963) "L'équipement ménager dans la famille," unsigned review, *Population* 18, no. 2: 387.

Ross, K. (1995), *Fast Cars, Clean Bodies: Decolonization and the Reordering of French Culture*, Cambridge, MA: MIT Press.

Rouaud, J. (1993), *60 ans d'arts ménagers Tome 2: La consomation*, Paris: Syros.

Segalen, M. (1994), "The Salon des Arts Ménagers, 1923-1983: A French Effort to Instill the Virtues of Home and the Norms of Good Taste," *Journal of Design History* 7, no. 4: 267–275.

Valentin, B. (2013), *Innovation et expérimentation dans le logement social de demain*, Master's Thesis: Marne-la-Vallée.

Villette, A. (1991), *J'étais maire de Fresnes*, Paris: Editions Ouvrières.

Werner, F. (October–December 1984), "Du ménage à l'art ménager: L'évolution du travail ménager et son écho dans la presse féminine française de 1919 à1939," *Le mouvement social* 129: 61–87.

# INDEX

Note: Page numbers in **bold** refer to illustrations

Addison, Joseph 20
Alberti, Leon Battista 211
Albrecht, Donald 149
Álvarez, Darío 150
Anderson, Benedict 76
*Antoinette* (magazine) 220
apartments
    Haussmannian 95, 96, 98, 99, 100, 101, 102, 109, 111
    "radiant apartment" 221–2
*Apollo's Cortege* (Sert) 134–5
Appia, Georges 219
Archer, James Abbot 205–6
architecture and sensation 18–19
*À Rebours* (Huysmans) 59, 60–1, 62–8, 108–9, 131
Aristophanes
    *The Clouds* 75
Art Deco movement 147, 148, 194
artifice and the Decadent movement 60, 62, 63, 64, 66
*Art in the House* (Havard) 32–3, 34
artistic dress 127
artists' homes 179–88, **181, 183, 186**
*Art Nouveau Bing* 32, 41
    see also chambre à coucher (Gaillard)
Art Nouveau movement 31, 119, 120, 125, 126
Arts and Crafts movement 119, 125, 126, 143
*Arts ménagers* (magazine) 219, 220
Astruc, Henri 187
Autant-Lara, Claude 145, 147
autobiographical books and selfhood 87, 88–9
Aynsley, Jeremy 193–4

*Bal du Moulin Rouge* (Chéret) 109, **110**
*Ballet Mécanique* (film) 149
Ballets Suédois 192
balls (masquerade) 47–9
Balzac, Honoré de 59, 169
Barillet, Pierre 203–4
Barney, Natalie 138
Baschet, René 157, 165
Bastide, Jean-Francoise de
    *La Petite Maison* 18–19, 20, 21
bathrooms at "Villa Windsor" 212–13
Baudelaire, Charles 60, 63, 64, 65, 96, 192
Baudrillard, Jean 61, 63, 65, 67
Beardsley, Aubrey 131, 132, 135–41
    *The Dancer's Reward* 138, **139**

*Design for Tailpiece or Fin* 138, **140**
    *The Peacock Skirt* 137, 137–8
Beaunier, André 114
bedrooms
    conjugal 33–4, 37, 43–4
    Duke and Duchess of Windsor 210–12
    as erotic spaces 15–17
    Gaillard's *chambre à coucher* 31, **31**, 32, 34–8, **35, 36,** 37, **38,** 41–2, 43–4
    hygiene in 32–3
    see also boudoirs; cabinets
Benjamin, Walter 1, 29, 59, 76, 77, 104
Bergson, Henri 30, 43
Berman, Marshall 66
Bernheim, Hippolyte 39–40
Bertrand, Antoine 67
Bing, Siegfried 31, 32, 34, 41, 119
biographical books and selfhood 87, 88–9
Blondel, Jean-François 205
*The Bolt/Le Verrou* (Fragonard) 16, **16**
Bonnier, Louis 32
Börlin, Jean 192
Boucher, François 15, 49
Boudin, Stéphane 205, 210
*Le Boudoir* (Moreau Le Jeune) 21–2, **22**, 25
boudoirs 17, 18–23, 33
    see also bedrooms; cabinets
Bourcet, Pierre-Jean de 85
bourgeois society
    arts patronage 83
    defiance of 60, 120, 123, 124
    Jules Massenet 161–2
    and Modernism 194
    as the subject of art and writing 95, 99, 100
Bourget, Paul 60, 157
Boyer, Jean-Baptiste de
    *Thérèse Philosophe* 20–1, 24–5
Boylesve, René 197
Breward, Christopher 193
Brockhurst, Gerald Leslie 208–9
brothels 19, 49, 140, 141
Brumbragh, Thomas B. 208
Brunel, Pierre 65
Brunet, P. 47, 53–6
Bruno, Giuliana 14, 17
Bullock, Nick 218, 225
busts 51, 83–92

# Index

*The Cabinet of Dr. Caligari* (film) 147
cabinets 19–21, 33
   *see also* bedrooms; boudoirs
Calan, Madeleine 220
Calinescu, Matei 62, 64, 132
Canudo, Ricciotto 144
Cardon, Émile 99
Cardon, Paul (Dornac) 158
Carrouges, Michel 78
Castellane, Boni de 192, 193, 197–8
Castle, Terry 204
Catelain, Jaque 145
Cavalcanti, Alberto 145, 147
Certeau, Michel de 220
*chambre à coucher* (Gaillard) 31, **31**, 32, 34–8, **35, 36, 37, 38,** 41–2, 43–4
Champier, Victor 167, 168, 169, 170, 172–5, 176–7
Charcot, Jean-Martin 30, 39, 64
Chareau, Pierre 145, 148, 150, 181
Charlaine, P. 197
Chéret, Jules 107, 108–12, 114
   *Bal du Moulin Rouge* 109, **110**
   *La Pantomime* **113**
cinema and Modern architecture 144–52
clothing and social mobility 126–8
*The Clouds* (Aristophanes) 75
Club des Amis du Septième Art (C.A.S.A.) 144
Collot, Marie-Anne 90–1
Colomina, Beatriz 194
Colonna, Edouard 32
*Le Comte Pierre-Jean de Bourget et sa famille* (Landon) **85**, 85–6
Condillac, Etienne Bonnot de 18
*Confessions* (Rousseau) 88–9
conjugal bedrooms 33–4, 37, 43–4
conspicuous consumption 161, 165
consumerism 193, 199, 217, 222, 226
Coolus, Romain 122, 124
Corbin, Alain 33, 139
Cornforth, John 205
correspondence (Baudelaire) 65
costumed balls 47–9
*Country Life* 209–10
Crauzat, Ernest de 107
Crébillon fils, Claude Prosper Jolyot
   *Le Sopha* 19
Cubism 148–9, 150

Daly, César 171
Danceny, Chevalier (fictional character) 14–15
*The Dancer's Reward* (Beardsley) 138, **139**
dandyism 132, 191–200, 207
*Dangerous Liaisons* (film) 14–17, **16**, 21
Darnton, Robert 13
Davidson, Bessie
   *Portrait de Famille D.* 1
decadence, origin and definitions of 60

Decadent movement
   *À Rebours* (Huysmans) 59, 60–1, 62–8, 108–9, 131
   and lesbian aesthetics 131–41
   and nature and artifice 60, 62, 63, 64, 66–8
Delaunay, Robert 148
Delaunay, Sonia 148
Deleuze, Gilles 78
Dell, Simon 197
depopulation crisis in France 33, 38, 44
*Design for Tailpiece or Fin* (Beardsley) 138, **140**
Diaconoff, Suellen 23
Diana (goddess) 51
Diderot, Denis 90–1
Didi-Huberman, Georges 64
Dietz, Bettina 205
distribution in interior decoration 171, 172
Dormoy, Marie 187
Dornac (Paul Cardon) 158
"doubled" interior 119, 124, 128
dress and social mobility 126–8
Dreyfuss, Carle 176
Du Barry, Madame 15, 19, 174, 206
Ducasse, Curt John 209
Dumas fils, Alexandre 157, 162

*Eaux-Fortes* (Beardsley spectacle) 135–41
*eaux-fortes* (literary genre) 136
Edward, Duke of Windsor 203–14
eroticism in interior spaces 15–23, 78–9
erotic novels 13
   *La Petite Maison* (Bastide) 18–19, 20, 21
   *Thérèse Philosophe* (Boyer) 20–1, 24–5
*Essai sur les jardins* (Watlet) 18, 25
Esseintes, Jean Des (fictional character) 39, 60–1, 62–8, 108–9, 131
evolutionary regeneration (Transformism) 31–2, 37, 43
*Exposition Universelle*
   1889 31, 111, 168
   1900 31, 32
Expressionist movement 147

Fayed, Mohamed Al 206, 210, 211
Felski, Rita 193
Fénéon, Félix 109, 113
Fernbach, Amanda 138
Ferry, Jules 157, 162
Feure, Georges de 32, 41
Field, Richard 97
Fizdale, Robert 126
Fleury, Maurice de 110–11, 113–14
Forain, Jean-Louis 111, 133
Fouillée, Alfred 32
4D design 72–5
four-dimensional thinking 73, 74, 75
"Four Marvellous Kitchens" 223–5
Fragonard, Jean-Honoré 15
   *The Bolt* 16, **16**
Frears, Stephen 14, 15, 18, 21

# Index

French design and craftsmanship 2
French identity and the interior 217, 221, 223–4, 225
French society in the 19th century 29–30, 44, 98
French understanding of the interior 1–2
Fresnes housing development 222
Fromentin, Charles 161–2, 165
Fry, Edith 1
Fuller, Richard Buckminster 72, 73–4, 75
furniture as an extension of self 49

Gabriac, A. de 136
Gailhard, Pedro 161
Gaillard, Eugène
    *chambre à coucher* 31, **31,** 32, 34–8, **35, 36, 37, 38,** 41–2, 43–4
Gallé, Émile 40
Garelick, Rhonda 193
gendered spaces
    the kitchen 219–22, 223, 224, 225–6
    in the 19th century 124–5
George, Waldemar 187
*Gesamtkunstwerk* 119, 135, 143, 148
Ghendt, Emmanuel de
    *Le Midi* 21, 24, **24,** 25
Giard, Luce 220
Girardin, René Louis de 89, **90,** 91–2
Girardin, Stanislas de 90
Glick, Elisa 193
Gold, Arthur 126
Goncourt, Edmond de 39, 96
    *La Maison d'un artiste* 49, 59, 114
Goncourt, Jules de 39, 96
Gordon, Beverly 49
Gorska, Adrienne de 182
Gourdan, Marguerite 19
Grand-Pierre, Henri 133
Greene, Gena 49
Groom, Gloria 124, 125
Guevrekian, Gabriel 150, 151
Gurney, Edmund 42

Halicka, Alice 180
Hamon, Philippe 60
Hampton, Christopher 14, 15
Hardy, P. 197–8
Harvey, Karen 17, 21
Haussmannian apartments 95, 96, 98, 99, 100, 101, 102, 109, 111
Havard, Henry
    *Art in the House* 32–3, 34
Hébertot, Jacques 192, 199
Helmholtz, Hermann von 42
Henry, Charles 109, 113–14
Hirsh, Sharon 76
historical revival in interior decoration 47–9, 53
Hoffman, Josef 143, 147
homosexual aesthetics and the Decadent movement 131–41

Horst P. Horst 203, 207
Hôtel Salomon de Rothschild **167,** 167–77, **173, 175**
Houdon, Jean-Antoine 89, 91
Huysmans, Joris-Karl 111, 112, 136
    *À Rebours* 59, 60–1, 62–8, 108–9, 131
hygiene and domestic interiors 32–3, 102
hypnosis 39
hysteria 39, 64

illusionist spectacles 62
"impolite" readings 13
    *see also* erotic novels
individualism 59, 60, 132
Ingram, H. Balch 1
interior decoration as an extension of self 49
interiority
    in autobiographical writing 87, 88–9
    Édouard Vuillard's paintings 120–1, 124, 126
    and portrait busts 83–92
    and Symbolism 75–7
*Interior with Three Lamps* (Vuillard) **121,** 121–2
*Intimités* series (Valloton) 95–104, **98, 102, 103**

Jaloux, Edmond 141
Jansen (decorating firm) 203, 205, 206, 208, 212, 213
Jarry, Alfred 72, 77–9
Jaubert, Abbé 170
Jeanmaire, Zizi 225–6
Jourdain, Francis 150, 181, 199

Kang, Minsoo 66
Kelly, Victoria 212
*The Kill/La Curée* (Zola) 50–3, 55
kitchen design 218–26
Kuenzli, Katherine 107
Kuffner, Raoul 185, 187

Laclos, Pierre Choderlos de
    *Les Liaisons Dangereuses* 14–15
Lamarck, Jean-Baptiste 31
Landon, Charles Paul
    *Le Comte Pierre-Jean de Bourget et sa famille* **85,** 85–6
*L'Architecture* (journal) 179
*L'Architecture d'aujourd'hui* (film) 145–6
*L'Architecture d'aujourd'hui* (journal) 146, 185, 187
Lawford, Valentine (Nicholas) 203, 207, 209, 214
Le Camus de Mézières, Nicolas 14, 18
Lecomte, Félix
    *Portrait Bust of Queen Marie-Antoinette* 87–8, **88**
Le Corbusier 75, 145, 151, 187
Léger, Fernand 71, 145, 148–9
Lempicka, Tamara de 182–4, 185–7
Leroy, Julien-David 18
lesbian aesthetics and the Decadent movement 131–41
Lescot, Claire (film character) 145, 146–8
Leymonerie, Claire 220
*l'habitation moderne* and the Rothschilds 171, 172

# Index

L'Herbier, Marcel
    *L'Inhumaine* 145–50, **146**
*Les Liaisons Dangereuses* (de Laclos) 14–15
libertine novels 13
    *La Petite Maison* (Bastide) 18–19, 20, 21
    *Les Liaisons Dangereuses* 14–15
*L'Inhumaine* (film) 145–50, **146**
Linkof, Ryan 206
Loos, Adolf 150
Loti, Pierre 48, 56
Lubey, Kathleen 20
Lurçat, André 180, 182, 187
Lurçat, Jean 148

"machine house". See *The Suspended House/La Maison Suspendue* (Nelson)
machines
    Alfred Jarry's pataphysical 78
    *À Rebours* (Huysman) 64–6
    *machines de théâtre* 61–3
    medical 64, 65
Mackintosh, C.R. 143, 147
Mairet, Henri 158, 163, 164
*Maison de l'Art Nouveau (Maison Bing)* 119, 125
*La Maison d'un artiste* (Goncourt) 49, 59, 114
Maison Jansen 203, 205, 206, 208, 212, 213
Maistre, Xavier de
    *Voyage autour de ma chambre* 87
Maleuvre, Didier 59, 63, 65, 66, 67
Mallarmé, Stéphane 150
Mallet-Stevens, Robert 143–5, 185, 187
    *L'Inhumaine* 145–50, **146**
    Tamara de Lempicka's apartment 182, **183**
    Villa Noailles 150–2, **151, 152**
Man Ray 150–1
Marcus, Sharon 96, 102
Maré, Rolf de 192
*Marie-Antoinette, Queen of France* (Millet) 83, **84,** 86–7
Marie-Antoinette portrait bust (Lecomte) 87–8, **88**
*Marie Claire* 218, 219, 220, 225
Martin, Reinhold 77
Marx, Roger 111–12
masquerade balls 47–9
Massenet, Jules 157, 161–2, 164, 165
Matthews, Patricia 76
Mauclair, Camille 187
Maupassant, Guy de 29, 64
Maxwell, Elsa 204
medical machines 64, 65
Meier-Graefe, Julius 32, 97
*Mélite* (fictional character) 18–19, 21
Mercier, Louis-Sébastien 19
Mérot, Alain 40
Merteuil, Marquise de (fictional character) 14–15, 21
Michel, Louis 145
*Le Midi* (Ghendt) 21, 24, **24,** 25
Milhaud, Darius 131, 145, 149

Millet, Anne-Flore
    *Portrait of Marie-Antoinette, Queen of France* 83, **84,** 86–7
Miró, Joan 71, 77, 78
misogyny and the interior 99–100
Modern architecture and the cinema 144–52
Modernism 66, 76, 96, 193, 194, 199, 217, 225
Mondrian, Piet 150
*Monsieur* 191–200, **195, 196, 200**
Montesquiou-Fézensac, Robert de 39, 67, 131, 132–3, 135, 136, 141
Montparnasse studio-houses 179–88, **181, 183, 186**
*Monument du Costume Physique et Moral de la fin du Dix-huitième siècle* 21–3
Monvel, Roger Boutet de 196–7, 198, 199
Moreau, Jeanne 224–5
Moreau Le Jeune
    *The Boudoir* 21–2, **22,** 25
Morgan, Michèle 225
Morris, William 125, 126
Moulignon, Henri Antoine Léopold de 170–1, 172
Mouret, Octave (fictional character) 100–1, 102
Mourey, Gabriel 33, 41
Mumford, Lewis 78
Musée Carnavalet 167, 169, 170, 172
Muter, Mela 184–5, **186,** 187, 188
*Les Mystères du Château du Dé* (film) 150–1, **152**

Nabis group 95, 96, 119, 120, 124, 125, 128
Natanson, Misia 120–8, **121, 122**
Natanson, Thadée 97, 99, 122, **122,** 124, 126
nature
    and the Decadent movement 60, 62, 63, 66–8
    and the interior 31–2, 34–7, 41–2
    and René-Louis de Girardin 92
Nelson, Paul
    *The Suspended House/La Maison Suspendue* **71,** 71–9, **73**
Néronde, C. de 162–4
neurasthenia 39, 111
neurosis 29–30, 64, 65
New Dandy 191–200
New Interior 119, 125
New Woman 53, 120, 123, 128
Noailles, Charles de 150, 151
Noorsen, Einar (film character) 145, 147, 148, 149
*Nos Contemporains chez eux* (photographic series) 158
Nouvel-Kammerer, Odile 33
Nutz, Thomas 205

Ochsé, Julien 135, 136
Ohnet, Léon 170, 174
organicized interiors 31–2, 34–7, 41–2
Orloff, Chana 180–2, **183,** 184, 185, 188
Ozenfant, Amédée 187

Padiyar, Satish 13
Page, Geneviève 224, 226

# Index

*La Pantomime* (Chéret) **113**
*Paris Match* 217–28, **223**, **224**
Parshall, Peter 96
Patachou (singer) 225
pataphysics and *The Suspended House* 72, 77–9
Pater, Walter 209
Pawley, Martin 74
*The Peacock Skirt* (Beardsley) **137**, 137–8
Percival, Melissa 15
Pérez-Gómez, Alberto 79
Perret, Auguste 145, 146, 180, 182, 184, 185, 187
Perriand, Charlotte 221
Perrier, Edmond 31–2
Perrot, Michelle 56
Petit, Roland 225–6
*La Petite Maison* (Bastide) 18–19, 20, 21
photography, development of 158, 168–9
"Picasso kitchen" 224, 226
Piles, Roger de 18
*pochoir* technique 193, 194
*Point de Lendemain* (Vivant Denon) 26
Poiret, Paul 48, 56, 144, 145, 192, 193–4
Ponsard, Justin 170
population regeneration in France 33, 38, 44
Porel, Paul 163
pornographic texts 21
portrait busts 51, 83–92
*Portrait de Famille D.* (Davidson) 1
posters 107–14
*Pot-Bouille* (Zola) 95–6, 100–4
promiscuity and the interior 102–4
Proust, Marcel 39, 124, 135
Prouvé, Jean 221
*la psychologie nouvelle* 30, 38–41
psychophysics 109, 113
Puvis de Chavanne, Pierre 112

Quick (art critic) 194–5, 198

"radiant apartment" 221–2
reading of books 13, 23
Reclus, Elisée 32
Redon, Odilon 67
Régnier, Marie de 141
Réjane, Gabrielle 162–4, 165
Résidence de Tourvoie 222
*La Revue Blanche* 96, 124, 125
*Revue des arts décoratifs*
    *L'Habitation Moderne* series 167, 168, 169, 172, 176
*Revue Illustrée* 48, **48**
    photo-interview series 157–65, **159, 162, 163**
Rice, Charles 119
Riffaterre, Michael 67
Roberts, Mary Louise 123
Robinson, Joyce Henri 107, 112
Roche, Daniel 23
Rosner, Victoria 214
Ross, Kristin 218

Rothschild, Madame la baronne Salomon 167–77
Rothschild, Salomon-James de 168, 176
Rousseau, Jean-Jacques 22, 86, 91–2
    *Confessions* 88–9
Roux, Marcel 222
Rudolph, Nicole 218

Saccard, Aristide (fictional character) 50, 51
Saccard, Maxim (fictional character) 50–1
Saccard, Renée (fictional character) 50–2
*Salome* (Wilde) 132, 136, 137–8
*Salon des arts ménagers* (SAM) 217, 218, 219, 220, 221, 222, 223, 225, 226
Sandier, Alexandre 158
Sans-Gêne, Madame 162, 163
Sapphic Modernism 132
Sardou, Victorien 159–60, 164, 165
Schleuning, Sarah 2
Schwartz, Vanessa 76
seduction and space 19–25
Segalen, Martine 220
selfhood
    and biographical writing 87, 88–9
    and portrait busts 83–92
sensation
    and architecture 18–19
    in modern urban life 111
sensationalist theory 2, 18, 25
Sert, José-María 133
    *Apollo's Cortege* 134–5
Sidlauskas, Susan 54
Silverman, Debora L. 31, 38–9, 120
simulacra (Baudrillard) 63
Simultaneism (Delaunay) 148
Singer, Winnaretta 131–41
social mobility through dress 126–8
Socrates' "nest" 74–5
Solidor, Suzy 184
*Le Sopha* (Crébillon fils) 19
Soulier, Gustave 35–6
Sparke, Penny 124, 126
Stahly, François 225
Starobinski, Jean 40–1
Stead, Evanghelia 67
Stoclet Palace 143–4
studio-houses in Montparnasse 179–88, **181, 183, 186**
suggestion (psychological) 39–40, 41
*The Suspended House/La Maison Suspendue* (Nelson) **71**, 71–9, **73**
Symbolist movement 38–9, 75–7, 126, 132, 136
sympathetic vibrations 42
synesthesia 64–5

*Le Tapissier Décorateur de Paris* (Ch. Juliot) 53–6, **54, 55**
Tardieu, Eugène 160, 165
technology and *Paris Match* 222, 223, 225, 226, 227
Texier, Edmond 96
*théâtres de machines* 61, 62

# Index

*Thérèse Philosophe* (Boyer) 20–1, 24–5
Tiersten, Lisa 53, 124
Tourette, Gilles de la 39
Transformism (evolutionary regeneration) 31–2, 37, 43
Trémicour, Marquis de (fictional character) 18–19

Ubu, Père (fictional character) 72, 77, 78

Vabre, Valérie (fictional character) 102
Vaillant, Odile 151
Valbert, Georges 29
Vallotton, Félix 127–8
    *Intimités* series 95–104, **98, 102, 103**
*Vallotton and Misia in the Dining Room at Rue Saint-Florentin* (Vuillard) 127
Valmont, Vicomte de (fictional character) 14–15
Vanderbilt family 1
Veblen, Thorstein 161
Velde, Henry van de 119, 125, 126
Verne, Jules 157, 162
Vian, Boris 217, 226
vibration
    in decorative art 41–2, 43–4
    the universe as a network of 42–3
Vidal, Jerome Léon 168
Villa Noailles 150–2, **151, 152**
"Villa Windsor" 205–14, **208, 209, 210, 211, 213**
Vivant, Dominique, Baron Denon
    *Point de Lendemain* 26
*Vogue* 203, 206–7, 208
Volanges, Cecile des (fictional character) 14–15
Voltaire 89–90
*Voyage autour de ma chambre* (Maistre) 87

Vreeland, Diana 203, 206–7
Vuillard, Édouard
    *Interior with Three Lamps* **121,** 121–2
    Misia Natanson as his muse 120–8
    *Vallotton and Misia in the Dining Room at Rue Saint-Florentin* 127
    *Woman in Blue with Child* 123

Wagner, Otto 143
Wagner, Richard 135
Wagrez, Jacques 48
Wallis, Duchess of Windsor 203–14
Watlet, Claude-Henri
    *Essai sur les jardins* 18, 25
Weill, Alexandre 100
Weill, Berthe 185
Weir, David 66, 132
White, Nicholas 101
Wiene, Robert 147
Wilde, Oscar 67, 131, 136
    *Salome* 132, 136, 137–8
Wilson, Elizabeth 126
Windsor, Duke and Duchess of 203–14
Wolfe, Elsie de 203, 204, 210
*Woman in Blue with Child* (Vuillard) 123
wood, design qualities of 41–2
woodcuts. *See Intimités* series (Valloton)

Young, Paul 20

Zimm, Malin 63
Zola, Émile 29, 44, 64, 157, 161
    *The Kill/La Curée* 50–3, 55
    *Pot-Bouille* 95–6, 100–4

www.ingramcontent.com/pod-product-compliance
Lightning Source LLC
Chambersburg PA
CBHW080537300426
44111CB00017B/2772